Property of
FAMILY OF FAITH
LIBRARY

W9-BIF-567

www.wadsworth.com

wadsworth.com is the World Wide Web site for Wadsworth Publishing Company and is your direct source to dozens of online resources.

At *wadsworth.com* you can find out about supplements, demonstration software, and student resources. You can also send e-mail to many of our authors and preview new publications and exciting new technologies.

wadsworth.com
Changing the way the world learns®

Family of Faith Library

Assessment in the Classroom

ANNIE W. WARD
University of South Florida, Emeritus

MILDRED MURRAY-WARD
California Lutheran University

Wadsworth Publishing Company
I⟨T⟩P™ An International Thomson Publishing Company

Belmont, CA • Albany, NY • Boston • Cincinnati • Detroit • Johannesburg • London
Madrid • Melbourne • Mexico City • New York • Pacific Grove, CA
Scottsdale, AZ • Singapore • Tokyo • Toronto

Education Editor: Dianne Lindsay
Assistant Editor: Tangelique Williams
Marketing Manager: Becky Tollerson
Project Editors: Jennie Redwitz, Heidi Marschner
Print Buyer: Barbara Britton
Permissions Editor: Robert Kauser
Production: Matrix Productions Inc.
Copy Editor: Patricia Herbst
Cover Design: Bill Stanton
Compositor: Pre-Press Company
Printer: RR Donnelley / Crawfordsville

COPYRIGHT © 1999 by Wadsworth Publishing Company
A Division of International Thomson Publishing Inc.
I(T)P® The ITP logo is a registered trademark under license.

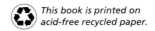
This book is printed on
acid-free recycled paper.

Printed in the United States of America
1 2 3 4 5 6 7 8 9 10

For more information, contact Wadsworth Publishing Company, 10 Davis Drive, Belmont, CA 94002, or electronically at
http://www.wadsworth.com

International Thomson Publishing Europe
Berkshire House
168-173 High Holborn
London, WC1V 7AA, United Kingdom

Nelson ITP, Australia
102 Dodds Street
South Melbourne
Victoria 3205 Australia

Nelson Canada
1120 Birchmount Road
Scarborough, Ontario
Canada M1K 5G4

International Thomson Editores
Seneca, 53
Colonia Polanco
11560 México D.F. México

International Thomson Publishing Asia
60 Albert Street #15-01
Albert Complex
Singapore 189969

International Thomson Publishing Japan
Hirakawa-cho Kyowa Building, 3F
2-2-1 Hirakawa-cho, Chiyoda-ku
Tokyo 102, Japan

International Thomson Publishing Southern Africa
Building 18, Constantia Square
138 Sixteenth Road, P.O. Box 2459
Halfway House, 1685 South Africa

All rights reserved. No part of this work covered by the copyright hereon may be reproduced or used in any form or by any means—graphic, electronic, or mechanical, including photocopying, recording, taping, or information storage and retrieval systems—without the written permission of the publisher.

Library of Congress Cataloging-in-Publication Data

Ward, Annie.
     Assessment in the classroom / Annie W. Ward, Mildred Murray-Ward.
           p.   cm.
     Includes bibliographical references.
     ISBN 0-534-52704-3 (alk. paper)
     1. Educational tests and measurements.   2. Grading and marking (Students).   3. Examinations.
     I. Murray-Ward, Mildred.   II. Title.
LB3051.W336   1999
371.26—dc21
                              98-41405

Brief Contents

Contents

Preface

This book is primarily intended to be used in an introductory course in educational measurement. Students will get more out of the text if they have had some teaching experience—at least an internship. For some of the students this course will be the only course in educational measurement they will take. For others it will be followed by more advanced or more technical courses. In addition, some of the chapters—especially those on test construction, observation, portfolios, and use of assessment results for grading and study of individual students—may be used as the foundation for in-service training programs.

The focus of the book is on the full range of classroom assessment, and the text is addressed especially to classroom teachers at all levels of education. However, school administrators, counselors, and others who work directly with students will also find the information useful. In addition, those who conduct in-service programs will find some of the chapters very useful. Our goal is to help educators, whatever their current assignment, use a variety of assessments to plan for instruction, evaluate the success of the instruction, and evaluate the progress of individual students and groups of students.

Teachers need to know how to develop tests and other assessments that meet accepted standards and how to combine the scores in a useful way. They also need to be informed consumers of tests and test reports, and they need to use the results of a variety of assessments as teaching tools and as the basis for evaluating and reporting student progress. To accomplish these tasks, teachers need to know some basic concepts and to understand how to avoid common problems. Those who work in multicultural classrooms and with mainstreamed students also need to understand the problems that affect assessment in those settings.

Administrators and counselors must know how classroom assessment is done in order to assist teachers and to interpret and use the information themselves. They also need to understand external tests and testing programs. Administrators are often responsible for managing external testing programs that carry very high stakes, so they need to be familiar with these programs. In addition, administrators are responsible for evaluating teachers and other people on their staff. Counselors and school psychologists use information from teachers' assessments, along with the results of external tests, in their work with individual students.

ORGANIZATION OF THE BOOK

The organization of this book is very different from that of most introductory textbooks in educational measurement. We start with issues that are likely to be of concern to educators. Chapter 1 reviews the question of how much and what kind of training in assessment teachers need. Chapter 2 discusses some currently "hot" issues related to educational measurement, about which there is much public concern and, at times, great controversy. The third chapter reviews the history of the development of concepts and techniques of educational measurement, and the fourth chapter explains the basic concepts of educational measurement. These chapters make up Part One.

Part Two covers the preparation of a variety of classroom assessments that are consistent with current views of teaching and learning. The emphasis in this part is on *how to,* with lots of examples. The first chapter in Part Two gives directions for planning assessments, relating the assessments to teaching and to the goals and objectives of education, with attention to the complex environment of the classroom and the varied purposes that must be served by classroom assessment. The other chapters in Part Two deal with specific types of assessments: paper-and-pencil tests; performance and production tasks; observation, both formal and informal; and portfolios.

Each of these chapters presents numerous examples of these various types of assessments, discusses the purposes for which each is appropriate, and provides detailed instructions for preparing and scoring them. Many sample items of all types are provided, and scoring rubrics are provided for assessments that need them. In connection with each specific type of assessment the threats to validity and reliability are discussed, and ways to check and handle such problems are provided. The emphasis is on practical ways to obtain the information teachers need.

Part Three deals with issues involved in working with external tests: selecting and using nationally normed tests of all kinds, including those furnished by commercial textbook publishers and state and local educational agencies; working with mandated high-stakes testing programs; and understanding and using data from reports of clinical instruments. Chapter 10 presents an overview of external testing and the other three chapters in this part discuss specific kinds of external tests.

Part Four provides help in putting all the information together for reporting to students and their parents and for diagnosis and treatment of individual students. Chapter 14 deals with grading and reporting student progress and is written with consideration of the many purposes served by grades. Chapter 15 deals with the study of individual students, and the final chapter covers referrals for special education services. A variety of student data is provided in varying formats, and the reader is guided through the process of making sense of these data.

SPECIAL FEATURES OF THE BOOK

This book has two aspects that distinguish it from other textbooks in educational assessment: (1) what is included that is *not* in most other books and (2) what is *not* in this book that most other books have.

New Material Included

Part One: Chapter 1	What Will You Learn from This Book?
Chapter 2	Current Issues and Controversies (Students are usually concerned about these issues and eager to discuss them.)
Chapter 3	Historical Roots of Assessment (This chapter helps students understand where the concepts came from and how certain practices developed.)
Part Two: Chapter 9	Portfolio Assessment
Part Three: Chapter 11	Discussion of evaluating and using *textbook tests*
Part Four: Chapters 15 and 16	Preparing student profiles and making referrals

Material not Included

Unexplained technical jargon

Newly coined terms to replace the old ones

Complicated mathematical formulas

We do not have separate chapters on *validity* and *reliability*. These concepts are discussed in many places in the book, and procedures are described in the chapters dealing with specific assessment techniques.

We feel that these additions and omissions are a strong point for the students to whom the book is addressed. Another important feature is the emphasis on the *use* of information. This emphasis is found throughout the book, but it is almost the entire message of Part Four.

Some of the content is entirely new. Much of is it not new, but our emphasis is different. Most measurement professionals have always advocated fitting the assessment to the instructional purpose and to the intended student behavior. What is new is our emphasis on curriculum issues and our provision of lots of structure to help students learn how to carry out the tasks we suggest. This book also differs from many other introductory textbooks in educational measurement by its lack of technical discussions of statistics. We present and explain the concepts without using elaborate formulas, and we have kept the mathematics to a minimum.

The book makes use of advance organizers to alert the reader to the important information to be presented. There is an introduction to each part and each chapter has a preview, followed by a list of major topics.

Many forms are provided to assist educators in carrying out the tasks, and examples of various types of assessments are liberally provided.

A summary and study questions conclude each chapter. Also appearing at the end of each chapter is a special section titled "For Your Professional Growth," which describes activities that will help students extend their knowledge and explore school, district, and community resources. Some of these activities are designed to be carried out in their own classroom. For readers who do not yet have a classroom, the instructor will be able to suggest alternative procedures.

The book emphasizes practicality and requires no previous preparation in either statistics or psychology. We emphasize high standards for all educational measurement, and we try to help educators avoid common problems, but we purposely avoid technical jargon and complicated mathematical computations. Our feeling is that teachers are turned off by these and do not use them. Administrators and counselors who need them will learn them in other courses.

Some of the material in this book has been presented in papers delivered at professional conferences or has appeared in bulletins published by the authors. However, all of it has been extensively expanded and revised.

ACKNOWLEDGMENTS

We are grateful for all the help we have received over the years from the measurement professionals cited in the various chapters of this book and for our interactions with many of them. However, our most important sources of information as to what we should include in this book and how we should present the materials have been the practicing teachers, administrators, and counselors who were students in our introductory classes and whose response to the materials has helped us evaluate their usefulness.

We are especially grateful to a group of teachers and master's degree candidates at California Lutheran University who provided student profiles for Chapter 15 and case studies for Chapter 16. Thanks to Elizabeth Brown, Kathleen Bordner, Gayle Pinkston, Linda Johnson, Maurene Everakes, and Maxine Fowles for their help in showing the reader how to "put it all together."

We wish to thank the reviewers for their helpful comments: Tim Anderson, Nebraska Wesleyan College; Helen Baldwin, MacMurray College; Victoria B. Damiani, Indiana University of Pennsylvania; Alan Davis, University of Colorado at Denver; James Earl Davis, University of Delaware; Bruce Frazee, Trinity University; Loyde Hales, Portland State University; Ron Hambleton, University of Massachusetts; Charles H. Hargis, University of Tennessee; Del Harnisch, University of Illinois—Urbana; Tim Heron, Ohio State University; Henry Leland, Ohio State University; Sandra Mathison; William E. McGraw, Jr., Southern Connecticut State University; William L. Merrill, Central Michigan University; Pat Sellers,

Indiana University at Purdue—Ft. Wayne; Fred Taylor, Illinois State University; and Peter Wood, Bowling Green State.

We would especially like to thank the graduate assistants at California Lutheran University, Clay Carter, Gayle Pinkston, and Lisa LaMontage, for their assistance in locating information and for their reactions and candid response as teachers to the materials in the book. Kathleen Roam of the Volusia County (Florida) Schools has also been very helpful as a reader and as an assistant in producing some of the materials and Kimberly McMonigle has been invaluable in helping with technical details in preparing some of the figures.

Annie W. Ward
Mildred Murray-Ward

PART ONE

࿎

Assessment
in Perspective

Assessment is part of life from the moment we are born, although we are not always aware of it because much assessment is informal. Assessment is part of the
responsibility of many professional occupations, but especially professionals in education. Educators face extremely important decisions daily, and we need all the
information we can get to help us. However, it is important that our information
is accurate and dependable and that it is the kind of information necessary for the
decisions we are making.

Some assessment decisions involve placement, admission to educational programs, or licensing for occupations. Some are mandated by government agencies
as a means of establishing accountability and, perhaps, increasing motivation.
However, the most important decisions in education involve students' learning
needs and planning for instruction.

Whatever the decisions, it is important for the assessments on which they are
based to be of high quality, so that we may use the results with confidence. Over
the course of the history of educational measurement, a body of knowledge and
theory has been developed to guide our practice. In addition, court rulings and laws
have defined allowable practices and constraints. Everyone who uses assessment information needs to be aware of the guidelines and laws that have been developed.

Although educators are not expected to be familiar with the complete body of
this knowledge, there are some basic concepts that we all must understand in order
to prepare assessments for our students, interpret other information correctly, and
avoid making bad decisions. In Part One we provide this kind of information. In
Chapter 1 we start with a discussion of the kinds of assessment activities teachers,
counselors, and administrators are responsible for and describe what they need to
know in order to meet these responsibilities. In Chapter 2 we present some problem areas that confront educators today. In Chapter 3 we provide historical perspective, and in Chapter 4 we end this section with a discussion of the basic
concepts of educational assessment. These four chapters provide a framework for
later sections covering the development and use of various types of assessments.

1

ॐ

What Will You Learn from This Book?

PREVIEW

Are you wondering why you are required to take a class in educational assessment? Have you heard that it is a boring course and that you will have to use complex mathematical formulas and learn a lot of things that have nothing to do with your job as a teacher, administrator, or counselor? We wrote this chapter partly to reassure you, because our approach to the subject is different from that of most other textbooks. We also want to explain why the material in this book is important to educators, so you will see how the course can be helpful. Let's look at some possibilities:

Jon S. teaches mathematics, and Lou M. teaches English at Central High School. Their students have been preparing portfolios of their work for the first quarter. Now it is time to assign grades. Jon and Lou are not sure about how to do this.

How should they proceed?

Lee G. is a newly hired counselor at Highlands Middle School. He has received several referrals from teachers concerning students who are having difficulty in their work.

What should he do with these referrals? Where can he find information to help him work with these teachers and students?

Celia S. is a kindergarten teacher at Newgate Elementary School. She has just been told by her principal that she should prepare to administer an early screening test to her students. The test has been mandated by the state legislature. The purpose of the test is to identify students who need additional prereading activities before entering first grade. The principal has arranged for a training session to prepare the teachers to administer and interpret this test.

What does Celia need to know?

This is Sara K.'s first year as principal of Newgate Elementary School. She needs to plan the training program for the kindergarten teachers.

What needs to be included in this training program?

Sara K. also notices that the district-wide achievement test in grades 3 through 6 is to be given in October.

What does Sara need to do to prepare for this testing?

Most educators work in an environment full of activities and face difficult problems and issues that need solutions. Teachers spend a large portion of each school day in assessing students' work and using that information to make decisions; however, much of the assessment is informal and largely unplanned. Administrators are faced with questions and problems that they have to handle by referring to assessment information. They are also responsible for providing inservice training for their teachers. Counselors and school psychologists use the assessment information in students' files and administer other assessments to help them work with teachers, parents, and students.

Unlike many activities for which educators have been well prepared, many educators receive little training in assessment processes and techniques. In general, educators receive only a small amount of formal training and some inservice training. Why is this so? What should educators know and be able to do? In this chapter we discuss these questions.

MAJOR TOPICS

The Use of Assessment in American Education

Why Do Educators Need Training in Assessment?

What Should Teachers Learn About Assessment?

What Are the Problems with Assessment Training?

THE USE OF ASSESSMENT
IN AMERICAN EDUCATION

You probably are aware that teachers and students spend a lot of time on assessment, but you may not be aware of how large a proportion of the school year and the school budget is involved. Stiggins (1988) and Schafer & Lissitz (1987) estimated that formal assessment activities such as testing, observation, and rating consume about 33% of a typical teacher's workday. The National Commission on Testing and Public Policy (1990) estimated that the equivalent of 20 million school days are spent each year by students taking tests, that perhaps 10 to 20 times that amount of time is spent in preparing for testing, and that 127 million U.S. students per year take standardized tests at a cost of about $1 billion annually. Wirth (1992) found that students in New York public schools were most likely to take 29 state-mandated tests during the years from kindergarten through twelfth grade, in addition to complying with local and national testing requirements. In addition to administering these external tests, teachers also spend many additional hours in preparing and using classroom tests and informal assessments of various kinds.

Madaus and Kellaghan (1992) found that teachers' own observations of students and students' class work had more influence on instructional decisions than did the results of district or state-mandated tests. They listed eight major conclusions about teachers' assessment practices, which we are summarizing here:

Teachers' Classroom Assessment Practices

1. From 2 to 15% of a student's day is spent in formal assessment procedures. These include teacher-made, text-generated, and district and state-mandated tests.

2. The amount of time students spend on testing increases with the grade level of the students.

3. Teachers value the assessment information they themselves generate more than they value information generated through mandated testing. However, teachers use both types of information to some degree.

4. Within the context of a lesson, teachers tend to use performance assessment more often than they use traditional test types and item formats. They use traditional items such as true-false and multiple choice in weekly or semester tests that occur outside actual instruction.

5. When teachers construct traditional test items, they tend to emphasize factual information rather than procedural or problem-solving skills.

6. Teachers in the upper grades tend to use information from their own assessments more often than they use commercially made tests.

7. Performance assessments tend to be most often used in language arts (e.g., writing), science (experiments), and social studies (class discussions).

8. Teachers tend to "record" information on students in informal ways—that is, in their memory, rather than in systematic, written records.

Let's examine the teacher assessment practices listed above. It is clear from the list that teachers use testing in their decision making and that many of these tests are teacher made, not commercially developed. Teachers also use performance assessments that they themselves create, along with more traditional assessments, although most teachers keep much of the information in their heads, instead of recording it systematically.

WHY DO EDUCATORS NEED TRAINING IN ASSESSMENT?

Assessment provides important information for teachers and students.

Assistance to Teachers. Assessment data helps teachers identify students' needs and select appropriate methods and materials. Assessments help teachers determine students' levels of mastery and identify students who need reteaching or referral to services such as special education or gifted programs. Some assessments help teachers understand students' preferences and attitudes. And, of course, teachers assign grades and make decisions about promotion on the basis of assessment information.

Assistance to Students. If teachers design their assessments so that they address important knowledge and skills, and if they explain to students the basis for their grades, this information can help students know what is important in their courses. The results of assessments help students know how well they are doing and help them decide where they need to put extra effort. These results can also help parents understand how well their children are progressing.

Educators other than teachers also have responsibilities related to assessment. Administrators have to schedule assessments, see that teachers receive inservice training, and handle public relations activities related to the various testing programs. Administrators also must discuss test information with parents and other community members. School counselors, too, have important assessment responsibilities—some are related to teachers' assessments, but many also involve external assessments.

TEACHER TRAINING IN ASSESSMENT

Assessment is a valuable teaching tool, and it is important that it be done well. Much of the responsibility for the quality of assessments rests with the teacher, and there seems to be an expectation that teachers should know how to develop and use good assessments. These expectations have grown recently with the increased interest in alternative assessment, which requires an especially high level of knowledge and skill.

Because assessment serves such an important role and takes up so much time, it is logical to expect a large part of teacher training to cover knowledge and skills in this area. Furthermore, many recommendations for teacher assessments assume that teachers know the important concepts about testing and assessment in general and that they understand how to apply the concepts. For example, recommendations that teachers use portfolios and performance assessments assume that they have had instruction about how to create such assessments. However, Revak (1995) found many studies suggesting the need for such alternative assessment but no mention of how and when teachers were trained in the new methods.

What Should Teachers Learn About Assessment?

Knowledge of assessment has been identified as one of six basic knowledge areas for teachers (Rosenfeld, Thornton, & Skurnik, 1987). The importance of assessment as part of the preparation of educators has long been recognized by many professional associations, for example, the National Education Association (1983), as an important element of all beginning teacher programs.

In 1990, the American Federation of Teachers (AFT), the National Council on Measurement in Education (NCME), and the National Education Association (NEA) agreed on seven standards of teacher competence in educational assessment of students.

Teachers should be skilled in

1. choosing assessment methods appropriate for instructional decisions;

2. developing methods appropriate for instructional decisions;

3. administering, scoring, and interpreting the results of both externally produced and teacher-produced assessment methods;

4. using assessment results when making decisions about individual students, planning teaching, developing curriculum, and school improvement;

5. developing valid pupil grading procedures, which use pupil assessments;

6. communicating assessment results to students, parents, other lay audiences, and other educators;

7. recognizing unethical, illegal, and otherwise inappropriate assessment methods and uses of assessment information.

This list includes skills that allow teachers to create assessments, use data from commercial and external tests, and communicate this information to a wide variety of audiences, including parents, other teachers, administrators, and the students themselves. (For the complete text of the AFT/NCME/NEA *Standards for Teacher Competence in Educational Assessment of Students,* see Appendix B.)

In 1988 the Joint Committee of Testing Practices in Education, made up of representatives from the American Education Research Association, the American Psychological Association, and the National Council on Measurement in Education, published the *Code of Fair Testing Practices in Education.* This code describes and clarifies the roles of professionals who develop and those who use educational tests (Joint Committee on Testing Practices in Education, 1988). A complete copy of this code is provided in Appendix C.

In 1995, the National Council on Measurement in Education published the *Code of Professional Responsibilities in Educational Assessment*, which is a code of ethics for professionals who are involved in educational assessment in any way. NCME members involved in educational assessment will:

1. protect the health and safety of all examinees;
2. be knowledgeable about, and behave in compliance with, state and federal laws relevant to the conduct of professional activities;
3. maintain and improve their professional competence in educational assessment;
4. provide assessment services only in areas of their competence and experience, affording full disclosure of their professional qualifications;
5. promote the understanding of sound assessment practices in education;
6. adhere to the highest standards of conduct and promote professionally responsible conduct within educational institutions and agencies that provide educational services; and
7. perform all professional responsibilities with honesty, integrity, due care, and fairness.

In addition to the general standards and codes mentioned above, some professional curriculum associations have created more specific sets of standards for assessing learning, as part of recent reform movements in the curriculum area. An example of this type of effort is the National Council of Teachers of Mathematics's (NCTM) *Curriculum and Evaluation Standards for School Mathematics* (1989).

Our own experience with teachers who have taken our measurement courses is that they want skills to use in their own classrooms and they recognize the need for training in techniques. They also want information about the commercially developed tests they administer. We also have found that teachers recognize their need for help with assembling information from a variety of sources to share with parents and to present to student study teams for possible referral of a student to special education.

What Are the Problems with Assessment Training for Teachers?

Assessment is an important part of a teacher's responsibility, and the public and teachers themselves expect teachers to know how to do it well. But what kind of training do teachers actually receive? The answer is very little.

Lack of Knowledge. There is considerable evidence that most educators are limited in their knowledge about tests and other assessments. For most prospective teachers, training in assessment is limited to what is required for certification, and states vary widely in their requirements. Some states require a certain number of hours in educational measurement, but others have no such requirement.

Impara, Divine, Bruce, Liverman, and Gay (1991) found that teachers report that their knowledge of tests and testing practices is limited. Furthermore, their studies showed that teachers have difficulty with specific interpretations of various types of scores. Carter (1984) studied the testing behaviors and knowledge of secondary teachers and found that they know little about good test-writing practices and do not understand the connection between the quality of their assessments and the consequences for their instruction and student learning.

Lack of Information about Important Issues. Another aspect of the problem is that educators' lack of knowledge makes them uninformed users of assessments, so they do not even know the critical questions they should ask about the instruments they use. In many cases, they do not understand how and why the quality of the assessments impacts the usefulness of the information attained from them. For external tests they need help with questions such as what is the correct method of administering the assessment, how appropriate is the test's norms group, and whether the test matches the curriculum.

Gullickson (1986) and Airasian (1991) found that most teachers, even those who have had a course in educational measurement, do not feel well prepared. They say that little discussion was devoted to informal assessment, and that few realistic examples were given. Also, many teachers do not see the relevance to instructional practice of assessment training, disagree with professors on the importance of certain key concepts, and claim that educational measurement is not put in context. Educators also complain that measurement courses provide little training in the topics they want, such as the relationship of assessment quality to purpose, how to communicate results, and the effect of the home and school environments on test results. Stiggins (1988) found that teachers' primary source of help with assessment is their colleagues even though these colleagues have little or no training.

REASONS FOR POOR PREPARATION

Why has such an important aspect of teacher preparation been left to chance and been so poorly supervised? In spite of the identified needs, only about half of the teacher-training programs require a course in educational measurement (Schafer & Lissitz, 1987). Furthermore, O'Sullivan and Chalnick (1991) found that only 16 of the 50 states and the District of Columbia require specific course work in educational measurement for teacher certification. Other states may require that teachers have a competency in this area, but it is unclear where in their preparation program teachers would receive the training.

Schafer (1991b) proposed that the real problem with assessment training for teachers lies with those people responsible for their professional education of teachers. He suggests that one reason for this situation is that teacher-training programs and credentialing and professional associations have not clarified the importance of assessment in everyday educational situations. He also suggests that the measurement community has not clearly stated what teachers really should know about assessment.

In many states that require training in assessment for prospective teachers, this training is placed in a curriculum or educational psychology course. This means that prospective teachers get some training, but it also means that assessment must vie for class time with topics such as learning theory and writing instructional objectives. This situation is even more critical than it may at first appear, because most teachers receive no course work in measurement after they leave their initial training program (Stiggins, 1987). The situation is often similar for educational administrators.

Stiggins (1991b) suggested that part of the problem may lie in the fact that schools focus on the process of instructional delivery, as reflected in number of hours of instruction and pupil/teacher ratios, rather than on outcomes. Stiggins also suggested that it may seem that teachers need little training in assessment because they use commercially developed tests and instructional programs that are "teacher-proof." They simply use the lesson plans and test materials provided and see little need to develop their own assessments. Another aspect of the problem may lie in teachers' consistent use of a single assessment tool, such as true–false questions, regardless of the educational objectives they are trying to achieve (Stiggins & Bridgeford, 1985). Because teachers keep using the same tools, which they believe to be adequate, they express no motivation to learn other procedures.

Another difficulty is that, even when teachers are required to take a measurement course, the training they receive is often not what they want or need. Most courses focus on traditional assessments, item construction, and technical information about validity and reliability (Schafer, 1991; Stiggins, 1991b). However, both Stiggins (1991b) and Airasian (1991) found that teachers really need help with evaluating informal sources of information such as student work and other input from teachers and parents. Teachers also need help in determining the relevance and validity (or usefulness) of test information collected by the school, district, or state, and they request help in evaluating tests and test materials found in the textbook series and instructional packages with which they work.

Our intent in this book is to provide a "toolbox" of assessment techniques and to suggest appropriate ways to use each of them. Almost no one will use every tool—you will find some tools more useful than others. The key to finding the appropriate tool is to think first about your *purpose*—what you are trying to do, what you need to know. Then you can decide which is the best tool to help you accomplish your purpose.

SUMMARY

- Assessment absorbs a large portion of the school day.
- Many educators have little training in assessment.
- A number of lists of skills and responsibilities have been prepared by teacher, testing, and curricular organizations to guide training.

STUDY QUESTIONS

1. What do you think teachers should know about assessment?
2. What do you see as your greatest need for knowledge in this area?
3. What are the greatest needs of your fellow teachers?

FOR YOUR PROFESSIONAL GROWTH

1. Look at the skills in the AFT/NCME/NEA list on page 7, and evaluate your own skills. In what areas do you feel well prepared? In which do you need more training? Look for a workshop on testing in your school district or community to meet your needs.

2. Look for opportunities to become involved in the scoring of alternative assessments. This activity will help you to see how experts create performance items and set up the scoring. It will also allow you to observe how to create such assessments for your own students.

3. Volunteer to sit on a test selection committee for your school or district. You will get a chance to see a number of different tests and evaluate their relevance to your curriculum.

2

ॐ

Current Issues and Controversies in Educational Measurement

PREVIEW

Many educators get their first experience in formal educational assessment in a situation that stirs up controversy and generates stories on TV and flaming newspaper headlines. Controversy swirls around the use of tests in high-stakes situations—situations that have important consequences for individuals, schools, school districts, states, and the nation. Many high-stakes situations arise because politicians like to use achievement test scores to point out the shortcomings of education. We read newspaper articles and watch news reports that focus on low test scores, the unfairness of tests, and cheating scandals. Critics use most of these stories to support the notion that schools are doing a poor job of educating children. Not only is test information used to confirm the writer's or speaker's belief that the schools are not doing their job, but many writers also expect tests to be an instrument of reform.

We are less educated than 50 years ago!

The scores are out and once again our children are the losers! What are teachers being paid for?

What the headlines do not make clear, and what politicians and the public do not understand, is that these issues are complex and that the interpretation of test scores is not a simple matter. Furthermore, there are unrecognized consequences of each proposed solution for each problem, and many attempts at reform have had disastrous consequences, some of which have sparked other controversies. The issues that we discuss in this chapter have been and continue to be the focus of much discussion and have no universally accepted solutions. For each of them, there are important subissues, and addressing them helps to build a rationale for the in-depth study of educational measurement. Unfortunately, understanding of the issues involves very technical points which you may not understand at this point and we will have to introduce some terms which will be unfamiliar. However, we are providing non-technical definitions and/or illustrations to help. As you go through the book, these concepts will become clearer and you may want to re-read this chapter later.

MAJOR TOPICS

Testing as an Instrument of School Reform and Accountability
    History of Reform Efforts
        The Push for a National Curriculum
        National Testing Programs
        Other Reform Efforts
    Subissues Related to Assessment
        Release of Test Scores to the Public
        Declining Test Scores versus the Lake Wobegon Effect
        Impact of Mandated Assessment Programs on Teaching
        Push for Performance Testing
Teaching to the Test: Coaching versus Cheating?
Fairness in Testing
    The Meaning of Test Bias
    Sources of Test Bias
    Access
    Testing Ethnic Minorities
    Gender Differences in Assessment
    Methods to Eliminate Bias
Changing Views of Thinking and Intelligence
    Definition of Intelligence
    Impact of Theories of Intelligence on Instruction

ISSUE 1: TESTING AS AN INSTRUMENT OF SCHOOL REFORM AND ACCOUNTABILITY

Because of the frequency and visibility of testing, it has become common practice to respond to a call for reform in education with a "new" assessment program. For example, President George Bush's *America 2000* program, announced as a strategy for reforming U.S. schools in the last decade of the twentieth century, included goals that require national assessment programs, and President Bill Clinton has proposed a Voluntary National Test. These are examples of high-stakes use of assessment results, which means that the consequences can be serious. Schools, school districts, teachers, and students would be held responsible for performance on the assessments, with little consideration of other factors that may have affected the test scores.

A serious problem with using assessments to hold schools and educators accountable is that the assessments become invalidated by that very action. If assessments are used in this way, educators have a strong incentive to use whatever means they have available to try to help students score well. Advocates of these high stakes programs think this is desirable. They ignore the fact that the assessment results may be invalidated by this kind of pressure.

Another method of trying to force reform in education that is strongly supported by some individuals is the requirement for a "national curriculum." By this term they mean that all schools all over the country would be responsible for teaching the same curriculum to all the students. Usually the plan for this curriculum also includes a mandated assessment program.

Some proposed reform efforts have not mandated. Instead, they have been experimental, and proposed programs have been given a limited tryout, with an evaluation built in.

Those who look for simple solutions to the problems of education do not understand the complexity of either the problems or the proposed solutions. In an editorial in the *Wall Street Journal*, Robert Carr wrote:

> The problems of America's schools stem in large part from causes deep in the national experience: urban blight, drugs, the erosion of the family and the long-standing failure to devote sufficient resources to the schools. In the face of these pressures, the schools have been called upon to take over roles formerly played by the family, churches, and other agencies, ranging from sex education to housing and feeding children from dawn to dusk—well beyond school hours. (1991, p. A17)

We review the major suggestions for reform in the following pages.

History of Reform Efforts

The Push for a National Curriculum.   In recent years there have been several attempts to institute a national curriculum. The proposals have ranged from a curriculum stressing "basic skills" and "minimum competencies," which were popular in the 1970s, to the ambitious *America 2000: An Education Strategy,* which was developed by the National Educational Goals Panel (NEGP) in 1991 (U.S. Office of Education, 1991). The original *America 2000* proposal was for six goals, later expanded to eight (NEGP, 1995), for all American schools. Progress toward meeting many of these goals was to be measured by a national examination. *Goals 2000* provided resources to states to develop standards and initiate reforms.

The problems associated with a national curriculum were addressed by a 1993 conference organized by the American Educational Research Association (AERA). The purpose of the conference was to provide congressional staff members and members of the press with the opportunity to hear what members of the educational assessment community had to say about critical policy issues related to the development of a common curriculum for the nation's 110,000 schools. The presentations of the various speakers at the conference were reported by E. W. Eisner in the *Educational Researcher* (1993). Our summary of this report follows:

1. The resources dedicated to developing a national curriculum would be better devoted to assisting communities not able to support conditions needed for quality education.

2. Given experiences with civil rights, the Smith-Hughes Act of 1917 (vocational education), and the National Defense Education Act (NDEA) of 1958, designed to strengthen high school curricula in physics, mathematics, chemistry, biology, and (later) English and social studies, curriculum reform should be done in the interest of creating a truly enlightened citizenry, not as a surrogate for directly addressing questions of national interest.

3. From a study of national curricula in Europe, conference participants concluded that a national curriculum results in a more uniform curriculum but increases lower-level cognitive activity. Also, a large bureaucracy is needed to administer national curricula programs.

4. Texas's incentive system resulted in many teachers who had devoted considerable time to the development of new teaching skills, assessment methods, and subject-matter knowledge having to deal with conflicts between their new skills and the demands of the bureaucracy.

5. Rather than devising a national curriculum, the public should support local communities and encourage professional groups like the National Council of Teachers of Mathematics.

In short, none of the presenters at this conference saw a national curriculum as a solution to the problems that beset American schools.

National Testing Programs. Because of the high consequences attached to the proposed testing programs, there is reason for great concern. The consequences may affect individuals, or they may impact the school, the school district, the state, or the nation. For individuals, test results are used for placement in special education programs, for the awarding of high school diplomas, for admission to college and to professional schools, and to determine who may enroll in programs for the gifted and in honors courses. For schools and school districts, news about test performance has led citizens to be concerned with how their schools are doing, and prompted politicians to exploit the results in various ways. In addition, the legal right of the public to this information has been established in the courts.

However, unless the tests reflected important goals of education, any decisions based solely on the test scores might have serious undesirable consequences. McLaughlin points out that

> teachers . . . worry that test-based accountability systems . . . will drive out the very kind of instruction that is most effective with low-achieving or nontraditional students—instruction that concentrates on concepts, discussion, and an active role (1991, p. 249)

For example, a school or school district may change teaching emphasis in response to poor scores on a test made up largely of low-level, specific skills, even though the district has adopted an integrated curriculum. There is a tendency to narrow the curriculum to only what is covered on the test, and even in some cases to limit teaching to practice on the specific kinds of activities covered in the test items.

Unfortunately, test data are almost always overinterpreted, and not enough attention is paid to the many variables that must be considered in interpreting the data correctly. The simple matter of the percentage of students tested, and of whether students in special education classes are included in the average scores, can make a great deal of difference in the results. There are also arguments about whether there should be a breakdown by gender, ethnicity, and language proficiency, and there is not even agreement as to what is the appropriate type of score to report and how much change is significant.

The only situation in which assessment for accountability purposes might improve the quality of student learning would be one in which the assessments are designed in such a way that practicing for and taking the tests actually enhances rather than impedes education. For many reasons, this does not happen very often.

Since the late 1970s, interest and practice in educational measurement have focused mainly on the use of standardized paper-and-pencil tests as a means of documenting student achievement for purposes of public accountability (Stiggins, Conklin, & Bridgeford, 1986). The professional literature of the 1980s dealt with issues and practices of large-scale testing programs using these tests, and much of it was critical of the tests.

As the emphasis on high-stakes external testing has increased, the term *testing* has largely been replaced by *assessment,* placing the emphasis on the regulatory function of the testing program. Also, many people think that an *assessment* program is something other than, or something more than, a *testing* program, and various kinds of performance assessments have been added to some of the programs. We use the term *assessment* in this broad sense. However, we also use *testing, educational measurement,* and *assessment* interchangeably.

Ironically, while there is pressure to increase external testing with a high level of accountability, there also is a countermovement, which decries the testing—blaming many of the problems with education on the pressures on students, teachers, and schools to do well on tests that critics claim do not measure the important objectives of education. Since tests are often used to evaluate teachers and schools, it is understandable that many teachers and school systems direct their teaching efforts to the specific knowledge and skills covered on the tests, even though these may not be what teachers consider important. The result is a perversion of the principles on which such tests are based.

Any time assessment data are reported, it is important that care is taken to provide enough information so that the audience can interpret the information correctly. Usually that does not happen, partly because the issues are complex and difficult to understand.

What the assessments are supposed to do is sample a large pool of objectives—the domain—so that inferences may be drawn from that sample and applied to the entire domain. It is clearly impossible to test in two or three hours all the knowledge and skills students should have learned (or should have been taught) at a given stage in their education. Furthermore, in many cases the intended domain of the assessment has never been adequately defined, or the domain has been systematically reduced until it includes only those elements that may be easily assessed. So the assessment is a sample of a domain different from the domain that the teachers are trying to teach.

Educational measurement has always had critics, although the focus of the criticism has changed from time to time. One of the strange contradictions of the current debate is that, in spite of the criticisms leveled at tests and testing, the almost automatic response to any criticism of the schools is to propose another testing program. Let's review some of those proposals.

Beginning in the 1970s, minimum-competency testing was proposed and tried as a method to ensure that every student attained the minimum basic skills believed to be necessary in order to get along in life. In the late 1980s and early 1990s these programs were expanded to include broader coverage and to provide for using the results to evaluate teachers, schools, school districts, and the entire educational endeavor, and to hold them accountable. The goal of these programs was to improve education.

In 1989 President Bush and the state governors proposed *America 2000*, a national strategy for addressing problems of American education. It had ten operational concepts and included new standards and a new voluntary nationwide examination, along with several types of awards and contracts for development teams to help local communities. The Goals 2000: Educate America Act was signed into law by President Clinton in 1994. It endorses national educational goals and provides grants to states and local communities. Unfortunately, the actual proposal for tests related to *America 2000* departed from these recommendations. (Shepard, 1991).

In addition to the unfairness and futility of trying to use a mandated external test as the major stimulus toward improvement of education, assigning high stakes to a testing program can have serious unintended consequences. A study by Mary

Lee Smith and Clair Rottenberg (1991) found that under the pressure of a high-stakes testing program, teachers and principals tend to do whatever is necessary to help their students score high. In their study, Smith and Rottenberg found some serious undesirable consequences of external testing, particularly with high-stakes tests. They concluded that, rather than improving teaching, high-stakes external testing narrows the curriculum and leads to concentration on only those skills perceived to be required by the test and to less attention to skills such as disciplined inquiry and critical thinking.

In another study Joan Herman and Shari Golan (1993) found that teachers say they feel a lot of pressure to see that students improve their scores. They say that they spend considerable time in preparing students for the tests, often seeing that students practice the tested skills, using practice exercises similar to those on the test, even though they think there is some discrepancy between what they think should be taught and what is covered on the standardized test. This study showed that the emphasis on testing does seem to lead to increases in test scores. Whether this outcome is desirable depends on whether you think the content and skills on the test are the important ones that students should be learning. There is also a question as to whether the students are really learning more or whether they are simply learning how to answer the specific questions asked on the test, because some teachers use items from the test itself as part of the instructional materials. Herman and Golan did not believe that focusing on testing is helping schools to improve student learning, and they question whether improving test scores really indicates students are learning more.

In spite of the problems and the legitimate criticisms that have been raised, the enthusiasm of politicians and reformers for the use of tests has not been dulled. Testing programs are still being proposed as a means of attaining a variety of difficult-to-attain goals. The hope is that a high-stakes testing program directed at desirable goals will automatically ensure that these goals will be reached.

Other Reform Efforts. Reform efforts have not been limited to curricula and assessments. In the 1970s, the U.S. Office of Economic Opportunity tried performance contracting. The idea was to see whether a private contractor could do a better job of teaching academically underprivileged children to read and write than the local public schools were doing. Payment was based on the number of students who made a preset gain of one grade equivalent per year. Meeting this standard turned out to be more difficult than the contractors had anticipated, and most of them suffered financial loss.

In the 1980s, the school effectiveness movement, based on studies of schools that seem to succeed with low-achieving students, attracted wide attention. In 1983, 875 school districts had such projects, and more were added later. Test scores were to be used to evaluate the effectiveness of these projects. However, many questions were raised about the projects themselves and, even more seriously, about the appropriateness of most available tests to assess the effectiveness of the program.

In the 1990s, a number of for-profit businesses returned to the idea of running schools for profit and promised achievement gains larger than those reached by traditional public administrations. Also charter schools, which may be either for-profit or not-for-profit, are supported by public school systems but are free of some of the constraints public schools operate under. Reports on the effectiveness of charter schools have been mixed, with some failing and abandoning the effort.

Subissues Related to the Use of Test Scores

Release of Test Scores to the Public. Even as late as the late 1970s only about half of the school systems enrolling 12,000 or more students released information about the school district's performance on standardized tests to the press. Today, almost all local school districts and national testing programs publish test results. Comparisons are made between local districts and national norms, between states, between districts within each state, and so on. This change occurred largely in response to a demand fueled by the actions of both governmental bodies and educational institutions. As we indicated above, test scores are now used as the principal indicator of how well an educational program is functioning, in spite of the fact that the scores are easily misinterpreted or misused.

Declining Test Scores Versus the Lake Wobegon Effect. Declining test scores have been the topic of numerous news reports for many years, and the results of national and international tests are emblazoned in the headlines of almost every newspaper. These declines have been the subject of many national, regional, and state conferences since the early 1970s. Furthermore, there have been a series of international studies that purport to show that American students are not as well educated as students of other countries. As a part of these concerns, many questions have been raised—about the quality of the tests, about the population of students tested, about the curriculum, and about the philosophy of education in this country.

Questions have also been raised about the fact that, as the push for accountability has grown, many states and school districts have been reporting steady gains in average test scores, so that most states are now "above the norm"—a phenomenon known as the "Lake Wobegon Effect"★ (Haney, 1988). These seemingly contradictory reports are discussed in this section.

Declining Test Scores. The big questions about declining scores are whether the decline is real and what are its causes if it is real. Federal government officials such as William Bennett (former Secretary of the U.S. Department of Education) and Diana Ravitch and Chester Finn (both former directors of the Office of Educational Research and Improvement) have claimed that achievement test scores over the years have substantially declined within the United States and in international comparisons.

★ Lake Wobegon is the mythical town in Minnesota from which Garrison Keillor broadcasts his weekly program on National Public Radio. In Lake Wobegon, Keillor proudly tells his listeners, all the children are above average.

Although we wish to present a complete picture of this issue, we strongly feel that many of these claims are not substantiated by real data. In our discussion, we draw from the work of many researchers and from federal reports. For an enlightening discussion of the entire area of the quality of American education, we recommend the very readable work of Berliner and Biddle (1995) titled *The Manufactured Crisis: Myths, Fraud, and the Attack on America's Public Schools* and the articles by Gerald Bracey in the September issues of *Phi Delta Kappan* for 1992 and 1993.

What has really happened to test scores? The document *A Nation at Risk* (National Commission on Excellence in Education, 1983) made a number of claims about the sad state of achievement of American students:

Claim 1: Student achievement across the nation has fallen below the achievement of students in the past.

Claim 2: College student performance has declined.

Claim 3: U.S. students fail to measure up academically to students in other industrialized nations.

Berliner and Biddle call these claims "myths." We will examine each of them in turn.

First, let's look at Claim 1. To address this point, most writers look at data from three sources: the *National Assessment of Educational Progress* (NAEP), college entrance scores obtained on the *Scholastic Assessment Test* (SAT, formerly the *Scholastic Aptitude Test*), and nationally normed commercial achievement tests. The SAT and NAEP scores did exhibit declines in the 1960s and 1970s. However, separate examinations of the SAT verbal and mathematics scales indicate small score decreases and a trend over the 40-year test period toward remarkably stable scores (Berliner & Biddle, 1995). Daniel Koretz (1992) thinks that the decline in scores on the SAT and its alternate, *American College Testing Program* (ACT), is real and substantial. He notes that these scores declined from 1974 to 1980, and acknowledges that they have improved somewhat since then but claims that the size of the improvement is not clear because some of it may be due to the use of unethical practices to prepare students for the tests.

The NAEP data show a slightly different pattern. A decline in test scores in both reading and mathematics occurred in the early 1980s. But the decline has been reversed, and the NAEP scores are currently at or above the levels recorded in the initial testing in 1971. Interestingly, these results also show gains for 9-year olds and for 17-year-old Hispanic and African-American students (Berliner & Biddle, 1995). However, Koretz (1992) notes that NAEP was started too late to capture all of the decline but acknowledges that African Americans and Hispanics have made consistent gains since 1950.

Wolf (1992) reports that state NAEP averages are highly correlated with many nonschool variables and that three nonschool measures have a correlation of .90 with the state NAEP scores: percentage white, pupil/teacher ratio, and percentage of seniors taking the test. He suggests that both the decline and the subsequent improvement are most likely the result of a combination of the effects of numerous factors, both educational and noneducational, such as the watering-down of course content, changes in ethnic composition, changes in family composition, amount of homework, Title 1/Chapter 1 programs, immigration, and desegregation.

In the latest NAEP reports on achievement in mathematics and science in 41 countries, the results are somewhat mixed. U.S. performance is now somewhat higher in both math and science than it was 15 years ago, but only equal to the performance of 20 years ago. The percentage of U.S. students meeting the performance standards is still quite low (16% in twelfth grade, 20% in fourth grade, and 23% in eighth grade). The performance in science is "average," although that in mathematics is below average (National Center for Educational Statistics (NCES), 1997).

The third indicator of decline used are nationally normed achievement tests. But in actuality, scores on these tests in reading and mathematics have *risen* since the 1980s about two percentile ranks per year (Linn, Graue, & Sanders, 1990). Some have dubbed this outcome an "inflation" of scores and are concerned that the gains are not real. We discuss this point in more detail in the next section, "The Lake Wobegon Effect."

In discussing the reasons behind declining test scores, Richard Jaeger (1992) points to the fact that schools actually have little control over factors that affect achievement, such as goals set by school boards, available resources, and the characteristics of students in local communities. He concludes that school bashing appeals to the public, grabs attention, and doesn't cost anything.

Now, let's look at Claim 2, that college student performance has declined. Some Americans feel that U.S. college graduates know less and are less well prepared for their places in the world than graduates in the preceding generation. However, the data—collected from the *Graduate Record Examination* (GRE), the *Graduate Management Admissions Test* (GMAT), the *Law School Admissions Test* (LSAT), and the *Medical College Admissions Test* (MCAT)—present a different picture. GRE and GMAT results show a drop in scores in the 1960s or 1970s, when a higher percentage of students began to take these tests, but continued increases for at least the last 20 years. The LSAT and MCAT have shown no declines even with an increase in students taking the tests (Berliner & Biddle, 1995).

Finally, let's look at Claim 3. Claim 3 states that U.S. students do not compare well with students in other industrialized nations. The evidence for this point comes from the International Association for the Evaluation of Educational Achievement (IEA), which in 1967 began testing students from 19 industrialized nations in order to compare achievement across these countries, and from studies conducted by the National Center for Educational Statistics, which recently completed studies in 41 countries. As reported above, the United States has not compared well with many other nations on these tests. How could such a thing happen? There are several possible reasons.

Critics of the schools state that American schools are simply inferior and American children don't learn as much as children in other countries. A possible explanation is that the cultures and the schools in the other countries are vastly different. Another possibility is that the comparisons across countries are not based on comparable samples of students. Some countries select only their best students to take these tests. Also, most of the nations with which the United States is compared use a systematically selective process that permits only a small percentage of children to reach high school and an even smaller percentage to attend college. In contrast, schools in the United States do not as readily eliminate children selectively from higher levels of education.

Furthermore, American children receive a different kind of education—one that offers experiences such as involvement in sports and other activities in which many students in other countries may not participate if they wish to have academic opportunities.

Finally, recent research indicates that U.S curricula are laden with more concepts and that more concepts are covered in a given class period and course than in other countries. So, less time is spent on each concept. Observers also found that instructional time in American schools is frequently interrupted by public address announcements and other distractions not permitted in the schools of other nations (NCES, 1997). Also, nothing in these assessments measures characteristics of American schools such as creativity and independent thinking (Bracey, 1992). In short, the situation in secondary schools of different countries is so different that it does not make sense to expect that students would all learn the same things. The tests being used in these studies are not broad enough to cover all curricula and the other aspects of the situation are not comparable.

Ironically, more positive comparisons for U.S. students have also occurred for some tests. Berliner and Biddle reported that Cogan, Tourney-Purta, and Anderson (1988) found that real differences between Japanese and American students on knowledge of global issues disappeared by the end of high school. Perhaps more importantly, a recent IEA study found that American 9-year-olds placed second highest in reading skills and American 14-year olds placed ninth. These are far cries from last place (Bracey, 1993).

The Lake Wobegon Effect. In the 1980s, many states and school districts instituted accountability systems using nationally normed standardized tests. During the first few years of these programs the majority of states and districts reported upward trends in their mean scores on the tests. In fact, all 50 states were above the average in the elementary grades. This situation was first reported in a study conducted by John Cannell, president of Friends of Education. In a report published by Friends of Education and summarized in an article published in *Educational Measurement: Issues and Practices* (1988), Cannell charged that "standardized, nationally normed achievement tests give children, parents, school systems, legislatures, and the press inflated and misleading reports on achievement levels" (p. 6). This position was further supported by Phillips and Finn (1988).

Cannell's report was reviewed by the U.S. Department of Education, and a meeting with Cannell and representatives from four major test publishers was convened. The summer 1988 issue of *Educational Measurement: Issues and Practice* was devoted to a report of this conference. There, you can read an edited version of Cannell's report, along with commentaries from representatives from the U.S. Department of Education and four major achievement test publishers. Some of the commentators argued that at least part of the gain is real.

The explanations given for spuriously high scores were summarized by Lorrie Shepard (1990). All participants agreed that part of the problem was outdated norms, and some suggested that normative samples have become biased by the greater participation rates of user districts. Another explanation was that of "teaching to the test," although the participants were not in complete agreement about whether the expression referred to teaching the domain of knowledge covered by the tests (which may be desirable) or to teaching specific content and even actual items from the test (which is not desirable) "Teaching to the test" is the next major issue that we discuss in this chapter.

Impact of Mandated Assessment Programs on Teaching. The prevailing priorities for education in the United States are dependent on what is happening in the rest of the world. We vacillate between a *cognitive* (hard-nosed, intellect-achievement oriented) emphasis and an *affective* (personal adjustment, feelings, play oriented) emphasis. Most people agree that there is merit in both emphases, but the one that has popular support at any given time depends on recent events. World War II, the launching of *Sputnik* in 1957, and the Cold War raised questions about the adequacy of the achievement of American children and led to international comparisons such as those conducted by the International Association for the Evaluation of Educational Achievement. In periods when these events were not raising alarms, American education tended to be "child centered" and concerned with producing "well-rounded" individuals.

Teachers are continually asked to adjust their priorities according to which philosophy is prevalent. Furthermore, there are costs associated with each philosophy. Preparing for and administering tests requires enormous amounts of time. The use of students' test scores to evaluate teachers and schools attaches very high stakes to the results and creates incentives to have the tests drive instruction. It is essential that this outcome be anticipated and that all high-stakes tests be carefully developed and their full effect be carefully evaluated.

The Push for Performance Testing. There is much evidence that teachers try to teach what is on high-stakes tests and that the use of tests for accountability purposes leads to narrowing of the curriculum and to "teaching (only) the test." One response to this situation has been a call for a change in the nature of the assessments. Terms such as *authentic, alternative,* and *performance-based* have been used to suggest that assessment programs should be modified to instruct students to construct responses that reflect the behavior that is called for in the objectives. This usually requires that students construct responses that are scored by human beings rather than by a machine. The argument is that, since the assessments drive instruction, they should be modified to model what is desirable in instruction (Resnick & Resnick, 1992).

For a number of years many states have included assessments of writing in their state testing program, and some states now include a portfolio assessment in writing, mathematics, or both. National development of performance standards and tasks is under way in many other subject areas.

There are many problems in using performance-based assessments in large-scale programs. The cost of scoring and the need for extended training of the scorers are major concerns. Also, the reliability of the scoring is often poor, and measurement error is high. Some advocates of performance-based assessment suggest that educators may have to sacrifice precision of measurement of individual performances in order to foster broad-based curricula for all.

ISSUE 2: TEACHING TO THE TEST: COACHING VERSUS CHEATING

As we said above, when testing programs have serious consequences, there is a tendency for teachers to try to maximize student performance. Some of these practices are desirable; some are not. The term *coaching* is used to refer to desirable practices; undesirable practices are called *cheating*.

Although it is generally agreed that coaching is good and cheating is bad, some teachers are not clear about how they differ. Both techniques are used to raise the students' scores on tests. What is the difference? *Coaching* is the teaching of test-taking skills to improve test performance. Because the teacher does not use actual test materials, coaching is considered ethical. It helps students work more efficiently so that their scores more accurately represent what they know. *Cheating,* in contrast, involves the use of the exact content and at times actual items from the test. It is considered unethical. Table 2.1 compares coaching and cheating.

Table 2.1 Comparison of Coaching and Cheating

Coaching (Ethical)	Cheating (Unethical)
Teaching content and skills covered on the test	Developing a curriculum based solely on test content
Training in test wiseness	Preparing and teaching objectives based solely on the test
Checking answer sheets for proper completion	Using actual test items or very similar items for student worksheets
Increasing student motivation on the test through appeals to parents, students, and teachers	Using artificial score-raising programs
Providing practice in handling a variety of item types	Excusing low-achieving students from taking the test

Appropriate Coaching Activities

If you want to help students do well on tests, what are the appropriate skills to teach them—other than the objectives of the course? Most coaching programs focus on *test wiseness,* defined by Millman, Bishop, and Ebel (1965) as a student's ability to use test features or the test situation to obtain a higher test score. Millman, et al. (1965), suggested teaching students to use information such as tricks for answering true-false items and eliminating obviously wrong responses to multiple-choice items, along with more general test taking skills.

If you provide your students with training in test-taking skills, will they really help your students score higher on tests? The answer is a definite *yes*—and no! Oosterhof (1990) summarized studies that showed that most students benefit from some coaching. In fact, according to Scruggs and Lifson (1985), many students learn test wiseness skills on their own. A study by Scruggs, White, and Bennion (1986) identified the situations in which coaching is most effective:

- The training works best with upper elementary students.
- Programs lasting four or more hours work best.
- Training is more effective in improving performance on mathematics tests than on reading tests.

Table 2.2 summarizes suggestions for improving test-taking skills from a number of sources, including Millman, Bishop, and Ebel (1965), Ebel and Frisbie (1991), Drummond (1992), and Linn and Gronlund (1995).

Table 2.2 Suggestions to Students for Improving Test-Taking Skills

Before taking the test

Enter the test situation rested, well fed, and prepared.

Ask in advance about the test content, item types, and scoring system.

Read or listen to directions and/or items carefully before beginning.

Using time effectively

Work quickly and pace yourself.

Answer time-consuming questions last.

Answer high-point-value questions and questions that you are sure of first.

Answer the specific questions posed by a short-answer or essay question.

Mark items for later review and possible change.

Avoiding errors

Follow directions carefully.

Estimate answers.

Proof your work.

Mark answers carefully.

Eliminate incorrect alternatives.

Know when to make "educated" guesses.

Knowing What the Teachers Want

Know the appropriate level of sophistication for your answer.

Respond to the teacher's scoring criteria.

Use "errors" in item writing to help your score.

If in doubt, choose "C" as the correct option in multiple-choice tests. It is the choice most often used by test-item writers.

Select the lowest multiple-choice option from numeric options.

Select the option cued in the stem of the test item.

If in doubt, select "false" over "true" when test items contain the words *always* and *never*.

ISSUE 3: FAIRNESS IN TESTING

As tests have come to be widely used for important decisions, the issue of fairness has been raised many times. It has been charged that tests are unfair, or biased, against certain ethnic and gender groups, and that this bias has resulted in members of these groups being treated unfairly. In response to these charges, procedures for investigating bias have been developed, and numerous studies have been made.

The importance of the fairness issue is highlighted when the charge is made, for example, that each year approximately five million students are inappropriately tested using standardized assessments (Torres, 1991). Torres and others suggest that the inappropriateness centers on a mismatch of language, cultural background, and command of English, and on misuse of age and grade norms. This is a matter of *validity*—that is, whether the test truly measures the intended variable. Some people suggest that a better term than *fairness* would be either *honesty* or *accuracy*. The problem with these terms is that a test may provide an accurate measure of what a student knows but the score may be misinterpreted or misused if allowance is not made for situations that make the test inappropriate.

Schools have reacted to questions of bias and fairness in testing in two quite different ways. Some school districts have decided to eliminate testing altogether. Other school districts add tests or other assessment procedures. The concern about lack of fairness in testing often leads to another troublesome situation—limited access both to testing and to the special services for which the tests are used to establish eligibility.

Types of Test Bias

The testing of ethnic minorities and other identified special groups has called attention to the issue of possible bias in the tests themselves. In general, bias is classified as predictive bias or item bias.

Predictive Bias. Tests are often used to predict later performance as, for example, when tests such as the SAT or ACT are used to predict college grade-point average (GPA). The tests are considered biased when they over- or under-predict performance for different groups of people. Wilder and Powell (1989) reported on a number of studies of the accuracy of predictions of success in first-year college mathematics courses for matched males and females with the same SAT mathematics scores. The criteria for success were course grades and class performance. It was found that, in general, SAT scores significantly underpredicted the success of the female students. What does this information mean to teachers and schools? It means that test scores used as the sole means to decide placement of students, especially in mathematics and science courses, may be unfair to females. On the other hand, many studies have indicated that, contrary to common expectations, selection tests overpredict the grade-point average of minority students (Linn & Werts, 1971). This may reflect the fact that grades, the criterion against which the test is validated, may also reflect cultural bias—perhaps even more than does the test.

Another issue in interpretation is accounting for ethnic group differences in scores on achievement tests. Traditionally, Asians score highest, followed by whites, African Americans and Hispanics, and Native Americans. Linn and Dunbar (1990) have shown that these differences are found consistently in long range U.S. educational statistics.

Item Bias.   There are two types of item bias: true bias and inflammatory bias. *True bias* is evident when variations in performance on various items are not related to the knowledge required by the items. It may be investigated by having items reviewed by members of various groups, but the final basis for deciding that an item is biased is a statistical one. For that reason, true bias is sometimes called *statistical bias.*

Inflammatory bias occurs when items that stereotype certain groups or are offensive to them are included.

True Bias.   To detect true or statistical bias, the examinees are divided into groups by ethnicity or gender or both, and the percentage of each group answering an item correctly is computed. However, differences between groups are not sufficient to establish that an item is biased. A procedure must be used that indicates whether the item score is lower than expected given the ability of the group.

Measurement specialists investigating item bias try to determine the reasons for the problem and correct it. Sometimes it is obvious that an item requires information that is irrelevant to the intent of the item. Consider this example:

SAMPLE ITEM 1

In a football game, a team scored two touchdowns and one field goal. The team failed to make the extra points but gained a total of 250 yards on passes. How many points did the team score?

| A 3 | B 15 | C 18 | D 253 |

If this item is intended to measure ability to select relevant information and solve an arithmetic problem, it is biased against anyone who does not understand the scoring system for American football. However, if the item is part of a test for coaches, it is not biased, because understanding of the scoring system is a part of what the test is intended to measure.

Statistical methods of investigating bias require an item to be administered to all groups for whom the test is intended. This may be handled in a field test; but many times a field test is not feasible, so item analyses are done after the test is administered, and biased items are discarded before the final score is determined.

Inflammatory Bias. The usual procedure for detecting inflammatory bias is to have a panel made up of persons from all groups review items to identify material that might be offensive. These items are rewritten to eliminate the offensive material. Here is an example of an item that such a panel would reject:

SAMPLE ITEM 2

Mrs. Lu works in a fortune cookie bakery. If she makes 25 fortune cookies in 10 minutes, how many will she make in one hour?

   A 25   B 35   C 150   D 250

All the information needed to solve the problem is provided, so this item is not truly biased against any group. The item exemplifies *inflammatory* bias because *Mrs. Lu* is working in a *fortune cookie* bakery. That combination of name and work site seems stereotypical. The bakery worker could just as well have been a Mrs. Jones or a Mr. Smith. Or, if *Mrs. Lu* is a name the test writer chooses to use in a mathematics item, why assign her to a fortune cookie bakery, instead of (for example) to the claims adjustment office of a car insurance company or to the assembly operation of a computer maker?

Inflammatory bias is usually detected by readers from various ethnic and gender groups who review test items to spot this type of bias and either recommend that an item be removed or suggest ways to revise it. Since no statistical information is required for this process, it usually takes place before a test is published or used.

Sources of True Bias

True bias stems from the coverage of the test, the test and item format, and the conditions under which the test is given and evaluated. We discuss each of these below.

Coverage. Coverage has to do with what is measured on the test, specifically, the content or subject area and the thinking skills to be used with the content. All tests have some type of content—in reading skills, mathematics, language, mechanical skills, speaking or listening, or reasoning, for example. What is learned and when it is learned are determined by the culture. In many countries, students learn to memorize information to be recalled and reproduced later in its exact form; in the United States, students are often asked on tests to recognize and select information. Some tests also require students to use information in creative ways, to solve problems, and to combine old information with new information.

Whether the coverage of a test is fair raises questions as to whether all examinees have had exposure to or opportunity to develop the knowledge and skills required for the test. For some ethnic groups, there is also a question as to whether they acquired the knowledge in their own culture or in the culture of the United States. For example, when reading tests are given to students in a class-room, it is assumed that everyone has had some opportunity to learn to read. But what of the student who was in a situation where there were no books or who did not attend school for a year? What if the test is in English, but the student can read only Korean? Is the test a "fair" assessment of the student? Some say *no* because the test assumes that all students have had an opportunity to learn the material covered by the test but this assumption has not been met. Others say *yes* because the test measures how well students read English, without considering how they acquired that ability. So, whether the test is judged to be biased depends on the purpose of the test.

Test Format and Testing Conditions.   Culture affects how people think and what they value as knowledge. The way people from different cultures respond to various kinds of test items is an important consideration in interpreting test results. Duran (1989) cites a number of studies that demonstrate that many peoples are unable to understand reasoning problems involving situations outside their actual life experiences. Formal linear thought and abstract and analytical reasoning are Western developments that are part of our testing and that may not be part of the culture of many people. Duran even suggests that demonstrating knowledge in a traditional Western testing situation may be a culturally developed ability.

Fairness also involves item types, testing conditions, and interpretation. Some people contend that multiple-choice items are easier for some groups than for others. Others point out that essay examinations penalize those who are not native English-speakers. Some countries, such as Japan, stress multiple-choice items on tests for important decisions such as university admission. Other countries, such as Great Britain, stress essay formats for such purposes (Cheney, 1991). In still other countries examinations are mostly oral.

Another aspect of the problem is the language of the test. Some educators contend that tests should be given in a student's native language because literacy is mastered in the first language. Others contend that if the test results are to be used in an English-speaking environment, performance on a test is meaningful only if the test is in English.

Royer and Carlo (1991) cite a number of studies of item interpretation problems with different ethnic groups. They offer the following example as an illustration of a supposedly unambiguous test-item sentence that actually is subject to differing possible interpretations (p. 88):

> **Example:**   **"They are eating apples."**
>
> Interpretation 1:   "A group of people are eating fruit."
>
> Interpretation 2:   "The apples are of the type that are eaten
>   as opposed to those that are used for cooking."

Language and culture affect the interpretation of test questions and the item content of direct translations. As Interpretation 2 in the example indicates, a fluent English-speaker with specialized knowledge of apples could interpret the sentence differently than someone who knows only that apples are fruit.

The conditions under which tests are administered is another consideration. In the United States, students are generally expected to perform most tasks under some time constraints and in isolation from others. In other cultures, strict time limits are not enforced, and many classroom tasks are completed in groups.

Scorer Bias. For performance tests and for tests administered individually by an examiner, the background and characteristics of the scorer or examiner may affect the interpretation of the responses, and the way the examiner interprets the responses is reflected in the score. Carlson, Bridgeman, Camp, and Waanders (1983) found that when the examiner and examinee are from different cultural groups, the fairness of the judgments about the examinee is harder to maintain. Cole and Moss (1989) cite instances in which the logic, writing ability, and oral language skills of children were judged differently by an examiner of the same ethnic, racial, or social class group than when they were scored by an examiner of a different group.

Finally, and most significantly, fairness questions involve the interpretation and use of results. Norm-referenced tests—for example, achievement tests like *Terra Nova*, formerly the *Comprehensive Tests of Basic Skills* (CTBS) and intelligence tests like the *Wechsler Intelligence Scales for Children* (WISC)—are used to compare a students' performance with the performances of other students in a norms group. The comparison group should be like the tested students in age, gender, ethnicity, and so on. The problem lies in whether there are enough people from a particular gender, age, and ethnic group in the norms sample to make comparisons valid. This problem became so acute that the *Larry P. v. Wilson Riles* (1972) case in California focused on the fact that the norms group for one intelligence test had very few students similar to the plaintiff, so the comparison of a student with the norms group was judged to be unfair and misleading.

Relationship of Bias to Access

Access is a two-edged sword. The first "edge" is the charge of too much access. It is charged that too many children of a given minority group have been tested for purposes such as referral for special education. This issue was brought to the attention of the public through a California Supreme Court case titled *Diana v. State Board of Education* (1970), which was a class action suit on behalf of Mexican-American students. The plaintiff in this case argued that these students were overrepresented in special education programs. The problem is alleged to have occurred because teachers and administrators sometimes see educational problems that are related to lack of fluency in English as being problems in intelligence. The response to this situation, as in the *Larry P.* case, has been to question the whole idea of testing these children. As a result of the *Larry P.* situation, many school districts in California stopped using any standardized intelligence tests for the purpose of identifying students for special education.

This policy has led to the other "edge" of the access sword: too little access—not testing children who need to be tested for services such as special education.

Children who are not tested when doing so is appropriate miss out on valuable services that they need to ensure that they receive the best education. In addition, testing often opens the door to other educational opportunities, such as entrance to programs for the gifted or college admission. Some educators feel that this situation has resulted in the underrepresentation of ethnic minorities in special education, gifted education, and language development courses. Several legal rulings in the late 1970s and the 1980s declared that the tests are not biased or have required school districts to include minority children in the testing and in the special programs for the educable mentally handicapped (e.g., *Mattie T. v. Holladay,* 1979, and *PASE v. Hannon,* 1980, a class action suit brought by Parents in Action on Special Education in Chicago).

Testing Ethnic Minorities

As the foregoing discussion indicates, the testing of ethnic minorities is an interesting and complex issue for educators. The United States has been a nation of immigrants since its beginning. So why has testing for minorities become such an important issue recently? There are at least four reasons.

First, the percentage of ethnic minorities in the school population is increasing dramatically. The largest increases are in the Hispanic and Asian populations. Many of these children come from poor, immigrant, limited-English-proficient (LEP) households. Using U.S. census data for 1980, Pallas, Natriello, and McDill (1989) estimated that by the year 2020 the total population of school-age children would increase from 62.8 million to 72.6 million and the percentage of minorities would increase from 27.1% to 46.8%. These statistics are especially significant in view of the fact that 1990 census data indicated that the *total* U.S. school-age population actually declined 5.8% from 1980. That decline is projected to continue, but the projections for the increases in minorities seem to be correct.

Second, all students, including ethnic minorities, are tested more frequently today than they were in the past. Children are tested for placement upon entering school, they are tested to evaluate gains in achievement from year to year, they are tested for entrance into special programs such as special education and gifted programs, they are tested to certify what they have learned through state assessment programs, and they are tested as a requirement to enter colleges and universities.

Third, testing carries important consequences for all students. It often determines which programs they are allowed to enter, the curricula to which they are exposed and, ultimately, it may determine possible careers and life experiences. In some cases a single test score determines whether students will be allowed to advance to the next grade, to graduate from high school, or to attend the college of their choice.

Test scores are also used to sort students for school programs. For example, some states have testing programs to sort kindergarten students into "transitional" (slow), "developmental" (average achievement), or "enrichment" (advanced) first grade programs. Such sorting affects the materials children see, parents' and teachers' expectations of achievement, and skills that students are required to learn. Test scores are also involved in major decisions such as placement in special education or second-language development programs.

Finally, options for students who don't pass tests or who score low are much more limited now than they were in the past. Formerly, those who had not mastered English or who were illiterate had many ways to earn their living and live their lives. Before the twentieth century many people worked on farms, in factories, or at manual labor jobs. The need for high levels of literacy and thinking skills was not as great as it is today. Today, literacy and the ability to think and solve problems are essentials for survival. Individuals without these skills have few options for good jobs or a high quality of life.

This situation has led to great concern about how assessment affects ethnic minorities in the United States. The long history of relatively low scores by African Americans, Hispanics, and Native Americans is undergoing some change. Progress has been made, especially by Hispanics and African Americans, and the achievement "gap" between these three groups and whites and Asian Americans is closing (Linn & Dunbar, 1990). However, differences still remain.

Gender Differences in Assessment

Another area of interest to educators is the matter of gender differences in test scores and how to interpret those differences. The issue involves especially science and mathematics tests and problem-solving tasks. One of the major studies of gender differences was conducted in connection with Project TALENT (Flanagan, 1982). Many studies have also been made of gender differences on the SAT—for example, Harris and Carlton (1993)—and with the *National Assessment of Educational Progress* (NAEP), summarized by Wilder and Powell (1989). These studies show that males generally outscore females on mathematics and science tests that present a problem situation in context. Females score better on content-free mathematics problems and specific skills tests. Females score better on reading and writing tasks, but longitudinal data show that males have narrowed the gap and most differences disappear with maturity. Males are better guessers and work better under time pressure in speeded tests than females. Some researchers suggest that the situation exists because males have more confidence in their abilities to answer correctly and don't change their answers or linger over individual items. Finally, males outscore females on spatial perception and rotation tasks (three-dimensional space); however, this difference also disappears with age.

Gender-related differences appear least pronounced among African Americans and are greater among Asian, white, Hispanic, and Native American populations, in that order. In other words, African American males and females score more similarly on mathematics than do Asian males and females or white males and females.

Differences in performance have significant consequences for females and males. First, because females generally score lower on mathematics and science tests, they are underrepresented in technical fields such as engineering, and they make up a relatively small portion of students in programs and institutions offering mathematics and science-related training. There are other consequences as well. Females generally score lower on the *Preliminary Scholastic Assessment Test*

(PSAT), the *Scholastic Assessment Test* (SAT), the *Graduate Record Examination* (GRE), and other major examinations that influence life choices. For example, Gronlund and Linn (1990) reported that because of females' lower scores on a test that was part of the National Merit Scholarship selection process, 61% of these scholarships were awarded to males in 1986.

Why do these differences in the test scores of males and females occur? There are many theories. Researchers point to biological differences, attitudes, attribution theory, differing educational experiences, and differing life experiences. Since lower scores are also associated with differences in students' high school preparation, many theories have been proposed to explain why females tend to take fewer mathematics and science courses (Flanagan, 1982).

Two attitude theories have been suggested by Chipman, Brush, and Wilson (1985) and by Horner (1970). Chipman et al. state that girls have been convinced that mathematics is not important to them. Horner suggests that girls are afraid of the success that high performance in mathematics and science might bring to them, and that these values and perceptions are formed through cultural experiences.

Attribution theorists focus on how much control individuals believe they have over their lives and choices. According to this theory, people attribute control of their lives to internal or to external forces. Internal-control people believe that they themselves control the events in their lives. External-control people believe that other people and outside forces control their fate. The problem with attribution theory is that researchers report contradictory results. For example, Weiner, Frieze, Kukla, Reed, and Rosenbaum (1971) state that girls attribute their success and failure to external causes and that girls believe their success or failure in math or science is caused by teachers and perhaps other students. But Frieze (1975) found that girls are internally controlled and blame themselves when they are unsuccessful.

Another group of theorists focus on life and educational experiences. Sadker and Sadker (1986) documented different treatment of girls in math and science classes. They found the atmosphere in these classes oriented toward males and teacher expectations and opportunities for discussion and questioning more limited for girls. Zill (1985) found that girls have different interests stemming from home and perhaps cultural experiences.

Attempts to Eliminate Bias and Ensure Fairness

How have we tried to ensure fairness and eliminate bias? In the 1950s, there was an attempt to develop an intelligence test in which items were based on life experiences of children in a lower-class section of a large city. This was the *Davis-Eells Intelligence Test*. Unfortunately, students from lower socioeconomic classes performed less well on this test than did students from affluent neighborhoods (Coleman & Ward, 1955).

Another approach, used with limited English proficiency (LEP) students, has been to create new tests in the language of the students under consideration— for example, the *Black Intelligence Test for Children* (BITCH), the *Spanish Achievement in Basic Education* (SABE), *Aprenda*, and the *Language Assessment System*

(LAS). However, most of these tests have failed to show evidence of equivalence with their English language assessment counterparts.

A third approach has been to eliminate from tests any items that show a difference between groups. The problem with this approach is that item differences between the groups tested may reflect differences in the variable of interest, so statistical procedures must be used that consider the overall ability of each group.

Other proposed solutions have focused on the way tests are used. Some institutions and agencies have tried using different prediction tables for each ethnic group, but this raises new problems.

One of the most promising solutions is the use of multiple criteria to evaluate students. Sometimes these systems are developed locally by teachers and psychologists, as for special education referrals. One commercial package, the *System of Multicultural Pluralistic Assessment* (SOMPA), incorporates scores on the *Wechsler Intelligence Scale for Children* (WISC) and information about the home, school, and health.

Guidelines for assessing Limited English Proficient (LEP) children have been developed. Lam and Gordon (1992) found that approximately 44% of the 50 states have lists of recommended tests for LEP children; however, 62% had no regulations indicating when exemptions from testing programs are appropriate, and only 33% had guidelines for handling these possible exemptions. Forty-one percent of the states in this study have a policy of no exemptions from mandated testing.

ISSUE 4: CHANGING VIEWS OF THINKING AND INTELLIGENCE

One of the most interesting and perhaps most important issues in education is related to changes in how we view intelligence. There is still no agreement on important points such as the exact nature of intelligence, its heritability, and whether intelligence can be taught. As we report in Chapter 3, researchers have been assessing intelligence for nearly a century. Nevertheless, many controversies remain. The furor over the publication of *The Bell Curve: Intelligence and Class Structure in American Life* by Herrnstein and Murray (1994) is only one indication that intelligence is still a basic issue at the heart of how we see ourselves and others.

Although the actual measurement of intelligence generally falls to psychologists, we, as educators, must face the implications of how to deal with children whom society deems to be intelligent or unintelligent. In this section we examine some of the many interesting aspects of this fascinating issue. We address the subject in greater detail in Chapter 12.

Definition of Intelligence

Defining intelligence and explaining its relationship to thinking is a complex task at best. Intelligence has been viewed by many as innate and therefore not teachable. At times, *achievement* and *intelligence* have been carefully differentiated. And at one time, calculation of the achievement quotient (AQ)—the ratio of the achievement age to the mental age—was recommended, although test specialists now agree that AQ is not a useful concept and is also misleading (Ebel, 1965). On the other hand, *thinking* has often been thought of as a set of discrete and (some think) teachable skills based on intelligence.

Early psychologists defined intelligence as a basic "ability to learn" that underlies school and other learning tasks (Schwarz, 1971). Furthermore, Schwarz reports, this ability was thought to be mainly genetic and involved abilities such as response time and dexterity. Ironically, Alfred Binet, whose work is considered to be the foundation of modern intelligence testing, strongly felt that intelligence was not fixed genetically but was malleable and influenced by education (Berliner & Biddle, 1995).

Spearman (1904) proposed the unitary concept of intelligence, which he called "g"—a general ability to learn. Later, Thorndike (1920), Thurstone (1938), and Guilford (1957) concluded that this general ability, or "g," is actually composed of many components or specific abilities. Cattell (1943), a student of Spearman and a colleague of Thorndike and Thurstone, attempted to resolve the dispute by proposing a theory of two types of intelligence: fluid abilities and crystallized abilities. *Fluid abilities* are the processes we use to think; *crystallized abilities* are the end products of thinking. (See Table 2.3 for a comparison.) Later, Cattell revised his theory to state that fluid abilities are innate (i.e., "intelligence") and that crystallized abilities are the results of interaction with home and school environments (i.e., "achievement"). Today, the theory of fluid and crystallized abilities has been joined by the triarchic brain theory of Sternberg (1984, 1985) and the seven intelligences of Gardner (1983), as well as by more complicated theories such as the 120 abilities proposed by Guilford (1957).

Lohman (1993) attempted to clarify the distinction between aptitude and outcomes (achievement) by returning to Cattell's fluid and crystallized abilities. Lohman states that crystallized abilities are the typical products of schools that stress manipulation of knowledge. Schools have been very good at addressing crystallized abilities; however, fluid abilities are among the most important outcomes of education, both in teaching and in testing. Lohman further suggests that fluid and crystallized abilities are at opposite ends of a continuum ranging from

Table 2.3 Comparison of Crystallized and Fluid Abilities

Crystallized Abilities	Fluid Abilities
General verbal ability	Perceiving relationships among elements
General achievement	Educing correlates in a situation
Vocabulary	Maintaining awareness of self in the problem situation
General information	Abstracting rules and concepts needed to solve problems
Arithmetic computation	Developing and maintaining memory
	Maintaining attention span
	Choosing and altering thinking strategies

"near transfer" (crystallized abilities) to "far transfer" (fluid abilities). He noted that the concept of the continuum is found in the writing of many psychologists, from Stern (1914) to Sternberg (1984, 1985). Snow (1980) says, "Both functions (i.e., fluid and crystallized abilities) develop through exercise, and perhaps both can be understood as variations on a central production system development" (p. 360).

Struggling to define intelligence is an interesting exercise, but the major concern of educators is the relationship between scores on intelligence tests and what students learn in school. Since intelligence has been defined to include skills and abilities that underlie school tasks, it is generally thought that the higher a person's intelligence quotient (IQ) is, the more likely the person is to learn in school. Interestingly, Binet's work on intelligence in the first part of the twentieth century began as an attempt to sort children for instructional purposes. What is often overlooked is the fact that scores on intelligence tests also reflect factors such as home environment and motivation, which can and do affect what and how much children learn. Cronbach (1977) stated that because fluid and crystallized abilities are the end products of interaction with the general environment and school activities, the abilities themselves can be learned in school.

Impact of Theories of Intelligence on Instruction

Recently there has been increased interest in making the concept of intelligence—specifically, fluid abilities—more meaningful to teachers. That concept strengthens the possibility of teaching thinking skills directly. Thinking skills are sometimes taught in programs that are separate from any course content or curricula. Examples of such efforts are those of *Instrumental Enrichment* by Feuerstein (1980) and Jensen and Feuerstein (1986) and the *Cognitive Curriculum for Young Children* by Haywood, Brook, and Burns (1992).

Reuven Feuerstein and his colleagues used the *Instrumental Enrichment Program* in connection with their work with children who were severely culturally deprived. He learned to work with these children and help them grow into fully functioning adults. This method uses specific materials and exercises to teach children to organize, see similarities and differences, and plan. Feuerstein feels that the nature of the adult–child relationship determines whether the child learns these skills. In administering the exercises, the administrator carries on a dialogue with the child—a dialogue that is actually a tutorial and may take several days. During this time, the student is presented with various tasks and is talked through them.

Feuerstein believes that these methods of working with culturally deprived, retarded, and autistic children should be used in classrooms. This would require teachers to receive specialized training and to have a sense of urgency and dedication.

One type of task used in Feuerstein's Learning Potential Assessment Device (LPAD) is the "Organization of Dots." See Figure 2.1. For these tasks, a picture with a scattering of dots is presented, and the student is instructed to connect some of the dots in a way that will draw certain figures. In Figure 2.1 the task is to connect the dots in a way that will make a square and a triangle, using each dot

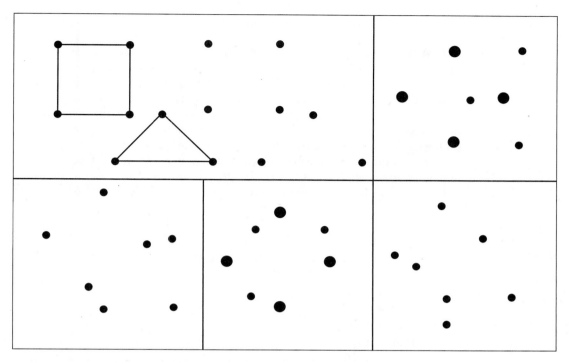

FIGURE 2.1 Exercises from the "Organization of Dots" from the Learning Potential Assessment Device

Reproduced by permission of the author, Reuven Feuerstein, from *Instrumental Enrichment: An Intervention Program for Cognitive Modifiability* (1980). Glenview, IL: Scott Foresman.

only once for the corners. The examiner guides the child through this task by questions, hints, and directions. The child must be guided to understand the rule that helps to solve the problem, which is that a square has four equal sides and four 90-degree angles. In addition, the child must find the square first, because it takes four dots to make a square but only three to make a triangle. If the child were to find a triangle first, the dots for the square might be used up, and the child would not be able to find the square. The examiner helps the student to understand the rules of shape and order, and, using the rules, the child spots the four dots that can only be a square and draws it and then finds and draws the triangle. Later, teachers may help students see that knowing definitions, such as those for shapes, and knowing the appropriate order of the steps in a task are important in school tasks such as solving mathematics problems and creating art objects.

It is easy to see how such thinking skills could be taught directly in the classroom. However, teaching these skills requires a great deal of time that would be taken away from other subjects. Furthermore, some educators feel that teaching thinking skills separately from content masks their usefulness to children and impedes their ready transfer to various subjects. Although Feuerstein does not recommend it, (Personal Communication, 1998), the solution might be to embed the skills in content by expanding in regular education activities the types of thinking required. In this case, students would be asked to solve problems, select a variety of thinking strategies to solve problems, and justify or explain their answers or solution strategies. Examples of curricula of this type may be found in integrated language arts programs, and in science, mathematics, and social studies curricula in many state model curriculum guides and frameworks. The instructional techniques and materials are also being promoted by many educational professional associations and some textbook publishers. Associations such as the National Council of Teachers of Mathematics and the Association for Supervision and Curriculum Development also provide concrete suggestions and materials to help teachers work with students on thinking skills that are part of fluid abilities.

SUMMARY

- Testing is often used as a vehicle to encourage educational reform and improvement.
- Because of the importance attached to test results, many educators have resorted to inappropriate methods of raising test scores.
- Charges are often made that tests are biased against certain ethnic and gender groups.
- The debate continues about the nature of intelligence and whether it can be taught.

STUDY QUESTIONS

1. What factors do you think have affected test scores in your setting?
2. How well does the testing in your school match the curriculum?
3. What can teachers do to be proactive about accountability issues?
4. Do you know of cases where teachers cheated in preparing their students for tests?
5. If you do, how did they cheat?
6. In your opinion, why did they cheat?
7. Do you think the tests you use are fair to all students?
8. If you do not, for what groups do you think tests are unfair?
9. On what do you base your opinion?
10. What does "intelligence" mean to you?
11. How does your view of intelligence affect your work with students?
12. Should teachers try to teach thinking directly or as a part of subject matter?

FOR YOUR PROFESSIONAL GROWTH

1. Ask your principal to make time at a faculty meeting to discuss one of the issues covered in this chapter. See how many different opinions are held by members of your faculty.

2. Check your school, district, or local university to see whether it offers any sessions on exploring or finding solutions to any of the issues discussed in this chapter. See what these training sessions offer for solving the problems.

3
ॐ

Historical Roots
of Assessment

PREVIEW

In this chapter we survey major events and the people that have influenced assessment as educators know it today. Of course, you can learn how to make and use good assessments without knowing anything about this history. But if you know where the procedures came from and understand how and why some procedures have changed, you will have a better understanding of why some practices are recommended and why others are unacceptable. For example, do you know why most measurement professionals do not recommend using only performance-based assessments?

As you read this chapter you will see some terms which may be new to you. At this point, you should simply try to understand the meaning of the terms in the context in which they are used here. They will be discussed more fully in later chapters.

INTRODUCTION

Assessment is so much a part of education today that we seldom question how tests as we know them came to be. As we reported in Chapter 1, assessment of students consumes a large part of a teacher's work day (Smith & Rottenberg, 1991) and the cost of the tests taken each year is very high (National Commis-

---

Earlier versions of this material were presented as papers at the 1993 Breivogel Conference sponsored by the Florida Educational Research Association, Gainesville, and at the 1995 annual meeting of the California Educational Research Association, Long Beach.

MAJOR TOPICS
Civil Service Tests in China
Other Early Performance Tests
University Examinations in Europe
Civil Service Examinations
Experimental Psychology
Achievement Tests
Intelligence Tests
Norm-referenced, Criterion-referenced
Nationally-normed Standardized Tests
Authentic Assessment
Alternative Assessment
Performance Based Assessment
Accountability
Minimum Competency

---

sion on Testing and Public Policy, 1990). At the same time, there is a great deal of criticism of the tests and much advocacy for change. A look at the historical background of the testing movement will help you understand how some practices developed and why there are some problems. Table 3.1 lists the major events and the dates of their occurrence.

Table 3.1 Events and Dates in the Development of Educational Testing

Events/Persons	Dates	
Beginnings		
Civil service testing in China	2200 B.C.–A.D.1905	
European civil service	1850	
Darwin's *Origin of Species*	1859	
U.S. Civil Service Board	1871	
Wundt's psychology laboratory	1879	
Galton's research	1882	
Cattell coins *mental test*	1890	
Achievement Tests		
Fisher's "scale" book	1865	
Rice's tests	1887	
Stone's arithmetic test	1908	
Thorndike's handwriting test	1910	
Buckingham's spelling test	1915	*(continued)*

Table 3.1 (continued)

Events/Persons	Dates
Multiple-choice machine-scorable items	1915
Trabue's language test	1916
Achievement test batteries	1923
Intelligence Tests	
Binet-Simon test	1905, 1908, 1911
Stanford Binet	1916, 1937, 1960, 1972
Army Alpha and *Beta*	1917
Otis Intelligence Test	1921
Wechsler-Bellevue Scale	1939
Army General Classification Test	1943
Wechsler Intelligence Scale for Children	1949
Wechsler Adult Intelligence Scale	1955
Wechsler Preschool and Primary Scale of Intelligence	1967
Aptitude Tests	
Primary Mental Abilities Test	1941
General Aptitude Test Battery	1946
Differential Aptitude Test	1966
Other Tests	
Rorschach's test	1921
Strong's vocational inventory	1927
Educational Research	
Rice's Bureau of Research	1903
American Educational Research Association	1915
National Council on Measurement in Education	1937
Theory and Standards	
Mental Measurements Yearbook	1935 (1st), 1998 (13th)
Educational Measurement	1951, 1971, 1989
APA *Standards*	1954, 1966, 1974, 1985
Code of Fair Testing Practices in Education	1988
Schools of Psychology	
Faculty psychology	1850–1920
Behavioral psychology	1920s–1980s
Cognitive psychology	1980s–1990s
Historical Events and Movements	
Launch of *Sputnik*	1957
Elementary and Secondary Education Act	1965
National Assessment of Educational Progress	1969
Minimal competency programs	1970s
Alternative, performance-based assessment	1980s–1990s
America 2000	1989
Goals 2000	1994
Voluntary National Test	1998

Like many other elements of education in the United States today, tests have ancient origins. It is interesting to review this early history and trace the development of ideas about what constitutes good practice. It may surprise you to learn that the history of testing spans more than 4,000 years. During this time, tests have undergone many changes. Many "new" testing procedures currently being advocated have already been tried numerous times in the past, and problems associated with them are well known, although some advocates of "new" practices choose to ignore them.

If we continue to ignore what is known about these problems, failed solutions of the past may be repeated when they are presented as "new movements" in assessment. It is wise to remember, in the words of philosopher George Santayana, that "Those who cannot remember the past are condemned to repeat it."

We review many important persons and events in this chapter but in the interest of brevity chose to omit many others. To learn more about this important part of the culture of education, you may want to read the sources that we cite in the references.

EARLY BEGINNINGS

In this section we discuss civil service testing in China, other early performance tests, and testing in early European universities.

Civil Service Testing in China

Testing was part of the culture of several ancient peoples. DuBois (1964, 1970) provides a description of a very early and long lasting testing program that began in China more than 4,000 years ago and lasted until the beginning of the twentieth century. When the testing was started, the Chinese did not have a hereditary aristocracy to provide a governing class, nor did they have a university system; therefore, they developed an elaborate examination system to select, promote, and retain public officials. The goal was to ensure a supply of government officials who would be well prepared for their duties through their own efforts and would demonstrate their proficiency by their performance on the tests. By 2200 B.C., key public officials were being examined once every three years. After three examinations, an official was either promoted or fired. There is no record of the content of or the methods used in these examinations, but the system seems to have worked satisfactorily, because it was continued for many generations.

In 1115 B.C., formal examinations were instituted for candidates for public office. The tests were "job samples," or performance tests, requiring candidates to demonstrate proficiency in five "basic arts"—music, archery, horsemanship, writing, and arithmetic. Knowledge of a sixth art was later added—skill in the rites and ceremonies of public and social life. Millions of men prepared for the tests, but relatively few achieved success. From time to time, the procedures were changed. A test on moral standards was included about 165 B.C. At various times the tests also included geography, civil law, military matters, agriculture, and the administration of revenue.

By A.D. 1370 three levels of examinations were well established: district ("Budding Genius"), provincial ("Promoted Scholar"), and national ("Ready for Office"). Those who passed at each level received suitable honors, but only the very few who passed the final examination received a position and a seat in the grand council on the Cabinet, thus becoming a "Mandarin." In the early 1900s leaders of China recognized that China lagged behind the West in military matters. The reason for this shortcoming was thought to be because government officials lacked knowledge about science and technology, since the qualifying tests did not cover these subjects. The attempted solution was to establish universities and technological institutes, but people aspiring to public office were not attracted to these institutions, preferring the old examination system with its emphasis on the arts and literature. So the examinations were abolished in 1905 as a reform measure (DuBois, 1964, 1970).

We can learn at least two lessons from the Chinese experience. One is that performance testing is a very old practice. Another is that testing programs that are not relevant to the needs of society will not survive indefinitely.

Other Early Performance Tests

The Chinese were not the only early people to use performance tests with very high stakes. One well-known performance test is reported in the Bible:

> And when any of the fugitives of Ephraim said, "let me go over," the men of Gilead said to him, "Are you an Ephraimite?" When he said, "No," they said to him, "Then say Shibboleth," and he said "Sibboleth," for he could not pronounce it right; then they seized him and slew him at the fords of the Jordan. (Judges 12:5–6, Revised Standard Version)

A later example of a performance test with high stakes was the "floating test," used by colonists in Salem, Massachusetts, to detect witches. People suspected of being witches were tossed into a pond. Those who floated were declared to be witches and were burned at the stake; those who sank and drowned were declared not to be witches. This was *really* a high-stakes test as well as a performance test! Unfortunately there were no winners.

University Examinations in Europe

Examinations were used in European universities during the Middle Ages. The earliest were oral law examinations at the University of Bologna in 1219. Louvain University used competitive oral exams in the mid-1400s to place students in the following categories: Honors, Satisfactory, Charity Passes, and Failures. By 1803 the use of written examinations was widely accepted, because of problems with the oral exam system (Popham, 1981). The universities' problems with oral examinations were similar to the problems evident in many current nonwritten assessments. Questions were raised about fairness of the oral examinations, and it was charged that some individuals received easier questions than others. There were also charges that the scoring was not always fair. It was difficult to answer such charges because there was no record of the examination. In spite of these criticisms, oral examinations are still widely used in many universities in Europe and in licensing examinations for some professions all over the world.

NINETEENTH-CENTURY DEVELOPMENTS

In this section we discuss civil service examinations, the development of experimental psychology, and early achievement testing.

Civil Service Examinations

The Chinese civil service examination system was admired in Europe and provided much of the impetus toward civil service testing there and in the United States. Westerners were impressed by the fact that competition was open, that distinction came from merit, and that the examination system produced a highly literate and urbane group of public officials. These are the same goals to which most current licensing and certification programs aspire.

The idea of an examination system for civil service employees had reached Europe by the 1800s, and in the 1850s the British began their own system. By the 1860s, interest had spread to the United States, and in 1871 President Ulysses S. Grant established the civil service board. The assessments that the board used contained short-answer items, biographical information, and a six-month, on-the-job performance rating (Popham, 1981). Three years after the establishment of the board, critics complained that the examination, though helpful in selection, did not predict job performance (DuBois, 1970). This issue is still a problem for employment and licensure examinations.

Development of Experimental Psychology

Modern psychological and educational testing developed from several movements that arose during the nineteenth century. The primary impetus for these developments was the application of the scientific method to the study of human beings. The power of the biological and physiological sciences, based on the scientific method, caused psychologists to abandon their philosophical leanings and begin to look for "hard indicators" of psychological traits.

Charles Darwin's publication in 1859 of *The Origin of Species* dealt with individual differences among members of a species. The English biologist, Sir Francis Galton was stimulated by Darwin's work to gather data on both physical and psychological traits of human beings. In 1882, he established a laboratory in London, England, where he explored individual differences among related and unrelated individuals on tests of perception and sensory discrimination, believing that such tests were indicative of intellect. He also pioneered in the development of rating scales and questionnaires and developed statistical methods for the analysis of data on individual differences. His student Karl Pearson expanded these procedures, paying special attention to correlation methods. Pearson's studies led to the development of many statistical procedures still used to analyze and describe human traits (Thorndike, Cunningham, Thorndike, & Hagen, 1991; Anastasi, 1988).

Meanwhile, in 1879 in Leipzig, Germany, Wilhelm Wundt established the first experimental psychology laboratory. In the late 1880s, James McKeen Cattell, an American, one of Wundt's students, returned to the United States and began to spread Wundt's ideas. Cattell coined the term *mental test* in an article he wrote in 1890. The tests to which he referred were similar to those conducted by Galton. Cattell's students administered these tests to large numbers of students, but the results were disappointing. The data were inconsistent from one occasion to another, and the scores were not related to any criteria of great interest. In short, the scores lacked both reliability and validity.

One of Cattell's students was E. L. Thorndike, now known as the "father of modern psychological and educational testing." At Teachers College at Columbia University he established a department in which the early leaders in educational and psychological measurement were trained. Thorndike continued to pursue Cattell's interest in the study of individual differences, and he and his students at Columbia University fostered the standardized educational testing movement in the United States (Anastasi, 1988).

The chief contribution of psychological laboratories to modern educational and psychological measurement was the recognition of the importance of placing strict controls on a variety of factors that could affect the behaviors to be examined. Measurement of learning, for example, required objective indicators of change. Standardized items and administration became a necessity.

Early Achievement Testing

Prior to 1850, achievement assessment relied almost totally on oral examinations conducted without attention to standardization or uniformity in questioning or procedure. Although such procedures provided an opportunity for teachers to determine some of what individual students had learned, the results were inconsistent and provided no basis for the comparison of students. Such comparisons were needed for decisions about students' entrance into academies and colleges and for assigning grades (Thorndike et al., 1991).

In order to develop a dependable basis for comparing students, oral examinations were gradually replaced by written essay examinations. Written tests allowed presentation of the same tasks to all students and allowed each pupil to use a full examination period to formulate and record responses. However, the essays also presented problems. Readers of the essays often used different criteria for different students, changed their standards for acceptable answers, or were influenced by extraneous factors such as neatness, legibility, and length of the responses. Educators today face the same problems when scoring writing and other performance-based assessments.

An early attempt to standardize scoring criteria was made in the mid-1860s by Rev. George Fisher of Greenwich, England. Fisher collected samples, or "specimens," of students' academic performance in writing, spelling, mathematics, and grammar and composition. He arranged these specimens in a "scale" book and assigned values to each specimen using a scale ranging from 1 (the best) to 5 (the worst). This was the first use of "anchor papers" for scoring educational measurements (Cadenhead & Robinson, 1987).

Joseph Mayer Rice, a pioneer in achievement testing, was interested in applying research methods developed by the psychological laboratories to the improvement of education. During the late 1880s, Rice was exploring methods to improve school efficiency. He started by preparing a standardized spelling test which was administered to 33,000 children. He later developed and administered such tests in arithmetic and language. His intent was to gather information about the effect on achievement of variables such as "amount of instructional time." An important feature of Rice's work was that by administering the tests to large numbers of students over several grade levels, he was able to develop academic expectancies—that is, grade equivalents—for each grade level (DuBois, 1970).

TWENTIETH-CENTURY DEVELOPMENTS AND CONCERNS

Within the twentieth century, there have been four distinguishable periods of test development. The first, from 1900 to 1915, was a time of pioneering work, during which the profession of educational and psychological measurement began to take shape. The period from 1915 to 1930 saw the rapid development of techniques for group testing of intelligence and achievement, as well as other types of assessment devices. From 1930 through the 1960s, there was great expansion of the use of tests and of technology that permitted the development of massive group testing programs. This period also included the development and refinement of psychometric theory, along with the beginning of criticism of the tests and of the uses made of them. A number of federally sponsored programs led to the use of tests as instruments of accountability. Since the 1960s, tests have been widely used and are frequently seen as the vehicle for change in education; however, serious questions have been raised about the effects of testing, and changes in procedures have been widely advocated.

We present the information about twentieth-century developments in two sections. First, in this section, we survey developments and concerns by time periods. In the next section we trace major developments and concerns through the century.

Pioneering Period, 1900–1915

At the turn of the twentieth century, the mind was thought to have certain faculties, such as memory and reason, that were to be trained. Theorists who supported this notion were called faculty psychologists. Between 1850 and 1920, faculty psychology guided much of the curriculum development effort in the schools and almost all of the test development.

In France, Alfred Binet and Theodore Simon pioneered the development of intellectual tasks, from which early group tests of intelligence were derived. Intelligence tests were first administered to groups during World War I, when the U.S. government needed to sort men for military assignments. These tests were known as *Army Alpha* (verbal tests) and *Army Beta* (nonverbal version).

Also during this period, standardized educational achievement tests began to appear. These included C. W. Stone's 1908 arithmetic test, E. L. Thorndike's 1910 handwriting scale, B. R. Buckingham's 1915 spelling tests, and M. R. Trabue's 1916 language tests. In addition, Thorndike used Rice's technique of setting expectancies based on the actual performance of students from different grade levels. He also adapted Fisher's ideas of "specimen" papers to set criteria for the score categories (DuBois, 1970).

Rapid Development, 1916–1929

Between 1916 and 1929, in the aftermath of the *Army Alpha* and *Beta* tests, there was tremendous growth in the number of intelligence tests, and achievement batteries made their appearance. Tests of specific aptitudes also were developed.

In addition, tests of other variables began to appear. Hermann Rorschach introduced his projective personality test using inkblots in 1921. Harold Seashore developed a music test in 1919, and Edward Strong published the first vocational interest inventory in 1927 (DuBois, 1970).

Rapid Expansion and the Beginning of Criticism, 1930–1959

Between 1930 and 1959, tests became an accepted part of the American culture in education and psychology, and there was a relatively quiet period in American education (Findley, 1963). World War II provided great impetus for the development and use of tests of many kinds. In 1943, the Office of Strategic Services (OSS), which later became the Central Information Agency (CIA), developed and administered personnel tests that used scenarios and real-life situations to assess recruits' ability to plan and carry out military intelligence work. In addition, the old *Army Alpha* and *Beta* tests were expanded into the *Army General Classification Test*, which had sections on reading vocabulary, mechanical ability, clerical ability, code learning, and oral trades. This work led to the development of tests of specific aptitudes.

This period saw changes in emphasis in testing. One change was the return to global assessments of a large range of educational skills. Another change was the use of new tests of basic skills and reasoning and the widespread use of "power" (untimed) instead of "speeded" (timed) tests. The field of psychology also changed its approaches, using more global projective assessment methods (Thorndike et al, 1991; Findley, 1963). Also during this period, psychometric theory and concepts of standards were developed, and psychometric concepts such as validity and reliability were discussed in books and journals.

Continued Expansion and
Mounting Criticism, 1960 to the Present

Since 1960 there have been contradictory movements, many of them political in nature. The greatest contradiction, discussed in Chapter 2, can be seen in calls for mandatory, high-stakes testing programs, spurred by political forces, and the increasingly vitriolic criticism of tests.

MAJOR DEVELOPMENTS
OF THE TWENTIETH CENTURY

In this section we present the major events in testing, organized by type of development.

Intelligence and Aptitude Testing

Early attempts to measure intelligence by means of tests of abilities such as sensory discrimination and reaction time were abandoned when researchers found little relationship between such tests and other indicators of intellectual behavior such as grades. However, there was much concern about individuals who were unable to function acceptably, especially children unable to function acceptably in school.

In the early part of the twentieth century, there was great interest in describing amounts and types of deviation (Thorndike, et al., 1955). German psychologist Hermann Ebbinghaus, Belgian psychologist O. Decroly, and French psychologist Alfred Binet and his coworkers devoted many years to ingenious attempts to measure physical attributes thought to be related to intelligent performance. Most of their early studies focused only on sensory and motor characteristics. When they realized that the simple functions being studied provided little useful information, they began to study the end products of intellectual functioning and to develop test items that more closely resembled the behavior in which they were interested. Binet and Theodore Simon prepared a series of tasks for testing children who were not doing well in school in order to describe the nature of their difficulties.

The Binet-Simon instrument, published in 1905, contained 30 problems (items) arranged in order of difficulty. The tests included verbal, sensory, and perceptual tasks and yielded a "mental level" score. Revisions published in 1908 and 1911 expanded the first test. Henry Goddard, director of the Vineland Training Institute, translated the 1908 and 1911 Binet scales into English and made some other slight changes. In 1911 William Stern, a German, termed the score on the Binet-Simon test a "mental age" and divided it by the chronological age to derive the "Intelligence Quotient" (IQ) score (Wolf, 1973). Lewis Terman of Stanford University revised the Binet-Simon test and published the revision in 1916 as the *Stanford Binet Intelligence Test*. He and his coworkers collected standardization data on a sample that included normal, defective, and superior children and adults (Hothersall, 1984).

Originally, the test employed many of Binet and Simon's concepts and test items. In 1937 and again in 1960 and 1972, the *Stanford Binet* was revised by Lewis Terman and Maud Merrill. Since then, there have been many other revisions, normative data have been collected, and statistical methods have been applied to investigate the qualities of the instrument (Anastasi, 1988).

The *Stanford Binet Intelligence Test* is individually administered by a trained examiner. Group intelligence tests, which could be administered to members of a large group simultaneously, developed from work on the *Army Alpha* and *Army Beta* tests. These tests were developed after the American Psychological Association set up a committee, headed by Robert Yerkes, to determine how the association might help in the war effort. The tests were based on the kind of tasks used in the *Stanford Binet,* and they featured multiple-choice items, which had been developed by Arthur Otis, a student of E. L. Thorndike.

The *Army Alpha* and *Beta* provided information that was used to make personnel decisions such as rejection or discharge, assignment to service, and admission to officer training. The *Army Alpha* was a general-purpose test. *Army Beta* was a nonverbal test developed for use with the foreign-born and illiterates. The *Otis Intelligence Test*, derived from the *Army Alpha,* was later released for public use, and large numbers of Americans took the test. Scores were reported as an intelligence quotient (IQ). This was the beginning of the American fascination with "IQ" (Anastasi, 1988).

Four other individual intelligence scales were developed during the 1930s through the 1960s by David Wechsler and his associates. The *Wechsler-Bellevue Scale* was developed in the 1930s and was widely used during the late 1940s for testing veterans of World War II. The *Wechsler Intelligence Scale for Children* (WISC) was published in 1949, the *Wechsler Adult Intelligence Scale* (WAIS), a revision of the *Wechsler-Bellevue,* was published in 1955, and the *Wechsler Preschool and Primary Scale of Intelligence* (WPPSI) was published in 1967. Each of these tests has a separate scale for verbal and performance tasks; in addition, each scale has numerous subscales that are separately scored to provide a diagnostic profile in addition to Verbal, Performance, and Total (Full Scale) IQ scores (Nunnally, 1972). Scores are not reported as mental ages, but deviation IQ (DIQ) scores are reported. The DIQ is a scaled score based on the mean and standard deviation of the distribution of raw scores of individuals of a given age group. (See Chapters 4 and 12 for additional information on this type of scoring.) This work led to the development of tests of specific aptitudes, in the expectation that such tests could assist in selection of careers and occupations.

There have been many multiple-factor theories of ability, ranging from Charles Spearman's two-factor theory first proposed in 1904, to J. P. Guilford's threefold "structure of the intellect" scheme, yielding 120 potential factors, which was proposed in a series of papers published beginning in 1956. *The Primary Mental Abilities Test* was developed in 1941 for use with children ages 5 to 7, 7 to 11, and 11 to 17. *The General Aptitude Test Battery* (GATB), developed in the 1950s by the U.S. Employment Service, has been widely used, and much validation information has been collected. The *Differential Aptitude Test* (DAT) was developed in 1966 for use in counseling programs in secondary schools.

Educational Achievement Tests

During the 1920s, multiple-choice machine-scorable items, invented by Arthur Otis in 1915 and used in the *Army Alpha* and *Beta* tests, were used in preparing group tests of intelligence and educational achievement. Test publishers developed and distributed so-called achievement test batteries, which covered such subjects as reading, arithmetic, language usage, social studies, and science. Norms were developed to establish the grade equivalent of scores on the various tests.

The growth of behavioral psychology in the 1920s impacted on the characteristics of the new tests. Behaviorists believed that people learned best when tasks were broken down into smaller skills that could be arranged in hierarchies. This idea, emphasizing basic facts and skills, spread to education and to teaching methodology and, consequently, to testing. This influence on testing lasted until the late 1980s (Stiggins, 1991a).

National Events Influencing Educational Assessment

Sputnik. In 1957, an event that greatly influenced American education occurred: The Soviet Union launched *Sputnik,* the first man-made, earth-orbiting satellite, thereby launching American education into a period of self-doubt and self-criticism that has lasted to the present time. Many people questioned the quality of American education, asking, "If the U.S. educational system is so great, why were we not the first to produce such a satellite?" The entire educational process was subjected to critical scrutiny, and many educational reforms were inaugurated. The question for educational testing was: Why didn't our testing show us the "inferiority" of our schools? The solution to this dilemma was to advocate more testing.

Elementary and Secondary Education Act. In 1965 the Elementary and Secondary Education Act (ESEA) was passed into law. The act required all schools receiving federal funds for education to show evidence that they were accomplishing educational goals with these monies. There was a demand for "accountability," which persists to this day. The federal government specified the kinds of evidence that would be accepted as proof of the effectiveness of federally funded programs. The evidence was to be the results of educational tests administered to children in recipient schools. School districts were required to administer tests, analyze the results, and report the results to Washington.

Educational change programs included programs for limited English proficient (LEP) students, minority persons, the gifted, the physically and mentally handicapped, preschool children, and adults. All of these programs required program evaluations that centered on test data. Thus, tests had to be administered often and for a number of purposes. Teachers became the primary administrators of such tests, even though most of them had little or no training in test use and test construction.

During this period, enthusiasm for assessment was so strong that misuses became common. Test results were often accepted as totally definitive indicators of achievement and intelligence. Scores were used for many inappropriate purposes, and criticism began to mount. Heredity-environment issues were hotly debated. Students were often grouped and tracked solely on the basis of test scores. Questions were raised about the limited scope of the content and skills covered on the tests, and about the efficacy of the underlying philosophy on which the quantification of behavior was based. Such criticisms are still with us.

National Assessment of Educational Progress.   Along with requirements for more testing for program evaluation, interest grew in educational progress within the United States as a whole. In 1969, federal legislation was passed to begin the *National Assessment of Educational Progress* (NAEP). NAEP tested a national sample of students aged 9, 13, and 17 years and adults aged 25 to 36 in reading, mathematics, writing, science, citizenship, literature, social studies, career and occupational development, art, music, history, geography, and computer competence. Items included short answers, essays, observation, questionnaires, interviews, performance tasks, and sample products (Linn & Gronlund, 1995).

Demand for Accountability.   The 1970s saw a shift of focus from the federal to the state level and the advance of the accountability movement and of minimal competency testing. During this period, an increasingly disgruntled public, impatient with what were perceived as small educational gains, demanded clear "evidence" of educational attainments. The evidence was to be in the form of tests and test scores, and high stakes were attached to the results, so the results carried severe consequences for schools and teachers (Jaeger & Tittle, 1980).

Schools, districts, and states began to develop tests or use commercially developed instruments to hold schools accountable for their use of public funds to educate children. The results were frequently published in the press with the names of schools and districts prominently displayed. However, these tests provided little information to help teachers use the test results to improve their instruction or diagnose students' needs. The most widely used educational tests are standardized and norm referenced—that is, students are tested on a common broad knowledge base, and their scores are compared or referenced to the scores of a wide variety of students from many locales.

Part of educators' response to the public's demands for accountability has criticism of the tests used. Since the early 1970s, the use of tests has continued to grow, and the criticism has become increasingly insistent. Critics claim that the tests were deliberately designed to be so general in content coverage that they do not reflect the curricula that teachers in any specific school district are teaching. Behavioral learning theorists warn that the standardized, norm-referenced tests are incomplete and inconsistent in examining skills. Their disenchantment with the tests reflected their experience with programmed instruction and teaching machines, which break learning into small, sequential steps in order to "guarantee" students' mastery of the concepts under study. Students taught by these methods sometimes failed to show mastery on the standardized, norm-referenced tests, which are directed at broader objectives (Glaser, 1963).

Criterion-Referenced Tests. One solution offered for the problem of the broad-range standardized tests was a new test that measured exactly what was to be taught. Dubbed "criterion-referenced tests" by Glaser, later writers have used other terms such as curriculum based assesment (CBA), these tests examined students on carefully specified content. The content often came from lists of skills, such as those for "minimum competency" (Madaus, 1983). Scores were interpreted in terms of mastery of objectives, rather than normatively—that is, students were compared not with other students across the country, but with some standard of mastery of the specified content. The criteria were in the form of cut scores, which are based on a prescribed amount of content mastered. If a student's score was above the cut score, the student was considered "competent." If the student's score was below the cut score, the student was supposed to receive remedial instruction on the content of the "missed" item.

For a time, the percentages of "minimally competent students" in each school, district, and state were publicly announced. Many school districts began to spend a large part of their resources and classroom time working on the "minimal" knowledge and skills, to the detriment of the rest of the curriculum. Furthermore, because the measured skills and knowledge were often tested and taught as discrete pieces of information, students were unable to put the knowledge and skills together into cohesive, useful bodies of learning. Schools were producing readers who could identify individual words but could not comprehend connected text, or who could recognize good grammar and syntax but could not write coherent paragraphs. Experts from the fields of mathematics, science, and the social sciences reported similar problems. The old criticism of narrow content had re-emerged.

Alternative, Performance-Based Tests. Since the 1980s, criticism focused on the almost exclusive use of multiple-choice tests in the United States. Critics insist that a different type of assessment should be employed. Many of the "alternative" assessments being advocated are very much like those used in earlier periods and have the same problems that they had. Many of the advocates, however, seem unaware of these problems.

The assessments currently being recommended are termed "authentic," "alternative," or "performance-based." This emphasis began during the 1980s, largely at the insistence of cognitive psychologists. These psychologists believe that children learn best with content and procedures grouped and organized (Lane, 1989; Glaser, Lesgold, & Lajoie, 1987). They also believe that assessments that fragment learning do not accurately assess what children really know.

The cognitive point of view is reflected in changes such as the return to the teaching of writing as a *process,* asking students to actually write rather than simply to recognize good writing or components of it. Mathematicians and scientists have also begun to look at the teaching of their fields from the constructivist perspective, which requires students to construct their own knowledge of how math and science work. There are now arguments about the extent to which students' construction of knowledge should be checked against knowledge from other sources.

Teachers have been urged to change their modes of teaching, deemphasizing lecture and increasing the use of projects, experiments, and productive tasks. Some critics have used this movement to support their criticism of traditional (i.e., norm-referenced, multiple-choice) tests because they do not reflect achievement in these activities. Traditional tests also are criticized because of the types of tasks and item formats used. Critics state that the tasks, typically multiple choice, assess only surface learning of facts. Shavelson, Baxter, and Pine (1992) called such test items "surrogates" to the real tasks of students. Some educators demand tasks that are "alternatives" to the more traditional multiple-choice tests, tasks that are more similar to actual or "authentic" work of students. Such tasks involve samples of writing, completion of experiments, creation of products such as reports and speeches, and problem-solving activities (Wiggins, 1989).

Today, some educators and educational agencies are busily developing "authentic" or "alternative" assessments. Although some of the new tasks are more appealing to students and teachers, there are problems. Many of the items are poorly written and, in spite of the writers' intentions, tap only low-level skills. In addition, the problems that led to the eager adoption of multiple-choice items in the 1920s have resurfaced: bias in scoring, unreliability of scorers, poor model answers, unclear scoring criteria, and introduction of irrelevant factors such as response length and handwriting. As a result, at the end of the 1990s we seem to be returning to the wide use of multiple-choice items, along with some alternative assessments.

Development of the Field of Educational Research

One major result of interest in studying education outcomes and procedures was the organization of research efforts. In 1903, Rice established the Bureau of Research and began to publish *The Forum,* which reported scientific studies of education. The name of the bureau was soon changed to the Society of Educational Research, which was the forerunner of the American Educational Research Association (AERA), organized in 1915. AERA continues to foster research and evaluation in education, holding an annual convention at which symposia, invited addresses, and papers are presented. Many books and journals in the area of educational research and testing have also been published. The National Council on Measurement in Education (NCME) started in 1937 with a group of professors of educational measurement. It was called the National Association of Educational Measurement until 1942, when the name was changed to the National Council on Measurement *Used* in Education. The name was changed again in 1961 to the present name (Lehmann, 1990), and attempts have been made to recruit members from the schools and state departments of education.

Development of Standards and Codes

As part of the movement to foster more critical use of tests and to improve test quality, new research publications appeared. In 1935, Oscar Buros began publishing the *Mental Measurements Yearbook*. This book contained a listing of tests in print and, beginning in 1937, included critical reviews of the listed instruments. The yearbooks have been issued approximately every five years; the thirteenth yearbook was published in 1998.

The first edition of *Educational Measurement*, edited by E. F. Lindquist, was published in 1951; the second edition, edited by R. L. Thorndike, was published in 1971; the third edition, edited by R. L. Linn, was published in 1989. Each of these volumes provides a comprehensive guide to educational measurement as practiced at the time of publication. All have been sponsored by the American Council on Education.

Measurement professionals worked to codify standards for tests and test use. In 1954 a joint committee of the American Psychological Association, the American Educational Research Association, and the National Council on Measurement in Education published the first *Standards for Educational and Psychological Testing*. These standards, now known as the "APA *Standards*," were revised in 1966, 1974, and 1985 (American Educational Research Association, American Psychological Association, & National Council on Measurement in Education, 1985), and another revision is under way. Standards for training teachers to develop and use assessments were developed jointly by the American Federation of Teachers, the National Council on Measurement in Education, and the National Education Association (1990). The *Code of Fair Testing Practices in Education* was published in 1988 (Joint Committee on Testing Practices, 1988), and the *Code of Professional Responsibilities in Educational Measurement* was published in 1995 (National Council on Measurement in Education, 1995).

Development of Technology: Scoring, Analysis, and Administration

The ability to score multiple-choice items objectively was hailed as a great improvement over the unreliability and biases of human scorers. Use of these items also reduced the scoring time and made possible large-scale testing programs. During World War II, IBM developed a test-scoring machine, further reducing the time needed to score large numbers of tests. More recently, development of electronic data-processing equipment has greatly expanded the possibilities for scoring, analysis, and preparation of tests. Other technical advances have made it possible to administer tests by computer and score them immediately.

Computerized item bank programs make it possible to construct multiple forms of equivalent tests in only a few minutes. Also available are banks of items at many grade levels in a variety of subjects (Ward & Murray-Ward, 1994). For a list of item banking programs and items currently available, see Appendix G. Many group tests are now administered individually by computer and scored immediately—resulting in a great saving of time for the agency and convenience for the examinee.

Current Issues

The most serious issues of the 1990s were the subject of Chapter 2. Let's simply review them here:

- There is a strong push for a national curriculum and for a national test as a means of improving teaching and learning. The *America 2000* project began in 1989, followed by *Goals 2000* (1994), and a voluntary national test has been proposed. There is also a strong impetus toward including performance assessments in many high-stakes mandatory testing programs.

- Because of the high stakes attached to many of the tests, there is great concern about the extent to which schools are spending time and other resources to teach students how to score well on specific tests instead of teaching them broader knowledge and skills.

- The effect of ethnic and gender differences on test items and on test results has been studied in many contexts, and methods for detecting bias have been developed and used in many programs.

- The nature of intelligence and the extent to which intelligence can be taught is being examined again.

SUMMARY

- Performance testing is very ancient, beginning in China more than 4,000 years ago.
- Early Civil Service tests in Europe and America were modeled after the Chinese System.
- Modern psychological testing began in experimental laboratories of Europe with tests of intelligence.
- Early achievement testing started in the United States.
- World War I and World War II led to great expansion of testing and development of new testing techniques.
- Standardized, norm-referenced achievement testing developed rapidly through the 1970s.
- High-stakes testing has expanded from early in the 1970s to the present.

STUDY QUESTIONS

1. Do you see any similarities between the civil service tests of the Chinese and the performance tests that we administer today?

2. What is high-stakes testing?

3. Can you think of some high-stakes examinations taken by students you work with?

4. Have you been involved in scoring that required the use of "specimen" papers?

5. If you have, were there any problems in using the specimens?

6. How could these problems have been prevented?

7. Has your school been involved in a testing program that has high stakes for the school and for teachers? What was the result of the program?

8. Do you think intelligence tests should be used in schools? Give reasons to support your answers.

9. How can information from nationally normed achievement tests be useful?

10. To what extent do you think educators are using lessons from history as they develop new tests and other assessment methods?

FOR YOUR PROFESSIONAL GROWTH

1. Arrange to discuss the history of testing in your school district with the test director. Find out when testing began in the district and how the program has changed during the past 20 years.

2. Find out whether there is a file of old standardized tests in the district. If there is, look at the tests to see how they have changed through the years.

4

Basic Concepts

In order to develop and use assessments appropriately, you must understand certain basic concepts and terms. The first of these is the important concept of measurement—what it is, how measurement in education and psychology differs from that in the physical world, and the purposes for which measurement is used in education. Then there is terminology that is used in discussions of tests and other assessments. And you also must understand what characteristics assessments must have if they are to serve the purposes for which you wish to use them.

In this chapter we present many concepts and terms that may be new to you and some familiar terms that are used in special ways in discussions of educational assessment. We suggest that you try to understand each one in context as you study the chapter. As you read later chapters, you may want to turn back to this chapter to refresh your understanding. Also, the Glossary lists terms and definitions to make it easy for you to look up a term at any time.

We deal first with the meaning of measurement and how measurement concepts apply to educational assessments. Then we present the terminology of assessment. The last section of the chapter deals with the characteristics of assessments if they are to be useful and not misleading and with standards that have been established for developing and using assessments.

MAJOR TOPICS

The Nature of Measurement
Purposes of Measurement in Education
Levels of Measurement
Terminology
Requirements for good assessments
   Validity: Relevance, Usefulness
   Reliability: Dependability
   Fairness
Published Standards for Assessments

NATURE OF MEASUREMENT

Measurement is the process of determining the amount, extent, or other category of a variable. It involves assigning numbers or symbols to objects in some meaningful way, following agreed-on rules. It may involve simply classifying individuals or objects according to some criterion, such as social class or gender, or it may involve comparing and ranking them.

The variables that are measured are *attributes,* or characteristics of objects or individuals, such as height, weight, or amount of information learned; they are not the objects or individuals themselves. We may measure variables such as the *length* of a room, the *duration of time* an individual needs to complete a task, or the *number of items* a student answers correctly. Some variables may be measured directly, for example *length, weight,* or *time.* Other variables must be measured indirectly, that is, by their effects. Temperature, for example, may be measured only by measuring the height of a column of alcohol or mercury in a tube. Similarly, a student's overall achievement may be measured only by measuring performance on a test or other activity from which we infer his or her achievement.

PURPOSES OF
MEASUREMENT IN EDUCATION

Assessment should be an integral part of instruction. Indeed, there is a predictable instructional cycle in which assessment information on which to base subsequent decisions is needed. Figure 4.1 shows how assessment information is used to modify instructional activities and make decisions about students. This figure also demonstrates how important assessment information is, why it must be valid and accurate, and how instruction and assessments together create a smooth and effective instructional cycle for a student.

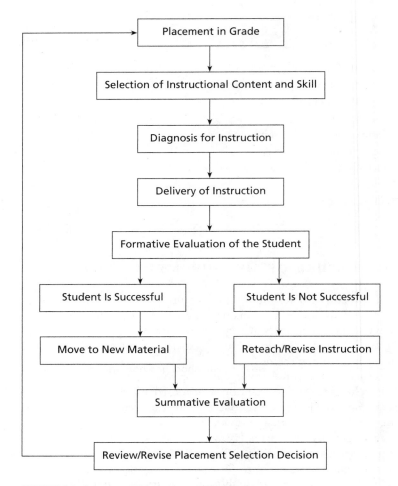

FIGURE 4.1 Assessment in the Instruction Cycle

The results of measurement are useful only if educators do something with the information. In education we may use measurement when evaluating individuals or programs. Two major types of evaluation are formative and summative.

Formative or Summative

Teachers use *formative evaluation* to monitor the instructional process of individuals or groups. Formative evaluation may precede instruction and takes place throughout a course of study. It provides feedback to guide instruction.

Summative evaluation is used to determine the status of individuals or groups. It is the basis of decisions about the adequacy of performance when considered over a long period of time or unit of instruction, such as a semester, year, or a program of study (as for awarding degrees, diplomas, or licenses). Summative evaluation usually occurs after instruction has been completed. It sums up what has happened. Summative evaluation is used when a teacher gives a semester or quarterly examination and assigns grades. It may also precede instruction to provide information about where to begin.

Table 4.1 summarizes the characteristics of formative and summative evaluation. Notice that they differ chiefly in purpose and time frame. The same type of reporting may be used for both, although the content of the reports would be different.

Table 4.1 Comparison of Formative and Summative Evaluation

	Formative Evaluation	Summative Evaluation
Purpose	Provides feedback to guide instruction	Provides evaluative information about outcomes
Time frame	Continuous	At the beginning and end of a period of instruction

Types of Reports	Informal
	    Conferences
	    Notes
	
	Formal
	    Checklists
	    Conferences
		For students
		    Conferences
		        Report cards
		        Profile charts
		    Promotion or nonpromotion
		    Graduation or nongraduation
		    Admission or rejection
		For school or school system
		    Recognition
		    Censure

Table 4.2 lists the purposes of assessment and gives some examples of ways in which assessment data might be used and some types of assessment data that teachers, other school personnel, and state or national officials might use. Each of the purposes listed in the table is discussed below.

Placement or Selection

To make decisions about placement and selection, teachers and other school professionals such as administrators, counselors, and school psychologists need assessment information in order to identify the best educational program for a student. The program may be in special education, a different grade, or a remedial or accelerated course. In higher education, selection also involves admission to a college or program. Assessment data used for placement or selection may come from a variety of tests and evaluations of student work.

Diagnosis

Diagnosis is often a part of placement decisions. It also may be used anytime there is a need to identify students' special strengths and weaknesses, so the teacher can

**Table 4.2 Purposes of Assessment, Examples
of Uses, and Examples of Assessment Techniques**

Purpose	Uses	Techniques
Placement or Selection	Referral to special education Placement in grade level Placement in instructional group Admission to college Admission to a program	Individual intelligence tests Individual achievement tests Group commercial achievement tests Student work samples Classroom observations
Diagnosis	Selection of instructional materials Determination of where to begin in instructional sequence	Textbook tests Student work samples Commercial diagnostic tests in mathematics, reading, etc. Student performance of skills in reading, music, physical education, etc.
Evaluation of instruction	Evaluation of teachers' instructional skills Evaluation of quality of commercial or locally made materials	Student work samples Student portfolios Classroom observations Commercial achievement tests
Certification	Awarding diplomas Evaluating mastery of basic competencies	Commercial or state or locally developed achievement tests Student work samples Student performances Student portfolios
Accountability	Evaluating a state's, district's, or nation's achievement of educational goals	Commercially developed tests Student performances Student portfolios
Re-examination for placement or selection	Review of student's placement in special education Re-evaluation of student's placement in remedial or accelerated instruction	Commercially developed tests Student work samples Student performances Student portfolios Classroom observations

decide what instructional materials would work best for the student. For diagnosis, the primary types of data needed are samples of student work and scores on group tests. The results from individual tests administered by a school psychologist may also be useful.

Evaluation of Instruction

An important focus for this purpose is to be sure that instructional materials used with students and the methods used by the teachers are the best choices for and most effective with students. The assessment data may come from commercially developed tests and from evaluation of student work. Students who do poorly may be retaught with a different approach or new materials.

Certification

In general, certification of students, as for graduation, is the task of schools, districts, or states, but teachers help to determine whether students have passed courses or have met minimum competency requirements that are part of the requirements for graduation or for promotion to the next grade. Data for this purpose may come from a variety of tests, such as competency examinations, and from evaluation of student work. A recent development has been the use of student portfolios as a part of the information used.

Accountability

Because schools are agencies of communities, they must be responsible for their work with students. As we discussed in Chapter 2, there is a continuing push to establish a national curriculum and use national testing programs to hold school districts and teachers accountable for student learning. Also, local school districts and state education departments often use an assessment program to check schools to determine whether students are meeting achievement goals. The assessment information generally comes from tests and samples of student work, including portfolios. Now many school districts use school and district report cards, which provide important indicators of school success, such as test scores, attendance, and graduation rates. For a discussion of such reports, see Chapter 14.

Re-examination for Placement or Selection

As a regular part of monitoring students' progress, their work is evaluated frequently to determine whether they should stay in or leave special programs such as remedial, language development, and accelerated courses. Depending on the type of decision to be made, assessment data may be generated from tests and from a variety of student work and observations.

Now that we have distinguished between formative and summative evaluation and have examined the purposes of assessment, let's consider several situations to see how assessment information is used in actual classroom events:

Situation 1. Students are assessed several times during the year with a variety of assessments. The teacher uses the results to determine how the students are progressing and to identify which students need additional instruction and in which topic. Progress—or lack of it —for each student and for the class is noted. This is a *formative* use of measurement.

Situation 2. Students take a test that predicts performance in an advanced class in mathematics. Students who pass the test are permitted to take the class; those who do not pass the test must take a different class. This is a *summative* use for placement.

Situation 3. Students in a history class take a test at the end of each chapter and at the end of each unit. These scores are averaged to determine what grade students get on their report cards for the grading period. This is a *summative* use. The information may also be used *formatively,* as when the teacher uses it to identify content and skills that need to be retaught.

State assessment programs, national testing programs, and some district-wide testing programs are usually summative. Administrators and politicians are very much concerned with these programs. Recent efforts to use a national testing program as a means to improve teaching and learning are an attempt to change the purpose from summative to formative. You may want to review Chapter 2 for more information about this situation.

LEVELS OF MEASUREMENT

Measurement has been defined as "assignment of numerals to objects or events according to rules" (Stevens, 1946). Numerals are symbols for numbers, and there are rules that govern how these numerals are assigned. In educational assessment, a numeral may represent the *raw score* on a test, which is the number of items answered correctly. Or the numerals may come from a rating scale—such as one rating students' performance on a scale from 1 to 5, so that the numerals represent varying levels of performance. The numerals may also be obtained from transformation of raw scores to *scaled scores,* in an effort to equate scores on different assessments by putting them on a common scale. The source of the numbers and the type of scale used affect the interpretation that can be made.

This concept was explained by a committee of the British Association for the Advancement of Science and developed by Stevens (1946), who identified four *levels* of measurement: nominal, ordinal, interval, and ratio as listed in Table 4.3. The level of the measurement determines which mathematical operations may

Table 4.3 Levels of Measurement Scales

Level	Definition	Example of Scales
Nominal	Classification	Gender group Ethnic group Student ID number
Ordinal	Rank order	Senior class rank Percentile rank Rating scales
Interval	Rank order with equal units but no true zero	Deviation IQ Scaled scores SAT scores
Ratio	Interval data with equal units and a true zero	Raw scores Number of books read

be performed with the numbers. For each, a variety of scales have been developed. This is an important concept, because it has been necessary to devise scales for educational and psychological measurement that yield defensible interpretations of assessments, although often the test user does not understand the scales.

In the remainder of this section we describe scales for the different levels.

Nominal Measurement

Nominal measurement assigns objects or individuals to categories. The only mathematical operations that can be performed are counting and computing the percentage in each category and determining the *mode,* the most frequent category. Interpretation must be limited to description. The symbols (usually numerals) that are used to represent each category and the order in which the numerals are used are arbitrary. For example, on a survey form we might use "1" to indicate male and "2" to indicate female. Here the "1" would not be less than "2"; it would simply be a separate category. For nominal measurement, letter symbols can be used in place of numerals ("A" for male, "B" for female). A nominal scale is used in many situations to indicate variables such as ethnicity and categories of occupation.

Sometimes nominal distributions are very informative. For example, if you are trying to evaluate the effect of an intervention program, you might compare the percentage of students with the unwanted behavior before and after the program. The data may be broken down further by gender or ethnic group. Example 1 shows how the data might appear when separated by gender group. In this example 40 students (20 boys and 20 girls) responded to a survey on school attitudes.

Example 1					
Percentage of students marking an item from a survey—"I like to come to school":					
	OVERALL (*N* = 40)		BOYS (*N* = 20)		GIRLS (*N* = 20)
	Yes	No	Yes	No	Yes	No
Beginning of year	40%	60%	20%	80%	60%	40%
End of year	65%	35%	60%	40%	70%	30%

What can we learn from the numbers in this example? Here are some possibilities: Overall, more students liked school at the end of the year than at the beginning of the year. What can we learn about this group if we separate the results by gender? Few boys liked school at the start of the year, but many changed their minds by the end of the year. The majority of the girls liked school at the start of the year, and even more liked it at the end. If we are trying to evaluate a program that is directed toward encouraging students to stay in school, all of this could be important information.

Ordinal Scales

An *ordinal scale* indicates how individuals stand in relation to each other. Ordinal scales include the concepts of *equal to, less than,* and *more than.* Mathematical operations can show the relative position of individuals (rank order); however, the steps between ranks are not equal, so it is not possible to discuss meaningfully *how much* higher or lower one individual is than another when only rank order is available. Examples of rank-order scales include ratings of individual items on teacher rating scales and scoring systems that use rubrics to score alternative assessments.

In Example 2 the heights of eight students are listed. They are ranked in order from shortest (1 in the *Rank* column) to tallest (rank 8). Notice that sometimes the difference in the height of individuals in adjacent ranks varies from 1 to 4 inches. For example, George at 5'10"(rank 6) is 1 inch taller than Sara (rank 5), but Sara at 5'9" (rank 5) is 4 inches taller than Juan (rank 4). Of course, in most cases students are not listed by heights. A teacher would rearrange the students by height to see the difference. Because ordinal scores do not have equal units, they cannot be added. Therefore, it is not correct to compute the average of ordinal scores. Instead, the appropriate statistics for ordinal data are the *median* (or middle score) and the *mode* (the most frequent score).

Example 2		
NAME	**HEIGHT**	**RANK**
Alicia P.	5'1"	1
Helen B.	5'2"	2
Jean J.	5'3"	3
Juan G.	5'5"	4
Sara T.	5'9"	5
George S.	5'10"	6
John H.	5'11"	7
Joe J.	6'0"	8

Ordinal scales are used for reporting students' academic rank and for ranking schools and school systems. *Percentile rank,* which translates simple rank order into a position in a group of 100 and indicates the percentage of students at or below that position, is a commonly used ordinal scale. More information about percentile scores is presented in Chapter 11. Another common ordinal scale is the class rank on grade-point average (GPA), which some schools use for purposes such as identifying the valedictorian.

Interval Scales

Interval scales are similar to ordinal scales but have an additional important characteristic. The interval—the distance between any two adjacent numbers on the scale—is the same throughout the scale. The starting point (that is, the zero point) and the interval values are arbitrary. A true zero would indicate a total absence of the trait or characteristic being measured. An ordinary Fahrenheit thermometer is a good example of an interval scale. The zero point is set arbitrarily, so that the freezing point is 32 degrees and the boiling point is 212 degrees. On a Celsius thermometer the freezing point is set at zero, and the boiling point is 100 degrees, so 32 degrees Fahrenheit is equal to zero degrees Celsius and 212 degrees Fahrenheit is equal to 100 degrees Celsius. The zero point on neither thermometer means an absolute absence of temperature or heat.

In educational measurement, one interval scale is the *standard score* scale. It uses the arithmetic average (or mean) of the norms group as the reference point and the standard deviation as the interval. Scores are expressed as *deviations,* or differences, from the mean, in units of the standard deviation. Such scales use equal intervals and do not use a true zero which would indicate the total absence of the trait. The mean and deviations are set at some convenient value to make the scores easy to handle. Some commonly used standard scores are the deviation IQ (DIQ), used with the Wechsler intelligence tests, and *Scholastic Assessment Test* (SAT) scores. The mean Wechsler scores are set equal to 100, and the interval or standard deviation (SD) is set at 15. So a score that is 1 SD above the mean would have a DIQ of 115. The mean SAT score is set equal to 500, and the SD is set equal to 100. Figure 4.2 illustrates how this works.

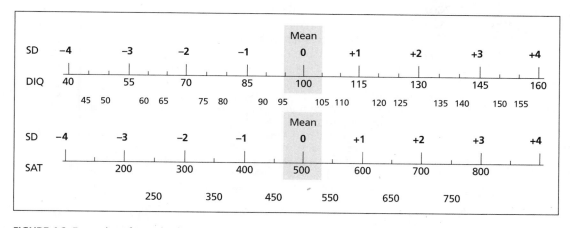

FIGURE 4.2 Examples of Standard Score Scales

Ratio Scales

Ratio scales have both equal units and a true zero. With the use of ratio scales it is possible to speak of one object as weighing twice as much or being half as heavy as another object. Many physical properties—for example, height, weight, velocity—have ratio scales. In education, the only ratio scores are raw scores or counts of things like number of books read or number of absences during a semester, for which there can be a score of zero. The raw score scale has a zero point only for the items on a specific assessment or test. It does not have a zero point for the characteristics being measured.

In measurement of most human characteristics there is no true zero point, because the characteristics exist to some extent in every individual. It is not possible to speak of one individual as having "twice as much" or "half as much" of a variable as another individual, or of a person's mathematics knowledge as being a percentage of his or her reading skill. It is possible to compare individuals only as to relative position or category.

In the problem below we have placed a data set in the box, along with instructions and some questions to help you think about how the four levels of measurement differ. (See Chapter 11 for more discussion of the different types of score forms.)

Measurement Scale Problem

You have the following information about the top group of seniors at a school:

NAME	GENDER	ETHNIC GROUP	GPA	D	RANK
Alicia P.	F	Asian	5.0	_____	1
Joe J.	M	White	4.9	_____	2
Juan G.	M	Hispanic	4.2	_____	3
George S.	M	White	3.9	_____	4
Sara T.	F	White	3.8	_____	5
Helen B.	F	African American	3.7	_____	6
John H.	M	African American	3.6	_____	7.5
Jean J.	F	White	3.6	_____	7.5

Directions
1. Tabulate the number of students by gender and ethnic group. What level of measurement is this?
2. Calculate the difference between each GPA and the next one. Record this information in the column labeled "D."
3. What is the relationship between a gain in GPA and the rank order?
4. Are the differences in GPA the same for each change in rank order?
5. Can you calculate the mean rank for each ethnic and gender group? Why or why not?
6. Can you calculate the mean GPA for each ethnic and gender group? Why or why not?

TERMS USED TO REFER TO ASSESSMENTS

Many terms are used to refer to educational measurements: Sometimes they are called "tests," other times we speak of "evaluations," and we also use the word "assessments." The term *assessment* often has a modifier such as *authentic, alternative,* or *performance.* Unfortunately, different people use these terms to mean different things, so it is easy to become confused. Although the meanings of these terms

Terms Used to Refer to Educational Assessments	
Measurement	Domain
Test	Authentic assessment
Assessment	Alternative assessment
Evaluation	Performance measurement
Variable	Criterion-referenced measurement
Attribute	Norm-referenced measurement
Trait	Mastery
Construct	Critical Thinking

overlap to some extent, each term has a special connotation. We have already used some of these terms in this book. At this point we will review them and add some other important related terms.

Educational Measurement

The expression *educational measurement* is a general term that refers to the entire field of tests and other assessments used in education. Educational measurement usually involves measures of ability, achievement, and/or personal characteristics.

Test

The word *test* is reserved for a measurement procedure that is formal—that is, the examinee perceives the procedure as a "test." A test may be distinguished from procedures such as informal observation and ratings. Tests may be written, oral, or performance based.

Assessment

The word *assessment* is currently used as a synonym for *educational measurement*. The original meaning of *assessment* is "the valuation of property especially for the purpose of taxation." When the term was first used in connection with education in the *National Assessment of Educational Progress* (NAEP), the intent was (and still is) to suggest a broad range of measurement procedures, not only paper-and-pencil testing, and to include some judgment about the quality of progress being made by a student or by schools, which incorporates the idea of "evaluation."

Thus, *assessment* now has two very different connotations: (1) The use of *assessment* in place of *testing* places emphasis on accountability and evaluative uses of testing. (2) Critics of traditional tests use *assessment* to suggest that an assessment program should be something more than a testing program made up of multiple choice items. In this book we primarily use the term *assessment* in the second sense. But we also use *testing* and *educational measurement* in the same broad sense. *Traditional assessment* refers to procedures most commonly used since the 1920s. These assessments are usually multiple choice, but they may also be true-false, matching, fill-in-the-blanks, short answer, or completion items.

Recently *authentic, alternative*, and *performance-based* have been used to describe *assessment*. Some people use these modifiers interchangeably; others use one term for all three concepts. However, there are some differences that we think are important.

An *authentic assessment* grows out of instruction and is integrated with it (Wiggins, 1989). This is certainly desirable, and we feel that all assessment can and should be authentic. Unlike some people, we do not automatically eliminate traditional tests from the authentic category, because we feel that many traditional procedures can be authentic. We also know that many of the "new" procedures are not automatically authentic, because they fail to meet one or more of the criteria for good assessments (discussed later in this chapter).

The term *alternative assessment* usually refers to assessment procedures other than traditional test items, and this is how we use the term. Alternative assessments include performance-based assessments as well as observation, rating scales, and portfolios. Some people use *alternative assessment* as a synonym for *authentic assessment,* thus implying that traditional assessment is inauthentic. We reject this usage, because we feel that both traditional and alternative assessment can and should be authentic.

Performance-based assessment, also called *performance assessment,* is one type of alternative assessment. We limit our use of this term to assessment that involves a performance, such as delivering a speech, playing a musical piece, or repairing a machine. Performance and production assessments are discussed in Chapter 7.

Evaluation

The term *evaluation* includes assessment but also refers to making judgments. In education, judgments may be made about the performance of a student, teacher, school, district, and so on. And judgments may be made about the quality or worth of an educational program or procedure.

Criterion-Referenced and Norm-Referenced Interpretation of Scores

Criterion-referenced interpretation (also known as *objectives-referenced* or *domain-referenced interpretation)* provides information about what percentage of objectives and which objectives have been met by students. *Norm-referenced interpretation* provides information about how the performance of a student or school or school district compares with the performance of other students or schools or school districts (that is, the norms group), to provide a basis for inferring what is a reasonable expectation for the student or school.

Mastery is associated with criterion-referenced interpretation of test scores. Washburne (1922) and Morrison (1926) advocated teaching until all students meet desirable criteria of mastery. Carroll (1963) proposed a model of learning that suggested that, if the kind and quality of instruction and the amount of time for instruction are appropriate for individual students, almost all students may be expected to achieve mastery. Bloom (1968) and Carroll (1989) reaffirmed the position that provision must be made for variation in time if most students are to attain mastery. An unfortunate consequence of the interest in mastery was the focus on basic skills, which led to a narrowing of the curriculum in some instances (see Chapter 2). Curriculum-Based Measurement (CBM) and Curriculum-Based Assessment (CBA) are terms used to refer to assessment procedures that are based directly on the curriculum and that yield information to monitor students' progress toward goals of the curriculum. At present it is used primarily in classes for students with disabilities (King-Sears, 1994).

Critical Thinking

Recently concern with mastery of a limited list of topics and skills has been somewhat replaced with renewed interest in higher-level cognitive skills, which are never completely mastered. These skills involve mental processes more complex than recognition or recall; for example, analysis and problem solving. One consequence of this change has been a recommendation to replace traditional testing with types of assessment that some people consider to be more authentic. However, as we have said, we reject the idea that traditional assessments cannot be authentic.

Variable

Literally, *variable* means "something that varies." In psychology and education the term is used to refer to a characteristic or trait of people or organizations. In education we are usually interested in variables such as students' knowledge about one or more subjects or their interests or attitudes. We also may be concerned with variables called *attributes* or *traits*.

Construct

This term is used to refer to variables, attributes, or traits that have to be inferred because they cannot be observed or measured directly. Except for physical attributes such as height and weight, most human traits are constructs. In order to measure them we have to measure behavior or the product of behavior that reflects the trait of interest, and we infer the individual's status on that trait. Achievement is an example of a construct, as are personal traits such as ambition, tolerance, and optimism.

Domain

A *domain* is a set of content and skills in some discipline or area of study. A domain in mathematics might be knowledge of all basic mathematics facts and the four basic operations. A domain in social studies might be all of the information about the Civil War. The term *domain-referenced* (sometimes *criterion-referenced*) alludes to a way of interpreting scores. When a test is based on a domain-referenced model, the items are supposed to be selected, or sampled, from the domain of all possible items. If this is done, when a student performs well on the test, we may "refer" this performance back to the domain of interest and estimate what proportion of the domain the student knows. Chapters 5 and 6 provide additional information about this concept.

STATISTICAL TERMS

To understand this text, you need not learn complicated statistical formulas or perform complicated mathematical operations. But there are a few statistical terms with which you need to be familiar. Two of the most important statistical concepts are central tendency and dispersion or variability. Measures of central tendency provide a convenient way to describe the average score, middle score, and most common score. Measures of dispersion indicate how spread out the scores are.

Measures of Central Tendency:
Mean, Median, and Mode

In Table 4.4 you see the terms statisticians use for measures of *central tendency*. There are three measures of *central tendency*—*mean, median,* and *mode.*

The *mean* is what you get when you simply add up some scores and divide by the number of scores. The mean is also known as the *arithmetic average.* Since you cannot add categories or ranks, you need something other than the mean to describe the central tendency of categorical and ranked scores. That's where the median and mode come in. If you have a group of scores that are in rank order but the ranks are not evenly spaced, you use the *median,* which is the middle score. If you are trying to sum up the results of a rating scale, you cannot use either the mean or the median. All you can do is to find the *mode*—the category that is chosen most frequently.

Table 4.4 Measures of Central Tendency

Measure	Level of Data	Procedure
Mean	Interval Ratio	Add scores and divide by the number of scores.
Median	Ordinal Interval Ratio	Place scores in order from lowest to highest and find which score is halfway through the distribution.
Mode	Nominal Ordinal Interval Ratio	Count the cases in each category and find the category with the greatest number.

Measures of Dispersion:
Standard Deviation, Interquartile Range, and Range

In some classes you may find that test scores are mostly bunched together; in other classes there are great differences between the highest and lowest scores. Sometimes you might want to compare two or more classes as to the spread of achievement. What you would use is a measure of *dispersion*. The two ways to calculate measures of dispersion are presented in Table 4.5.

Table 4.5 Measures of Dispersion

Measure	Level of Data	Procedure
Standard deviation	Interval, ratio	Subtract each score from the mean. Square the differences Add the squared differences. Divide by the number of scores and take the square root.
Interquartile range	Ordinal, interval, ratio	Find the score below which 75% of the scores lie. Find the score below which the bottom 25% lie. Subtract the lower score (25th percentile) from the upper 75th percentile. The *quartile deviation* is one-half of the interquartile range.
Range	Ordinal, interval, ratio	Subtract the lowest score from the highest score.

The Standard Deviation is one measure of dispersion. It describes how much scores are dispersed from the mean. It refers to the fact that the distribution of scores is divided into 8 equal units or "mile markers." The number of points in an SD refers to the number of points you need to get to each major score division. When scores are more spread out from the mean they have a large SD. For example, if a teacher gives a test to two groups of students and one group's SD is 5 and the other's is 10, the group with the SD of 10 has a wider spread of scores. SDs are used in the creation of many score forms that make it possible to combine scores on different assessments.

The Normal Distribution or Curve

When you give a test, the scores of most students are somewhere near the mean score, but a few scores are much higher and a few scores much lower than the mean. When a test is given to a large enough group, the scores fall in what is called a *normal distribution,* which appears as a *bell-shaped curve.* When the scores are plotted on graph paper there is a bulge at the center of the curve, and the tails dwindle down to near zero. In other words, the curve is shaped like a bell.

The mean is at the center of this distribution, and the distribution is divided into eight sections of one standard deviation each. There are different percentages of the distribution within each section, depending on how far the section is from the mean. Figure 4.3 shows a normal distribution or curve.

For interval scores, the best measure of dispersion is the standard deviation. If you look at the normal distribution in Figure 4.3, you will see that there are eight equally spaced divisions called standard deviations of all the number lines, four on each side of the mean. Approximately two-thirds of the distribution will lie between one standard deviation *below* the mean and one standard deviation *above* the mean.

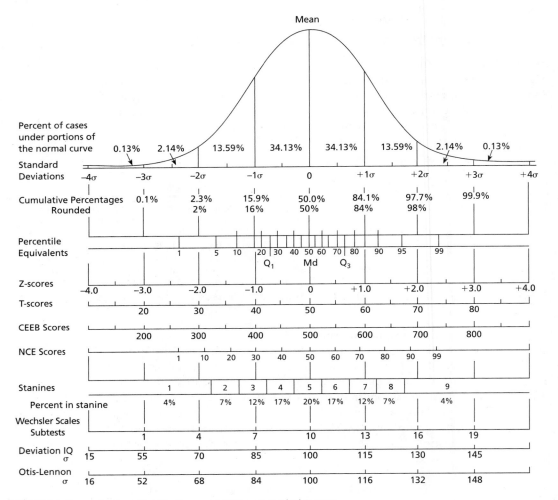

FIGURE 4.3 Normal Curve Distribution and Common Scaled Scores

Source: *Methods of Expressing Test Scores.* Test Service Bulletin, January 1955 by the Psychological Corporation, No. 48. Reproduced by permission of Harcourt Brace Educational Measurement.

From Figure 4.3 you can see how the different types of scores relate to one another. If the distribution is normal, you can easily translate a percentile score into a standard score and vice versa. For example, a DIQ of 115 has a percentile rank of approximately 84. An SAT score (one of the CEEB scores) of 600 also has a percentile rank of 84.

Correlation Coefficient

A *correlation coefficient* is a statistic that indicates the degree of relationship between two or more sets of data. One of the most common uses of the correlation coefficient is to investigate the validity and reliability of a test. There are many ways to do this. For reliability, you may either give two or more forms of the same test to the same group of people or give the same test to the same people at different times and compute the correlation coefficient between the scores. Another way is to use only one form of a test, split the items into halves, and then compute the correlation coefficient between the scores on the halves.

To investigate the validity of a test you may correlate the scores on one or more preassessments with one or more indicators of the same trait or of a trait to which the assessment is supposed to be related. An example is correlating a test like the Scholastic Assessment Test (SAT) with students' college grade-point averages.

Correlation coefficients may be either positive or negative. A *positive* correlation indicates that low scores on one variable go with low scores on the other variable and high scores on one variable go with high scores on the second variable. A *negative* correlation indicates that low scores on one variable go with high scores on the other variable and vice versa. A negative correlation might exist between grades and the number of days absent.

The scatterplots in Figure 4.4 demonstrate how this works. Correlation coefficients run in size from -1.00 to $+1.00$. The higher the number is, the closer is

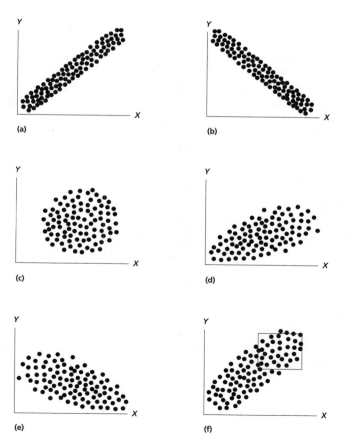

FIGURE 4.4 Scatterplots of Linear Relationships Between Two Variables

the relationship, whether it is positive or negative. Scatterplot (a) shows a positive correlation of +1.00. Scatterplot (b) shows a negative correlation of −1.00. Scatterplot (c) shows a correlation of "0." Correlations of +.60 and −.60 are pictured in Scatterplots (d) and (e), respectively.

Scatterplot (f) shows one kind of problem in working with correlations. The size of the correlation is affected by the range of scores on either or both variables. If every individual in a group makes the same score on one or both of the variables, then there would be a zero correlation with any other variable. This exact situation is not likely to happen, but something similar does happen frequently. A college or university may require a very high score on the SAT for admission, perhaps a total score of 1350. When the SAT scores are correlated with grades, the correlation coefficients are quite low. What we have is a scatterplot limited to a small section of the possible scores, similar to the boxed area in Scatterplot (f).

CHARACTERISTICS OF GOOD ASSESSMENTS

If assessments are to be really useful, they must be valid, reliable, fair to all students, usable, and timely. Testing experts have standards and procedures for evaluating the extent to which tests exhibit these characteristics. We are introducing these terms here. In later chapters, when we discuss specific uses of assessment tools, we describe methods of building these qualities into the assessments. We also describe how to evaluate the qualities.

Validity

Validity is the term used by testing experts to refer to the extent to which the test or other assessment instrument truly measures what it is used to measure, that is, how accurate or relevant it is. Validity is not usually a problem in physical measurement, because (for example) a measure of length is not easily confused with a measure of weight. However, in educational settings the distinctions may be less clear. A teacher may want to measure a student's high-level knowledge but choose an assessment that measures something very different. For example, a teacher may intend to test students' problem-solving ability but use items that require only simple calculations.

Even worse, some assessment scores may reflect the scorer's bias more than the students' achievement. This is a special concern when assessments require the use of human judgment for scoring. This may happen in individual tests, or in some rating scales, or in the scoring of performance assessments, as, for instance, if you allow poor handwriting to affect the score on a writing sample. We address these concerns in Chapters 6, 7, 8, and 9.

For classroom testing to be useful, the assessments must be completely relevant to what is being taught. Relevance is best accomplished by carefully articulating the desired learning outcomes and developing measures that assess those goals. We discuss this process, which we call "defining the domain," in Chapter 5.

You also should be sure that assessments are appropriate for the students who take them. For example, if students have not had an opportunity to learn the material or if a mathematics test has problems written in English but the students have not yet learned English, the test will not be a valid measure of their ability to solve mathematics problems.

One of the strongest arguments being made for alternative assessments is that they may be more valid than traditional assessments such as multiple-choice tests. However, simply changing the type of assessment does not ensure all the good effects some advocates of alternative assessment suggest. Judy Arter cites as possible problems with validity of alternative assessments:

The performance may not be representative of the student's usual or best performance.

The criteria may not be appropriate for the task.

The task may be poorly chosen.

There may be aspects of the assessment that keep the student from performing well.

The evaluation and conclusions may reflect biases of the evaluator.

Reliability

The consistency or dependability with which an assessment measures whatever it is supposed to measure is called *reliability*. An assessment that measures the desired characteristic but gives inconsistent results from one measurement to another is unreliable. Imagine trying to measure the length of an object with a rubber ruler in which the ruler is stretched on some occasions and relaxed on others!

There are two aspects of reliability: (1) the accuracy and consistency of the scoring and (2) the extent to which different assessments of the same variable yield the same results, or items within the same test agree with each other. A frequent cause of unreliability in scoring classroom assessments is that the teachers doing the scoring become overtired and change their standards. Some tired teachers overlook errors that they are very careful about when they are fresh. Some become more demanding as they tire. In either case, standards change in the course of the scoring. We discuss these problems and suggest ways to avoid and correct them in later chapters.

To minimize problems of this kind, large-scale assessment programs use carefully developed *rubrics,* or scoring guides, and the scoring is carefully monitored. Each product is scored by more than one judge, and there is a provision for rescoring products for which there are differences. Teachers should use rubrics to score classroom assessment when the scoring involves more than simply marking answers right or wrong according to a key.

One great advantage of machine-scored multiple-choice tests is that they may be scored with a high degree of reliability. However, the test may not be reliable if scores on the various items do not agree with each other or if scores on different forms of the test do not agree. Also, the test may not be valid if the scoring key is marked incorrectly, if more than one option could be the correct answer, or if none of the options is really correct.

Measurement error is actually a discrepancy between the score information a teacher collects for a student, such as a score on a social studies test, and what the student *really* knows about the content area, in this case social studies. It may surprise you to learn that all assessments have some error or discrepancy because of the factors that lead to unreliability. When an assessment is very reliable, *measurement error* is low. If reliability is low, the measurement error is high. The theory of true and error score accounts for the error in test scores. According to this theory, the *observed* score—the score we actually get—is composed of the student's *true* score, plus or minus some error. The true score is a hypothetical score that would be obtained if the assessment were perfectly reliable. However, the only estimate we have of the true score is the actual, or observed, score.

A procedure has been worked out to estimate the amount of error in a given assessment and to use that estimate to determine the probable range within which a student's true score lies. Using the reliability coefficient, which ranges from -1.00 to $+1.00$, we estimate the standard deviation of the errors, which is called the *standard error of measurement* (SEM). Then we use the percentages under various sections of the normal curve, and using the actual score as the mean, we estimate the probable range for an individual's true score. We know that the probability is approximately 68% that the true score lies within $+1$SE or -1SE of the observed score, and we know that the probability is 99.7% that it lies within $+2$SEs or -2SEs. In reality, the SE applies only to scores at the mean, and it increases somewhat for scores as they approach the extreme of the distribution. The important point to remember is that any score is an *estimate* and indicates a *range,* not a fixed point.

In addition to measurement error, other situations may lead to errors in scores. For example, error resulting from fatigue, fear, or too little studying can lower scores. Cheating or guessing can artificially raise scores. Teachers can contribute to the problem through inaccurate or inconsistent scoring, thus raising or lowering students' observed scores.

Relationship Between Reliability and Validity

Obviously, a lack of reliability will affect the validity of a measurement. When assessments are made by judges, as when a group of teachers score writing samples or portfolios, different judges may have different standards and may use different criteria in scoring. Also, some judges may have different standards early in the morning and late in the afternoon, or their standards on Monday may be different from their standards on Thursday. Or, the scoring standard may change as a teacher tires, creating not only a problem of reliability but also a problem of validity.

Other Desirable Characteristics
of Classroom Assessments

Validity and reliability are the most important characteristics of any assessment. However, other considerations, if ignored, may cause problems with either validity or reliability.

Fairness. Recall from Chapter 2 that the possibility that an assessment is biased against gender or ethnic groups is of great concern. Many procedures have been developed to check for fairness. The final decision as to whether an assessment is biased depends on the purpose of the test.

Practicality. Another important concern is that of *practicality*, also termed *utility* or *usability*, which was once considered to be a prime criterion for selecting a test or other assessment and is still very important. There are two aspects of practicality. One has to do with whether the assessment is doable: how realistic it is to try to include certain kinds of evidence under the circumstances of a program of instruction. Sometimes, you might be able to find a substitute for a procedure that is simply not practical. For example, you might be able to score a random sample of each student's work, or keep a folder of all such work and score only the work of students who are having problems. This might make it possible to use more written assignments than would be practical if you tried to score every paper for every student. Or you could have an in-class assignment that requires students to do whatever they are supposed to have been doing, and score only that assignment.

The other aspect of practicality is whether the assessment serves the purpose for which it is intended and whether some other procedures would serve the purpose equally well or better. For instance, sampling may be used if the diagnosis is only for schools or school districts. But if the purpose of the assessment is to provide diagnostic information for individuals, the assessment must include all individuals on every task.

Timeliness. *Timeliness* refers both to the frequency of assessment and to the rapidity of turnaround of test results back to students. If assessments are administered frequently, they may be brief because there can be a large number of them. No one assessment has to be extremely long in order to ensure dependability.

PUBLISHED STANDARDS
FOR ASSESSMENTS

Professionals in educational and psychological measurement have identified the characteristics of good assessments and have developed guidelines and procedures for preparing and using them. Most of the standards were developed for large-scale testing programs. Nevertheless, some of the concepts and procedures are useful for classroom teachers, and all of the standards become important if you are asked to serve on a committee to review and select a test or test battery for your school or school district or to participate in scoring a performance assessment. In Part Two of this book, the procedures for developing, scoring, and using each type of classroom assessment were written with the standards in mind. Part Three, which deals with external assessment programs, discusses the standards and how they apply to external assessments.

Four documents serve as references for standards in psychological and educational measurement. The provisions of each are summarized below. Most of these standards are directed toward the selection, administration, and interpretation of standardized tests, but many also apply to classroom tests. There is also a set of standards for teacher competencies in educational measurement.

The APA *Standards*—their formal title is *Standards for Educational and Psychological Testing* (American Educational Research Association, American Psychological Association, & National Council on Measurement in Education, 1985)—were developed by three national organizations of measurement professionals from the fields of education and psychology. The *Standards* provide guidelines for developing assessments and evaluating them for validity and reliability. They also deal with the use of test scores in counseling and evaluation and with testing special populations. The *Standards* are updated periodically.

The *Standards for Teacher Competence in Educational Assessment of Students,* prepared by the American Federation of Teachers, National Council on Measurement in Education, and the National Education Association (1990) is included as Appendix B.

The *Code of Fair Testing Practices in Education,* prepared in 1988 by the Joint Committee on Testing Practices, deals primarily with the selection and use of external tests; however, many of the suggestions also apply to assessments developed by classroom teachers. This code summarizes the responsibilities of both the test developer and the test user. The intent was to translate relevant parts of the APA *Standards* into language that the general public can understand. The code is included in this book as Appendix C.

The *Code of Professional Responsibilities in Educational Measurement* (National Council on Measurement in Education, 1995) was developed by the NCME Committee on the Development of a Code of Ethics as a guide for people who develop, market, select, administer, and use assessments.

The standards and the codes suggest that procedures be followed that will ensure that assessments meet acceptable standards of validity, reliability, and fairness, and that evidence be provided to support the claims. Commercially available tests should report sufficient information about validity, reliability, and bias that potential users can judge how well they meet the standards.

The standard for validity requires evidence of a test's content and skill coverage. The content covered by an assessment should be appropriate for the instruction. This does not mean that content must have been explicitly taught; rather, the content must be material to which the intended skills may legitimately be applied. Furthermore, all types of content to be learned by students should be represented in the assessment process, even though different procedures may be used to assess content of different types.

It is also important for the assessment procedures to cover all the skills that are included in the curriculum goals. If the goals emphasize high-level skills, such as extrapolation, evaluation, and problem solving, but the assessments cover only recognition, the assessments are not valid.

The standard for reliability requires that whenever an assessment is used, an attempt should be made to estimate its reliability. Estimates of reliability for multiple-choice tests are easy to make, and scoring programs routinely calculate the reliability coefficient. It is much more difficult to estimate the reliability of essays and other performance tests. The most common procedure involves using at least two judges and comparing their judgments. More specific suggestions are provided in later chapters.

Evidence of fairness should be both statistical and judgmental. Statistical checks of how members of different groups perform can be made, and judges from different groups can simply review items. These procedures, too, are covered in later chapters.

SUMMARY

- Understanding educational assessment requires understanding the nature of measurement, the different types of scales, and many statistical concepts.
- Standards for tests and testing have been developed by such professional organizations as American Federation of Teachers, National Education Association, American Educational Research Association, National Council on Measurement in Education, and American Psychological Association.
- Good assessments must meet high standards for validity, reliability, and fairness.

STUDY QUESTIONS

1. Why is it often appropriate to use in a national or state assessment program assessments different from those used most frequently by classroom teachers?

2. What is the most important characteristic of an assessment?

3. Why are multiple-choice tests used widely in state and national assessments?

FOR YOUR PROFESSIONAL GROWTH

Check your local professional library or the library at a local university or college to locate the AERA/APA/NCME *Standards for Educational and Psychological Testing*. Also, find a copy of a recent *Mental Measurements Yearbook*.

1. Think about a test that you use in your classroom or one that you have used in the past. Does this test meet the criteria in the *Standards?*

2. Examine the technical manual of a test used in your school district. Does the information in the manual meet the *Standards?*

3. Look up reviews in the *Mental Measurements Yearbook* for a test that you have used or one that you have seen results from. What does the reviewer say about the test?

PART TWO

∂ℜ

Preparing Classroom Assessments

As you learned in Chapter 1, much of a teacher's day is spent in assessment activities. Of this time, most is devoted to teacher made assessments, both formal and informal. In spite of (or maybe because of) this, many teachers complain that they dislike assessments of any kind. Part of the problem may lie in the fact that teachers receive little training in assessment and do not consider assessment to be part of instruction.

In Part Two we discuss planning for and developing classroom assessments. We give you a "toolbox" of assessments and show you how to use the various tools. Chapter 5 covers planning for an assessment: identifying the purpose, the content and skills to be covered, and the mode of assessment to be used. The other chapters present instructions for preparing and using specific types of assessments.

These chapters will help teachers understand the importance of planning for and integrating assessment with other classroom activities. Furthermore, the information in Part Two can help counselors and administrators understand the assessment tasks that teachers face. In addition, the information may help administrators and counselors handle their own assessment tasks. For example, a counselor will find this section of the book helpful in understanding teacher-generated assessment information about students, and he or she may find the material in Chapter 8 on observation and rating scales helpful in constructing his or her own assessments of student behavior.

Principals, too, should find these same elements helpful in communicating with parents about assessment information generated by teachers. In addition, the material on observation and rating scales may be used as a resource for creating and using faculty and student observations.

Here is the model of assessment development that we use in this book:

Model of Assessment Development
Plan
Define the purpose of the assessment
Define the domain of the assessment
Define the content domain
Define the skills domain
Select the mode of assessment
Prepare the test blueprint and item specifications
Write items
Try out and evaluate items
Score
Interpret scores

5

ॐ

Planning Classroom Assessments

PREVIEW

The first step in preparing an assessment is planning.

The focus of this chapter is on planning assessments of achievement, although some of the suggestions will also be useful for assessing variables such as interests and preferences.

MAJOR TOPICS	
The Planning Process	Terms:
Purposes of Assessment	Construct
Assessment Domain	Domain
The Taxonomy:	Taxonomy
Content	Blueprint
Skills	Specifications
Deciding What to Assess:	
Content	
Deciding What to Assess:	
Skills	
Deciding How to Assess:	
Translating Instructional	
Objectives Into Assessments	

THE PLANNING PROCESS

The various tasks involved in planning an assessment of achievement are listed below:

Planning an Assessment
Identify the purpose of the assessment.
Define the domain.
Start with the instructional objectives.
Decide what to assess.
What content should be covered?
Which skills should be required?
Decide how to assess.
What types of items or tasks should be used?
Finalize the assessment blueprint and item specifications.

Notice that the end product is an assessment blueprint, which will guide your work on various assessments.

For a preview of what an assessment blueprint looks like, see the assessment blueprint for a teacher certification examination as presented in Figure 5.1. Notice that it contains a breakdown of *content* by topics and subtopics and gives percentages for each topic and subtopic. It also has a breakdown of *skill levels* for each topic. This blueprint was developed by a group of educators and served as a guide for developing a written examination, so the method of assessment is not indicated. If you are developing an assessment blueprint for a unit of study in your class, and if you want to use several different types of assessments, you will need to add a column for that information.

In this chapter we take you through the steps of planning for assessments, whether you are planning for an entire course, for a single unit, or simply for a test on a single lesson. First, you must be clear about the purpose of your assessment, because that decision should guide all other decisions. Next, you have to decide what should be assessed. We call this step "defining the domain" of the assessment, and it includes making decisions about what content and skills are to be covered. The domain should incorporate the desired instructional objectives; that is why we start with them. However, you may find that you need to work on the objectives before you can use them as the basis of your assessments. Finally, you have to decide what assessment procedures to use. Valid assessments require students to demonstrate the behavior that is the target of instruction. This requirement means that a variety of assessment procedures must be used, and each procedure must be appropriate for the content and skills to be learned.

Topics and Subtopics	Percentages						
	Skill Levels					Totals	
	1	2	3	4	5	Topic	Subtopic
A. The Student						44	
1. Human Growth and Development		6	2	8	10		26
2. Behavior Management and Control	2		2	8	6		18
B. Instruction						50	
1. The Learning Process		2	6	3	4		15
2. The Teaching Process	2	2	2	6	6		18
3. Goals and Objectives	1	1	3				5
4. Measurement and Evaluation			3		7		10
5. Reports and Records		1		1			2
C. Legal and Societal Requirements for Schools and Teachers						4	
1. Role of Education in U.S. History and Current Culture			1				1
2. Laws Related to Students, Teachers, and Schools	1	1					2
3. The School's Response to Social Change			1				1
D. Personal and Professional Development of Teachers						2	
1. Initial Certification and Certificate Renewal	0.5						0.5
2. Professional Renewal				0.5			0.5
3. Professional Development		1					1
TOTAL	6.5	14	20	26.5	33	100	100

FIGURE 5.1 Assessment blueprint for a teacher certification examination

IDENTIFYING THE PURPOSE
OF AN ASSESSMENT

The first task in planning an assessment is to identify its purpose. Just as you think about individual lesson plans in the context of an instructional unit, you must be clear about the role of an assessment in the context of instruction. And you must think about the purpose or objective of an assessment just as you would think about the purpose of an instructional procedure. Here are some important questions to ask yourself:

1. Will the assessment be used to identify students' learning needs, to assign grades, or to make promotion decisions?

2. Will it be used to guide instruction for a class or for specific individuals?

3. How often will the assessment be used?
4. Will it be a pretest at the beginning of the year or the beginning of a unit?
5. Will it be part of daily, weekly, or monthly assessments?
6. Will it be part of an assessment package used in determining the course grade?

The use to be made of the assessment is a very important consideration in selecting and organizing the specific materials to be included. The purpose may be *formative,* which includes such uses as diagnosis and placement, or it may be *summative,* as for the purpose of assigning grades or determining whether students have "passed" the course. We discussed these terms in Chapter 4. If the assessment is *formative*, you will probably use focused content and skills with many subparts. *Summative* assessment generally requires a large range of content and skills and may have fewer detailed subparts.

DEFINING THE DOMAIN OF AN ASSESSMENT

Most test professionals agree that it is essential to define the domain, even though they may use different terminology. Hopkins, Stanley & Hopkins (1981), for example, say, "all good achievement tests should be based on either explicit or implicit objectives or topics in a table of specifications." Ebel (1980) suggested that a domain definition should include an outline of knowledge or aptitude to be tested, numbers of items for each type of knowledge, and sources and explanations for the selection of item types. In addition, he recommended that the domain definition should indicate what is to be done with the knowledge, such as "demonstrating understanding of terms, facts, and generalizations"; "predicting outcomes"; "providing explanations"; and "solving problems."

Cronbach (1971) recommended that the test developer begin with a blueprint that crosses content with levels of behavior "response process categories"— that is, types of thinking required to successfully answer the resulting test items. In addition, he advocated the use of detailed directions to item writers for structuring the *stimuli* and the *options,* including directions for writing both the correct response and the distractors, which should incorporate common misconceptions.

We recommend a model for assessment development that uses both an assessment blueprint and item specifications to define the domain. Our recommendations are in keeping with those made by Cronbach and Ebel. Before we discuss specific procedures, we review the definition of some terms introduced in Chapter 4, and we introduce some new terms. Then we discuss curricular issues that you should be concerned with when planning assessments.

Later in this chapter we present a taxonomy of content and skills, and then we present information about selecting content and skills that are appropriate for the objectives. Finally, we go through the process of preparing an assessment blueprint, starting with a list of objectives for a course. But first, some terminology.

Definition of Terms

Construct. In Chapter 4 you learned that a *construct* is the variable, trait, or attribute measured by a test or other assessment procedure. The construct to be assessed is dependent on the purpose of the assessment. It may be very restricted, as "mastery of addition and subtraction of numbers from 1 to 10," or it may be quite broad, as "achievement in geometry."

Domain. The concept of a *domain* comes from science, where it is defined as "the total body of information for which a theory is expected to account." This concept has been adopted by test specialists to refer to the content universe or construct that an assessment is supposed to sample. Behaviors demonstrated on an assessment are samples of a domain and may be used to define status in it. It is important not to confuse this use of *domain* with the use of the term in the *Taxonomy of Educational Objectives. Handbook 1. The Cognitive Domain* (Bloom, Engelhart, Furst, Hill, & Krathwohl, 1956), commonly referred to as "Bloom's taxonomy," to differentiate the cognitive, affective, and psychomotor domains. The creators of that taxonomy used the word *domain* to mean a broad set of behaviors. We use the term to refer to content and skills specifically defined to describe the variable of which the assessment is a sample.

To sample a domain, you must know what the pieces of the domain are; that is why domain definition is such an important part of planning for an assessment. Once the domain is defined, then rules for creating items that fit the domain are prepared.

Taxonomy. The term *taxonomy* comes from natural science and refers to a hierarchy that is organized in some meaningful way. The taxonomy that is currently most used in connection with educational objectives is Bloom's taxonomy. However, we have developed a somewhat different taxonomy that we find more useful.

Assessment Blueprint. By *assessment blueprint* we mean an outline of the content and skills to be covered on an assessment, along with the proportion of the assessment to be devoted to each topic and skill. The method of assessment is also indicated.

Item Specifications. *Item specifications* are directions for creating items for an assessment. Their purpose is to ensure that items fit the blueprint and measure the intended content and skills.

Relationship of Curriculum Goals to Assessment

Assessment should be rooted in curriculum issues. National standardized tests are often criticized for not fitting what is (or should be) taught in a school year or grade level. For example, state curriculum frameworks generally dictate the content of science and social studies courses. The state content sequences may not match the content in the science and social studies sections of nationally normed achievement tests, which thus would be invalid for use in some states. On the other hand, many people are now proposing changing assessments as a way to change the curriculum and methods of teaching, because it is easy to establish that teachers "teach to the test" (see Chapter 2).

Ideally, the domain of a classroom assessment should be defined by the objectives of instruction—that is, the intended outcomes—and the question of what is to be taught and how it is to be taught should have been resolved before assessments are developed. In other words, assessment should develop from the curriculum, rather than the other way around. However, we have found that teachers often do not have clear objectives for their teaching. Or objectives are not stated in a way that lets them serve as a basis for assessment.

The problem is that very few statements of objectives can be used as the basis of assessment without some editing. Many teacher guides for textbooks and teacher lesson plans do not list learning objectives at all, or the so-called objectives are not outcomes but are simply descriptions of class activities, such as

The student will read *The Little Drummer Boy*.

The student will do research for his project.

Another problem is that many curriculum guides that do list objectives in terms of student outcomes list only low-level objectives, such as

Give an example of the conversion of one form of energy to another.

Convert measurements within the metric system.

To be really useful, both in instruction and in assessment, objectives must be stated in terms of student outcomes, and the outcomes must be important. In order to address important outcomes, the objectives must be more than a list of unorganized skills and simple tasks. The pieces must be organized in some way that makes clear how the elements fit together. The most effective procedure for preparing a workable list of objectives is to start with a list of the major concepts or the major tasks for students and then identify the content and skills associated with each major concept or task. This is the process that is recommended in the report of the Mathematical Sciences Education Board (1991), and it is the approach we recommend to identify the content to be covered in an assessment. Later in the chapter we show you how to do this.

Schools of Psychology and Curriculum Goals

How do you decide what curriculum issues are important? The emphasis in curriculum development in American education is closely related to the prevailing emphasis in educational psychology at a given time. At times the emphasis is on basic skills; at times it is on higher-level thinking skills. The change in emphasis is related to the school of psychology in favor: some form of faculty psychology, behaviorism, or cognitive psychology. Table 5.1 indicates the focus of education that has resulted from each, and we discuss each one briefly below.

Table 5.1 Relationship of Schools of Psychology to Education

School of Psychology	Emphasis	Focus of Education
Faculty psychology	Mental faculties	Memory, reasoning, thinking
		General mental processes
Behaviorism	Specific skills	Part to whole
		Hundreds of specific skills
		Mastery of skills
		Immediate goals
Cognitive psychology	Mental processes	Whole to part
	Information processing	Problem solving
		Concept development
		Learner-generated solutions
		Long-term goals

But first let us assure you that we are not advocating any particular viewpoint about psychology or learning theory. What we are trying to do is to help you translate your own ideas of what is important for students to learn into good assessments.

Faculty Psychology. Early in the twentieth century, psychologists and educators believed that the mind had certain faculties, such as memory and reason, that were to be trained and that the skills to be developed by education consisted of various mental processes. This view is not too different from current ideas about teaching and assessing thinking. Faculty psychology was abandoned as the basis of curriculum development because of declining acceptance of that school of thought and the growing influence of behaviorism.

Behaviorism. In the 1920s, behaviorists such as John B. Watson and Ivan Pavlov set the foundation for working on specifically defined skills, such as "Add 2 plus 2." Each course had hundreds or even thousands of specific objectives, and the focus in education was on seeing that every child attained mastery of so-called basic skills, which were believed to be the cornerstone for the rest of education. Later behaviorists such as B. F. Skinner used assessment as part of programmed learning and teaching machines. Later movements such as criterion-referenced test interpretation, mastery, and minimum-competency testing are closely related to early behaviorist objectives, although the objectives for these programs are not so narrowly defined as those of the 1920s.

The sheer task of keeping up with all of the objectives, along with the formulation of other theories of learning that included the generalization of behavior, led to use of more generalized (but difficult to assess) statements of objectives, such as, "Understand" and "Apply principles to concrete problems." Bloom's taxonomy, published in 1956, advocated the statement of educational goals as "behavioral objectives" and was in part a reaction to such ambiguous statements (Bloom et al., 1956).

Cognitive Psychology. Cognitive psychology has its roots in nineteenth-century Europe, and its ties with educational and psychological assessment were close. Studies by Binet, Ebbinghaus, Galton, Spearman, and Piaget make this relationship clear (Snow & Lohman, 1989). Cognitive psychology is concerned with attention, perception and memory, thinking, and organization, retrieval, and use of knowledge. Problem solving is seen as both a function and an activity; thus, it is a central concern of educational measurement. Arguments about the extent to which intellectual skills can be directly taught have resurfaced, and the consensus is that they can and should be part of the curriculum.

Although the terminology has changed, the cognitive psychology view of learning is close to that of faculty psychology. Focus on cognitive psychology has led to renewed interest in performance assessments and in the teaching of thinking skills. Cognitive psychology is also one of the bases of the constructivist view of learning (Fosnot, 1993). The recent resurgence of interest in the works of Ausubel (1963) and Bruner (1966) also reflects the growing interest in the constructivist view of learning.

A TAXONOMY OF CONTENT AND SKILLS

When you analyze the content of the domain, you will find it helpful to use a classification scheme that facilitates thinking about all aspects of the discipline.

Many of you are familiar with the *Taxonomy of Educational Objectives* (Bloom et al., 1956), so you know how it works. We have developed a taxonomy that is similar to Bloom's but differs from it in important ways. The major difference is that our taxonomy has two major divisions: (1) content and (2) skill. Bloom's taxonomy commingles them. We developed our taxonomy after trying to use Bloom's for a number of years. Like several other educators (e.g., Roid & Haladyna, 1982), we found that the blending of content and skill level created problems. The revision of Bloom's taxonomy, which is now under way, divides that taxonomy into (1) the knowledge dimension and (2) cognitive processes.

When you identify content for a course, it is important not to confuse *content* categories with *skills* categories. We believe that you get a more meaningful description of the domain of an assessment when the domain definition separates the two aspects, although at some point the interaction of the two concepts has to be described.

We present our taxonomy in Tables 5.2 through 5.6. Table 5.2 lists the content categories of Bloom's taxonomy and our taxonomy. In Table 5.3 we define the content categories of our taxonomy. Our skills categories are listed in Table 5.4 and defined in Table 5.5, and the interrelation of content and skills is presented in Table 5.6. In Tables 5.2 and 5.4 we also list the categories from the Bloom taxonomy, so that you can see the relationship.

Categories of Content

When we use the term *content*, we are referring to what some people call *knowledge* or the *knowledge base*. However, sometimes—notably in the Bloom taxonomy—the word *knowledge* is used to refer to the lowest level of the skills dimension. Also, the term *knowledge* is frequently used to refer to basic skills, as opposed to higher-level skills. Therefore, to avoid confusion, we chose the term *content* for the base of knowledge that is distinguishable from the skills dimension of a domain.

If you are familiar with Bloom's taxonomy, you may find it helpful to note the similarity between our content taxonomy and the categories of knowledge in Bloom. See Table 5.2. The major difference, which is not obvious from Table 5.2, is that Bloom's taxonomy lists all the categories of knowledge under the lowest skill level, which is called "Knowledge," but we suggest that there are many levels of both content and skills and that the various categories of content may be assessed at many levels of skills. We are using essentially the same three broad headings as Bloom—"Elements" (Bloom's "Specifics"), "Ways and Means," and "Universals." However, we include *conventions, symbols,* and *components* under "Elements"; in Bloom's taxonomy they are listed under "Ways and Means." We also provide more "Ways and Means" than Bloom and add *standards and ethics* to the "Universals" category. Table 5.3 provides definitions and examples of the various categories of content and should help you understand what we mean by each of the terms.

Table 5.2 Content Classification in the Bloom and the Ward and Murray-Ward Taxonomies

Bloom Taxonomy	Ward and Murray-Ward Taxonomy
1.0 Specifics	**Elements**
Terminology	A. Terms
Facts	B. Facts: Dates, Events, Persons, Places, Number Facts
	C. Conventions
	D. Symbols
	E. Components
2.0 Ways and Means	**Ways and Means (Transactions)**
Conventions	
Classifications/Categories	
Trends and Sequences	F. Trends
Methodology	G. Research Findings
Criteria	H. Rules and Laws
	I. Techniques
	J. Criteria
3.0 Universals and Abstractions	**Universals**
Principles and Generalizations	K. Principles
Theories and Structures	L. Theories
	M. Standards and Ethics

Table 5.3 Definitions and Examples of Content Terms in the Ward and Murray-Ward Taxonomy

Terms	Definitions	Examples
Elements		
A. Terms	Generally accepted key terms	Definition of assessment and measurement
B. Facts	Established and generally accepted dates, events, persons, places, etc.; Also includes "number facts"	Dates and people in the history of the measurement of intelligence
C. Conventions	Characteristic ways of treating and presenting ideas and phenomena	Rules of grammar in English; conventions in mathematics; use of specialized phrases
D. Symbols	Symbols other than words that are used to represent ideas or relationships	Symbols used to represent mathematical concepts, such as M or X
E. Components	Pieces and parts of larger concepts and their relationship to each other	Provisions of the theory of relativity
Ways and Means (Transactions)		
F. Trends	Processes, directions, and movements of phenomena with respect to time	Changes in definition of intelligence; changes in curricular emphasis
G. Research Findings	Results of empirical inquiry	Research on attribution theory
H. Rules and Laws	Legally or scientifically established procedures related to the behavior of individuals or phenomena	Statutes and constitutional and case law; natural laws, such as gravity
I. Techniques	Methods and procedures employed in a given discipline	Methods of inquiry in science; teaching methods
J. Criteria	Standards by which facts, principles, opinions, or conduct are tested and/or judged	The probability level for acceptance of a null hypothesis; standards for educational and psychological tests
Universals		
K. Principles	Abstractions that summarize phenomena used in explaining, describing, predicting, or in determining the most appropriate action	Peter Principle; Principle of Parsimony
L. Theories	Bodies of principles and generalizations that present a clear, systematic view of complex phenomena	Theories of teaching and learning
M. Standards and Ethics	A combination of principles, theories, and knowledge of ways and means that guide practice, especially professional practice	Standards of ethics for teachers

Skills Classification

It is usually fairly easy to identify important content, but sometimes it is more difficult to think about the skills. What do you want students to be able to do with the content: simply recognize terms or apply concepts in order to solve complicated problems?

Table 5.4 Skills Classification in the Bloom and the Ward and Murray-Ward Taxonomies

Bloom Taxonomy	Ward and Murray-Ward Taxonomy
1.0 Knowledge	1.0 Recognition
2.0 Comprehension	2.0 Inference
2.1 Translation	2.1 Translation
	Examples, Illustrations
	Context Clues (Cloze)
	Classification
	Translation/Transformation
2.2 Interpretation	2.2 Interpretation
	Main Idea/Theme/Author's Purpose
	Summarization
	Generalization
2.3 Extrapolation	2.3 Extrapolation
	Causation
	Prediction
	Implications
3.0 Application	(See 2.3, 3.0, 4.0, and 5.0)
4.0 Analysis	3.0 Analysis
	Analogies/Ratios
	Matrices/Series
	Sequencing
	Outlining
	Structure
	Facts, Assumptions, Hypotheses, Opinions
	Internal Consistency
	Viewpoint
5.0 Synthesis	(See 2.2, 2.3, 3.0, 4.0, and 5.0)
6.0 Evaluation	4.0 Evaluation
	Comparison with Specified Standards
	Comparison with Unspecified Standards
	Contribution to Theme/Purpose/Effect
	Compare/Contrast
	5.0 Problem Solving
	Incorporating: Problem Identification
	Selection of Correct Principle
	Embodiment of Correct Principle

Students may process information at many levels. To teach and test higher-order skills, you have to understand what they are. Instruction is likely to be most effective if the teacher is clear as to what the student is supposed to know and be able to do at the end of instruction. Useful instructional objectives focus on outcomes and start with identification of the major concepts—what the Mathematics Sciences Education Board (1991) calls the "big picture."

In our skills taxonomy (see Table 5.4), we use "Recognition" as the lowest level. "Inference," the next level, involves doing something with the knowledge—translating, interpreting, extrapolating. "Analysis" involves breaking a whole into its parts; "Evaluation," making comparison and rendering judgments. "Problem Solving" requires the use of many lower-level skills to analyze a problem, identify

Table 5.5 Definitions of Skill Categories in the Ward and Murray-Ward Taxonomy

Category	Definition
1.0 Recognition	Recognize or reproduce information in essentially the same form in which it was originally received.
2.0 Inference	Recognize information when it is presented in a different form. This is the level called "Comprehension" in the *Taxonomy of Educational Objectives* (Bloom et al., 1956).
3.0 Analysis	Identify the organizing structure and relate details to the effect or outcome. Most of the material will be verbal communications, but the materials may come from science, mathematics, social studies, philosophy, or the arts, as well as from reading and literature.
4.0 Evaluation	Compare information with a standard, specified or inferred, and judge its adherence to that standard; evaluate information in terms of its contribution to a theme/purpose/intended effect.
5.0 Problem Solving	Given a description of a problem situation, identify the appropriate solution.

Table 5.6 Interrelation of Skills and Content in the Ward and Murray-Ward Taxonomy

Skills	Content		
	Elements	Ways and Means	Universals
1.0 Recognition	√	√	√
2.0 Inference	√	√	√
3.0 Analysis	√	√	√
4.0 Evaluation			√
5.0 Problem Solving			√

causes, evaluate possible solutions, and select the most appropriate one. The skills categories are listed in Table 5.4 and defined in Table 5.5. The interaction of content and skills is indicated in Table 5.6. The difference in skill levels will become clearer in the next four chapters as we go through the process of preparing assessments of various kinds.

DECIDING WHAT TO ASSESS: CONTENT

In this section we describe the process of identifying and organizing the content to be covered in an assessment.

Procedures for Defining the Content Domain

We start the definition of the content domain definition by preparing a *content outline*, which organizes the content into logical units and specifies the percentage to be devoted to each section. A content outline may be developed for a course as a whole or for a specific unit, depending on the purpose of the assessment.

It is important to organize the content in such a way that overlaps and gaps in the list of content can be noticed and corrected. This is especially important for tests used summatively—for example, a unit test or a final examination. If you get used to thinking about the content of your courses in this way, it should be easier for you to keep the major issues in mind and to check on whether students are getting them. Teachers who teach in the same grade or department may want to do some of these analyses as a group and perhaps even develop an item bank that all of them can share. If so, then they will not have to do the whole job from scratch each year.

Steps in Defining the Content Domain

Here, we describe four specific steps to take to define the content domain. Procedures for defining the skills domain and completing the Assessment Blueprint are presented in the next sections.

Steps in Defining the Content Domain
1. Identify the construct for the assessment. 2. Identify and collect sources of information. 3. Identify and organize the content. 4. Assign weights.

Step 1: Identify the Construct for the Assessment. The *construct* is the variable (quality, skill, etc.) that the assessment is intended to measure. Constructs may be very broad—such as "achievement in mathematics" or "achievement on Unit II" —or quite narrow—such as "number combinations from 0 through 99." The construct provides the framework for specifying the domain to be covered.

It is also important to clarify how scores on the assessment are to be used. Will they be used to guide instruction (formatively) or to evaluate performance after instruction (summatively)? Is the concern with overall achievement, with attainment of specific objectives, or with a combination of the two? The answers to these questions should guide you in selecting and organizing the content to be covered in an assessment and in deciding whether the coverage should be broad or limited.

Step 2: Identify and Collect Sources of Information. Development of assessments in education usually starts with a given—often a list of state-mandated or district-adopted skills. Also, instruction is usually dependent on the specific textbook series used and, in some cases, national organizations develop and promote lists of skills or concepts to be included in instruction for certain subject areas. These materials may be useful to teachers who are developing assessments and should be incorporated whenever they are useful.

Step 3: Identify and Organize the Content. Although skills and content, or both for chapters or units may be outlined in the teachers' manual for a textbook, most of the material will require additional organization before it will be useful as the basis for developing assessments. There is often much overlap in individual skills, and often one or two of the statements subsume the entire domain even though many of the elements are also listed separately. Such overlap is apparent in the example of objectives for a chemistry unit presented later in the chapter.

A worksheet for an assessment blueprint is presented in Figure 5.2. On this worksheet, content is listed from top to bottom on the left side, and the skill levels run in the columns across the top. To use Figure 5.2 for making a content outline, you first would identify the major topics and then list subtopics. When doing this, be aware that the concept of universals—whether principles, theories, or standards and ethics—is especially important if test items are to address knowledge of more significance than only the elements.

You may want to make copies of this form to use as a worksheet, or you may want to make a similar form that better fits what you are teaching. Of course, you can simply use plain paper, but sometimes a form helps to remind you of a term or category you might otherwise forget.

Step 4: Assign Weights. With the topics appropriately organized, it is easy to decide how important each of them is—that is, how much weight to give to the major components and elements of each topic and subtopic. We stress the importance of this step because you need to think about what you teach, what is required of your students, and how much instructional time and effort to place on each piece of content. For example, if you are giving an assessment for summative purposes, you would not want to stress content on which you spent little instructional time.

| Major Topics and Subtopics | Total | Percentages of Topics By Skill Level | | | | | Type of Assessment |
		1	2	3	4	5	
1.0							
1.1							
1.1.1							
1.1.2							
1.1.3							
1.1.4							
1.2							
1.2.1							
1.2.2							
1.2.3							
1.2.4							
2.0							
2.1							
2.1.1							
2.1.2							
2.1.3							
2.1.4							
2.2							
2.2.1							
2.2.2							
2.2.3							
2.2.4							
3.0							
3.1							
3.1.1							
3.1.2							
3.1.3							
3.1.4							
3.2							
3.2.1							
3.2.2							
3.2.3							
3.2.4							
4.0							
4.1							
4.1.1							
4.1.2							
4.1.3							
4.1.4							
TOTAL	100%						

FIGURE 5.2 Assessment Blueprint Worksheet

How will you express the weights? You have two choices. You can use *percentages* for the various items of content on the blueprint if you don't know how long a test will be or if you want to use more than one type of assessment. But if you know you will be using a test of 50 items (for example), you can use the *number of items* to be allocated to each topic and subtest.

DECIDING WHAT TO ASSESS: SKILLS

Completing the content outline is the first step in preparing the assessment blueprint. The next task is to identify skills to be assessed and allocate weights to them. There are spaces on the worksheet in Figure 5.2 to help with this task. The content outline goes into the columns at the left side of the worksheet. Then the skill levels are entered across the rows under the appropriate heading.

It is important that the skill to be measured is clearly identified and that items and tasks are carefully written so that they evoke the desired skill. For example, an item may ask that the examinee *recognize* the definition of a term, or it may require the examinee to *make a prediction* from a series of events. Clearly there is a difference in the cognitive level of these skills.

Identification of the skills to be assessed involves identifying the processes the examinee should be able to use to manipulate and interact with the content. For some topics there will be only one skill level. Other topics may be addressed at several skill levels.

Two issues are involved in identifying skills: (1) Some of the skills should call for higher-level thinking. (2) The skills must be operationally defined, in order to communicate what is meant. The definitions and examples of skills provided in Table 5.5 may be helpful. It is important to tap higher-level critical thinking skills with your classroom assessments. We offer some general suggestions below, and in the next chapters we offer more specific help in addressing higher-level skills when you are developing various kinds of items and exercises—especially in Chapter 6, which deals with paper-and-pencil tests.

Assessment of Critical Thinking

If students are to learn critical thinking skills, it is important that assessments require those skills. Many people believe that you cannot use multiple-choice tests to assess higher-level skills. It is true that most of the items in many minimum-competency or basic skills examinations are at the recognition or literal knowledge level, but it is also true that multiple-choice items do not have to be so limited. Furthermore, poorly conceived and poorly developed open-ended alternative assessment procedures also fail to tap higher-cognitive levels and complex skills. The examples in Figure 5.3 illustrate this point.

In both low-level items in Figure 5.3, the task for the student is simply to read the problem, do a simple calculation, and either select or write the answer. The task and thus the skill level are the same whether the student is *selecting* the correct answer on the multiple-choice item or *writing* the answer. The student might report the steps she or he completed in solving the problem in either case.

LOW-LEVEL ITEMS

Multiple-Choice Item	**Open-Ended Item**
Tommy has 7 pennies, and he finds 3 more. How much are his pennies worth now?	Tommy has 7 pennies, and he finds 3 more. How much money does he have now?
A a nickel	How did you get your answer?
B a dime	
C a quarter	
D a dollar	

HIGHER-LEVEL ITEMS

Multiple-Choice Item	**Open-Ended Item**
A gardener applies manganese to a plant that has been turning yellow and dropping leaves.	A gardener applies manganese to a plant that has been turning yellow and dropping leaves.
What will probably happen to the plant?	What will probably happen to the plant?
A Insects will be attracted to the plant.	How did you get your answer?
B The plant will become dormant.	
C The plant will grow new, green leaves.	
D The plant will grow flowers.	

FIGURE 5.3 Examples of Low-Level and Higher-Level Test Items

The situation is different with the higher-level items. On both the multiple-choice and the open-ended item the student is required to make a prediction, which is an *inference* skill. However, the question "How did you get your answer?" is too vague. Different students will interpret the question differently, so the task will not be the same for all students. To be certain of eliciting the process you want the student to use, you would have to ask a much more focused question, such as "Describe the chemical process that would cause the change you predict."

As these examples suggest, problems in assessment are not so much with the type of measurement procedure as they are with poorly defined goals and objectives and with poorly written assessment items. Simply asking "How did you get your answer?" does not make an item high level. The answer that the majority of the students gave to the low-level open-ended item in Figure 5.3 was "I just knew it."

The Need for Operational Definitions

To determine the skill level of a test item, you need to be clear about what test behavior you need to "see" in order to be certain that the students can perform the skill. This is called an *operational definition*—that is, defining the variables in terms of the procedures used to measure them. Only with such definitions can clear communication be established. Robert Ebel (1980) explained why we need such clear definitions of our variables:

> Any characteristic of people or materials must be defined unambiguously before it can be measured validly. An unambiguous definition of a quantitative characteristic must be an operational definition: it must describe in some detail the means by which one gets the numbers that purport to measure the characteristic in question.(p. 1)

Whether you are trying to measure requisite knowledge and skills or are observing actual performance, you must know what is to be measured—that is, have an operational definition of it—before you can determine how best to measure it. The most satisfactory way to operationalize skills is to prepare item specifications. Many large testing programs do this.

Item specifications provide an operational definition of the way the content and skill are to be measured. Figure 5.4 presents a set of item specifications for a multiple-choice item at the "Analysis" level. Notice that the specifications provide an operational definition of the content and skills and information about what the stimulus should be like, how the question should be posed, and what the criterion for a correct answer is. There is also a sample item. Specifications like this are a great help in writing items at the level you want.

Skill: **Content:**	Comparison/Contrast Techniques
Skill Statement:	Given the specification of two or more factual, fictional, pictorial, or auditory products, identify factors that are similar or that are different.
Stimulus Attributes	
Format:	A direct question asking how two trends, research findings, techniques, criteria, principles, theories, or standards are *alike* and/or how they are *different*.
Response Attributes:	Statements of possible likenesses and/or differences.
Options	
Correct Response:	The statement that fits the stimulus.
Other Options:	Statements that are incorrect or irrelevant to the stimulus.
Sample Item:	In what way are *conditioning* and *learning* alike, and how are they different?
	A Both are like in all respects; there are no differences except for the terms.
	B Both are involved with psychomotor processes, but learning involves higher-level processes than conditioning.
	C Both involve behavior change, but only learning involves understanding reasons for behavior.
	D Both involve cognitive processes, but only learning depends entirely on self-reinforcement.

FIGURE 5.4 Specifications for a Multiple-Choice Item

Steps in Identifying Skills

The steps in identifying skills are listed below; then each step is discussed.

Steps in Identifying Skills
1. Identify possibilities for skills associated with each type of content to be covered.
2. Make a choice of skills.

Step 1: Identify Possibilities for Skills Associated with Each Type of Content. When you are trying to decide what skill levels you might use for each piece of content, you may find that it helps to review Tables 5.4, 5.5, and especially Table 5.6, which shows which skills categories may be used with each content category. Notice that for any category of content there are many possible skill levels that might be used. For "Universals," for example, all levels of skills may be tapped. If the content covers a certain theory, the student could be asked to do any of the following:

State a component of the theory. (Recognition)

Restate a component of the theory in other words. (Inference)

Identify a situation in which the theory applies. (Analysis)

Compare or *contrast* the theory with another theory. (Evaluation)

Apply the theory to solve a practical problem. (Problem Solving)

Step 2: Make a choice of skills. You may wish to use only one or two of the possible skills, or you may want to use all levels. The choice will depend on several considerations:

1. What is the intended level of the test? What levels of skill is it reasonable to expect of students?

2. How many items will be directed at the piece of content?

3. What types of items are appropriate for the specific content and skills to be covered?

Question 1: What is the intended level of the test? What levels of skill is it reasonable to expect of the students? The answer to this question depends on whether the class is a beginning class or an advanced one. It also may depend on the purpose of the assessment. An assessment that is used formatively to guide instruction might be quite different from one that is used in part to assign grades in the course.

Question 2: How many items will be directed at the piece of content? If several items are to be devoted to a specific piece of content, you may want to prepare the items at varying skill levels in order to see which levels students are able to handle. However, if only one or two items are to be used, you will probably want to make those items at a fairly high level, unless students are just starting to study the topic.

Question 3: What types of items are appropriate for the specific content and skills to be covered?   If your content is organized by broad categories, you probably can use assessment items at all levels of skill. However, some of the subtopics may be assessable at only a few skill levels.

DECIDING HOW TO ASSESS

The assessment of human performance has a long and varied history ranging from early tribal initiation rituals to present-day mass administration of standardized achievement tests to high school students, massive testing programs to license practitioners of many professions and occupations, and proposals for national testing programs. Most of the current large-scale testing programs rely on machine-scorable multiple-choice tests, but there is substantial interest in alternative types of assessments.

As you learned in Chapter 3, alternative assessment is not new. So, you may ask, why did multiple-choice testing become the most frequently used assessment? There are many answers to this question. One is that multiple-choice tests and other structured response tests are by far the easiest to score, and multiple-choice items are much more flexible than other structured response items. However, that is not the primary reason. In the early part of this century, concerns about the unreliability of scoring and fairness in testing were very serious. All assessment in psychology and education was "alternative"—that is, it used methods other than multiple-choice tests. The few studies of teachers' grading practices made prior to 1920 revealed great variations between the grades that different teachers assigned to the same student's answers in a variety of subject areas (e.g., Starch & Elliott, 1912, 1913a, 1913b). Later studies confirmed the findings of scoring problems.

The great advantage of multiple-choice tests is that the scoring is objective and easily accomplished. This has made large-scale testing programs possible. In the early days of multiple-choice testing, teacher practice was not much influenced by the high regard in which such tests were held. However, as the national tests gained more prestige and high-stakes decisions came to be associated with them, teachers began to emphasize in their instruction those skills that they perceived to be emphasized on the tests. The situation with essay tests and writing is a good illustration of this. A study of the relationship between essay scores and multiple-choice tests of writing skills on the *College Entrance Examination* found a very high correlation between the two (Godshalk, Swineford, & Coffman, 1966). As a result of this study, the essay test became an optional part of the *College Entrance Examination.* Consequently, teachers placed less emphasis on writing and more on handling multiple-choice items. In recent years, the need to include some non-multiple-choice assessments has been recognized, if only as an incentive to ensure that teachers teach skills not easily assessable by multiple-choice tests.

At the present time, some critics are advocating the complete elimination of all multiple-choice tests, overlooking the difficulties associated with other types of assessments, some of which led to the initial development of the multiple-choice tests. Regardless of the type of assessment, an important consideration is that assessments should tap more than low-level skills. The tasks should require both application and integration. Written tests should ask questions that require the type of thinking to be demonstrated; other assessments should require the demonstration of the target behaviors; and all assessments should avoid extraneous interference that makes the scores invalid.

Articles by Stiggins and Bridgeford (1985) and Stiggins, Conklin, and Bridgeford (1986) indicate that these criteria are seldom met in classroom assessment. As a help with this problem, we present in this section an overview of assessment possibilities, along with an indication of their respective strengths and weaknesses.

Types of Assessments

Assessment options are many and varied. They range from observing actual performance through simulations with observers and simulations with written questions, to tests that ask questions about the knowledge required to perform the necessary tasks acceptably. Furthermore, there are many dimensions on which assessments may vary: test versus nontest; written versus oral; assembled versus unassembled; constructed response versus open-ended response.

We like to think about all of the assessment choices discussed in this section using the metaphor of the toolbox. The types of assessments are the tools. You choose the best tool for the job—assessment purpose and conditions.

The major classes of assessment techniques are listed in the box below:

Classes of Assessment Techniques
Paper-and-pencil tests:
Objective (structured response)
Open-ended (unstructured response)
Oral tests
Assessment of performance
Assessment of products
Observation
Retrospective ratings
Portfolios

Each technique may vary as to other dimensions. For example, testing may be written or oral; written tests may be objective, completion, or essay; objective tests may be multiple choice, matching, or true/false; observation may be either direct or retrospective. Another way of looking at assessment possibilities is to consider the various combinations of types of stimuli, or tasks, and modes of response for test items, as suggested by Table 5.7. Each type of stimulus may be used with all of the response modes.

Table 5.7 Stimulus Type and Response Mode

Stimulus Type	Response Mode					
	Performance		Oral		Written	
	Unstructured	Structured	Unstructured	Structured	Unstructured	Structured
Real life	√	√	√	√	√	√
Simulations	√	√	√	√	√	√
Oral	√	√	√	√	√	√
Multimedia	√	√	√	√	√	√
Written	√	√	√	√	√	√

The third way in which assessments may vary is in the scoring procedure. They may be scored by hand or by machine. Scores may be numerical or descriptive; they may be global or analytic; and they may be unidimensional or multidimensional.

The purpose for which an assessment is to be used and the conditions under which it is to be administered are important considerations in the choice of an assessment. As a practical matter, for summative assessments administered to a large number of people, written, structured-response tests are by far the most common, economical, and efficient method of assessment. Furthermore, this type of testing (usually multiple choice) has the following advantages over other types of assessment, including other types of written exams:

Advantages of Structured Response Examinations
Broad sampling of the domain
Objectivity of scoring
Reliability of scoring
Ease of evaluation of items
Ease of checking on item bias

Because of the many advantages, most large-scale testing programs in the United States have opted for the broad coverage and economy of multiple-choice tests, a form of structured-response test. At times these are supplemented by more direct measures, such as a writing assessment or an observation system.

A variation of multiple-choice testing that is used for some programs involves *simulation,* in which a variety of techniques is used to present information to which the examinee responds by answering a series of multiple-choice questions. This technique is sometimes used in computer administration of examinations, but it may also be used with written examinations with the use of scenarios, films, or videotapes to present the stimulus.

A point to keep in mind is that many desirable outcomes or skills are not *directly* assessable by multiple-choice tests—for example, "Write a technical report based on statistical data." Recalling the toolbox metaphor, and trying to find the most appropriate tool for our task, we know that the most valid way to find out whether someone has this skill is to have him or her actually write such a report. However, this would be an expensive procedure and scoring might not be reliable. Furthermore, there may be dozens of such reports and other procedures the applicant needs to know how to do, but the time required to assess all these procedures directly would be prohibitive. So we look for other tools. We find that we can use a variety of procedures to test a group of "enabling" or "requisite" skills. For the technical report writing skill, one might use requisite skills such as these:

Enabling Skills for *Writing a Technical Report*

Interpret data presented in a table or graph.

Select a conclusion that can correctly be drawn from the data presented in a table or graph.

In the described research study, identify the procedure that is missing (or erroneously carried out).

The many possibilities of assessment are summarized in Table 5.8. Notice that each assessment method has both advantages and disadvantages. The greatest trade-offs are between immediacy or real-life assessment on the one hand, and economy and breadth of domain sampling on the other.

Steps in Selecting an Assessment Method

In determining the most appropriate method of assessment, these steps must be carried out:

Steps in Selecting an Assessment Method

1. Determine the assessment purposes and resources.
2. Study the assessment options.
3. Consider the advantages and disadvantages of each option.
4. Make a tentative choice of types of assessment to be used.
5. Prepare item specifications.

Table 5.8 Assessment Options

Techniques	Advantages	Disadvantages
I. Tests		
A. Written Test	Economical, efficient	May not be valid for all objectives/skills
1. Structured response (multiple choice, matching, T-F)	Can sample wide range of knowledge and skills in a short time period Encourages examinees to develop broad background of knowledge and skills Measures low-level skills efficiently Can measure high-level cognitive skills Scoring is objective, rapid, and efficient	Preparation time is lengthy Writing good items requires technical skill Poorly written items may cause problems in interpreting results
2. Open-ended	Encourages examinees to organize their ideas Writing the items does not require as much time as writing structured-response items	Coverage of content and skills may be limited
B. Oral test	May assess skills not addressed by other assessment methods	Cannot cover the domain Scoring may be unreliable and invalid
C. Situational test	Can be (or simulate) a real-life situation	Coverage of domain is quite limited Unless multiple-choice version is used, scoring is difficult, requires a great deal of time, and may be both unreliable and invalid Valid scoring requires trained observers with good recording skills
II. Other Assessments		
A. Direct observation/ Performance test	Direct method of obtaining information	Time-consuming, therefore expensive Observers may not use common referents Preparation and scoring requires high level of skill
B. Retrospective ratings	Can subsume and generalize long experience Economical	May be invalidated by response set of raters
C. Product examination (includes portfolios)	Can be (or simulate) a real-life situation	Coverage of domain may be quite limited and may vary with each examinee
D. Self-reports	Economical	May be invalidated by dishonesty, lack of insight, and response set
E. Interviews	Provide opportunity to observe skills not otherwise assessable	Difficult to standardize Scoring is difficult Situation may not be typical

Step 1: Determine the Assessment Purposes and Resources. The most appropriate types of assessment to be used in a classroom situation depend on the purposes of the assessment. There are several questions to consider when you are making this decision:

Questions
1. How will the assessment be used?
2. How can the important qualities best be assessed?
3. How many students must be handled each year?
4. What resources are available for preparing assessments and training those doing the assessments?

Question 1: How will the assessment be used?   Remember, there are basically two major purposes for assessment. *Formative* assessment is used to monitor the instructional process, to determine whether learning is occurring as planned. *Summative* assessment is used to determine the status at the end of instruction and usually involves high stakes of some type such as assignment of grades and promotion and retention decisions. Some assessments are used for both purposes, as when assessments are used for a placement decision; then the results of the assessments are used to plan the instruction for the student.

Question 2: How can the important qualities best be assessed?   Tests are most appropriate for assessing knowledge, including principles, theories, and standards. But a decision as to whether an individual can carry out certain procedures must be based on observation of behavior, on inspection of a product of that behavior, or on ratings by someone who has observed the behavior over a period of time.

Question 3: How many students must be handled each year?   Some courses are limited as to the types of assessments they can use because of the large numbers of students assessed each year. Observation of performance and inspection of products require a large block of time for each person evaluated. Also, it is difficult for judges (teachers) to maintain objectivity and a high degree of reliability when large numbers of people must be processed; therefore, it is necessary to spend extensive time in training and monitoring the scoring. On the other hand, some programs are so small that costly test development is difficult to justify.

Question 4: What resources are available for preparing assessments and training those doing the assessments?   All assessment tasks must be carefully prepared if they are to work well in identifying competence. Multiple-choice examinations require much time to prepare, but scoring is easy and can be done in a short period of time. Open-ended items, observation, and product examinations are relatively simple to set up but require much time to carry out and score, and judges must be carefully trained and monitored. Ratings and self-reports are fairly easy to develop and score but may not be valid. Whatever assessment procedures are used, all those responsible must be trained and monitored. The school or district must consider what resources can be devoted to the process.

Step 2: Study the Assessment Options. When looking at Table 5.8, consider each assessment type as it would apply to your situation. For some courses, written tests alone are quite adequate, and some written tests will be desirable for most courses. Other types of assessments will be essential in some courses and highly desirable in others.

Step 3: Consider the Advantages and Disadvantages of Each Option. Table 5.8 makes it clear that objective tests can cover a lot of material in a short period of time and can be scored easily and accurately. Also, contrary to common perception, they can measure very high-level thinking skills. Unfortunately, writing good objective tests requires a great deal of time and sophistication, and poorly written tests may provide misleading information.

Observation of performance and examination of products (including essays and portfolios) are necessarily limited in scope and require a great deal of time and sophistication to administer and score. Poorly conceived observations may be even more misleading than poorly written tests, products may be very limited, and there is seldom time to sample all skills and knowledge that an individual acquires. The best procedures usually combine objective testing and some type of more direct assessment.

The various options also should be considered with regard to the criteria for good assessments presented in Chapter 4.

Step 4: Make a Tentative Choice of Type(s) of Assessment to Be Used. The decision about which type of assessment to use should rest primarily on considerations in assessing achievement in the subject area and on practical concerns. The first decision is what to use: testing, evaluation of performance, examination of products, observations, ratings and portfolios. Then several choices must be made about subcategories. For example, if the decision is to use testing only, the next question is whether to use oral or written tests, multiple-choice or essay questions. Next, you must decide to what extent some simulations will be included in the examination and how they will be presented.

The discussions in other sections of this chapter may help answer these questions. The worksheet in Figure 5.2 provides space for recording these decisions.

Step 5: Prepare Item Specifications. In addition to the assessment blueprint, many test development specialists recommend that item specifications also be developed to provide specific instructions for writing items that fit the blueprint. *Item specifications* are detailed directions for the stimulus, responses, and scoring criteria and include a sample item.

Review the item specifications in Figure 5.4. It can serve as a model. Many large testing programs use something similar to guide item writers.

You probably will not want to write all the specifications you will need for all your assessments. You may be able to adapt some of those that we provide in subsequent chapters of this book, as well as those in other publications—for example, Roid & Haladyna (1982) and Ward & Murray-Ward (1992).

TRANSLATING INSTRUCTIONAL OBJECTIVES INTO ASSESSMENTS

Teacher-made assessments are usually used to determine whether students have learned a body of content. Logically, then, most teachers begin with a list of *instructional objectives*—the content and skills that they plan to teach or have taught. This makes good sense; however, the form in which most objectives are written makes it difficult to use them for test writing.

Figure 5.5 shows a list of objectives for a chemistry unit. Notice the problems with this list: Some of the objectives do not seem to fit the title of the unit; there is no indication of which are the major concepts; and many of the objectives are written at the lowest cognitive level. You would have trouble using this list as a guide for planning instruction, and you would have a similar problem if you tried to use it as the basis of an assessment program.

---

1. Define *chemistry.*
2. Show how the following terms fit into the scientific method:
   a Experiment   c Hypothesis
   b Law   d Theory
3. Distinguish between *matter* and a *substance.*
4. Name and characterize the three states of matter.
5. Classify samples of matter as *homogeneous* or *heterogeneous.*
6. Identify *physical changes* of matter.
7. Classify samples of matter as a *substance* or a *mixture.*
8. State the difference between an *element* and a *compound.*
9. Write the symbols of common elements; write the names of elements from their symbols.
10. Distinguish between *potential* and *kinetic* energy.
11. Give an example of the conversion of one form of energy into another.
12. State the *law of conservation of energy.*
13. Classify changes in matter as *physical* or *chemical.*
14. Define a *chemical reaction.*
15. State the *law of conservation of mass.*

FIGURE 5.5 Original List of Objectives for a Chemistry Unit on Matter, Change, and Energy

Figure 5.6 shows a content outline that works better. The objectives listed in Figure 5.5 have been organized by topics and subtopics, and percentages have been assigned to each. For example, subtopics for the topic "Energy" are "States of energy," "Conversion of energy," and "Conservation of energy."

Topics	Subtopics	Percentages	
		Topic	Subtopics
Chemistry		3	
Scientific Method		2	
Matter		40	
	Substances		2
	Properties of matter		9
	States of matter		8
	Solutions: homogeneous vs. heterogeneous		1
	Changes in matter		20
	Physical changes		
	Chemical changes		
	Chemical reactions		
Elements and Compounds		5	
Energy		35	
	States of energy	10	
	Potential energy		
	Kinetic energy		
	Conversion of energy	12	
	Conservation of energy	13	
Mass	Conservation of mass	15	
TOTAL		100	

FIGURE 5.6 Well-Organized Content Outline. Developed from Figure 5.5.

The blueprint form has spaces for the content and skills to be assessed and the relative weights of both. If more than one type of assessment task is to be used, the blueprint may also include this information. Figure 5.7 presents the completed blueprint for an assessment in the chemistry unit.

We strongly recommend the procedure described here for all assessment programs. We think that teachers can and should use at least rudimentary blueprints for their classroom assessments, perhaps working in teams by departments or grade levels to do so.

Major Topics and Subtopics	Total	Percentage By Skill Level					Type of Assessment
		1	2	3	4	5	
1.0 Chemistry	3		3				Multiple choice
2.0 Scientific Method	2			2			Multiple choice
3.0 Matter	40						
3.1 Substances		3	2				Multiple choice
3.2 Properties		3	2	1			Multiple choice
3.3 States of matter		3	2	1			Multiple choice
3.4 Solutions		3	1	1			Multiple choice
3.5 Changes							Performance
3.5.1 Physical			1	3	2		
3.5.2 Chemical			1	3	2		
3.5.3 Reactions			1	3	2		
4.0 Elements and Compounds	5		5				Multiple choice
5.0 Energy	35						Multiple choice
5.1 States of energy			2	3	3	2	
5.2 Conversion of energy			3	3	3	3	
5.3 Conservation of energy			4	3	3	3	
6.0 Mass: Conservation of mass	15			7	5	3	Performance
TOTAL	100%	12	27	30	20	11	

FIGURE 5.7 Completed Assessment Blueprint for the Unit on Matter, Change, and Energy

SUMMARY

- Good assessment requires careful planning.
- Assessment planning starts with specification of the domain.
- Start with major concepts and identify content and skills for each of them.
- An assessment blueprint is used to indicate the distribution of both content and skills.

STUDY QUESTIONS

1. What is the domain of an assessment?

2. Why is the definition of a domain important?

3. Where should the domain of a classroom assessment come from?

4. Why is a taxonomy of content a useful concept?

5. How can preparation of a content outline improve an assessment?

6. Why is the percentage of the total test that is assigned to each piece of content important?

7. What levels of skill are most difficult to assess?

8. How are skill levels related to content levels?

FOR YOUR PROFESSIONAL GROWTH

1. Think about one area of your curriculum or a chapter in a textbook that you use in one of your classes. Has there been a change in the content or skills emphasized in this course? How has the assessment for this material changed?

2. From a professional library, check out an issue of a curriculum journal such as *Educational Leadership* or *Phi Delta Kappan*. What major curriculum issues are discussed in that issue? What implications does this discussion have for assessment?

3. Choose a unit of instruction or a textbook chapter and prepare a content outline for it.

   Identify the major topics and list them in a format similar to Figure 5.2. Extend the form if you need more space.

   Fill in subtopics for each topic.

   Decide on the percentages (or number of items) for each topic and subtopic.

4. Decide which skills should be involved with each piece of content, and assign weights for content and skills for each content row.

5. For each row on the blueprint, record the type of assessment you will use.

6

༄

Paper-and-Pencil Tests

PREVIEW

In Chapter 5, we introduced the *toolbox* metaphor in thinking about methods to assess students. By far the most frequently used tool is the paper-and-pencil test. There are many reasons why this is so. In the first place, such tests can cover a wide range of objectives. Second, they are relatively inexpensive to construct, administer, and score. Finally, they produce a record of the assessment.

The two major categories of paper-and-pencil tests are unstructured response and structured response. Unstructured-response tests include short-answer and essay items. The most useful structured-response test, which is also called an objective test, is the multiple-choice test. Objective tests also include true-false and matching items.

MAJOR TOPICS

General Considerations for Preparing Written Tests
Overview of Paper-and-Pencil Tests
    Unstructured-Response (Open-Ended) Items
    Multiple-Choice and Other Structured-Response Items
    Construction Items
Choice of Item Type
Developing Assessment Tasks
    Steps in Developing Assessments
    Guidelines for Writing High-Level Items
Preparing Unstructured-Response Items
    Short-Answer Items
    Essay Items
Preparing Structured-Response Items
    Multiple-Choice Items
    True-False Items
    Matching Items
Preparing Construction Problems
Trying Out Items and Exercises
Setting Up an Item Bank

GENERAL CONSIDERATIONS
FOR PREPARING WRITTEN TESTS

Teachers assign many written tasks, but not all of them are tests. For a written task to be considered a test, all students must respond to the same instructions and must do so under the same conditions. When a task is a test, and when a task is presented to students as an evaluative device, it should meet these criteria for good assessments:

Criteria for Good Assessments

Validity: An assessment should address important goals that are relevant to instruction.

Reliability: An assessment should be consistent and dependable.

Objectivity: Assessment tasks and scoring procedures should be designed in such a way that scores are based on the same standards for all students and all scorers.

Fairness: Scores should be based on criteria that are applied consistently to all students. All students should have an opportunity to learn the material covered by the test.

OVERVIEW OF PAPER-AND-PENCIL TESTS

Many kinds of tasks may be presented on written tests. The items may be multiple choice or short answer, simple or complex. Structured-response (or objective) tests present students with items that have a list of responses from which they are to select the correct answers. Unstructured-response (open-ended) items require students to write their answer or to draw a picture or make a graph. Many times the same objective may be assessed by any type of item.

Unstructured-Response (Open-Ended) Items

Unstructured-response items require the examinee to write or produce the answers and require a human being to score them. Some of these items are called *short-answer* or *essay items*. Others require the examinee to make a chart or draw a picture. Sometimes an unstructured-response task is a long, complex assignment, such as a term paper, rather than an item on a test. These tasks are called *production* or *performance assessments*, and preparing and scoring them are covered in Chapter 7. In this chapter we discuss only short-answer, essay, and construction items.

Unstructured-response items may simply require the examinee to respond with a word, phrase, or number, or they may require long, complex responses. Scoring simple short-answer items is not much more complicated than scoring objective items, except that it cannot be done by machine. In contrast, scoring the complex items—essay questions—requires a lot of time. It requires that the scoring criteria be prepared in advance and that the scorers be trained. To ensure fairness, it is also desirable to monitor the scorers' performance to check that they maintain the same frame of reference throughout the scoring. You should set up a system of monitoring your own classroom assessments so you can be sure that you are being fair to all students.

Multiple-Choice and Other Structured-Response Items

The most useful and flexible objective item is the multiple-choice item. For an *objective* item there is one correct answer, and the scoring is often done by machine.

Multiple-choice tests were developed as a solution to a practical problem: the need to score the tests of large numbers of examinees in a short period of time. This need arose during World War I, and since then the multiple-choice format has come to dominate testing in education, civil service, and licensing. The advantages of multiple-choice testing include the objectivity of the measurement, the ease and accuracy of scoring, the ease of evaluating the reliability of the measurement, and the amount of content that may be covered in a short time. True-false and matching items share these advantages, but they are limited to the assessment of low-level skills. Multiple-choice items can measure very high-level skills if they are well written.

The advantages offered by objective items are important considerations for large-scale testing programs, because broad coverage of the curriculum and ease and speed of scoring are important. For testing in a single classroom, the distinction is less important, because the lengthy scoring process can be balanced by a shortened time for developing items and multiple assessments may be used in place of a single long one.

Many educational objectives, especially those in mathematics and science, require the student to "construct a graph" or "construct a table" from a given set of data. These objectives may be assessed either by having students do the construction or by using multiple-choice items that require them to select the correct or best example of the construction. Figure 6.1 presents items that require the student to construct the response.

1. Shade in two-thirds of the figure below.

   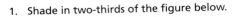

2. The picture below is one half of a symmetrical figure. Draw a picture of the complete figure.

3. Look at the figure below. Draw another figure that is *congruent* with this figure.

4. The percentages of income spent on major categories of expense by the average American family are listed below. Fill in the circle graph showing this information. Be sure to label each part of the graph.

Category	Percentage
Rent	50%
Food	30%
Clothing	5%
Transportation	6%
Miscellaneous	9%

   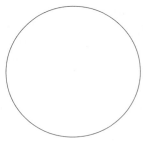

FIGURE 6.1 Examples of Simple Unstructured-response Items

With multiple-choice items, these objectives become, "Identify the graph or table for the data set given." Figure 6.2 presents a multiple-choice form of the same items as those in Figure 6.1. Similarly, in language arts classes, outlining is frequently listed as an objective. When testing is limited to multiple-choice items, an example of a correct answer is provided along with options that are incorrect. Obviously these items do not address exactly the same skills, but the substitution may be necessary in a very large testing program. In classroom testing, however, students can actually write out the responses or construct the tables and graphs.

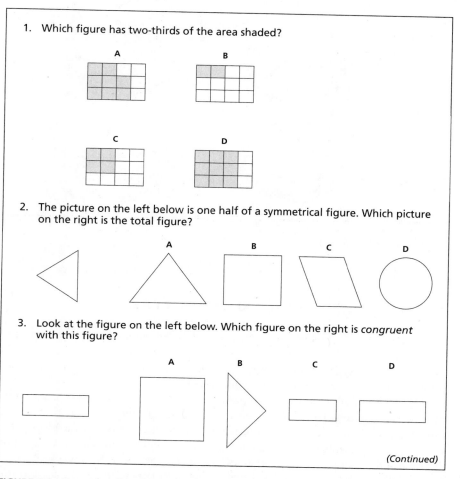

1. Which figure has two-thirds of the area shaded?

   A   B

   C   D

2. The picture on the left below is one half of a symmetrical figure. Which picture on the right is the total figure?

   A   B   C   D

3. Look at the figure on the left below. Which figure on the right is *congruent* with this figure?

   A   B   C   D

   (Continued)

FIGURE 6.2 Examples of Multiple-Choice Construction Items

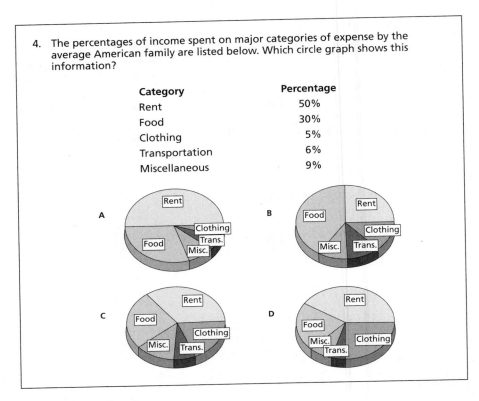

4. The percentages of income spent on major categories of expense by the average American family are listed below. Which circle graph shows this information?

Category	Percentage
Rent	50%
Food	30%
Clothing	5%
Transportation	6%
Miscellaneous	9%

FIGURE 6.2 *continued*

CHOICE OF ITEM TYPE

Table 6.1 summarizes the advantages and disadvantages of objective and unstructured-response items. Because multiple-choice and essay are the most frequently used types of items, we spend most of this chapter discussing them, although other types of items are also addressed. Both kinds of items may address very high-level skills when they are presented in the context of appropriate stimulus material. Considerations to keep in mind when deciding whether to use multiple-choice items or unstructured-response items are listed in Table 6.2.

Figure 6.3 presents sample items at the various skill levels in both unstructured-response and multiple-choice formats. Notice that for items at the lower skill levels, the stimulus of the item may be the same for both the multiple-choice and the unstructured-response items. With higher level skills, more than one multiple-choice item is often needed to cover all that a single open-ended item can cover.

Both objective and unstructured-response items should be written thoughtfully, paying attention to the details that help to ensure that the items measure what you intend. Many of the suggestions for creating item stimuli and stems apply equally to both unstructured-response and objective items. The only task you

Table 6.1 Advantages and Disadvantages of Objective and Unstructured-Response Items

Item Category	Item Types	Advantages	Disadvantages
Objective	Multiple choice Matching True-false	Ease of scoring Objectivity of scoring Accuracy of scoring Can measure large number of objectives in a short time Can measure high-level thinking	Difficulty of writing good options Difficulty of writing high-level items Difficulty of wording items to minimize guessing
Unstructured response	Short answer Essay Construction	Good "face validity" Can offer windows into thinking processes: to tap planning, organization, integration, and effective expression of ideas Requires less preparation time because of fewer items	Time and effort for scoring Subjectivity in scoring Possibility of judges' unreliability in scoring Difficulty of assessing reliability and item performance May be influenced by bluffing or by poor writing skills Small number of possible tasks

Table 6.2 Decision Criteria for Multiple-Choice and Unstructured-Response Items

Use Multiple-Choice Items When . . .	Use Unstructured-Response Items When . . .
The test is to cover a large number of objectives. There is time to prepare good items. *or* There is a bank of items that can be used. Machine-scoring facilities are available. *or* Keys can be made easily for untrained scorers. Time for administration is short. Scores are needed immediately.	There is a short time to prepare items. There is a longer time after the test for scoring. Trained scorers are available. There is a long period of time for testing. *or* The test can be given in several sessions. *or* A number of short tests can be given. The group of students is small. There is a need to examine many aspects of student writing.

eliminate if you choose unstructured-response items is developing the options. You still have to develop scoring guides, and doing that requires the same careful analysis as does writing options for objective items.

The major advantage of the unstructured-response item is that it can provide the examinee the opportunity to decide what to say—that is, what ideas are most relevant—and how to say it, and to express the ideas effectively. It is not appropriate to use items of this type simply to ask *what, who, where,* and *when* questions. Objective items can easily be constructed to measure these questions, and they can be scored easily.

DEVELOPING ASSESSMENT TASKS

The best assessments are those that have been thoughtfully developed to measure the content and skills that are of concern. What is missing in objective items is the opportunity for students to express their own ideas. If you want to assess this skill on your classroom tests, an unstructured-response test will be more valid. Whichever type of item you decide to use, it will be necessary to provide stimulus information that lets students demonstrate the skills you are concerned with. This is especially important for higher-level skills. For the higher-level questions in Figure 6.3, notice that you have to provide some information and ask questions in a way that elicits the intended skill.

An advantage of unstructured-response items is that they allow for scoring responses based on the organization and presentation of information, rather than just on the correctness of the information—for example, in stating and defending an opinion on an issue for which there is no single acceptable response. Such items may also ask the student to defend both sides of a contradictory issue. Additional suggestions for writing items are provided later in the chapter.

Both unstructured-response and objective tests are often developed without proper care to ensure that the items address skills other than those at the lowest level—simple recognition or recall. The need to address higher-level thinking skills has always been recognized by some members of both the teaching and the measurement professions. But as multiple-choice tests have become more widely used, the large majority of items on such tests have tapped the lower cognitive levels. Unfortunately, many of these tests have had high stakes attached to them, so there has been a strong incentive to coach and drill students and other prospective examinees on tasks that resemble the test items, often to the detriment of other, more important, objectives.

Here are four suggestions for producing quality test items of all kinds:

Steps in Developing Assessments

1. Start with a test blueprint.
2. Prepare the answer you expect.
3. Prepare stimulus material that is needed and write a question or instructions that will elicit the expected answer.
4. Write the options for multiple-choice items; prepare the scoring guides for essay and construction items.

---

1. **Literal Knowledge:** *Recognize or reproduce information in essentially the same form in which it was originally received.*

   EXAMPLES

   Unstructured-Response Items

   1. What part of the brain regulates the heart beat?
   2. What does the term *fortitude* mean?
   3. What percent of 400 is 10?

   Multiple-Choice Item

   What part of the brain regulates the heart beat?

   A Cerebellum

   B Cerebrum

   C Medulla

   D Pons

2. **Inferential Knowledge:** *Translate and interpret information; identify examples or illustrations; make predictions and identify causes.*

   A. **Interpretations:** *Restate information in a different modality or in different terms of the same modality.*

   EXAMPLES

   Stimulus 1 and Question

   What conclusion can be drawn from the graph below?

   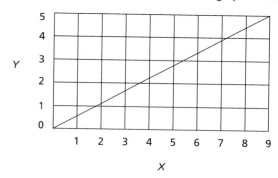

   Multiple-Choice Options

   A There is no relation between X and Y.

   B Y increases at the same rate as X.

   C Y decreases as X grows larger.

   D Y increases as X does, but at a slower rate.

   Stimulus 2 and Question

   Read the paragraph below; then answer the questions.

   The American makes, and is forced to make, a long and tedious business of getting fit, whereas a Canadian merely has to exercise and sleep a trifle more than usual.

   What is the author's purpose?

   Multiple-Choice Options

   A To entertain

   B To inform

   C To incite some action

   D To support a position

   (Continued)

FIGURE 6.3 Definition of Skills and Samples of Items at Different Taxonomic Levels

B. **Examples and Illustration:** *Given a term or concept, provide an example of it. Given an example of a term or concept, identify the term for it.*

EXAMPLES

Question

Name three components of the blood.

Multiple-Choice Options

A Corpuscles, marrow, hydrochloric acid

B Erythrocytes, leukocytes, plasma

C Proteins, sugars, minerals

D Salt, oxygen, hydrogen

C. **Extrapolation:** *Go beyond the information given. Extend the time dimension backward to identify causes or forward to identify effects and make a prediction. See implications of the information given.*

EXAMPLES

Stimulus and Question

Read the paragraph below; then answer the questions.

> When the Brown family returned from vacation, they found that a rose bush that they had planted just before leaving home was brown and dead-looking.

What is the most likely reason for this?

Multiple-Choice Options

A Lack of water

B Lack of copper

C A fire

D A storm

3. **Analysis:** *Identify the organizing structure and relate details to the effect or outcome.*

EXAMPLES

Stimulus

Read the passage below; then answer the questions.

> A plaintive murmur rose in the night; a murmur saddening and startling, as if the great solitudes of surrounding woods had tried to whisper into his ear the wisdom of their immense and lofty indifference.
>
> Sounds hesitating and vague floated in the air round him, shaped themselves slowly into words, and at last flowed on gently in a murmuring stream of soft and monotonous sentences.
>
> Harlan, motionless and shadowy, sitting with bowed head under the stars, was speaking in a low and dreamy tone. It was he who was murmuring.

Unstructured-Response Items

1. What mood does the author convey with this passage?

2. How does he convey this mood?

Multiple-Choice Item

How does the author let you know that he feels compassion for Harlan?

A He uses soft words that make you feel quiet and accepting.

B He describes what has happened to Harlan.

C He uses words that paint a picture of the scene.

D He concentrates on sensory details of the scene.

(Continued)

FIGURE 6.3 *continued*

4. **Evaluation:** *Compare information with a standard, specified or inferred, and judge its adherence to that standard; evaluate information in terms of its contribution to a theme/purpose/intended effect.*

EXAMPLES

Stimulus

Read Susan's letter to her parents; then answer the questions.

> *Dear Mom and Dad,*
>
> *Our cabin is so close to the lake that we can swim three times a day. We have a swell rowboat that we can use to go for a ride or to go fishing. We eat all the fish we catch. Nothing could taste better.*
>
> *There are many pine trees here, so there are lots of pine cones on the ground. We have collected several bags of cones to take home. Up the pretty little road there are wild berry bushes, and we like to pick and eat the berries. First, we had blackberries and now raspberries—all delicious!*
>
> *It's so peaceful and quiet here. Just the songs of birds, the sighing of the pines, and at night, the lapping of the waves on the shore. And the stars seem so bright. I love to sit on the pier and watch them.*
>
> *I miss both of you and even Tommy. However, I am really enjoying camp. Thank you for sending me.*
>
> *Love,*
> *Susan*

Unstructured-Response Items

What kind of person is Susan? List her attributes; then, for each attribute, indicate the parts of her letter that tell you about it.

Multiple-Choice Item

Which part of the letter tells you that Susan likes the outdoors?

  A The activities she describes   C The kind of food she likes to eat

  B The way she misses her family   D The kind of animals she likes

---

5. **Problem Solving:** *Given a description of a problem situation, identify an appropriate solution.*

EXAMPLE

Stimulus and Questions

Read the paragraph below; then answer the questions.

> *When the Brown family returned from vacation, they found that a rose bush that they had planted just before leaving home had many brown leaves and buds had dropped off.*

Unstructured-Response Items

1. How should the Browns decide what to do *first* to try to save the rose bush?
2. Who might be able to help them decide what to do?
3. What else should they do?
4. How will they know that what they are doing is helping?

Multiple-Choice Items

1. What is the first thing the Browns should do to try to save the rose bush?

  A Water it.   C Move it to another spot.

  B Put some fertilizer on it.   D Cover it up.

2. Who might be able to help them decide what to do?

  A Florist   C Grocery manager

  B Gardener   D Veterinarian

FIGURE 6.3 *continued*

Step 1: Start with a Test Blueprint. A test should sample the domain of content and skills covered by instruction. In Chapter 5 we provided directions for identifying the content and skills, identifying the desired balance for each, and preparing the assessment blueprint. A blueprint is just as important for a test partially or totally comprised of unstructured-response or construction items as it is for an objective test. Remember that if you plan to use different kinds of items, you should note them in the blueprint.

It is also important to remember that, for a large unit of instruction, you get a better sample of the domain if you use a large number of questions, rather than a few long questions. But if the test is to cover a single, short unit of instruction, a single, carefully prepared question or exercise may be appropriate, although usually you will need many items to cover all the objectives.

Step 2: Prepare the Answer You Expect. If this seems like working backward, it is! Think about it this way: The answer is what you are trying to elicit with the item, so you need to be very clear about what the answer is, in order to write the right question. For multiple choice items, write the correct answer. For unstructured-response items, write out a model response.

Step 3: Prepare the Stimulus Material and Write a Question. To assess higher-level thinking, instead of simply requiring recognition or memory of bits and pieces of information, you will need to provide some stimulus material. This material can include a problem situation or scenario, a picture, a drawing of science apparatus, and so on. The students' task should be to process the information, not to guess what situation the teacher has in mind. The type and amount of stimulus material you need for each item depend on the level of skill you are trying to test. Some suggestions for writing item stems that require high-level thinking are discussed in the next section of this chapter. Note that the stimulus must present the material that the student needs to answer the item.

Step 4: Write the Options (Multiple-Choice) or the Scoring Guide (Unstructured-Response). For multiple-choice items, write the correct answer exactly as you want it to appear; then write the other options in the same format. For example, if your correct answer is a complete sentence, then all other options should be complete sentences.

For unstructured-response questions, you need to prepare a scoring guide. For short-answer questions, the guide will usually be fairly simple. However, if you have a complex question for which there are several important points, you should prepare a guide that lists the points that should be covered and indicates how much weight each point should have. This guide is discussed in more detail later in the section on unstructured-response items and in Chapter 7.

Guidelines for Writing High-Level Items

We have been emphasizing the importance of teaching and testing high-level skills. Now we are going to give you some specific suggestions to help you do this, starting with five general suggestions for all types of items. Specific suggestions for each of the major types of items are presented in the next sections.

Guidelines for Writing High-Level Items

1. Make stimuli lifelike.
2. Ask questions about novel situations, not those provided in a text book or discussed in class.
3. Word the questions so that they require high-level thinking.
4. Consider the use of "progressive" items.
5. Supplement items with probes.

Guideline 1: Make Stimuli Lifelike. It is easy to write items that ask only for bits and pieces of information and can be answered with a single word or phrase. Items of this type require only recognition and leave little room for reasoning. It is harder to write items that require the application of knowledge. This requires a stimulus that sets up a lifelike situation and can be done in several ways.

Using Written Scenarios. The simplest way to increase the complexity of the stimulus is to use a written description of a situation in which there is a problem. Such descriptions are called *scenarios.* A scenario will work best if you pattern it on real life and provide enough detail to make it lifelike. Students should have to sort out possibilities, evaluate the effect of various facts, anticipate the possible effect of courses of action, use criteria to evaluate possible courses of action, or do any combination of these.

A point to remember is that many times you can often base more than one question on a well-written scenario. We give you some examples later.

Using Real-Life Materials and Simulations. Teachers can use real specimens for a test, even when the questions and options are multiple choice. For example, if you teach science, you can present plants to be identified, slides to be evaluated, or chemicals to be tested. The results are recorded on an answer sheet.

There are several ways in which you can set up the materials for students to observe and respond to them, depending on what the materials are. For example, you can set up a viewing table and give students a page of questions, with either multiple-choice responses or a space for open-ended responses. Then students can walk by the table, view the exhibit, and mark their answers on their answer sheets. If you want to do this, you can divide the test into at least two sections and let most of the group work on the other portion while individuals or small groups take turns using the viewing table. Of course, all of this has to be carefully monitored so that everyone has a chance to get to the viewing table and to avoid students' "sharing" of information during the test.

Other methods of presenting stimuli allow the entire class to respond to the items at the same time. These methods include the use of videotapes, movies, or slides of situations, objects, or materials. Language teachers often use tape recordings of conversations; music teachers use recordings; art teachers use pictures or other visual materials. In any field, videotapes or films may be used to present information.

Variations of this type of stimulus presentation are sometimes used when tests are administered by computer.

Guideline 2: Ask Questions about Novel Situations, Not Those Provided in a Textbook or Discussed in Class. In order to test for students' ability to apply learning and to transfer it to other situations, some of your questions must require students to deal with situations that have not been specifically taught. The situations should be similar to those studied, so students can transfer their learning to them, but they should not be something for which the answers can be memorized.

Guideline 3: Word the Questions in a Way That Requires High-Level Thinking. To tap higher-level thinking skills, the stem of the item must ask for that type of skill. If the stem asks "Which term means_____?" the allowable answers will be only terms. To facilitate testing higher-level skills, you must phrase the question in such a way that students have to use the intended mental process to answer the question. Look again at Figure 6.3, which presents examples of both unstructured-response and multiple-choice items for all taxonomic levels. Notice the difference in the way the question is asked at the different levels. You may want to study these items to get an idea of how to phrase your questions in a way that elicits high-level thinking.

Guideline 4: Consider the Use of "Progressive" Items. Sometimes, in addition to presenting a real-life or simulated stimulus, you may want to ask a series of questions about the situation, supplying additional information before each question. The problem with this procedure is that later information may clarify the correctness or incorrectness of earlier responses. For example, the first question may present a situation and ask what other information is needed. Then additional information is presented, and a question is asked about a tentative diagnosis of the cause. Next, the diagnosis is given, along with a question about what the first treatment should be. The results of a treatment are given, and a question is posed about next steps.

This technique is used frequently in examinations in medicine and science. It is a good testing technique to identify at what point the examinee is confused about a series of procedures. However, an examinee can use clues presented in later items to correct answers to previous items, which would invalidate the procedure as a source of information about the area in which the examinee is having problems.

If you want to use progressive items, work out a way to administer such items by computer, or use a special answer sheet that makes erasures very obvious and invalidates the second choice. Both of these strategies are feasible if there is a need for this kind of information.

Guideline 5: Supplement Items with Probes. Another way to look at several aspects of examinees' responses is to use probes along with the items. This can be done with both multiple-choice and unstructured-response items. The items are asked as usual, with spaces on the answer sheet for the responses or with multiple-choice options. In addition, for at least some of the items, space is provided for examinees to explain their answers, with a question such as "How did you get your answer?" or "Why is that true?"

It is important for the probes to be carefully written and used only with high level tasks. To ask a simple arithmetic computation question and follow with the question "How did you get your answer?" is nonsensical. The only reasonable answer is "I just knew it." Sometimes probes are given orally, in a one-on-one situation. This may be especially useful for students who are having difficulty with tests. However, such oral probes are more properly considered teaching rather than testing.

PREPARING UNSTRUCTURED-RESPONSE ITEMS

As a general rule, reserve unstructured-response items for the skills that are difficult to test adequately with multiple-choice or other objective items. In this section we present ideas for creating two types of unstructured items: short-answer and essay. Construction items are discussed later in the chapter.

Short-Answer Items

Short-answer items test only low level skills, and for those skills, you could use objective items, which would shorten your scoring time considerably. However, if you want to use short-answer items, here are some samples of the kinds of short-answer items you might use:

Who discovered the use of insulin for diabetes?

What is the holy city of both Judaism and Christianity?

What is the chemical formula for ammonia?

You could address these questions very easily in matching items, and the items would not be much more difficult to write than these were. In the section on matching items we show you how to do this. The only advantage we see in using short-answer items, aside from the speed with which you can write them, is that you can see whether students can spell names and terms correctly—and maybe that's important!

Essay Items

Well-written essay tests can address high level skills that are difficult to include in objective tests. You can require students to remember information and to process it and organize it and then present it in a logical and coherent manner. However, writing essay questions requires a great deal of skill, and scoring them requires careful analysis and much time.

What many teachers prefer to do is to make a few large assignments each year on which students spend a lot of time and which teachers score very carefully. However, if you have a small group of students and if you prefer to spend time in scoring rather than in writing items, you may want to include some essay items on all your tests. We still advise that you use objective items for all those skills for which they are best suited.

Although writing essay questions is somewhat easier than writing multiple-choice tests, it still requires time and thought to be sure you ask the right questions. Preparing scoring guides also requires care. Both of these processes are presented below.

Five guidelines for writing essay questions are listed below and then discussed:

Guidelines for Writing Essay Items

1. Ask questions about major concepts.
2. Require students to apply their knowledge, not simply to report facts.
3. Define students' task as completely and specifically as possible.
4. Ask many short, specific questions, rather than a few general questions.
5. Decide in advance which variables will be considered in scoring and let students know.

Guideline 1: Ask Questions about Major Concepts. The best assessments are those that focus on important concepts, not minor details. It is not that you don't want students to learn the specific information; you want them to learn it in context. Before you start to develop an essay assessment, you need to review the objectives of the course and have them firmly in mind as you plan and prepare your items. We discussed this at length in Chapter 5, so you should have this information well in hand.

Guideline 2: Require Students to Apply Their Knowledge, Not Simply to Report Facts. Don't ask students to tell you what is in the textbook or what you did in class. Instead, pose a situation that will require them to use the information and, perhaps, to reorganize it.

Guideline 3: Define Students' Task as Completely and Specifically as Possible. The statement or the question must be sufficiently specific and detailed to eliminate ambiguity but at the same time give students sufficient opportunity to demonstrate their knowledge and skill. Avoid use of general words like *discuss*, or *explain* unless some delimiting words or phrases follow. The object is for all students to understand what the task is. The following examples should help:

Too general: Discuss the American Revolution.

Better: Which cause of the American Revolution is similar to a cause of the United States Civil War? How is it similar and how is it different?

Also, you might get additional help by reexamining the items in Figure 6.3.

Guideline 4: Ask Many Short, Specific Questions, Rather Than a Few General Questions. As a rule, the more questions you have, the more reliable your scores will be, and the test will be more valid because you will cover the objectives more thoroughly. We are *not* suggesting that you use a lot of short-answer questions. What we are suggesting is that your essay items be focused and that you do not try to cover the entire course in a single general item. Remember that we have already suggested that you also consider using a number of objective items so you can cover your instructional objectives more thoroughly.

Guideline 5: Decide in Advance which Variables Will Be Considered in Scoring and Let Students Know. Students need to know what components of their responses will be considered in the scoring. They also need to know to what extent English mechanics, handwriting, and artwork will be considered in scoring. Unless the test is in English or art, these factors should not affect the score, although it is good practice for teachers to mark mistakes. Another possibility is to score and report on the mechanics, handwriting, and artwork separately, especially if the school has a policy that all teachers should foster good communication. The rating for this assessment component can be reported to the English or art faculty, for example. If these qualities are included in the score for an achievement test in some other content area, they will invalidate the score, and the end result will not really be a measure of achievement in the intended area.

It is also important to give students some idea of the weight the various items will have, so they can allocate their time appropriately. Doing this is especially important if several essay items are to be answered in a given period of time. Decide on answers to these questions:

Are the items of equal value?

Is one item more important than another?

For essay questions, you will usually want the scores to indicate the completeness and accuracy of the answer. Also, some of the questions may have greater weight than others.

Essay items should be scored as objectively as possible, so that the scoring is fair to all students. It is not fair to give one student credit for an answer but not give another student credit for the same or an equivalent answer. What is an equivalent answer? Think about the matter in advance, and be very clear about what is the important information that must be included in a correct answer. Also, consider the various ways in which that information may be stated and the kinds of errors students might make—the common misinformation or misconceptions some students might have—so that these are noted when the item is scored.

Many times teachers score student papers without doing any preparation. And to make bad matters worse, often they change their procedures or their standards or both in the middle of the process. Another mistake many teachers make is to score all items for a given student at the same time. It is much better to score the papers for all students on a single item and then take the next item and score all students' paper on that item, and so on.

Get in the habit of preparing scoring guides and sharing them with the students. If you do this, then it should be much easier to answer questions about where scores come from and what they mean. We are assuming you will not simply mark each paper "correct" or "incorrect," after you have spent so much time developing the items and considering what should be in the responses. You will want to assign a score to each item on each paper that indicates how well the student did on that particular item.

Before starting to score the papers, prepare a scoring guide. Here are some suggestions:

Preparation of a Scoring Guide for Essay Questions

1. Decide what weight each question has.
2. For each question, list the most important points.
3. List subpoints for each point.
4. Assign weights to each point and subpoint.
5. Prepare a sample of a perfect answer.
6. Prepare a list of alternative ways of stating each correct answer.
7. Prepare a list of common errors and mistakes.

After listing the important points and skills to be covered, you can develop some descriptive statements for determining what score you will give each student for each item. First, of course, you will have to decide what your range of scores will be and whether each item will have the same range. Our preference is to use a 5-point rating scale for each item, with the descriptions, or rubrics, looking something like those in Figure 6.4. The rubrics in Figure 6.4 may be used for many items similar to the two included in that figure. If some items have more weight than others, simply multiply the rating of individual items by a weighting factor, such as 1,2, 3, etc.

If you want to use a rating system similar to this, you can simplify your job and build in some validity and reliability checks by using what we call the "stack" system. You read the response to one item on one paper, assign a tentative score to it, and start a pile for that score on that item. Then you score the next paper and the next, placing each paper in the appropriate stack. When all papers have been scored for that item, you review the stacks to be sure that the papers in each stack are of about the same quality. If you find any papers that are in the wrong stack, you change the stack they are in. When you are satisfied, you mark each paper with the score for that item. Then you go to the next item. The stack procedure helps improve both validity and reliability.

In place of rubrics, you can use a point system, perhaps starting with a checklist and then counting the number of checks to determine the score.

EXAMPLES OF ESSAY ITEMS:

1. Explain how hurricanes that strike the east coast of the U.S. develop and why they take the paths they do.

2. Why should everyone be concerned about which fertilizers farmers use on their crops? Explain what happens to the fertilizer and how that affects people who live other places.

SCORING RUBRICS

5 Shows understanding of all major content and processes.
Applies principles correctly in all important respects.
Expresses ideas in a way that communicates well.

4 Knows most concepts and principles.
Usually applies principles correctly but occasionally misses something.
Expresses ideas so that they are understood.

3 Understands most major concepts and processes.
Knows most principles and applies some of them correctly.
Expresses ideas correctly but not elegantly.

2 Understands some concepts.
Knows some principles but does not apply them.
Has difficulty in expressing ideas.

1 Understands very few or none of the major concepts.
Does not know principles.
Cannot express ideas.

FIGURE 6.4   Sample Rubrics for an Essay Item

PREPARING STRUCTURED-RESPONSE ITEMS

Multiple-Choice Items

The general suggestions provided in the overview earlier in this chapter are important if you want to write multiple-choice items that assess important skills. These include preparing an assessment blueprint and then providing good stimuli for students to use when responding to the questions. It also is important to ask the right questions. Here are six steps for constructing good multiple choice items:

Steps for Preparing Multiple-Choice Questions

1. Start by writing the correct or best answer. Be sure to state it correctly and in the correct grammatical form.
2. Create the stimulus.
3. Write questions that require high-level thinking skills.
4. Identify common errors and misunderstandings.
5. Write options that would appeal to students who have one or more of those misunderstandings.
6. Avoid common errors in item writing.

Step 1: Start by Writing the Correct or Best Answer. This works, even though it may seem like working backward. If you write the correct answer first, you set the goal for students. The answer then provides a guide for the stimulus, allowing you to write a stimulus that will elicit the answer from the student. In addition, the correct answer will help you frame parallel, plausible options for students who do not know the correct answer.

Step 2: Create the Stimulus. Suggestions for preparing stimulus materials are presented in an earlier section of this chapter. The same suggestions will work for multiple-choice items.

Step 3: Write Questions that Require High-Level Thinking Skills. In writing multiple-choice questions, it is important for you to ask questions in such a way that they require students to engage in the kind of mental processes you want to assess. No matter how elaborate your stimulus is, if a question asks for facts or details, the student will simply provide them. If you want students to solve a problem, you must ask for a *solution*, not for the name of a person.

Avoid writing the stem in such a way that you confuse students. We recommend that you make all stems a complete sentence, usually a question. Incomplete sentences and fill-in-the-blanks often are confusing. Another practice that you should avoid is the use of a negative in the stem. When the stem is negative, it is almost impossible to write options without using double negatives and convoluted wording.

Figure 6.5 shows a poorly constructed item and the revised version of it. The stem of the poor item is an incomplete and negative sentence. In the improved version the stem is a question and the word *not* has been eliminated.

Poor Item

The statement that is *not* true about the AFL is

    A They did not admit skilled workers.

    B They did not admit unskilled workers.

    C It was founded by Samuel Gompers.

    D It was organized into separate craft unions.

Improved Item

Which statement correctly describes the AFL?

    A Only skilled trades workers were admitted as members.

    B Both skilled and unskilled workers were admitted as members.

    C It was made up only of people from the mining industry.

    D It was made up only of people from the textile industry.

FIGURE 6.5   Examples of Poor and Improved Multiple-Choice Items

In order to write multiple-choice items that call for high-level thinking skills, you must be creative. Most inexperienced item writers write only items that require simple recognition and memory. Strictly speaking, the only behavior that a student can demonstrate on a multiple-choice item is to *recognize* **an example** of:

Analysis	Paraphrase
Classification	Prediction
Drawing conclusions	Finding a solution
Definition	Translation
Extrapolation	

Many desirable outcomes or skills are not directly assessable by multiple-choice tests. However, a skilled item writer can word the question so that it taps one of the high-level skills and presents options that are examples of the skill that is elicited by the question. This is a central notion in writing good multiple-choice items. Look at this objective:

"Describe what will happen in an experiment and explain why."

Obviously, this objective cannot be tested in a single multiple-choice item, but much of the content and skills related to the objective may be approximated by a series of multiple-choice items, such as these:

"What is the most likely effect of _____ ?"

"What is the process that occurs when _____ ?"

Step 4: Identify Common Errors and Misunderstandings. Incorrect options should be plausible but not tricky. Misconceptions held by poor students make good options.

Step 5: Write Options Likely to Appeal to Students Who Have One or More of Those Misunderstandings. When constructing the incorrect options, consider the common misunderstandings students have about the subject of the item. Be sure to write the incorrect options in the same grammatical form as the correct answer. If the correct answer is a complete sentence, all options should be complete sentences. If the correct answer is a phrase, all options should be phrases.

Step 6: Avoid Common Errors in Item Writing. The way in which options for a multiple-choice test are written greatly affects its validity. Inexperienced teachers are likely to make mistakes that either make an item ambiguous or provide help to examinees who really know nothing about the material covered in the item. So the tasks for the teacher are to facilitate the task of responding for the student who knows the material and to avoid giving unwarranted help to the student who is ignorant.

Suggestions for avoiding problems with options for multiple-choice items are summarized in Figure 6.6.

1. Write the correct or best answer. Be sure to state it correctly and in the correct grammatical form.

2. Consider what are the common misunderstandings students have about the subject of the item. Write options that will appeal to students who have one or more of these misunderstandings.

3. Prepare three other options in the same grammatical form. If the correct answer is a complete sentence, all options should be complete sentences. If the correct answer is a phrase, all options should be phrases.

4. Be sure that all options are plausible—that they are not so obviously wrong that the item is a giveaway.

5. Have other teachers take the test and see whether they mark the correct answer. If they do not, ask why they chose the answer they did.

6. Avoid "none of the above," "all of the above," and "both A and B" as options.

   EXAMPLE:

   What do those who work for "equal rights" believe in?

   A Equal rights are guaranteed by the Constitution.

   B Women should be treated as a minority.

   C Both A and B

   D None of the above

7. Avoid giveaways. Grammatical clues, use of absolutes such as *always* and *never*, and clang associations often give away the correct answer or steer examinees away from incorrect options. Also, be careful not to make the correct option longer or shorter than other options.

   EXAMPLE (Clang association)

   When John realized he was lost, he re-examined a map.

   What is the meaning of *re-examined* in the sentence above?

   A threw away

   *B examined again

   C looked for

   D bought

   EXAMPLE (Longest option)

   What is a way to improve the *reliability* of a test?

   A Shorten it.

   *B Make it longer and keep all items in the same content domain.

   C Use essay items.

   D Use true-false items.

FIGURE 6.6 Suggestions for Preparing Options for Multiple-Choice Items

True-False Items

As we indicated earlier, we do not recommend the use of true-false items.

Perhaps you like true-false items because you think they are easy to write. You simply take statements out of the textbook and change about half of them to make them incorrect; and voilà, you have a test. The problem, however, is that these items are usually poor and ambiguous and measure unimportant objectives and skills. Some people like to use true-false items because they say they can cover a very large amount of content in a short period of time. But in most courses there is little content that is absolutely true or false. The best answer for questions on this kind of content would be "It depends," but that is not an option with a true-false item.

Our final objection to true-false items is that they are very susceptible to guessing. With only two possibilities, the student has a 50% chance of getting the right answer. That does not leave much room for real knowledge to affect the scores.

In light of these serious problems, we recommend that you limit your use of true-false items. If you use them, follow the suggestions listed in Figure 6.7 to minimize the problems.

---

1. Avoid broad statements.

    Poor Example: *The governor of a state is elected to that office. (Usually true, but not always.)*

    Better Example: *The constitution of Florida describes how governors are elected.*

2. Avoid qualifiers.

    Poor Example: *The governor of a state is always elected to that office.*

        (The *always* gives away the fact that the statement is not true.)

    Better Example: *The constitution of Florida describes how governors are elected.*

3. Avoid double negatives.

    Poor Example: *None of the employees is unnecessary.*

        (Very confusing. May be misread.)

    Better Example: *All employees are needed.*

4. Avoid long, complicated statements.

    Poor Example: *Election procedures developed during the early days of the country require many steps and discourage many people from running for office.*

        (Such statements have many problems:

        They are hard to follow.

        There is more than one idea in the statement, so part of it may be true and the rest false.)

    Better Example: *The procedure for electing the governor requires that many steps be taken at the prescribed time.*

FIGURE 6.7 Suggestions for Writing True-False Items

Matching Items

Usually matching items are used to assess knowledge of simple relationships and offer an efficient way to do this. There are many kinds of important associations in most fields. We list some of them in Table 6.3.

Table 6.3 Types of Matching Stimuli and Their Associations

Stimulus	Association
Person	Accomplishment
Dates	Events
Rules and laws	Provisions
Terms	Definitions
Objects	Classifications
Principles	Examples
Statement	Interpretation

The problem comes if matching items are used as the exclusive method of assessment, because many important aspects of student achievement cannot be assessed in this way. Usually matching exercises can be prepared quickly. To prepare good matching items, however, requires care and thought. We offer seven guidelines to help.

Guidelines for Creating Matching Exercises

1. For each set of matching items, limit all items to a single type of relationship and content area.
2. Indicate how often an option can be used.
3. Keep each set of matching items short.
4. Indicate in the headings and the directions the basis for the match.
5. Order responses logically.
6. Keep all items in a set together on the same page.
7. Have at least one more option than you have items.

Guideline 1: For Each Set of Matching Items, Limit All Items to a Single Type of Relationship and Content Area. If you are matching people with their accomplishments, it is preferable for all the accomplishments to have something in common, such as a field or a time period.

Guideline 2: Indicate How Often an Option Can Be Used. Most of the time an option may be used only once, but sometimes item writers allow each option to be used "more than once," and it is important to say so. Also, it is a good idea to state that not all options will be used.

Guideline 3: Keep Each Set of Matching Items Short. It is better to have several short sets of items than a single long set in which the type of relationship varies within the list. Another consideration, if you want to be able to score your test by machine, is that each set of items should not have more options than there are response spaces on your answer sheet. This number is usually five, which suggests that you should have no more than four items in a set with five matching options.

Guideline 4: Indicate in the Headings and the Directions the Basis for the Matching. Example: "Match the definition in the column on the left with the term in the column on the right."

Guideline 5: Order Responses Logically. If options are arranged in alphabetic or numeric order, there is less chance that students will miss one, or that they will get unintended clues from the way the options are listed.

Guideline 6: Keep All Items in a Set Together on the Same Page. This will prevent students from missing some of the choices.

Guideline 7: Have at Least One More Option Than You Have Items. The point of this recommendation is to minimize guessing by eliminating the possibility of having students get the last item in a set by a process of elimination. Figure 6.8 provides examples of matching items. The POOR EXAMPLE shows some of the major problems seen in poorly constructed matching items. First, there is not a single type of relationship between the two sets of data, and the directions do not indicate what is the basis for the matching. Instead, there are presidents, explorers, inventors, and generals and there is no logical order to either the items or the options. Second, the number of items and options is too long to fit the usual machine-scorable answer sheet. Furthermore, there are the same number of items and options, so that the final choice is made by eliminating the other options.

The "better items" correct some of these problems. Both items indicate in the directions what is the basis for the matching and limit the possibilities. Both include one more option in Column B than the number of stimuli in Column A.

TRYING OUT ITEMS AND EXERCISES

If you write your items carefully, following the guidelines provided here to avoid common problems, the quality of your items should be fairly good. However, items that appear acceptable in an armchair review sometimes perform poorly when taken by examinees. In high-stakes testing programs it is essential to give items a real tryout to provide data to be used for estimating certain psychometric characteristics of the items and tests, such as *item difficulty, item discrimination, functioning of distractors,* and *reliability.* Allowable values are established, and items that do not fit the established parameters are flagged, studied, and perhaps eliminated.

The same procedures are highly desirable for any assessment, including all classroom assessments that are used to make summative evaluations.

POOR EXAMPLE

Directions: Match the items in Column A with those in Column B.

A	B
1. Christopher Columbus	A Started mass production of automobiles
2. Theodore Roosevelt	B First to circumnavigate the globe
3. Martin Luther King, Jr.	C A king of England
4. Robert E. Lee	D Leader of the Rough Riders
5. Henry Ford	E President of the U.S. during the Civil War
6. Magellan	F Civil Rights leader
7. Henry Tudor	G Leader of the Confederate army
8. Abraham Lincoln	H Discovered America

BETTER EXAMPLES

1. *Directions:* Match the person in Column A with his area of exploration or discovery in Column B. You may use each option only once, and one of the options will not be used.

A	B
1. Christopher Columbus	A Alaska
2. DeSoto	B Around the world
3. Henry Hudson	C Canada
4. Magellan	D The Caribbean Islands
	E The Mississippi River

2. *Directions:* Match the person in Column A with his role in American History in Column B. You may use each option only once, and one of the options will not be used.

A	B
1. Dwight Eisenhower	A First President of the United States
2. Ulysses S. Grant	B President of the Confederacy
3. George Washington	C President during World War I
4. Woodrow Wilson	D General during the Civil War
	E General during World War II

FIGURE 6.8   Examples of Matching Items

If a school district has a district-wide test development program and keeps an item bank, it should be possible for all items to be tried out before they are widely used. For a single teacher working alone, the best tryout might be to have another teacher or an older student respond to the items. However, you may have a hard time finding someone to do this unless you and a fellow teacher agree to review each other's items.

If you cannot work out anything better, you can try out the items yourself— but not at the time you write them. You have to get a little distance from them. Write the items one week, and try to answer them the next. You may find they are not quite as good as you thought they were. At the very least, the first time an item is used can serve as the tryout, and if you keep a record of how items perform, then you can improve them before they are used again.

EVALUATING ITEMS
AFTER AN ASSESSMENT

When you try out items or use them in a test, you may notice problems with some of them. There may be some that very few students answer correctly, or good students may miss some items while poor students get them right. When this happens, examine each item to see whether there is some problem with the way the question is stated or whether some important information is missing. When problems are found, correct them before the item is put into the item bank for future use.

Some programs for machine-scoring of tests will give you an item analysis that helps you identify problems with items. If you don't have access to that kind of program, you can easily look for the problems yourself. The easiest thing to look for is simply what percentage of students got the item right. If fewer than half of the students got an item right, there may a problem with the way the item is written. First, look at the stimulus. Does it tell students what information they are supposed to be looking for? Consider these items:

Poor Example

1. Richard Nixon

   A   was the twenty-third President.

   B   made an important trip to China.

   C   was governor of the largest state.

   D   is the only President to resign from office.

Better Example

2. Who is the only president who has resigned from office?

   A   Calvin Coolidge

   B   Warren Harding

   C   Richard Nixon

   D   Franklin Roosevelt

With the first item, students do not know what question is being asked until they read all the options. It is better if the stimulus allows students to formulate the correct answer so all they have to do is to find it among the options.

Next, look at the options. Even if the stimulus makes the task clear, the options may need some work. Look at the correct option. Does it make sense? Does it need to be re-worded? Now look at the other options. Did a large number of students choose some option other than the correct answer? Is that option worded in such a way that it could be considered correct? Perhaps you need to rewrite that option.

SETTING UP AN ITEM BANK

You can save a lot of time and have better tests if you set up an item bank. It may be simple or elaborate, depending on your resources.

Items may be typed on a card and stored in a shoe box or printed on paper and stored in a notebook. However, many teachers now have access to a computer, which is a great help in formatting and storing items so they can be retrieved for new tests and in keeping records of how each item performs. There are now many item banking programs and even a few item-creation programs, especially in mathematics and science, that teachers may acquire for use with their classroom examinations. See Roid (1989), Hiscox and Brzezinski (1980), and Ward and Murray-Ward (1994a, b). Also, Appendix G has information about sources of programs and item banks.

However you set up your item bank, try to keep a record of information about how the items perform, updating the record every time each item is used. The information may simply be recorded on the back of the item card, or, if you use a computer, it may be put on a file in the computer. We suggest that the following information be recorded:

1. Date of administration
2. Examinee group
3. For multiple-choice items
   a. Percentage getting item correct
   b. Percentage choosing each option
4. For essay and construction items
   a. Distribution of scores on the item
   b. Problems students had with the item, if any

SUMMARY

- Preparation of good test items of all types requires that the stimulus material be carefully prepared so that the question or instructions make it clear exactly what is called for in the item.

- With structured-response items, the options must all be parallel and the correct answer must be clearly correct.

- Items of any type should address higher-level skills—skills higher than recognition or recall.

STUDY QUESTIONS

1. Why did multiple-choice items become so widely used?
2. What is the most serious problem with true-false items?
3. What is the best procedure to use to develop matching items?
4. What is an item bank? How could you use an item bank?
5. Identify the most serious problem with this unstructured-response item:

   "Tell about the beginning of the Civil War."

FOR YOUR PROFESSIONAL GROWTH

1. Write items for sections of the blueprint that you prepared in Chapter 5. Try to write both multiple-choice and unstructured-response items. You may also write matching items for low-level skills. Try to write items at different skill levels.
2. Have someone else review your items.

7

࿎

Performance and
Production Tasks

PREVIEW

In this chapter we explore another set of measurement tools, which have increased in popularity recently. The increased use of performance tasks and production tasks has been one response to the criticism of multiple-choice testing. Resnick and Resnick (1985) argue that assessments drive instruction, so they should model what is desirable in instruction. Grant Wiggins (1989) made a case for what he termed "authentic" assessment, by which he meant assessments that are a sample of whatever students should be learning. In a book on authentic assessment, Hart says,

> An assessment is authentic when it involves students in tasks that are worthwhile, significant, and meaningful. Such assessments look and feel like learning activities, not traditional tests. They involve higher-order thinking skills and the coordination of a broad range of knowledge. They communicate to students what it means to do their work well by making explicit the standards by which that work will be judged. In this sense authentic assessments are *standard-setting*, rather than *standardized*, assessment tools. (Hart, 1994, p. 9)

The most valid assessments require students to demonstrate the type of behavior that is the target of instruction. Although, as we indicated in the previous chapter, you can approximate the targeted behavior very closely with objectively scored tests, that is an *indirect* measurement, rather than a *direct* one. Since most instruction is intended to help students *do* something, it is important that you also include some assessments that measure directly the extent to which they are successful. This requires assessment of actual performance. However, in many cases the performance yields a product, and it is the product that is scored, not the performance itself. Currently, the term *performance test* is used to cover assessment of both performance and production tasks. Performance and production assessments are most meaningful and convey the most information if they are carefully planned and if the scoring process is as objective and dependable as possible.

Preparation of performance tasks and production tasks is similar, and the same considerations must be handled in both. The chief difference is in the time at which the scoring occurs. When the focus is on *performance*, scoring occurs at the time of the performance. With *production tasks*, scoring occurs after the task is finished.

Performance tasks require the student to do something. *Production* tasks require the student to create a product. Even though these are different processes, the procedures for creating the tasks and for scoring them are very similar, so we discuss them both in this chapter.

MAJOR TOPICS
Definition of Terms
Performance Test
Production Task
Standardization
Preparation of Performance and Production Tasks
Steps in Preparing Tasks
Methods of Scoring Performance and Production Tasks
Holistic (Global) Scoring
Analytic Scoring
Primary Trait Scoring
Domain Scoring
Score Scales
Ensuring Validity, Reliability, and Fairness
Common Scoring Problems
Constant Errors
Judge-Specific Errors
Avoiding Problems in Scoring

DEFINITION OF TERMS

Performance Test

A *performance test* is a test that requires the student to demonstrate a targeted behavior. The term was originally used for a test that required the examinee to perform one or more operations under observation and under standard conditions. Performance tests may be used to assess many kinds of interactions with other people, with equipment or machines, or with situations. One example of a performance test outside the school setting is the road test for a driver's license.

Performance tests are used extensively in vocational education and such courses as art, music, and physical education. These tests often require the examinee to carry out some type of complex operation under observation, such as operation of a piece of equipment, while the performance is rated. Performance tests have been used to assess such divergent variables as "executive ability" and "reaction to stress." A group of performance tasks, such as the ones used to qualify individuals for administrative positions in school systems, is often assembled and administered at an assessment center. Perhaps the most frequently assessed performance in most classrooms is a speech or oral presentation.

A test using performance tasks should be differentiated from naturalistic observation, in which an individual is simply observed as he or she performs (see Chapter 8). The situation is not standardized or controlled, as it is in a performance test.

Production Task

A *production task* is a standardized task that requires the examinee to produce something. The production task most commonly used in schools is an essay test or writing sample, which is often assigned as a term paper or research report. However, a production task may involve other types of products, such as a painting, an exhibit, a machine, a computer program. Often a given task calls for both performance and a product. Many of the assessments used in vocational training, music, art, and licensing may be of this nature.

Standardization

If performance and production tasks are standardized, all students respond to the same instructions and do so under equivalent conditions. Whether the task itself is standardized, the reliability of the scores requires that scoring procedures be standardized—that is, that the same criteria be used for everyone.

PREPARATION OF PERFORMANCE
AND PRODUCTION TASKS

Developing performance and production tasks involves two important, intertwined procedures: preparing the tasks and planning the scoring. Judith Arter suggested that the decision about where to start depends on where you are. When you have a good idea of what a good performance looks like, you start there. But if you are not clear about this, start with the task and develop the scoring criteria as you look at students' actual performance (Arter, 1993).

Steps in Preparing Tasks

We begin our discussion with task preparation, but some of this discussion also impinges on scoring, which we discuss later in the chapter. The steps in preparing tasks are listed below and discussed. Most of these suggestions were originally developed to be used in large-scale assessment programs, but we have tried to adapt them to an individual classroom situation.

Steps in Preparing Tasks

1. Identify the purpose of the assessment.
2. Determine which tasks are to be used—that is, what the product or performance is to be.
3. Decide under what conditions the task is to be performed.
4. Decide how many scorers will be used and what their qualifications will be.
5. Prepare instructions for the examinees, examiners, and scorers.
6. Have the tasks reviewed and modify them as necessary.

Step 1: Identify the Purpose of the Assessment. As with all assessments, you must first identify your purpose, both to yourself and to your students. Remember that the purpose drives all of the other decisions educators must make when selecting and using any assessment. Notice that many of the examples in this chapter focus on writing in "on demand" situations. In these situations, students must produce their writing products without a chance to revise later, thus excluding part of the writing process. If educators are interested in assessing the entire writing process, they must state their purpose and modify their procedures accordingly.

Step 2: Determine Which Tasks Are to Be Used; That Is, What the Product or Performance Is to Be. Tasks should be *relevant* to the content and skills to be assessed, and *representative* of the content and skills. Furthermore, any procedure you use for any assessment purpose, other than a rough estimation of skills mastered, must be based on a *standardized* situation and set of instructions, so that all examinees are assigned the same task and scored by the same criteria. Otherwise, there is no way the scores may be interpreted either across examinees or in reference to a standard. If one person builds a mousetrap and another paints a picture, or if one person is put into a stressful situation and another is asked to prepare an income tax return, it is difficult to score the products on a common scale.

It is also important that each examinee receive precisely the same type and amount of help. Therefore, the allowable prompts and probes must be carefully specified in advance. Sometimes, when you need to develop a number of tasks—for example, if you want to use alternative but comparable tasks for different classes—it is a good idea to prepare task *specifications*, which provide instructions for creating the tasks. They are similar to the item specifications described in Chapters 5 and 6.

Figure 7.1 is an example of a set of specifications for a writing task. The "Performance Objective" tells what student behavior the item will be directed toward. The description of the stimulus indicates what should be in the instructions and how they should be stated. Then, the conditions under which the task is to be administered are specified. Finally, information about the scoring procedures is provided. Although you may not always write such complete specifications for your production and performance items, you need to have all this information well in hand when you are preparing them.

PERFORMANCE OBJECTIVE: Write a narrative based on personal experiences, interviews, or both.

STIMULUS: The prompt will instruct students to write a narrative paper based on their own experience, real or imagined, or on the experience of someone they know well.

CONDITIONS

1. To be written under quiet conditions in 35 minutes in a regular class period.
2. May be written in either black pen or #2 pencil.
3. May be written in either cursive or manuscript writing.
4. Booklet with lined paper is provided.
5. A separate sheet of paper is provided for making rewriting notes that will not be scored.
6. Students are allowed to use a dictionary.
7. Directions are presented to students both orally and in writing.
8. Directions may not be amplified.
9. Students will be told when only 5 minutes of testing time remains.

SCORING PROCEDURES

Type of Scoring: 4-point scale for each of three domains:
content, organization, conventions

Scorers: Two teachers trained in the scoring procedures

Scoring Standards

A sample of papers will be selected randomly and each paper will be scored by two raters.

Papers for which there is a discrepancy will be discussed, and a consensus will be reached as to the score.

Three papers at each score level for each domain will be selected to use as anchor papers.

FIGURE 7.1 Example of Specifications for a Writing Sample

If you want to test whether students can generalize and apply knowledge, the tasks used in assessment should be new situations, not some that you have taught in class. For example, in using the specifications in Figure 7.1, you would make it clear that the personal experience should not be something that has already been discussed in class. Figures 7.2 through 7.5 are examples of items that you might want to use as models for preparing tasks. Notice that each of these specifications describes the scoring criteria, under *performance criteria*, although the actual scoring procedures are not presented until later in this chapter.

Step 3: Decide Under What Conditions the Task Is to Be Performed.

Decisions must be made about the setting, time limits, availability of various aids, method of presentation, and so on. Is the task to be done at home or in class? Are there to be time limits? What materials are to be used? Look again at Figure 7.1. It provides a list of conditions for a writing sample that can serve as suggestions when you write the conditions for your specifications.

OBJECTIVE: Tell how to do something.
MODE: Narrative
AUDIENCE: A young child
FORM: Essay
STIMULUS: Written instructions

ITEM

We sometimes think that everybody knows how to do simple things like tying a shoelace. But a young child might not be able to do this simple thing. Imagine that you must explain to the child how you tie your shoelace. Think about what you need. Think about what you do first. Think about how you want the shoe to look when you have finished.

Write an essay in which you explain to a young child how you tie a shoelace. Include all the items needed. Start with the first step and continue until your shoe looks the way you want it. Be certain the child knows what the shoe should look like when he is finished.

Your essay will be scored on how clear your description is, how well organized the discussion is, and how well you express your ideas.

PERFORMANCE CRITERIA

Accuracy and clarity of description

Logic of organization and use of transitions

Effectiveness of the writing—

    Use of complete sentences

    Use of some complex sentences

    Use of action words

FIGURE 7.2 Sample Production Item

Step 4: Decide How Many Scorers Will Be Used and What Their Qualifications Will Be. For many classroom assessments, the only possible scorer is the teacher. But at least two scorers are preferable and it may be that you can work out an arrangement with one or more other teachers to cooperate in the scoring. Teachers' aides or other school personnel might help with the scoring of some of the performance and production tests if they are trained and carefully monitored. For district-wide or school-wide assessments, the scoring may be handled by a specially selected and trained team of teachers.

Step 5: Prepare Instructions for the Examinees, Examiners, and Scorers. Figures 7.1 through 7.5 provide examples of how the instructions might be prepared. The instructions to the students should describe the task unambiguously. Students should be told what the scoring criteria will be—especially which, if any, factors will not be considered. See the item in Figure 7.2 to see how this might be done. Often, it is better to write the instructions after you develop the scoring criteria. When you know what the scoring criteria will be, as you will when you have had experience in scoring, you may even give students a copy of the scoring rubrics.

OBJECTIVE: The student will locate sources of information and ideas relevant to a specific problem.

ASSESSMENT STYLE: Written presentation

ITEM

AIDS is a topic that is of concern to almost everyone today. Medical research has some answers related to the transmission of AIDS, but not a lot of information about what causes it or what kinds of treatment should be used with people who have AIDS.

Pretend that a magazine has asked you to write an article comparing what we know about AIDS today with the state of knowledge about AIDS 10 years ago. To complete this assignment you should do the following:

1. Find the most recent articles or other sources of information about AIDS, its causes, factors that place people at risk, and treatment methods. Each source of data should be listed, along with a summary of all sources.

2. Select the five best articles or other sources from those published during the past year.

3. Follow the same procedures to select the best five articles published 10 years ago.

4. Write your article, comparing the two sets of articles and/or sources. Tell how medical knowledge about causes, risk factors, and treatment has changed in the past 10 years.

5. Address your article to the people who would read the magazine. Limit your article to 4 double-spaced pages. Include illustrations and/or charts, if they will help you communicate more clearly.

6. List your sources at the end of the article.

PERFORMANCE CRITERIA

Number and variety of sources

Quality of information

Variety of media used in the article

Appropriateness of style and content of article

Clarity and effectiveness of the presentation

FIGURE 7.3 Sample Production Item

Instructions for the examiner (the teacher, in the case of classroom testing) should describe under what conditions the task is to be presented, how the task is to be presented, and how to handle questions. If aides or other teachers help to monitor the test, there should also be instructions about what comments may and may not be made to students. It is very important that all students take the test under the same conditions. This means that neither the teacher nor anyone else should provide help to some students that is not provided to everyone. The following guidelines for examiners are commonly used for testing of all types.

Guidelines for Examiners

- The examiner *may*

  Reread a portion of the instructions

Encourage students to continue to work on a task

Quietly redirect the student's attention back to the task

- The examiner *may not*

Reword the instructions

Provide another demonstration

Provide verbal or behavioral clues about the quality of the student's performance

---

OBJECTIVE: Students will produce a product or a presentation that demonstrates that they have developed meaning from, and can communicate ideas through, the use of a variety of algorithms.

ASSESSMENT STYLE: Written production

ITEM

As Easter approaches, many people color eggs. The history of coloring eggs is a long one, and the eggs are considered to be a symbol of "new life" in the spring. You are planning to color eggs for an Easter egg hunt. You have the following information:

Eggs cost $1.07 per dozen.

A dye kit costs $2.35.

A basket costs $1.15.

Plastic "grass" to go in the basket costs 65 cents.

You can get other supplies you need from home at no cost.

The dye kit contains only the primary colors: red, blue, and yellow. You are to dye one-half dozen eggs in the primary colors and one-half dozen in orange, green, and violet. There is to be an equal number of each color.

Think about this information and write a short story about how you will proceed and what the costs will be. Be sure to answer these specific questions:

How will you make the orange dye?

How will you make the green dye?

How will you make the violet dye?

How many eggs of each color will you have when you are finished?

What will be the total cost?

What will be the average cost of each egg?

Be sure to answer every question. Be sure your mathematical calculations are complete and accurate. Use complete sentences in your story.

PERFORMANCE CRITERIA

Accuracy and completeness of mathematical calculations

Understanding of the properties of color mixing

Ability to write complete sentences, describing the actions needed

---

FIGURE 7.4 Sample Production Item

OBJECTIVE: Students will produce a product or presentation that demonstrates that they have drawn meaning from reading several kinds of materials, for a variety of purposes.

ASSESSMENT STYLE: Oral report

ITEM

During the school year, each of you has kept a list of books that you have read for pleasure, either at home or during independent reading periods. Select from that list one book that you would like to talk about. Think about the following questions:

1. Why did you select this particular book?
2. What was it about this book that made you remember it?
3. Would you recommend this book to another student? If so, why? If not, why not?
4. Have you read any other books by this author? If so, how was this book like or different from the others?

Be prepared to talk about the book you have selected during one of our reading report periods.

PERFORMANCE CRITERIA

Your report should show the following:

You have a preference for certain kinds of books.

Your experience with books, in general, helped you to select this book.

You got some meaning from this book.

This book is appropriate for students like you.

You know how to organize a report and make clear to others what you have learned.

You can use appropriate language in making your report.

FIGURE 7.5 Sample Performance Item

In preparing students for a performance or production task, you should discuss the scoring methods or rubrics with the students, even soliciting their input. We discuss rubrics in the next section of this chapter. Sandra Schnitzer (1993) described her experiences as a teacher when she and an associate involved students in making decisions about the scoring standards for a project in advanced biology. She

Advantages of Discussing Rubrics with Students

1. When students are involved in creating rubrics, it sharpens their understanding of the criteria and their importance in the product or performance.

2. When students know what the rubrics are, they can focus their attention on the criteria you think are important.

concluded that, as a result of this experience, students learned to synthesize and integrate what they had learned and to take responsibility for their own learning.

Step 6. Have the Tasks Reviewed and Modify Them as Necessary. You may be perfectly clear about what you want students to do and what you will consider an appropriate response. However, the students do not have access to all the background material in your head. It would be grossly unfair to expect students to read your mind. And it is disconcerting to discover during the scoring process that some students performed extremely well on a task that is not the one you intended them to do!

To prevent this dismaying occurrence, try out the tasks, if possible. Studies of writing assessments have shown that the way a writing task is presented—that is, the specific instructions and the amount of background materials provided—makes a difference in average performance of students on the task. In addition, it has been found that an individual may differ greatly in his or her ability to handle one type of writing task in contrast to another type of task. It seems reasonable to think that the situation will be the same for other production tasks and for performance tasks. If trying out is not possible, then try to get other teachers to review your items and make suggestions for changes before the items are actually used. Also, reviewing items and rubrics with other teachers will help you to align your teaching with important aspects of content.

METHODS OF SCORING
PERFORMANCE AND PRODUCTION TASKS

The three major issues in the scoring of performance and production tasks are (1) method of scoring, (2) type of score scale, and (3) avoidance of problems affecting validity, reliability, and fairness.

There are basically four scoring methods used to score performance and production tasks: holistic, analytic, primary trait, and domain. Most of the formal studies of scoring methods have been done in the context of writing assessment, but we can generalize some of the information from these studies to the scoring of other types of tasks. The directions for all of these scoring methods include rubrics, which describe the qualities of the products to be scored at each level.

The *analytic* method provides the most information but requires the most time. *Holistic* scoring is fairly easy to do and is quite satisfactory for many situations, but it does not provide the diagnostic information most teachers want. *Primary trait* scoring focuses on the purpose for the task and success in attaining that purpose. *Domain* scoring is a compromise, offering separate scores for a limited number of major categories. The rubics may be so general that they could be used in any form of production task; for example, a *general writing* rubric with any writing assignment. A *specific* form of a writing rubric is limited to a specific type of writing; for example, expository or narrative writing.

Some scoring methods are directly interpretable because the ratings incorporate an evaluation of the quality of the performance. On the other hand, some scales simply provide a number of points, which means that an additional step must be taken—setting a value on the total scores. What constitutes an acceptable performance? What is outstanding? A judgment must be made about these questions in order to interpret the performance.

The scoring rubrics provided in Figures 7.6, 7.7, and 7.12 are *generalized*—that is, they may be used for scoring a wide variety of products or performance tasks. Figures 7.8 and 7.9 are *task specific* and are appropriate for only a single task.

A brief survey of major issues related to each scoring method follows.

Holistic (Global) Scoring

Holistic scoring is based on the assumption that the components of a task are so closely interrelated that there is little point in trying to separate one element from another. Instead, anchor points are described, and illustrations of products or performances to be scored at the various anchor points are provided.

In holistic scoring, a single score that incorporates all aspects of the criteria to be considered is assigned to each response. It is usually desirable to write a brief description of the product or performance at each point of the scale, and to select illustrative products for each point. For example, to score writing samples, anchor papers are selected to represent each score point and are used as reference (comparison) papers. In large-scale testing programs, copies of the anchor papers may be embedded in the papers being scored so that each scorer scores them. That way, a check can be made on the consistency of the scoring, identifying "score scale drift." Score scale drift occurs when judges change their application of scoring standards over the course of the scoring. For example, a judge may assign higher scores to papers scored late in the day because she is tired.

In your classroom you can use this same process of preselecting samples of products at different score levels to serve as anchors, and you can check your scoring periodically against these samples. Another possible procedure is to sort the products into score groups as you score them, as we described in Chapter 6 for scoring essay items. When you have scored all the papers, you can review each group to see whether all products in the group are indeed at approximately the same level.

An example of a holistic score scale is presented in Figure 7.6. Notice that there is a written description for each score point.

Score	Definitions of Score Categories
7	The essay is unified, sharply focused, and distinctively effective. The ideas are rich, concrete, plentiful, appropriate, and deep textured. The writer uses an abundance of specific, relevant details, including concrete examples, that clearly support generalizations.
	A wide variety of sentence constructions are used. Appropriate transitional words and phrases and effective coherence techniques make the prose distinctive. Usage is uniformly sensible, accurate, and sure. The mechanics, with some exceptions because of the pressure of time, are generally flawless.
5	The essay is focused and unified and it is clearly, if not distinctively, written. The writer presents a considerable quantity of relevant and specific detail in support of the subject. A variety of sentence patterns occur, and sentence constructions indicate that the writer has facility in the use of language.
	Effective transitions are accompanied by sentences constructed with orderly relationships between word groups. Syntactically, the essay is clear and reliable. There may be a few errors in spelling, capitalization, and punctuation, but they are not serious.
3	The essay has some degree of unity and focus, but each could be improved. It is reasonably clear, though not invariably so. The writer employs a limited amount of specific detail relating to the subject. Paragraphs are usually sufficiently united and developed. Sentence variety is minimal, and constructions lack sophistication. Some transitions are used, and parts are related to each other in a fairly orderly manner.
	The essay is syntactically bland and, at times, awkward. Usage is generally accurate. There are some errors in spelling, capitalization, and punctuation that detract from the essay's effect, if not from its sense.
1	The essay lacks unity and focus. The writer includes very little, if any, specific and relevant supporting detail but, instead, uses unsupported generalizations. Underdeveloped, ineffective paragraphs do not support the thesis. Sentences lack variety, consisting of a series of subject-verb and, occasionally, complement constructions. Transitions and coherence devices are not discernible.
	Usage is irregular and often questionable or wrong. There are serious errors in mechanics.

FIGURE 7.6 Holistic Rubrics (for a Writing Sample)

Analytic Scoring

Analytic scoring may use either a checklist or a component rating scale.

Checklists. A checklist may be prepared for scorers to use when looking for the elements that are to be considered. Sometimes, scorers are asked to simply check whether an element is "present" or "absent" or "satisfactory" or "unsatisfactory." At other times, scorers not only check the presence or absence but, in the case of a performance, they may also indicate the order in which the behavior occurred. The score for each component is the number of "present" or "satisfactory" ratings or, perhaps, the number of times the actions occurred in the correct order. Samples of checklists are provided in Figures 7.7, 7.8, and 7.9.

```
┌──────────────────────────────────────────────────────────────────┐
│                                      STUDENT _____      │
│                                                                    │
│  _____  Prints words neatly.                                       │
│  _____  Stays on the line.                                         │
│  _____  Leaves even margins.                                       │
│  _____  Uses upper and lower case letters correctly.               │
│                                                                    │
└──────────────────────────────────────────────────────────────────┘
```

FIGURE 7.7 Example of a Simple Checklist (for Primary Handwriting)

```
┌──────────────────────────────────────────────────────────────────┐
│                                      STUDENT _____      │
│  _____  Correctly names parts of the microscope.                   │
│  _____  Focuses microscope so that specimen is seen clearly.       │
│  _____  Adjusts microscope for high and low power.                 │
│  _____  Prepares slide of potato that reveals cell structure.      │
│  _____  Identifies cell coverings in stained potato.               │
│  _____  Distinguishes between potato cells and salt crystals.      │
│  _____  Makes simple drawing of potato cell.                       │
└──────────────────────────────────────────────────────────────────┘
```

FIGURE 7.8 Example of a Checklist (for Use of a Microscope)

Component Ratings. In another type of analytic scoring, the objective is broken into component parts, and each component is (supposedly) scored independently—that is, the score on one component should not influence the scores on the other components. For each component, the scoring may use a rating scale like the scales used for holistic scoring, in which case the total score is simply the sum of the ratings for the various components.

Another possibility is for each element to be assigned a weight and for scorers to be instructed to assign a value somewhere between zero and the maximum weight. The final score is the total of the points assigned. This method of scoring is called the point score method. To develop a scoring guide for this method of scoring, a list of the characteristics of an ideal response is made, identifying the major points to be considered, each followed by subheadings. Then the relative importance of each major point is indicated by assigning weights; weights are also assigned to the subheadings for each major point. In some cases, it may be important to indicate possible errors that students might make and assign negative weights to those points. Alternatively, such errors may simply be ignored. Figure 7.10 identifies the components and assigns weights to each, but it is not a complete scoring guide.

STUDENT_____		
Student Action	**Present**	**Sequence**
Takes slide	____	____
Wipes slide with lens paper	____	____
Wipes with cloth	____	____
Wipes with finger	____	____
Places drop of culture on slide	____	____
Places slide on stage	____	____
Looks through eyepiece	____	____
Keeps other eye closed	____	____
Turns to low-power objective	____	____
Turns to high-power objective	____	____
Keeps eye to eyepiece while adjusting	____	____
Removes slide from stage	____	____
Wipes objective with lens paper	____	____
Wipes with cloth	____	____
Wipes with finger	____	____
Wipes eyepiece with lens paper	____	____
Wipes with cloth	____	____
Wipes with finger	____	____

Student Characteristics	**Present**
Slow and deliberate	
Very rapid	____
Awkward	
Dexterous	____
Serious and task oriented	
Disinterested	____
Satisfied with poor performance	____
Careful, follows directions	
Careless, needs much supervision	____

FIGURE 7.9 Example of a Complex Checklist (for Use of a Microscope)

Primary Trait Scoring

The primary trait scoring system was developed by *National Assessment of Educational Progress* (NAEP) and was based on the theory that most writing is addressed to a specified audience and has an intended purpose. Tasks were developed to address a specific purpose, and the basic trait of a successful response was identified.

The scoring guide is directed to the primary trait of the assignment and has a score scale that outlines the characteristics of various levels of success on the trait. An example of a rubric for a primary trait score scale is presented in Figure 7.11. This type of scoring has not been widely used outside the NAEP.

OBJECTIVE: Write a character study.
WRITING MODE: Creative writing

SCORING RUBRIC

Ideas		**20 points**
Creative presentation	5	
Variety of character traits presented	10	
Vivid mental pictures	5	
Organization		**10 points**
Logical presentation of topics	2	
Definite pattern discernible	5	
Conclusion follows from details	3	
Development		**20 points**
All details relevant	10	
Use of a variety of literary devices	5	
Variety in sentence structure	5	
Conventions		**10 points**
Grammatical constructions	3	
Spelling	2	
Punctuation	3	
Handwriting	2	

FIGURE 7.10 Example of an Analytic Scoring Rubric (for a Writing Sample)

OBJECTIVE: Write a paper to persuade the reader to accept a clearly defined point of view and/or course of action.
WRITING MODE: Persuasion

SCORING RUBRIC

1 **Little or no evidence of the skill**
  Inappropriate language for the intended audience.
  Few or no supporting arguments.
  Details lacking or irrelevant.

2 **Marginal evidence of the skill**
  Language somewhat appropriate for the intended audience.
  A few supporting arguments.
  Some details but few are relevant.

3 **Competent performance**
  Clear and appropriate language for the intended audience.
  Most supporting arguments are plausible and relevant.
  Most details are relevant.
  Evidence of some innovative thinking.

4 **Outstanding performance**
  Clear, interesting, and appropriate language.
  Many plausible and relevant supporting arguments.
  Ideas are creative and well-expressed.

FIGURE 7.11 Example of a Primary Trait Rubric (for a Writing Sample)

Domain Scoring

The domain scoring system is a compromise between analytic and holistic scoring. It yields a separate score for each of a number of specified domains that are more broadly defined than are the points for analytic scoring. Figure 7.12 presents a rubric for a three-domain scoring scheme used by one testing program to score writing samples. There is a 4-point score scale for each of the three domains to be scored. Figure 7.13 provides rubrics for a 3-domain scheme to score word problems in arithmetic.

SCORE SCALES

The number of points on the scale should be limited to the number of differentiations the scorers may be expected to make. It is usually possible to identify easily "Totally incompetent" or "Unsatisfactory" performance on the one hand, and "Extremely competent" or "Outstanding" performance on the other. The difficulty arises in the center of the scale. Some rating scales simply lump everything between the two extremes into an "Average" or "Acceptable" category, yielding a 3-point scale. Other scales provide a category between each extreme and the middle, thus providing a 5-point scale.

When a scale has an odd number of points, there is a tendency to assign the middle point for a very large number of the products or performances. This may be quite all right. It has been found, however, that scorers make finer discriminations when there is no central point, so that all products are scored in such a way that the score indicates at least a tendency toward either satisfactory or unsatisfactory performance. The scale can be even further subdivided, but it is doubtful that scorers can really make meaningful discriminations between more than four or five categories.

In designing scales for your assessments, you should use the number of points that seem reasonable to you, defining each point so that you can discriminate between each of them. Regardless of the number of categories, each must be defined in terms of examinee behavior, and one or more examples must be provided. Sometimes you may want to extend the scale by allowing an undefined point between each defined point as in Figure 7.6. This undefined score may be used for products in between the two described scores.

For some performance tasks, the scoring consists of simply recording some information about the performance, rather than evaluating the performance. Examples of this kind of report are provided in Figure 7.14.

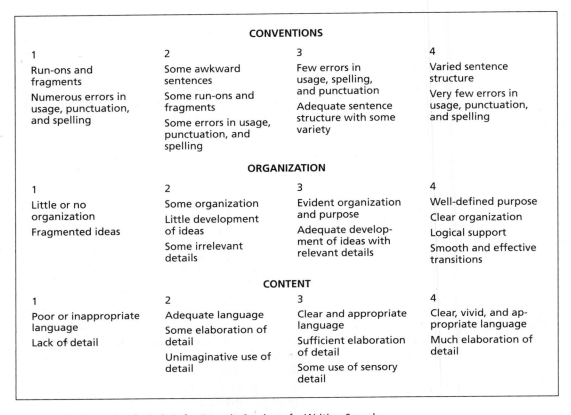

CONVENTIONS

1	2	3	4
Run-ons and fragments	Some awkward sentences	Few errors in usage, spelling, and punctuation	Varied sentence structure
Numerous errors in usage, punctuation, and spelling	Some run-ons and fragments	Adequate sentence structure with some variety	Very few errors in usage, punctuation, and spelling
	Some errors in usage, punctuation, and spelling		

ORGANIZATION

1	2	3	4
Little or no organization	Some organization	Evident organization and purpose	Well-defined purpose
Fragmented ideas	Little development of ideas	Adequate development of ideas with relevant details	Clear organization
	Some irrelevant details		Logical support
			Smooth and effective transitions

CONTENT

1	2	3	4
Poor or inappropriate language	Adequate language	Clear and appropriate language	Clear, vivid, and appropriate language
Lack of detail	Some elaboration of detail	Sufficient elaboration of detail	Much elaboration of detail
	Unimaginative use of detail	Some use of sensory detail	

FIGURE 7.12 Example of a Rubric for Domain Scoring of a Writing Sample

UNDERSTANDING OF THE PROBLEM
1   No attempt or complete misinterpretation
2   Misinterprets most of the problem
3   Misinterprets some of the problem
4   Understands all of the problem

PROCEDURES
1   No attempt or procedure completely wrong
2   Procedure partially correct but with major flaw
3   Procedure correct except for minor flaw
4   Procedure correct

CORRECTNESS OF SOLUTION
1   Answer totally wrong
2   Major computation error
3   Minor computation error
4   Solution is correct

FIGURE 7.13 Example of a Rubric for Domain Scoring of Word Problems in Arithmetic

1. On a typing test, the time in minutes and seconds used to type a standardized passage is recorded; then the average number of words per minute is computed.
2. On a physical fitness test, a student is asked to run a standard mile, and the time is recorded in minutes and seconds. The pulse rate before and after the run may also be recorded.

FIGURE 7.14 Examples of Records of Performance

ENSURING VALIDITY, RELIABILITY, AND FAIRNESS

It has often been demonstrated that the scoring of performance and production tasks is invalidated through consideration of irrelevant factors. This problem may be minimized by thorough training and practice, using carefully developed instructions and examples, but it is never completely eliminated. The scoring procedure for large-scale testing programs must provide a way to detect and correct the problem. Some of the procedures used in large scale programs can be adapted for classroom assessments. The following list of procedures should help you:

Prevention of Invalidation of Score Scales

- Prepare operational descriptions of the points on the rating scale, or construct analytic checklists.

- Prepare illustrative prescored products or performance samples for each point on the scale.

- Ensure that the scorer understands the scoring rubrics.

- Mask the identity of the students whenever possible.

- Try to have every product or performance scored twice, preferably by two people.

- Monitor the interscorer agreement continually during the scoring process.

It is important that ratings on performance and production tests reflect the students' true capabilities rather than some other variables. Validity requires that the tasks be a sample of some domain of interest, so that performance on the tasks can be generalized to that domain. Reliability requires that the scoring procedure be consistent over time and across scorers. Fairness requires that the tasks are not biased against any individual or group of students and that they are scored in an objective and unbiased manner.

In performance and production assessments, validity is the extent to which the assessment corresponds to the criterion activity. Reliability, on the other hand, is dependent on the degree of control over extraneous variables, such as the setting and the standards of the scorers. So in many cases these are competing concerns. To the degree that a task is a sample of a real-life situation, there is often a loss of control over variables such as variations in the setting, the degree of interaction with other individuals, the objectivity of the scoring, and interpersonal and intrapersonal variations in the scorers.

The experience of the state of Vermont is instructive. In 1988, Vermont instituted a state-wide assessment program that focused primarily on performance assessment and involved evaluation of student portfolios in writing and mathematics. The goals of the program were twofold: to provide quality measurement and to improve instruction. This program was carefully monitored by a group of external evaluators, who concluded, "the Vermont experience has begun to make concrete the conflicts between the basic goals of this and similar programs and illustrates the need to make difficult compromises between them" (Koretz, Stecher, Klein, & McCaffrey, 1994). The interrater reliability ranged from .35 to .45 within each dimension of writing, and from .34 to .50 within each dimension of mathematics. These reliabilities are not sufficiently high for the scores to be used for individual interpretation. But the evaluators concluded that the program was apparently a powerful tool for encouraging teachers to change practices. Many teachers, however, seemed to lack an understanding of exactly how to go about teaching some of the goals of the program, and there were great variations among teachers' practices, both in teaching and in selecting materials to include in student portfolios.

A major threat to validity, reliability, and fairness in performance and production tests is that irrelevant factors too often influence the scoring process. In the classroom, the matter of whether you like a student or how the student does on other tasks may influence your scoring unless you are very careful. In large-scale testing programs with multiple scorers, there is also a need to be aware of the possible sources of scoring errors and to take steps to guard against them. In both situations, the solution to the problem is to prepare the tasks carefully and to specify in advance what qualities are to be considered in the scoring, providing a good description and perhaps a sample of what the scores should represent. However, when the task is too standardized, it may lose some of its authenticity. There are no simple solutions to this dilemma. All you can do is to be aware of the problem and work out the best compromise possible.

Common problems in scoring performance and production tasks are discussed in the next section, and specific suggestions for preparing the tasks and scoring rubrics are provided.

COMMON SCORING PROBLEMS

The fact that performance and production tasks must be scored by human beings makes the scoring vulnerable to the usual problems such judgments involve. Some of the errors are constant, affecting the ratings of all ratees; others are specific to individual scorers. These errors should be anticipated and steps should be taken to minimize them. The way the rating scales are written can help. If you are sensitive to the possible problems, you may be able to avoid at least some of them.

Constant Errors

Constant errors are potentially present across all ratings and must be anticipated and guarded against. There are two kinds of constant error: generosity error and the halo effect.

The *generosity error* is the tendency to give all except the very worst ratees a high rating. It is found in almost every situation, not only in schools. It has been found, for example, that supervisors rate more than 90% of their employees at the highest point of the rating scale and teachers generally rate all except their most difficult students very highly.

The *halo effect* obscures the patterns of individual behavior and lets irrelevant variables such as a student's personal attractiveness and handwriting influence the scores. It leads to all qualities being rated very similarly. You may think, for example, "Sarah is a good student" (or a nice one, or an accommodating one), and check her at the high end of the ratings for every point, ignoring the fact that Sarah is not really excellent on every criterion.

Judge-Specific Errors

Errors specific to specific judges are of two types. *Intrajudge errors* are errors resulting from changes in the standards used by an individual judge over time. They can happen as teachers become tired, bored, or irritated with the quality of the material or performance they are scoring. Some scorers simply vary from one student to another, using a different standard for each performance or product rated.

Interjudge errors are errors resulting from differences between scorers as to the standards they are applying. For example, one scorer may tend to rate everyone high, and another may tend to rate everyone low. Sometimes a scorer decides the standards are not correct and arbitrarily changes them. A scorer in one state assessment project decided unilaterally that handwriting should be weighted heavily in the scoring, even though the rubrics did not provide for that element.

If you are the only scorer for your tests, you may not be aware of such problems, because you will not know how your scores would compare with those of another teacher. That is why we recommend that you try to work out some kind of cooperative arrangement with at least one other teacher.

AVOIDING PROBLEMS IN SCORING

Several devices are available to minimize the errors in scoring performance and production tasks for large-scale assessment programs. We are describing some of them so you can adapt them to your own classroom assessments.

The best prevention of scoring problems begins with the preparation of the tasks, spelling out very carefully the conditions under which the task is to be administered and writing complete scoring rubrics so that the criteria for the various ratings are clear. For performance tasks, this usually involves a written description of what a performance at each level looks like. For production tasks, samples of products at various levels may be prepared and kept to be referred to during each new scoring task. In large high-stakes assessment projects at the district, state and national level scorers must be carefully trained and evaluated. Scorers who are not able to attain and maintain an objective, consistent perspective are dismissed.

When you have a product such as a term paper to score, one way to keep the same standards for each score level throughout the scoring process is to go through the papers very quickly and select a few at each score level. As you score the other papers, reread the selected papers and use them periodically. If you decide that you made a mistake in your selection of comparison papers, you should go back and rescore everything, using the new standards. Scoring other types of products is more complex, but the basic idea of periodically comparing products at the same score level still is a good idea.

Scoring performance tasks is a different matter. You cannot go back and rescore the performances. All you can do is to have a good set of descriptions for each score and consult the descriptions before you do each rating.

SUMMARY

- Performance and production tasks are important types of assessments.
- In order to ensure validity and reliability, tasks must be carefully prepared and scorers must be carefully trained.
- Teachers who use performance and production tasks in their classrooms should be aware of potential problems so they can guard against them.

STUDY QUESTIONS

1. What are the major differences between performance tasks and production tasks?
2. What are the advantages of using performance and production tasks over other types of assessment tools?
3. What are the major causes of problems with the validity and reliability of performance and production tasks?

FOR YOUR PROFESSIONAL GROWTH

1. Prepare a production or performance task for one of the sections of your blueprint. Specify the stimulus, conditions, instructions, and scoring procedures.
2. Ask another teacher to review your task specifications.
3. Administer the assessment to a class and score it, using your rubrics.
4. Evaluate the process:
   a. Are your scores valid?
   b. Did you maintain the same standard throughout?
   c. Did you stick to the written descriptions for the scores?
   d. Are your scores consistent?
   e. Are your scores fair to all students?

8

૩ક૦

Direct Observation and Retrospective Reports

PREVIEW

In Chapter 7 we presented two major types of assessment tools that depend on human judgment—performance and production tests. Here, we continue our exploration of assessment tools with a discussion of some less formal procedures that also rely on human judgment. The judgments may be made by students, teachers, other school personnel, or community personnel; and the judgments may be made about students, teachers, programs, activities, or the whole area of education. Some of these procedures assess performance; others deal with attitudes, preferences, and habits. Observation is part of all these judgmental procedures, and some kind of record is made of the observations at some time.

Why should an educator be interested in learning about these procedures? They are useful tools, yielding information that you can use directly in your teaching or in other work with students. For example, information about how students feel about various classroom activities can help teachers decide which instructional activities to use. You could simply ask for a show of hands; however, some students might be hesitant to show their enthusiasm for activities that class leaders do not endorse, so you might not get the correct information that way. Other educators may be interested in using the procedures to investigate student response to many aspects of the school. Also, sometimes you may need help in understanding a student who is having a great difficulty of some kind. Some of the observational procedures and other kinds of reports from that student and from other students may help you understand what is going on and may provide a clue for helping the student.

```
┌─────────────────────────────────────────────────────────────────┐
│                         MAJOR TOPICS                              │
├─────────────────────────────────────────────────────────────────┤
│                                                                   │
│          Dimensions of Observation                                │
│              Observers                                            │
│              Targets of Observation                              │
│              Time Frames                                          │
│              Recording System                                    │
│          Direct Observation                                      │
│              Steps in Making Direct Observations                 │
│              Records of Direct Observation                       │
│              Sources of Error in Direct Observation              │
│          Retrospective Reports                                   │
│              Steps in Preparing Retrospective Reports            │
│              Types of Retrospective Reports                      │
│              Sources of Error in Retrospective Reports           │
│                                                                   │
└─────────────────────────────────────────────────────────────────┘
```

DIMENSIONS OF OBSERVATION

Observation is the most frequently used method of classroom assessment (Stiggins, Conklin, & Bridgeford, 1986). Teachers are continually observing students and drawing conclusions about them, although much of the time the observation is informal and the teacher is hardly aware of doing it. Students also observe and form opinions about themselves and other students.

Most classroom observation is informal and unsystematic, but observation can be systematized and made into an effective evaluation tool if a little care is taken. It is possible to use observation in a more formal manner, somewhat like a performance test, but without using the standardized situations that are part of performance tests. What is standardized is the way the observation is recorded, the specific variables that are evaluated, and the way the scores are derived and interpreted.

The best systems of assessment involve a variety of sources of data and data-gathering procedures. When you combine data from many sources, you can get a much more complete picture than when you must depend on a single source.

Observation as an assessment tool varies on many dimensions. There are many categories of *observers* and of the *targets* of the observation, the *time frames* may vary from immediate to retrospective, and the *recording system* may vary widely.

Observers

In a school setting, many people may be observers. Students may observe themselves, other students, the teachers, and other school personnel. Teachers and other school personnel observe the students, other personnel, the school and school system, and programs. Other people, such as parents and other community residents, observe various aspects of the school or school system and programs. Obviously, each of these different observers has a different perspective.

Targets of Observation

Usually the target of observation is a person. Students, teachers, and other school personnel may be observed to find out about their skills, abilities, and preferences. However, observation also may be directed at programs, procedures, or institutions.

Observers sometimes observe themselves and their own perceptions and performances. They also observe other people and programs.

Self-reports are one of the cheapest methods of assessment and usually are easily obtained. Self-reports are widely used to assess student attitudes toward, for example, specific school courses such as mathematics, science, or physical education, or toward a special program, as in Figure 8.1. Attitude scales may also be directed toward specific class activities, as in Figure 8.2.

NAME _____

Directions: Here is a chance for you to tell what you like about school and what you dislike. It is not a test. The right answer is your opinion. Before you start, put your name at the top of the page.

Which are your favorite courses in school? In the first column, put a "1" for the course you like the MOST, a "2" for the course you like next, and so on up to 5.

Which courses do you like the LEAST? In the second column, put a "1" for your least-liked course, a "2" for the next disliked, and so on up to 5.

There are spaces for courses not on the list.

IF YOU HAVE NOT HAD A COURSE, LEAVE THE SPACES BLANK.

Course	Like	Dislike
English	_____	_____
Arithmetic	_____	_____
Algebra	_____	_____
Geometry	_____	_____
Trigonometry	_____	_____
Mathematics	_____	_____
History	_____	_____
Geography	_____	_____
Sociology	_____	_____
Biology	_____	_____
General Science	_____	_____
Chemistry	_____	_____
Physics	_____	_____
_____	_____	_____
_____	_____	_____
_____	_____	_____

FIGURE 8.1 Student Self-Report of Preference for School Courses

---

CLASS _____

STUDENT _____

Directions: Look at the list of things we do in this class. Put a check mark by all the things you like to do in this class. Then draw a ring around the thing you like to do the most.

_____ Read at your desk.

_____ Have a class discussion.

_____ Work with a group of students on a project.

_____ Listen to the teacher tell us about something.

_____ Draw a picture about something we read.

_____ Make a speech about something we have done.

_____ Go to the library to work on a report.

_____ _____

_____ _____

_____ _____

FIGURE 8.2 Student Self-Report of Attitude Toward Class Activities

Self-reports are sometimes used to find out how students feel about their own achievement; and self-report instruments are often developed as part of the evaluation of a specially funded program, in an attempt to get information about students' response to the program. Teachers and other school personnel may also report their perceptions about their own abilities, attitudes, and skills.

Time Frames

Individuals may be observed by other people while they are engaged in some activity, or people may be asked to recall events and perceptions accumulating over a long period of time. The most direct assessment is to observe students as they engage in some activity. This is called *direct observation*.

Ratings that are based on recall, rather than on direct observation, are called *retrospective ratings*.

Recording Systems

Many observation scales try to quantify the observations; however, there is currently much interest in qualitative evaluation, or what is often called the "ethnographic" method. This method is somewhat like the holistic method of scoring production tasks (see Chapter 7). The observer simultaneously observes, interprets, evaluates, and records the behavior. Sometimes video recording is used, and the record is prepared from the videotape. The result is often a narrative description, although some abbreviations and shorthand notes may be made. Such procedures require careful training for the observers and are most useful in research situations in which multiple types of data are gathered. An evaluative rating scale may also be used in an ethnographic setting.

Both direct observation and retrospective reports may be made in either a *descriptive* (low-inference) mode or an *evaluative* (high-inference) mode. As you will see, some recording systems merely provide a record of events, and others require the observer to make judgments about the quality or value. We describe specific types of recording systems and provide examples in later sections of this chapter.

DIRECT OBSERVATION

Direct observation is the best source of information about such variables as work habits and social skills, so it is important for the observations to address the important aspects of those variables. It is also important for the observation records not to reflect irrelevant variables, such as a student's *personal attractiveness* when the intended variable is *work habits*.

Direct observation may be either systematic or informal. *Systematic observation* is planned, organized, and objective. The specific kinds of behavior to be observed are identified in advance, and a system of recording the observations is prepared. Arrangements are made to observe all students under the same conditions. The specific behaviors are defined, so that there is no question about what is to be observed. The advantage of systematic observation, as opposed to informal observation, is that it is focused, so it helps the observer obtain information that might otherwise be overlooked. Also, it may be recorded under both ecological and formal conditions.

Systematic observation is similar in many ways to a performance test, and the same type of scales used to score performance tests may also be used to score systematic observations (see Chapter 7). However, systematic observation differs from performance tests in that the situation is naturalistic—that is, it involves some activity that students engage in regularly, rather than a situation that is specially designed. For instance, students may be observed as they work together in groups on a science project or in physical education activities. It is important to predetermine which variables are to be assessed, what the important aspects of the variables are, and how various behaviors are to be rated. Often the observation uses time sampling, spending a predetermined time observing and recording the behavior of each individual student. If the observations require students to do something special, like perform a specific physical skill, it is a *formal* assessment. If the observation occurs during the normal course of instruction it is called an *informal* assessment. For some informal observations, no record is made until later. We discuss this type of observation under *retrospective ratings*.

Steps in Making Direct Observations

To use observation as an assessment technique, you must plan carefully when you prepare and conduct the observations or collect ratings of various kinds. The following suggestions may help:

Steps in Conducting Direct Observations
1. Identify the purpose of your observations   2. Create a list of meaningful and productive behaviors to be observed.   3. Prepare the observation form.   4. Coordinate the observations with instruction.   5. Train the observer(s).   6. Use multiple observers if possible.   7. Record the observation as the behavior occurs or immediately afterward.   8. Summarize and interpret the observation.

Step 1: Identify the Purpose of Your Observations. You must identify the purpose of your observations, because the purpose affects your choice of observation record, the targets of your observation, and even when or under what conditions you will observe. Ask yourself these questions:

- What is the purpose of the observation?
- Is the class to be observed as a whole, or will individual students be observed?
- Under what conditions will the observations take place?
- How long will the observation be?
- If students are to be observed individually, how long will the observations last?
- At what time of day will the observations occur?

Step 2: Create a List of Meaningful and Productive Behaviors to Be Observed. This process is similar to the process used to specify the content of an achievement test. These questions must be answered:

- What traits or qualities are to be considered in the observation?
- How are these traits defined?
- How are the observations to be recorded?

    On a checklist?

    On an evaluative scale?

    As a running description?

- Who will do the observation?

Step 3: Prepare the Observation Form. Start with the list of behaviors to be observed and prepare the observation form. For each type of behavior, provide a description. Add specific points if you need them. Some negative behaviors may also be included with the scale reversed.

The observation will be easier if you list the behaviors in the approximate order in which you expect them to occur. Figures 8.3, 8.4, and 8.5 serve as examples.

STUDENT _____

_____ Identifies numerals from 0 to 99.

_____ Counts to 100 by 5's.

_____ Groups objects into sets of 3, 4, 5, and 6.

_____ Identifies geometric shapes: square, triangle, rectangle, trapezoid, circle.

_____ Compares objects as to size.

_____ Compares objects as to weight.

_____ Identifies coins and bills.

_____ Identifies the amount of money represented by a group of bills and coins.

_____ Identifies similar, congruent, and symmetrical figures.

FIGURE 8.3 Simple Checklist of Skills in Mathematics

CLASS _____Painting_____   **STUDENT**_____

Directions: Indicate the order in which the student does the listed activities by putting a "1" by the first activity, a "2" by the second, and so on. If an activity is repeated, write a number for each time in the sequence it is done. If the student does something not on the list, add it to the bottom of the list and number it appropriately.

_____ Prepares the surface.

_____ Studies the subject.

_____ Selects materials.

_____ Makes a sketch.

_____ Works at painting.

_____ Examines work.

_____ Corrects work.

_____ Cleans brushes.

_____ Puts away materials.

Other Activities:

_____ _____

_____ _____

_____ _____

_____ _____

_____ _____

_____ _____

FIGURE 8.4 Checklist of Student's Class Activities

STUDENT _____   TEACHER _____

Directions: Select a student who is presenting behavior problems. Check each time the teacher uses each strategy. If the strategy used is not on the list, write it in the space provided in the middle of the page.

TEACHER'S STRATEGIES

_____ Ignores behavior.

_____ Looks at student and frowns.

_____ Moves toward student while continuing instruction.

_____ Stands near student.

_____ Addresses a question to student.

_____ Verbally reprimands student and continues instruction.

_____ Stops instruction and reprimands student.

_____ Appeals to student to change behavior.

_____ Directs student to leave the room.

OTHER STRATEGIES

_____ _____

_____ _____

_____ _____

_____ _____

STUDENT RESPONSE TO TEACHER'S STRATEGIES

_____ Stops behavior and participates in instructional activities.

_____ Stops temporarily, then resumes.

_____ Becomes verbally aggressive toward teacher.

_____ Becomes verbally aggressive toward another student.

_____ Becomes physically aggressive.

FIGURE 8.5 Observation Checklist for Teacher Behavior Response to Problem Behavior of Student

Step 4: Coordinate the Observations with Instruction. The observation should be conducted while regular classroom activities are going on; otherwise, it may not be a valid reflection of students' usual behavior. The exception is when a specific activity is set up as a performance test, as described in Chapter 7.

Step 5: Train the Observer(s). Whoever is to do the observation must be trained. The training should cover general observation skills and the procedures to be used with the specific observation record. If you are the observer, you must train yourself and practice before you actually do the observation. It may also help to work with another observer, so you can discuss any problems you might have.

Step 6: Use Multiple Observers, If Possible. When a great deal of human judgment is involved in an assessment, it is always preferable to have at least two observers, so you can check on the amount of agreement between them. Perhaps you can work with another teacher, or perhaps an aide or another person on the school staff can help.

Step 7: Record the Observation as the Behavior Occurs or Immediately Afterward. This step may require that someone other than the teacher do the observation and recording, depending on the activity being observed. If the recording must be delayed, the procedure becomes a retrospective rating, rather than a direct observation. A video camera may be used for immediate recording, and the written report may be prepared from the videotape. The advantage of doing it this way is that you may use someone else to do the taping and you may then view the tape as many times as you want to.

Step 8: Summarize and Interpret the Observation. The analysis should be directed to the purpose you had for doing the observation. It should answer the questions that prompted you to do the observation.

Records of Direct Observation

The three basic tools of direct observation are checklists, narrative reports, and evaluative ratings.

Checklists. The simplest and most objective way to record direct observations is to use a checklist and make a tally every time each behavior occurs. Or, alternatively, the behaviors may be numbered to indicate the order in which they occurred, as in Figures 8.4 and 8.6. The checklists may be fairly simple, covering only a few types of behavior as in Figures 8.3, 8.4, and 8.5. Other checklists are quite elaborate and provide for recording a full range of behaviors as in Figure 8.7.

You can use checklists to record observations of a wide variety of activities, such as errors in oral reading, incidents of disruptive behavior, carrying out the steps in a laboratory procedure in the right order, and the number and type of interactions between students and between individual students and the teacher. Figure 8.3 is a checklist of elementary mathematics skills and is very simple. The observation form in Figure 8.4 is fairly complex, and the one in Figure 8.5 for observing teacher behavior is quite complex. Figures 8.6 and 8.7 are forms for recording the order in which a student does something. Figure 8.6 is quite simple. Figure 8.7 is complex and includes some evaluative items in addition to the sequence.

Making complex observations requires a great deal of concentration by the observer, and you probably cannot handle this while you are simultaneously providing instruction to the rest of the class. However, recording behavior on a

---

STUDENT _____

Directions: Indicate the order in which the student does the listed activities by putting a "1" by the first activity, a "2" by the second, and so on. If an activity is repeated, write a number for each time it is repeated in the sequence. Each activity may have more than one number.

If the student does something not on the list, add it to the bottom of the list and number it appropriately.

_____ Big Blocks

_____ Sand Box

_____ Water Play

_____ Story Center

_____ Record Player

_____ Construction Block Center

_____ Computer

_____ Puzzles

_____ Stacking/Nesting Boxes

_____ Felt Board

_____ Chalkboard

_____ Easel

Other:

_____ _____

_____ _____

_____ _____

_____ _____

FIGURE 8.6 Tabulation of a Student's Activities

checklist is not extremely complicated, so you may be able to train an aide to be the observer. Then you can look at the checklists later and make an evaluative judgment about how well the student is doing. You can also compare behavior at one time with the behavior at an earlier time to see whether there has been any change.

A complex checklist can identify social interactions among students, which could be reported in the fashion used in Figure 8.8. Notice that the same information could be reported in a simple report that lists numbers of times contacted, as in Figure 8.9. This is a direct approach to sociometry, which often uses retrospective reports to collect similar data.

One form of a checklist often used in reading programs is the _running record_. One of these is shown in Figure 8.10. The teachers listens to a child read a literature selection and marks a check on a form for every correctly pronounced word and records the errors made. The teacher then summarizes the percentage and types of errors made (Clay, 1991).

```
STUDENT _____
```

Student Action	Sequence	Skills Needing Improvement (Check all that apply)	
Picks up slide	_____	Following instructions	_____
Wipes slide with lens paper	_____	Handling microscope	_____
Wipes slide with cloth	_____	Taking care of equipment	_____
Wipes slide with fingers	_____	Preparing slide	_____
Obtains bottle of culture	_____	Cleaning objective	_____
Places drop of culture on slide	_____	Adjusting microscope	_____
Adds water	_____	Identifying material	_____
Wipes off surplus fluid	_____	Cleaning up	_____
Wipes cover glass with cloth	_____		
Places slide on stage	_____		
Looks through eyepiece		**Characteristics of Student**	
with right eye	_____	**(Check all that apply)**	
with left eye	_____	Awkward movements	_____
Holds other eye closed	_____	Skillful movements	_____
Adjusts the focus		Hands steady	_____
Keeps eye on eyepiece	_____	Hands unsteady	_____
Takes eye away from		Slow moving	_____
eyepiece		Rapid moving	_____
Finds object	_____	Average speed	_____
Identifies material	_____	Follows instructions	_____
Removes slide from stage	_____	Needs extra help	
Cleans stage	_____	handling equipment	
Cleans slide	_____	and materials	_____
Asks for instructions	_____	Careful	_____
Says he or she does not know		Careless	_____
what to do	_____		

FIGURE 8.7 Checklist of Behaviors in a Laboratory Procedure

Narrative Reports. Sometimes, instead of using a simple checklist, the observer tries to observe, interpret, evaluate, and record the behavior. The record may eventually be turned into a narrative. Many times the observer uses abbreviations and shorthand notes while making the observations. This kind of observation tool requires careful training for the observers and is most useful for gathering information about a single individual, either a student or the teacher. However, the reports may also describe a whole class.

Anecdotal records are a form of narrative report. An *anecdotal record* is a report of a single, naturally occurring event. The event may be recorded because it is typical behavior or because it is atypical, something quite unexpected, as when a

Student Contacting	Student Contacted									
	Anne	Helen	Jean	Marie	Sara	Billy	Charles	Frank	Howard	James
Anne		///	//		/					
Helen	///		//						/	
Jean		///		/					//	
Marie	///		//				/			
Sara	//		///						/	
Billy			/					///		//
Charles				/		//				///
Frank			/			///			//	
Howard	/					//	///			
James							///	//	/	
Total times chosen	9	6	11	2	1	7	7	5	7	5

FIGURE 8.8 Tabulation of Social Interaction in a Classroom

student who has shown a total lack of interest in school volunteers one day to give a report on a science project he has read about.

Although anecdotal records usually describe unplanned events, the records should be complete enough to be meaningful when they are read at some later date. Figure 8.11 is an example of a simple anecdotal record. It includes the fol-

Student Contacted	Students Making Contact	Total Times Contacted
Anne	Helen, Marie, Sara, Howard	9
Helen	Anne, Jean	6
Jean	Anne, Helen, Marie, Sara, Billy, Frank	11
Marie	Jean, Charles	2
Sara	Anne	1
Billy	Charles, Frank, Howard	7
Charles	Marie, Howard, James	7
Frank	Billy, James	5
Howard	Helen, Jean, Sara, Frank, James	7
James	Billy, Charles	5

Student Contacting	Students Contacted	
Anne	Helen, Jean, Sara	
Helen	Anne, Jean, Howard	
Jean	Helen, Marie, Howard	
Marie	Anne, Jean, Charles	
Sara	Anne, Jean, Howard	
Billy	Jean, Frank, James	
Charles	Marie, Billy, James	
Frank	Jean, Billy, Howard	
Howard	Anne, Billy, Charles	
James	Charles, Frank, Howard	

FIGURE 8.9 List Report of Social Interaction (Using Data from Figure 8.8)

lowing information: identifying information, a description of the event, and an interpretation. It is important that the description and the interpretation be separated and clearly labeled, in order to allow the reader to interpret the facts. Notice that Figure 8.11 also has a plan of action.

Evaluative Ratings. Direct observation is often used to evaluate some aspect of student work, either that of a single student or of a group of students. It is especially useful to assess qualities such as leadership, playfulness, and tolerance for frustration. In most cases, you would not use observation to evaluate products such as a writing sample. Chapter 7 has suggestions for evaluating products.

Figure 8.12 is an evaluative scale for rating high school students in a nurses' aide program on their attitude toward patients, as observed by their teacher.

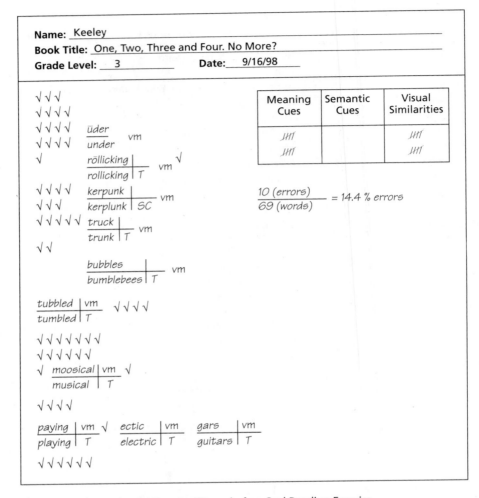

FIGURE 8.10 Example of a Running Record of an Oral Reading Exercise

Figure 8.13 is an evaluative report for a group of students, rating them on their group interaction skills. Notice that the description of points on the scale is similar to the rubrics used in the evaluation of performance and products.

Sources of Error in Direct Observations

Unfortunately, assessments that involve observation and judgment are open to many kinds of error that may keep them from being valid and reliable. Table 8.1 summarizes the sources of error in direct observations. If you are the person doing the observation and making the judgments, this information may help you guard against these problems.

NAME Billy Thompson   **DATE** 9/15/98

OBSERVER H. Smith   **TIME** 10:00 A.M.

INCIDENT

Billy arrived late this morning. He came into the room quietly and opened his book. His face was dirty and his hair was not combed.

When the class ended, he went to the restroom and he looked somewhat better when he came out.

I asked him quietly if something was wrong, but he said, "No, ma'am." His voice was very low, and he seemed near tears.

INTERPRETATION

Billy seems to have some problem at home, but I don't have enough information to know what kind.

PLAN OF ACTION

Talk to the Principal and Counselor to get more information.

FIGURE 8.11 Sample Anecdotal Record

NAME _____   **DATE** _____
RATER _____

Directions: Circle the number of the rating for the student named.

Rating	Behavioral Description
5 (Outstanding)	Anticipates patient needs, physical and emotional. Makes self available to patient. Allows patient opportunity to express feelings.
4 (Good)	Interacts with patients. Responds to patient requests. Goes beyond specific request.
3 (Acceptable)	Does assigned tasks. Responds to specific patient requests.
2 (Needs Improvement)	Unpredictable as to patient relationships.
1 (Unsatisfactory)	Does not relate to patients. Conversation with patients is mostly about self.

FIGURE 8.12 Evaluative Scale for Rating High School Students in a Nurse's Aide Training Program on Their Attitude Toward Patients

Directions

1. List the students who are being evaluated. These should be students who are members of the same group.
2. The groups should be work groups, not social groups.
3. Use the rating scale below to rate the students on the qualities of leadership, cooperation, accepting ideas of others, helping others to learn, and contributing to the solution.

RATING SCALE

1 = Little evidence of the skill

2 = Some evidence of the skill

3 = Much evidence of the skill

Student	Leadership	Cooperation	Accepting Others' Ideas	Helping Others	Contributing to the Solution
_____	____	____	____	____	____
_____	____	____	____	____	____
_____	____	____	____	____	____
_____	____	____	____	____	____
_____	____	____	____	____	____
_____	____	____	____	____	____
_____	____	____	____	____	____

FIGURE 8.13 Evaluative Report of Students' Group Interaction Skills

Table 8.1　Sources of Error in Direct Observations

Sources of Error in the Record Form

1. The form does not contain the behaviors the teacher wants to observe.
2. The record form is ambiguous, so the observer does not understand what is to be observed.

Sources of Error Within the Observer

1. The observer is not a good judge of the variables being observed.
2. The observer has insufficient information to make good judgments about what is seen.
3. The observer does not understand the observation technique or system.
4. The observer deliberately provides misinformation.
5. The observer makes different judgments from one time to another.
6. The observer tends to rate toward one end of the scale (too "generous" or too "severe").
7. The observer allows the halo effect to operate.

RETROSPECTIVE REPORTS

Have you ever been asked to fill out a form that asks for ratings of a person or product on one or more qualities? This tool is called a *retrospective* rating form, because the rating is done in retrospect—that is, it is a summary of the rater's impressions over time, rather than being based on a specific occasion. Retrospective reports are widely used in education, where they are usually called *rating scales*. In many schools teachers rate students regularly on variables such as "social growth," "work habits," and "attitudes." Also, retrospective reports by students, teachers, and parents are frequently used as part of the evaluation of specially funded programs, such as those for prevention of dropouts.

Some aspects of student development are not accessible to testing or to direct observation, and some direct observations are difficult and expensive to carry out. Therefore, educators often have to depend on retrospective reports for a great deal of important information. We ask people to tell us about their own thoughts, wishes, and experiences. We also ask them to summarize their experiences with other people, and we ask them about their experiences with various programs and institutions. A retrospective report is not so immediate as a report of direct observation, but sometimes it is all we can get. And if they are carefully handled, retrospective reports may provide valuable information.

Retrospective reports may be useful for summarizing a large number of observations over a long period of time. Furthermore, they may be used to assess almost every variable. Variables that are not directly observable may be assessed by asking people to think about their accumulated experiences and make some judgments about the abilities, attitudes, preferences, or habits reflected in those events. If several people are asked to evaluate the same people or programs, and if the reports are pooled, the information may be quite useful.

Steps in Preparing Retrospective Reports

The procedures for collecting retrospective data are listed and discussed below:

Steps for Preparing Retrospective Reports

1. Identify the purpose of the report.
2. Select a rating procedure.
3. Create a list of meaningful and productive behaviors to be rated.
4. Write the statements for the variables and arrange them in the manner required for the type of scale to be used.
5. Train the rater if necessary.
6. Use multiple raters if possible.
7. Summarize and interpret the ratings.

Step 1: Identify the Purpose of the Report. As we do with the other assessment tools mentioned thus far, we suggest that you begin by clarifying the purpose for yourself and for others who will make or use the ratings. Start by making a list of the variables—the objects, behaviors, and qualities—to be assessed, and define them specifically. These questions must be answered:

- What is the purpose of the assessment
- What are your main considerations in doing the report?

Step 2: Select a Rating Procedure. Will you use nominations, forced-choice questionnaires, narrative reports, or some type of evaluative report? Looking at the figures in this chapter may help you decide. It should be obvious that there are a great many possibilities. Several of them yield almost identical information, but some are unique.

The choice of a rating procedure depends in part on whether you are asking for descriptions or for evaluations. Evaluative ratings must have an evaluation system built in. Another consideration is whether you must take precautions against the halo effect and rater bias, in which case you probably will want to use forced-choice ratings.

Step 3: Create a List of Meaningful and Productive Behaviors to Be Rated. In this step you need to focus on exactly what behavior will be rated. You also should consider what you DO NOT want to rate. This is also the step where you decide whether you need to specify the degree to which a behavior is exhibited or has been mastered. Some of the figures in this chapter show some ways of noting the variation in behaviors.

Step 4: Write the Statements for the Variables and Arrange Them in the Manner Required for the Type of Scale to Be Used. When you first begin to prepare forms for retrospective reports, you may find it helpful to find a sample of the kind of form you want to use and adapt it to your needs. As you develop experience, you can become more creative.

Step 5: Train the Rater if Necessary. In a classroom, most of the time the raters are either the teacher or the students, although sometimes parents are asked to participate in a rating. Unless the rating scale is very complicated, perhaps all that is needed is a good set of simple written instructions. If the form is unusually complicated, it may be necessary to schedule a training program so you can be sure everyone understands what the terms mean and how to mark the forms.

Step 6: Use Multiple Raters if Necessary. If your purpose (in Step 1) is to collect information on an important problem, you should use more than one rater, in order to check the reliability of the ratings. If your purpose is to secure information about a single student's opinion, you need only one rater. However, if you want to know how other teachers or students view a student, you should get several people to do the rating.

Step 7: Summarize and Interpret the Ratings. If you are interested only in a single rating, you may skip this step. However, if there is more than one rater, or if there are several ratings over time, you will need to tabulate the ratings across all raters and look for patterns in the ratings. Answering the following questions might help:

- Are there any ratings in which all ratings agree or nearly agree?

- Are there any ratings in which there are pronounced differences of opinion?

- Do the differences seem to be related to the raters' position in the school or the conditions under which the ratings were made?

Types of Retrospective Reports

When you think about retrospective reports, you probably think of a rating scale, and that *is* one type of retrospective report. However, there are other kinds. Some of the most commonly used types of retrospective reports are described below.

Rating Scales. There are many kinds of rating scales which we are describing below. Simple instruments for indicating students' preference for classes and classroom activities were presented as Figures 8.1 and 8.2. More complex rating scales are presented later in this section.

Nominations. *Nomination* is a procedure that asks students to name other students who fit certain categories, such as "best student," "friendliest," etc., it is sometimes used to identify students who fit certain descriptions. Sometimes the instrument simply asks, "Guess who is _____?" Figure 8.14 provides two examples of such nomination instruments.

Sometimes the nomination technique is used to secure sociometric information, that is, information about the social interactions between students. When used in this way, nominations yield information similar to that which is obtained from some direct observations. The nominations are directed toward social relations, as in Figure 8.15, and the interrelationships are plotted on the same kind of charts used for sociometric observations as in Figures 8.8 and 8.9. Another type of third-party nomination is that by teachers of their students.

The nomination technique may also be used for students to evaluate teachers or programs or activities. See Figure 8.16.

Preference Records. Many retrospective reports, especially those involving self-reports, are directed at simply sorting individuals into categories according to their preferences or attitudes. Some of the well-known commercially available

NAME _____

1. Who is the most fun to play with?   _____
2. With whom do you like to work on homework?   _____
3. Who always knows the answers in class?   _____
4. Who knows how to make other people feel good?   _____
5. Who is always willing to help if you need it?   _____
6. Who does not think about anybody else?   _____
7. Who won't share anything?   _____
8. Who often makes other students feel bad?   _____

NAME _____

1. Who can state the problem clearly?   _____
2. Who asks the best questions in class?   _____
3. Who likes to do research to get more information?   _____
4. Who keeps suggesting another way to do something?   _____
5. Who is the best leader when you work in a group?   _____

FIGURE 8.14 Examples of "Guess Who?" Questionnaires

NAME _____

Directions: You have an opportunity to choose other students who will sit near you and work with you. Of course, you will not be able to have ALL your choices, but everyone will get some of their choices.

There are four questions below for you to answer by writing in the names of other students in this class.

List your four best choices for each question. You may list anyone who is in the class, even students who are absent if they are still a part of the class. Be sure to write the first name and the initial of the last name.

1. If you could choose the people you sit by in class, which ones would you choose?

   _____   _____

   _____   _____

2. Whom would you choose to work with on class projects?

   _____   _____

   _____   _____

3. Whom would you choose to be with during free play?

   _____   _____

   _____   _____

4. Whom do you really NOT want to be with in class?

   _____   _____

   _____   _____

FIGURE 8.15 Nominations: Sample Questionnaire

STUDENT _____

Directions: This questionnaire asks for your opinion about the courses and programs you have taken in this school this year.

Please answer the questions below with the name of a course or program you have taken.

1. In which course did you learn the most new material?   _____
2. Which course was most interesting for you?   _____
3. Which course was a waste of time for you?   _____
4. Which course was hardest for you?   _____
5. Which course would you like to take again?   _____

Have you been part of one or more special programs in the school?

YES   NO

If you answered "YES," please answer these questions:

Name of Program(s) (List all in which you have participated):

_____

_____

_____

1. In which program did you learn the most new material?   _____
2. Which program was most interesting for you?   _____
3. Which program was a waste of time for you?   _____
4. Which program was hardest for you?   _____
5. In which program would you most like to stay?   _____

FIGURE 8.16 Nomination Questionnaire for Evaluating Programs

instruments of this type are the *Strong Vocational Interest Inventory* (Stanford University Press), the *Kuder Personal Preference Record* (Science Research Associates), and the *Survey of Study Habits and Attitudes* (Psychological Corporation). These particular self-reports are widely used in counseling but are not so useful in the classroom setting, although they can provide information about how students see themselves and what their interests and concerns are. You may prepare similar instruments and use them to help you understand student attitudes and interests.

Several methods of response have been developed for the preference records. These are reviewed below.

Forced-Choices and Paired Comparisons. To eliminate faking on self-report inventories, a device called *forced-choice* was developed, with a variation called *paired-comparisons*. On some instruments, every option is paired with every other option, and the individual is forced to choose between paired options. On other instruments, the options represent different concepts. For example, in Figure 8.17, there are three choices for each item, and the choices for each item have a common framework. Sometimes the verbs differ and the objects remain constant; in other items, the verb remains constant and the objects change.

STUDENT _____

Directions: Each item has three choices listed. You are to mark ONLY ONE CHOICE in each group of three choices.

MARK THE THING YOU WOULD MOST LIKE TO DO.
Assume you CAN do everything, so it is just a matter of what you WANT to do.

1. ___ Build model cars
   ___ Work on a car
   ___ Read a story about cars

2. ___ Visit a factory
   ___ Visit a government office
   ___ Visit a library

3. ___ Go to an auto race
   ___ Go to Disney World
   ___ Go to Washington, DC

4. ___ Go swimming
   ___ Go camping
   ___ Go sightseeing

5. ___ Play baseball
   ___ Play tennis
   ___ Play football

6. ___ Eat at home
   ___ Eat at a short-order restaurant
   ___ Eat at the country club

7. ___ Watch TV
   ___ Read a book
   ___ Paint a picture

8. ___ Wear jeans
   ___ Wear a business suit
   ___ Wear party clothes

9. ___ Play cards
   ___ Play chess
   ___ Play video games

10. ___ Cook food
    ___ Serve food
    ___ Eat food

FIGURE 8.17 Example of a Forced-Choice Scale

Likert-Type Scales. A scale that is often used to measure attitudes is the Likert scale. For each statement there is usually a 5-choice scale, ranging from **SD** (strongly disagree) to **SA** (strongly agree). Other scales range from a negative such as "Strongly Dislike" to the strong positive of "Strongly Like." Sometimes a 4-point scale is used in order to force responses toward either the positive or the negative position. Likert-type scales for young children often use a happy face at one end, a sad or angry face at the other end, and a neutral face in the middle. Some of the statements may be positive and some negative. Figure 8.18 is an example of a traditional Likert scale. In scoring a Likert scale, numerical values are assigned to the response positions. For positive statements, "1" is assigned to SD and "5" to SA. For negative statements, the numbers are reversed: "5 is assigned to SD and "1" to SA.

STUDENT _____

Directions: Tell how much you agree with each statement by circling the letters that stand for your opinion.

KEY

SA	Strongly Agree
A	Agree
U	Undecided
D	Disagree
SD	Strongly Disagree

1. History classes are interesting.	SA	A	U	D	SD
2. The history textbook is fun to read.	SA	A	U	D	SD
3. History class assignments are boring.	SA	A	U	D	SD
4. History class projects are interesting.	SA	A	U	D	SD
5. The things we learn in history class are monotonous.	SA	A	U	D	SD
6. I like to read library books on history.	SA	A	U	D	SD
7. History is an important subject.	SA	A	U	D	SD
8. We don't need to study history.	SA	A	U	D	SD
9. I wish I could take something else instead of history.	SA	A	U	D	SD

FIGURE 8.18 Example of a Likert Scale (History)

Numerical Rating Scales. Some record forms are designed so that the observer evaluates the behavior, rather than simply reporting its presence or absence. Teachers may use ratings to assess student achievement. The numerical rating scales may assess the students' behavior; either the adequacy of performance or the manner and attitude with which the performance is carried out (or general "work habits"). Usually a 3-to-5-point rating scale is developed for each variable to be observed, and each point on the scale is defined. The scales used to rate performance and production tasks in Chapter 7 are examples (Figures 7.11 and 7.12). Scales similar to those may be used for both direct observation and for retrospective ratings.

Sometimes the numerical ratings are recorded on a graph that has a statement describing desirable qualities at one end, a statement describing undesirable qualities at the other end, and one or more points in between (Figure 8.19). The rater marks the point on the scale where the person or program falls. A graphic scale may be used to display any numerical rating or for Likert-type rating. It provides a picture that may make the ratings easier to interpret.

Sources of Error in Retrospective Reports

There are many possible sources of error in retrospective reports. Some are common to all retrospective reports; others are specific to the type of report. They are summarized in Table 8.2.

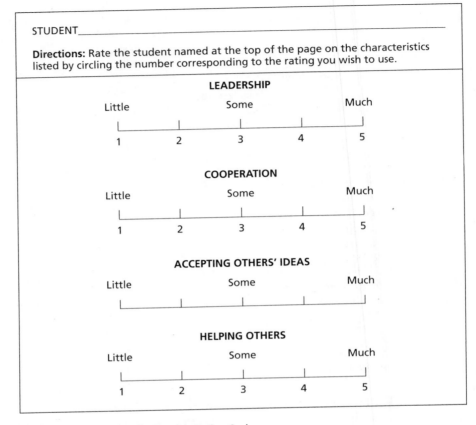

FIGURE 8.19 Example of a Graphic Rating Scale

Table 8.2 Sources of Error in Retrospective Reports

Sources of Error in All Retrospective Reports
1. The report form is ambiguous, so responders do not understand what is to be rated.
2. The form is not appropriate for the variable being rated.

Sources of Error in Self-Ratings
1. The individual is not aware of his or her true abilities or feelings.
2. The individual deliberately fails to tell the truth.
3. The individual feels differently from one time to another.

Sources of Error in Ratings by Others
1. The rater is not a good judge of the variables being rated.
2. The rater has insufficient information to make a good judgment.
3. The rater deliberately provides misinformation.
4. The rater makes different judgments from one time to another.
5. The rater tends to rate toward one end of the scale (too "generous" or too "severe").
6. The rater allows the halo effect to operate.

SUMMARY

- This chapter has presented procedures for a variety of assessments using observation.
- Some procedures involve *direct* observation, others are *retrospective*.
- Some procedures are *formal,* others are *informal.*
- Formal, direct observation yields the most dependable information, but the information may not indicate how the students usually behave.
- Retrospective reports are low cost and may be the only source of some kinds of information, but they may not be completely accurate and measurement error may be high.

STUDY QUESTIONS

1. How do direct observation and retrospective ratings differ? How are they similar?
2. For what reasons do teachers, counselors, and administrators use observation and ratings?
3. What are the major sources of error in these techniques?

FOR YOUR PROFESSIONAL GROWTH

1. Design an instrument for observing individual students during a group activity. The observation schedule may be a checklist, a narrative description, or a rating scale.
2. Design a self-report scale to identify students' preference for classroom activities. You may use a nomination questionnaire, a forced-choice scale, or a rating scale.

9

᷂

Portfolio Assessment

PREVIEW

As alternative assessment has gained popularity in education, a natural outgrowth has been a concern about how to collect and store the work of students as part of a total assessment package. Portfolios have become the device of choice for this purpose. They are currently being used to award final grades and diplomas, monitor student progress, determine readiness for activities, and hold schools accountable for their work with students.

MAJOR TOPICS
A Little Background
Definition of Portfolios
Planning and Creating Portfolios
Steps in Creating a Portfolio Assessment
Scoring Portfolios and Reporting Results
Choice of a Scoring System
Selection of Scorers
Weighting the Pieces
Sources of Error

A LITTLE BACKGROUND

There has been a great deal of interest in portfolio assessment in recent years, and many high stakes assessment programs in school districts and statewide now include portfolio assessment. Decisions based on these programs include promotion to the next grade and high school graduation. Interest in the use of portfolios in education developed in the 1970s and 1980s with the renewal of interest in the teaching of writing (Calkins, 1986; Graves, 1983). Literacy portfolios as described by Tierney, Carter, and Desai (1991) contain reading and writing collections of students' "real," authentic work, as opposed to "surrogates," or substitutes for real work. Portfolios have also been recommended as an assessment procedure in documents describing reforms in mathematics, science, and social studies—for example, the *Standards for Curriculum and Evaluation in Mathematics* by the National Council of Teachers of Mathematics (1989).

A portfolio can be used to secure a broader sample of students' work than would be possible from a single production task. Although alternative assessments such as writing samples do reveal a great deal about student achievement, they, like traditional assessments, are samples of learning taken out of the context of the student's learning life. A portfolio can be a sample of a student's regular class activities over an extended period of time.

Without the context of students' prior learning activities, it is difficult to diagnose or to hypothesize about why students perform in a specific way. Suppose you are interested in learning about students' ability to plan a task. You can give one assignment to sample this planning behavior by asking students to write down steps in planning, or you can observe and rate them.

The problem is that planning is a skill that develops over time. If students do not exhibit good planning in a given task, does that mean that they never plan or only that they did not plan this task well? If they show some faulty planning, did that happen because of the nature of the task, or do they always plan in this way? You need more information. One way to get that information is through keeping portfolios of student work.

Portfolios provide a means for collecting a variety of assessments over time in order to detect students' patterns of success and failure to achieve instructional objectives (Wiggins, 1989). For example, if your purpose is to make a judgment about a student's writing expertise in drafting, planning, and mechanics, you might state the student objective as follows: "The student will create a piece of narrative writing that includes good use of organization, voice, and mechanics." In addition, you may wish to examine the student's growth in writing over a period of six or nine weeks because you must conduct parent and student conferences on progress in writing. You will also use the information to diagnose and plan writing activities for the next nine-week period. In this situation, a single writing exercise might tell you how well students write at a given moment, but it does not reveal progress in learning to write well, nor can it reveal how the students thought through their work at the beginning of the task. A portfolio is a logical strategy to help you find out what you want to know, because it can contain the cumulative writing work of students along with their planning and drafting work. Thus, the teacher and students may see evidence of growth in the knowledge and practice of principles of good writing.

A number of people have written about the benefits of portfolios (for example, Wolf, 1989; Arter & Spandel, 1992; Linn & Baker 1992; Moss, Beck, Ebbs, Matson, Muchmore, Steele, & Taylor, 1992; and Gillespie, Ford, Gillespie, & Leavell, 1996). In general, the benefits include those listed in Table 9.1.

Potential problems with the use of portfolios also have been identified, especially when portfolios are used as an evaluative tool. For example, when portfolios are used as part of a state or district assessment program, the student products to be included in the portfolio are carefully specified so that the results will be comparable across all participating schools. One problem with this kind of high-stakes assessment program is that teachers and students may engage in practices that invalidate the scores. Gearhart and Herman (1995) found that some teachers use inappropriate methods to help students prepare for the high-stakes uses of portfolios. Others spend a great deal of time polishing the products so that the students, the teachers, and the school score well. This practice raises questions about whether the work was really the students' efforts and about the validity of portfolios as measures of students' achievement.

Another problem is that an assessment procedure that is intended to lead to more teaching time and less test-directed practice may in reality lead to considerable narrowing of class activities and threaten the validity of the entire assessment system. This outcome is similar to what happened in the case of high-stakes multiple-choice tests. (See Chapter 2.) Finally, Gillespie and colleagues (1996) and others identified some additional problems and costs of using portfolios. These are summarized in Table 9.2.

Table 9.1 Benefits of Using Portfolios

Instructional Benefits

> Facilitates integration of assessment with instruction.
>
> Promotes more valid assessment, better match with curriculum.
>
> Assesses a broad range of tasks and activities.

More Meaningful Process

> Permits more involvement by students in the assessment process by allowing them to select pieces when appropriate, evaluate their own work, and reflect on learning over time.
>
> Allows students to set more of their own educational goals.

Better Information for Teachers

> Helps teachers examine the processes and the products of learning.
>
> Reveals student development.

Positive Impacts on Teacher Behavior

> Influences the whole teaching/learning process.
>
> Helps teachers develop more accurate expectations of students.
>
> Facilitates teacher involvement in the assessment and scoring process.

Table 9.2 Problems in Using Portfolios

- Time for scoring may take time away from other instructional activities.
- Evidence of validity and reliability is difficult to obtain.
- Sophisticated testing knowledge on the part of the teacher is required.
- Contexts and purposes are often poorly defined.
- Information may be very detailed and of little interest to the public.

The benefits and problems listed in Tables 9.1 and 9.2 should help you to see that the use of portfolios is a complex, stimulating, and controversial area in assessment, which offers great possibilities, along with some potential problems.

DEFINITION OF PORTFOLIOS

What is a portfolio, and how is it different from a simple folder of student work? A definition we especially like has been suggested by Arter and Spandel (1992):

> A *purposeful* [italics added] collection of student work that tells the story of the student's efforts, progress, or achievement in given areas. This collection must include student participation in selection of portfolio content; the guidelines for selection; the criteria for judging merit; and evidence of student self-reflection (p. 36).

Using this definition, let's explore the differences between a portfolio and a simple folder of student work. The differences, gathered from a number of sources including Wolf (1989), Mumme (1990), Cheong and Shively (1991), and Nitko (1996), are summarized in Table 9.3. It should be clear from Table 9.3 that a lot of

Table 9.3 Comparison of Portfolios and Student Folders

Portfolio	Student Folder
Student work is purposefully selected to match instructional objectives.	Student work is whatever the students produce and is not necessarily tied to instructional objectives.
Content reflects students' effort in, progress toward and achievement of objectives.	Content is a sample of activities to date and is not selected because it reflects objectives.
Students' progress in mastering a *process,* such as critical thinking, problem solving, strategizing, and planning, is one of the criteria for judging items.	Products generally reveal completion of a task or product and not the process of working on the task.
Students help select content.	
Teacher uses selection guidelines and shares them with students.	Teacher generally controls content.
	If the teacher has selection guidelines, they usually are not known to students.
Criteria for judging items are set in advance and often are shared with students.	Criteria for judging usually are not set in advance and are not shared with students.
Students' self-reflection is presented through some means such as a journal.	There is no evidence of self-reflection.

thought and decision making goes into setting up a portfolio system. The work is collected for a specific purpose, and students participate in selecting, scoring, and evaluating the meaning of their work.

The prototype for the use of portfolios comes primarily from the writing and fine arts communities, where individuals routinely gather their best work into a folder or packet. The purpose is to present exemplary work samples to potential employers or judges in competitions. Portfolio-like documents are also used in other professions. Pilots and social workers, for example, keep portfolios of sorts, but the purpose is primarily to keep records of past work and experience.

PLANNING AND CREATING PORTFOLIOS

Portfolios are purposeful and require advance planning. Without this planning they become a simple folder of work (Valencia, 1990), and the major benefits from using them may be lost. Authors such as Clemmons, Laase, Cooper, Areglado, and Dill (1993), Popham (1995), and Nitko (1996) suggested a number of steps for creating a portfolio system. We combined a number of these suggestions to create a comprehensive set of steps to follow in creating a portfolio assessment. These are presented in the box below and then each step is discussed.

Steps in Creating a Portfolio System

1. Define your purpose.
2. Determine the content and skills to be assessed.
3. Determine whom you will assess and at what grade levels.
4. Determine what pieces you will collect.
5. Specify the number of times and how often work will be collected.
6. Make provisions to involve students in the system.
7. Set up the procedures for scoring portfolios.
8. Prepare everyone for the introduction of portfolios.
9. Plan for communicating results.
10. Plan for storing portfolios and sharing information with other educational professionals.

Step 1: Define Your Purpose. As with any assessment activity, you should start by defining your purpose. In Table 9.4 we list and describe some purposes you might have for preparing a portfolio. This list is primarily based on a review of the literature on portfolios carried out by Valencia and Calfee (1991). They found three basic uses, each of which serves different purposes. We believe this information will help you think about the other decisions you will have to make.

Is the portfolio intended to be a *showcase* of the students' best work? Is it to be used for *formative* purposes, to document student progress? Or will it be used as a *summative* evaluation tool? All uses are important, and sometimes part of the same

Table 9.4 Uses of Portfolios

A Showcase

The student places his or her best or favorite work in a showcase portfolio. Works-in-progress are not included. Reflection on why these works were chosen may be appropriate. The contents are not standardized, because each person is allowed to choose his or her own work for inclusion.

Documentation of Progress

The material for inclusion in a portfolio to document progress may involve student work as well as observations, tests, parental information, anything that describes the student. Student self-reflections and self-ratings may also be included. This is a *formative* evaluation process.

In addition, materials that are not necessarily the student's best work are included in order to show growth (or lack of it) over time. These portfolios work well as tools to communicate to parents about their children's progress, and they may be the basic source of information for a profile or referral.

Evaluation Tool

The contents of an evaluation portfolio are usually standardized, as is the scoring procedure. *Summative* evaluation uses of portfolios include promotion, retention, and pass/fail decisions about individual students, as well as summary reports for a given time period.

Program evaluations, and school, district, and state accountability requirements often use portfolios as the exclusive or major source of information about program effectiveness or curriculum improvement.

SOURCE: Based on "The Development and Use of Literacy Portfolios for Students, Classes, and Teachers," by S. W. Valencia and R. Calfee, 1991, *Applied Measurement in Education, 4*(4), 333–345.

portfolio may used for more than one purpose. In this case, it is best to sort the materials into specific sections, because the procedures differ for the various purposes. The portfolio contents, the people involved, and the time schedule for collecting the information vary with the purpose, as Table 9.5 makes clear. The purpose also determines whether the portfolio is scored and, if so, how it is scored.

Step 2: Determine the Content and Skills to Be Assessed. You will not know whether students have achieved what you hoped they would achieve unless you are clear about what you are looking for. What are your instructional objectives? What content and skills are students supposed to be learning?

We addressed this matter in Chapter 5, and you may wish to review that chapter. As a teacher, you want to be sure that you collect evidence of whether your students are attaining the objectives you feel are important. Recall that one of the main criticisms of traditional assessments has been that they tend to be used to measure what is convenient to measure, rather than learning outcomes that really count. Portfolios will suffer the same criticisms if teachers are not careful to define their teaching objectives and to collect evidence that helps them decide whether the students have achieved them. When Robert F. Mager wrote his landmark book on writing instructional objectives for programmed instruction, he suggested that in order to teach successfully, there are three requirements: *content*

Table 9.5 Relationship of Purpose to Materials, Persons Involved, and Time Schedule

Purpose	Materials	Person Selecting	Person Using	Time Schedule
Showcase	Best efforts of all kinds	Student Teacher	Student Administrators Teachers Parents	Continuous
Documentation of progress	Samples collected over time, may include standardized test scores, observations, ratings by self and others.	Teacher Student	Teacher Student Parents Counselor Other educators	Regularly scheduled dates
Evaluation	Special assignments	Teacher Student	Student Teachers Parents Administrators Public	Specially designated assessment date

to be learned, a *criterion* for achievement, and a *visible indicator* that achievement has taken place (Mager, 1962).

Step 3: Determine Whom You Will Assess and at What Grade Levels. If you are a classroom teacher, the matter of whom you will assess is easily answered. It will be your own students, of course. However, administrators and members of an assessment committee also may have to deal with this issue. Should all students of every grade be involved? If not, what grades and which students should be included? Portfolios have to be scored to be useful for evaluation purposes, so part of the consideration has to be what is practical. How can the scoring be handled in such a way that the scores will be valid and reliable? Is the purpose of the portfolio to evaluate individual progress, or is it to look at the achievement of the school or school system, so that a sample might be used?

The decision should be based on the purpose of the assessment. If you are planning to provide feedback to all students in your classroom and their parents, you will need to collect many pieces of work from those students. If you are collecting information for diagnosis, readiness, or referral to special education, you may decide to collect information only on selected students and only on specific content and skills.

School district and state portfolio programs may dictate the grade levels and frequency of collection of student work. Another consideration is the grade level at which the curriculum begins to emphasize the objectives that are supposed to be demonstrated in the portfolio.

Step 4: Determine What Pieces You Will Collect. The selection of items for the portfolio should begin with a review of the purpose. If the purpose of the portfolio is to serve as a *showcase,* then only samples of students' best work should be included. Because best work varies from person to person, it is not possible to prescribe and standardize the content to be included. But no work-in-progress would be included. Nor would there be scores from standardized tests. However, a great variety of student work might be included. In addition to written materials, such products as paintings, recordings, videotapes, or photos may be used to demonstrate the students' productions of such products as dioramas.

Contents of a portfolio to *document progress* should be chosen to reflect the trait for which progress (or lack of it) is to be demonstrated. Classroom behavior and effort might best be shown in observational records, work samples, and anecdotal records. General achievement might best be demonstrated through test papers, records of test scores, and work samples, including work-in-progress. A portfolio covering general achievement in a social studies class might contain writing samples, ratings of presentations, test papers, and evaluation of products such as dioramas, bulletin boards, or charts. Putting together a portfolio of this kind is very similar to preparing a student profile which we discuss at length in Chapter 15.

If the portfolio is to be used for *evaluation,* some of the materials might be the same as those used for documentation of progress. However, in this case it is imperative to standardize the contents and time schedule in order to keep judgments consistent so the scores may be interpreted correctly.

The key to portfolio content selection is the purpose of the portfolio. Most of the contents will be samples of students' work. However, student self-reports and ratings by others may also be appropriate for portfolios used to document progress.

Portfolios provide an opportunity to include student work that traditionally has not been considered. Table 9.6 lists some of the items we have seen in portfolios and heard teachers discuss in workshops and courses. This list is not exhaustive and we are often surprised by the creativity of teachers and students in developing new items. A number of the items listed in Table 9.6 are discussed in

Table 9.6 Possible Items for a Portfolio

Writing samples	Scores on traditional achievement tests
Lists of books read or materials used	Ratings and reports of observations
Journals and learning logs	Projects
Mathematics problem sets	Group activities
Students' reports	Cartoons
Worksheets	Models
Reports on laboratory experiments	Computer printouts and disks
Photographs of dioramas, bulletin boards, and other projects	Artwork
	Maps, charts, and diagrams
Reports of interviews with students and others	Tapes of choral or oral reading
Videos	Reports of investigations
Audiotapes	

detail in Chapters 6, 7, and 8, and a brief discussion of the usefulness of some of them is presented below.

Writing Samples. Writing samples can be collected to reflect the type of writing on which students are working. For example, if a student is learning about expository writing, samples of short summaries of library research could be placed in the portfolio.

Many teachers like to keep a final-draft section and a work-in-progress section in portfolios. Students may keep old copies to see their own progress and discuss their progress with the teacher.

Lists of Books Read or Materials Used. One objective that many teachers have set for students is to broaden their reading. It is helpful for children to experience a variety of genres in their reading. In a social studies or science unit, for example, students may be asked to use a variety of references such as almanacs, encyclopedias, biographies, atlases, and newspapers.

One way to check on the variety of materials that students are using is to have them keep a record of books they read or materials they use in their work. Some teachers also have students make a few comments about each selection.

Journals and Learning Logs. Journals and learning logs are important items in any portfolio because they offer a way to convey student self-reflection. Many teachers use dialog journals in which students record their own thoughts on one half of the paper and the teacher responds to students on the other half of the paper.

Curry (1989) suggested ways in which students may use a journal to think about their learning and reflect on their progress. Curry suggests that students be given a list of questions to be addressed in their journals. They might be encouraged to think about questions such as these:

1. What did I learn in _____ class today?
2. What do I need more help with?
3. What can I do to learn this?

Edwards (1992) suggested that a journal for a textbook assignment might be divided into several columns, which would help students organize their learning from an assignment. Such columns might be

What It Says	What It Means	How I Can Use It

For a problem-solving activity in mathematics, the column headings might be something like these:

What It Says	What It Means	Operations	Solutions

Mathematics Problem Sets. Mathematics problem sets can be useful to display student progress in all mathematical areas—from learning facts to solving complex word problems. Many teachers ask students to explain how they solved a problem and to show their work. These explanations may be written or discussed in person with the teacher, and notes may be recorded during the discussion, or the discussion may be videotaped or audiotaped.

Students' Reports.   The portfolio items that require the most work by students and is most dreaded by teachers is a written report. The portfolio affords the student and teacher a means to work on skills such as taking notes, consulting references, and summarizing research.

Worksheets.   Worksheets have been looked on with disfavor recently, but they do serve a useful purpose. They can help students practice skills they must use automatically such as math facts and recognition of sight words. In addition, worksheets can include complex problem-solving activities that allow students to work together or alone, and for some students it may be useful to have samples of the practice work.

Reports of Laboratory Experiments.   For years, secondary science teachers have had students record their laboratory work in biology, chemistry, and physical science classes. Teachers at the elementary level have discovered that these devices allow them to check on students' progress in conducting experiments and their understanding of the concepts behind the experiments. The reports may be useful additions to some portfolios.

Photographs of Projects, Dioramas, Bulletin Boards.   Photographs may be used as evidence of work that is impossible to store in a portfolio because of its size or shape. Photographs are particularly important when achievement of an objective requires construction of a product such as a diorama. The students' work may be evaluated by the number of elements contained in the display and their arrangement and relationship to each other.

Reports of Interviews with Students and Others.   Interviews may take several forms, depending on their purpose and the objectives they are designed to achieve. Teachers may conduct interviews with students when they want to document student progress. The results of the interview may be a video or audiotape or a written account of the interview. Winograd, Paris, and Bridge (1991) found a number of studies that demonstrate the usefulness of interviews in helping students become aware of and evaluate their own learning. In addition, students may wish to interview each other or other school or community members as part of reports, projects, or other data collection activities.

Videos.   Videos are interesting items for a portfolio. They can be used to show speeches, performance of music and acting, and even documentaries of students as they complete projects. For example, students may wish to videotape their work on projects such as the creation of a garden. In some occupations, videos allow professionals-in-training to show their personal interaction skills. In education, teachers are often asked to videotape lessons that show their teaching expertise.

Audiotapes. Audiotapes may be used to show performances that do not require visual presentation of skills. For example, an audiotape may be used to record an interview with a community member or to document group interactions in a discussion exercise.

Scores on Traditional Achievement Tests. Scores on standardized tests and on classroom tests will be part of most classroom portfolios, especially if the purpose of the portfolio is to show progress. Scores on these tests may provide important information because the tests present snapshots of student performance in a traditional testing context. It is important for teachers to examine student performance in this type of setting as well as in alternative ones. Chapter 6 provides many important points about writing items for classroom tests, and Chapter 11 presents information on interpreting commercially developed traditional achievement tests.

Ratings and Reports of Observations. Some objectives require direct observation and ratings by teachers, students, or administrators. For example, students may be rated in physical education concerning their physical fitness, in music concerning their expertise with a musical instrument, or in other classes on their ability to deliver a speech. Within a portfolio, rating sheets may add support for evaluations of student work or help explore complex learning such as planning, researching, or delivering a debate. Chapters 7 and 8 discuss these types of assessment in more detail.

Projects. Projects take many forms. They may include writing, data collection, field trips, and experiments, for example. Miller, Murray-Ward, and Harder (1994) suggested several activities that might be used as part of a project on the recent Columbus Quincentenary. This list of activities is printed as Figure 9.1. As you can see, a project covering these activities could yield an entire portfolio for a given grading period.

Group Activities. At times, teachers not only teach content, they also teach social skills. One of the most popular ways to do this is through cooperative learning. Effective cooperative groups require work on social skills such as sharing, allocating responsibilities, and helping one another. Forms for recording the level of cooperation and the contributions of each member may be used (see Chapter 7). Copies of these forms may also be included in a portfolio, if an objective is to develop cooperative skills.

Step 5: Specify the Number of Times and How Often Work Will Be Collected. As Table 9.5 indicates, the time schedule is very much a function of the purpose of the portfolio. If the purpose is to *showcase* outstanding work, the materials may be collected at any convenient time after the best examples of the student's work become available. If the purpose is to *document progress,* it is necessary to collect examples of the student's behavior over an extended period. The

1. A written report on events leading up to Columbus's voyage.
2. A dramatization of the landing of Columbus and reactions of Columbus's crew and the native peoples.
3. A bulletin board on some aspect of the period: time line of events, locations of native peoples, comparison of world maps of the time period and today.
4. A content journal featuring what the student is learning and the resources used.
5. An oral presentation of subsequent events after the voyage.
6. Reviews of books written about the events of the day.
7. A student-teacher conference interview reviewing and evaluating the entire project.
8. A simulation of the entire trip across the Atlantic.

FIGURE 9.1 Outline for a Project for the Columbus Quincentenary

From Miller, E., Murray-Ward, M. & Harder, H. (1996). *Reading and language arts for all students: A practical guide for content area teachers,* p. 296. Reprinted by permission.

evaluation use of a portfolio requires that the samples be collected from all participating students at the same time of the year and under the same conditions.

Step 6: Make Provisions to Involve Students in the System. One of the major strengths of using portfolios is the possibility of involving students in the portfolio assessment system. Students may help select the work to be included in the portfolio, although large-scale assessment projects using portfolios generally have some restrictions on content. Students may keep a journal that becomes part of the portfolio. They may also share their work and progress with others. In general this is accomplished in conference with the teacher, although student-led parent conferences are becoming popular as well. Some teachers also arrange for students to evaluate parts of their own portfolios, in order to encourage them to reflect on their work. Sometimes this reflection is written into a journal, or it may be done orally, either with the teacher or with other students.

To engage in meaningful self-analysis, most students need training and time to select work and reflect on it. Clemmons and colleagues (1993) suggested criteria for training students to evaluate their own writing. We use these criteria in our suggestions of ways to train students in the self-evaluation process. The suggestions are presented in Table 9.7.

Step 7: Set Up The Procedures for Scoring Portfolios. In a classroom, most of the individual pieces in a portfolio are scored at the time they are collected. At this point, the question is whether and how the portfolio as a whole will be scored. The choice of procedure depends on what you are trying to accomplish and what kinds of material you are scoring. We deal with these issues in the next section of this chapter.

Table 9.7 Suggestions for Teaching Self-evaluation

1. **Develop criteria for effective work on a product.** Involve students in generating the criteria. If that is not possible, students should at least see and understand the criteria before completing a product.
2. **Teach the process of self-evaluation.** This step involves using work samples and training students to "see" the difference between quality and marginal work. In addition, students are trained to examine work for strengths and weaknesses.
3. **Allow students to practice self-evaluation of their work on a regular basis.** Ask them questions about their thinking and provide feedback about the quality of their self-evaluations.
4. **Help students use their self-evaluations against the scoring criteria to set goals for themselves.** A useful exercise is to have students evaluate samples of student work and develop a set of learning goals for the fictional person who produced the sample.
5. **Use goal setting frequently in class activities.**

Step 8: Prepare Everyone for the Introduction of Portfolios. When portfolios are to be used for the first time, everyone involved should receive information about what portfolios are and how they will be used. Teachers can handle this task with their own students in their classes or homerooms. To inform parents, Farr and Tone (1994) suggested strategies such as sending them a newsletter to explain the meaning of portfolios and holding an open house to share information. When portfolio results are used in an entire school district or state, the public needs some training on portfolios as well. This might be done through news releases to local newspapers.

Step 9: Plan for Communicating Results. Of course, students are interested in their own progress, and parents are interested in their children's progress. Portfolios are a great departure from more familiar forms of feedback such as letter grades or percentages, so everyone will need information about what the information means. Clemmons et al. (1993) suggested the use of support groups and volunteer parents who assist other parents in learning about portfolios. Open houses, newsletters, and news releases may also be useful.

Step 10: Plan for Storing Portfolios and Sharing Information with Other Educational Professionals. Another aspect of communication is the storing and passing on of portfolio information to other schools. When portfolios were first introduced, the type of container was the first concern of teachers, and it remains a concern. Furthermore, because portfolios require such an investment of student and teacher effort, throwing them out at the end of the year or sending them home means that the school loses valuable information.

We recommend that teachers store the portfolios during the year and periodically send parts of each student's portfolio home. Some items could be returned to the school and others kept by students' families. When a student moves to the next grade or to a new school, some selected pieces could be kept at school in the portfolio. However, paper storage is a problem for most schools, so we suggest that a portfolio evaluation summary form be kept and all materials be returned to the student. That way, teachers at students' new schools can have high-quality information about each student without having to read volumes of material on each one. This is one situation where a single portfolio form would be very useful. A high-tech solution, proposed by Barrett (1994), is to store portfolios and portfolio evaluations on computer disks. The problem, of course, would be finding someone to enter the material on disks.

SCORING PORTFOLIOS
AND REPORTING RESULTS

The primary decision to be made about scoring portfolios for summative purposes is whether each portfolio is to be scored as a whole or whether the individual items are to be scored and the scores averaged in some way. To use a portfolio as a summative assessment instrument, you must score it in a way that ensures validity, reliability, and fairness. The same procedures and care must be used in assessing the total portfolio as are used in assessing individual projects. Furthermore, the way in which the scoring is handled will affect the type and amount of information that may be obtained from the portfolio.

Choice of a Scoring System

Care should be taken when a portfolio scoring system is being selected, because it has been found that students receive different results on their portfolios depending on how the total score is derived. The most unreliable and error-prone system is to average scores across different tasks scored with different criteria.

Figure 9.2 presents a form for evaluating a portfolio using holistic scoring across three writing assignments; the form also has a place for a general descriptive statement about the student's work. This evaluation form uses the same scale to rate all the pieces. Each section could be completed at the time the piece is scored, and then the scores could be combined for the total.

Figure 9.3 is an example of a domain rating form developed by Tierney, Carter, and Desai (1991). This figure rates the various qualities as "Strong Performance," "Acceptable Performance," or "Needs Improvement." Still another example, presented in Figure 9.4, was developed for the Kentucky portfolio project (Strobe, 1993). The Kentucky system assigns ratings as "Novice," "Apprentice," "Proficient," and "Distinguished" for five qualities that include awareness of audience and purpose, idea development and support, organization, sentence structure, wording, and surface features of the writing.

You may recall from earlier chapters that rubrics are of four general types—holistic, primary trait, domain, and analytic—and may be task specific or general in nature. It has been our experience and that of Arter (1993) that when teachers are permitted to select a type of rubric, they generally choose rubrics that are analytic, such as the domain scoring rubric, because they believe that they get more diagnostic information from the different parts of the rubric and that their

Evaluation of a Writing Portfolio						
Item/Project	Rating				Weight	Weighted Score
	Outstanding: 4 points	Acceptable: 3 points	Minimally Acceptable: 2 points	Poor: 1 point		
1. Narrative writing task						
2. Descriptive writing task						
3. Expository writing task						
Total rating						

GENERAL DESCRIPTIVE STATEMENT:

RATER: _____   DATE: _____

FIGURE 9.2 Sample of a Holistic Portfolio Evaluation Form

students are better able to react and improve their work with the specific information provided in this type of rubric. The choice of a rubric is especially important when you are scoring individual assignments or when your purpose is to document student progress; it is less important for a portfolio that is used for summative evaluation.

We believe that it is useful to provide information about the scoring system to students in advance. Our experience with our own students and conversations with teachers indicate that this practice leads to improved task performance. It is important that *all* students receive complete information.

Selection of Scorers

Portfolios used in classroom assessment are usually scored by individual teachers. For district-wide or state-wide assessment programs, scoring is usually done in networks to which teachers are assigned. Scoring rubrics must be carefully worked out for these programs.

Weighting the Pieces

If you have scores on each piece, you may want to give more weight to some pieces than to others. If your scores are all based on the same rubrics, you may simply multiply each score by the desired weight, add the weighted scores, and divide by the total of the weights. Figure 9.5 show how this works.

Continua of Descriptors		
Strong Performance (3)	**Acceptable Performance (2)**	**Needs Improvement (1)**
Versatility		
Wide variety of reading and writing across genre.	Some variety.	Little or no variety. Collection shows little breadth or depth.
Process		
Samples reveal discoveries or pivotal learning experiences.	Process illustrated in inflexible or mechanistic ways.	Minimal use of process to reflect on achievements.
Response		
Engaged with story. Discusses key issues. Evidence of critical questioning.	Personal reflection but focus is narrow.	Brief retelling of isolated events.
Self-Evaluations		
Multidimensional. Wide variety of observations. Establishing meaningful goals. Notes improvement.	Developing insights. Some specifics noted. Limited goal setting. Vague idea of improvement.	Single focus, global in nature. Goal setting too broad or nonexistent.
Individual Pieces		
Strong control of a variety of elements: organization, cohesion, surface features, etc.	Growing command evidenced. Some flaws but major ideas are clear.	Needs to improve: sophistication of ideas, text features.
Problem Solving		
Wrestles with problems using various resources. Enjoys problem solving and learning new ways.	Uses limited resources. Wants quick fix.	Seems helpless. Frustrated by problems.
Purposefulness/Uses		
Uses reading and writing to satisfy various goals including sharing with others.	Uses reading and writing to meet others' goals.	Apathetic, resistant.

FIGURE 9.3 Portfolio Assessment in the Reading-Writing Classroom

SOURCE: From *Portfolio Assessment in the Reading-Writing Classroom* (p. 134), by R. J. Tierney, M. A. Carter, and L. E. Desai, 1991, Norwood, MA: Christopher-Gordon Publishers. (Numeric values added.) Reprinted by permission.

Novice (1)	Apprentice (2)	Proficient (3)	Distinguished (4)
Awareness of Audience and Purpose			
Limited awareness of audience and/or voice and tone.	An attempt to establish and maintain purpose and communicate with the audience.	Focused on a purpose; evidence of voice and suitable tone.	Establishes and maintains clear focus; evidence of distinctive voice and/or appropriate tone.
Idea Development and Support			
Minimal idea development; limited and/or unrelated details.	Unelaborated idea development; unelaborated and/or repetitious details.	Depth of idea development supported by elaborated, relevant details.	Depth and complexity of ideas supported by rich, engaging, and/or pertinent details; evidence of analysis, reflection, insight.
Organization			
Random and/or weak organization.	Lapses in focus and/or coherence.	Logical organization.	Careful and/or subtle organization.
Sentence Structure			
Incorrect and/or ineffective sentence structure.	Simplistic and/or awkward sentence construction.	Controlled and varied sentence structure.	Variety in sentence structure and length enhances effect.
Wording			
Incorrect and/or ineffective wording.	Simplistic and/or imprecise language.	Acceptable, effective language.	Precise and/or rich language.
Surface Features			
Errors in surface features are disproportionate to length and complexity.	Some errors in surface features that do not interfere with communication.	Few errors in surface features relative to length and complexity.	Control of surface features.

FIGURE 9.4 Domain Scoring Guide

Reprinted by permission of the Kentucky State Department of Education.

	Rubric Score	Weight	Weighted Score
Assignment 1	3	3	9
Assignment 2	2	5	10
Assignment 3	4	2	8
		Total weighted score	27
		Sum of the weights	10
		Portfolio score	2.7

FIGURE 9.5 Example of Weighting Scores on Pieces of a Portfolio

Sources of Error in Scoring Portfolios

Since much of the material in the portfolio will have to be scored as products or performances, all the requirements for ensuring valid, reliable, and fair scoring will be present. This is an important irony because one of the primary claims for the use of portfolios is the increased validity of the measurement. Herman and Winters (1994) found little published evidence to support this claim. Furthermore, there is some evidence that the scoring of portfolios is not as reliable as first hoped and that the procedure used for a portfolio evaluation (averaged or global) can affect outcomes. Fairness also is a concern because of the possible "contamination" of student work through help from teachers and parents (Herman & Winters, 1994; Gearhart & Herman, 1995). Furthermore, in the overall analysis of the entire portfolio, in which someone looks at all of the student work, the potential problem of allowing irrelevant variables to influence the evaluations is of even greater concern. Such variables could include students' handwriting, the neatness of the items, and the length of each item. To avoid these problems, the suggestions for ensuring validity, reliability, and fairness in scoring production and performance tasks, presented in Chapter 7, should be applied in the evaluation of portfolios.

There are some other important questions to be answered about validity, reliability, and fairness. Of primary concern is the validity of the portfolio in terms of the selection of the contents and the scoring procedures. Brandt (1992) and Farr and Tone (1994) found that the reliability and validity of scoring depend on a match to instructional objectives and accurate scoring. Valencia and Calfee (1991) state that validity in portfolios can be ensured by careful attention to the representativeness of the portfolio tasks and their match to the objectives and purpose of the portfolio. In order to ensure validity of scoring, Farr (1990) suggests that the teachers make notes on the date and context of students' work. This information will help the portfolio scorer to understand the context of the assessments and conditions that could affect students' scores. For example, the teacher could note the date and indicate that a writing sample of a business letter was completed immediately *before* instruction on how to construct such a letter. Another sample could be dated and the teacher could note that this second sample was collected immediately *after* instruction on letter writing. Another sample could be dated and marked as collected *one month after* instruction.

Communicating Results

If students and teachers are the only stakeholders, you might use summary sheets or scoring rubrics for each item and an overall portfolio rubric. You might also consider a conference as an informal way to communicate results. However, when others outside the classroom are involved, we have new logistical problems. Parents will be interested in seeing the student's best efforts, and they will also be interested in seeing growth over time, so they would want to see drafts and a learning log.

The situation is even more complicated when information from portfolio assessments is summarized for the school and the district. For this situation, formal records and a uniform scoring system will be necessary. The focus will be primarily on the final product, not on interim indicators of progress.

SUMMARY

- Currently there is much interest in portfolio assessment.
- Portfolios may include a wide variety of student work at various stages.
- Portfolios must be carefully planned and the work must be collected according to the plan if the portfolios are to serve their purpose.

STUDY QUESTIONS

1. What are major advantages and disadvantages of portfolios?
2. What steps could you take to ensure valid, reliable, and fair portfolio scoring?
3. What are some logistical considerations of portfolio scoring and storage in your school?

FOR YOUR PROFESSIONAL GROWTH

Use the following steps to plan for the use of portfolios for a project in your class:

1. Set up the purposes for the objectives.
2. List the materials to be included and the source.
3. Design an evaluation sheet to be used in scoring the portfolio.

PART THREE

ॐ

External
Testing Programs

In Part Two we explored testing tools that are created by teachers, counselors, or administrators. However, there are many tools that have already been developed. These tools are *external tests*—external because they were created outside the school or district, usually by a company or professional association. In Part Three we explore the construction and use of these other tools.

There are two types of external testing programs. Group tests, the most common type, are usually standardized tests of achievement, although ability tests of various kinds and measures of attitudes and preferences also may be used. The other type of external tests is individual, or clinical, tests, which are usually administered by a school psychologist or other specially trained professional.

As a teacher, counselor, or administrator you may be involved in external group testing in several ways. You may be expected to administer a test that is part of a state or district testing program and to interpret the results to your students and their parents, or you may be asked to serve on a committee to evaluate and select tests to be used. You may be selected to be part of a team of scorers for some performance tests, or you may be asked to participate in developing some tests.

For individual tests, your responsibility as a teacher, counselor, or administrator is to interpret and use the information. You also may participate in the development of an Individualized Education Program (IEP) for some of your students—a program that will be based largely on the results of individual tests. The chapters in Part Three will help you carry out these responsibilities.

10

ॐ

Overview of External Testing Programs

PREVIEW

At the second teachers' meeting of the year, Mr. Taylor, the Associate Superintendent, distributes the calendar for the year, which includes four weeks marked off for testing. In October, the State Assessment tests will be administered to grades 4, 8, and 10. The nationally normed achievement test battery—a district-wide test administered to grades 1 through 8 and 10—is to be given over a two-week period in April, and a readiness test is to be administered to kindergarten students in May. In addition, the schedule notes that the SAT for college admissions will be administered on Saturdays seven times throughout the year, and the ACT is administered in the spring, summer, and fall. Before the rest of the schedule is discussed, some of the teachers ask, "Why do we have to have all this testing? What good does it do?"

How would you answer the teachers' questions?

As the scenario above illustrates, external testing requires an impressive amount of time in most American schools and consumes much of the educational system's resources. All of the tests mentioned in the scenario are *external*, which means that they are developed by someone other than the classroom teachers. If left to follow their own preferences, few classroom teachers would choose to administer external tests to their classes. Many teachers believe that time spent in testing might be better spent on other activities. This negative feeling is increased when teachers know that these tests may be used to evaluate them and their students and when they believe the evaluation will be unfair. Counselors and administrators, too, might prefer not to use these tests, because they consume large amounts of planning time, disrupt regular school-day activities, and are sometimes the center of difficult discussions with parents and teachers.

Why are tests used that many educators see little value in? Is there a good reason for using external tests? Can such tests be useful for educators? To answer these questions, we need to think about the various kinds of external tests and to understand the purposes for which they may be used. Many of these uses may have negative consequences, as we discussed in Chapter 2. For example, using tests as the sole criterion of accountability for students, teachers, schools, school systems, states, and the nation can lead to narrowing of the curriculum and to coaching (or "teaching to the test"), which invalidates the test. These consequences are so serious that we state unequivocally that no important decision in education should be based solely on a single test score. On the other hand, if a variety of test-generated information, properly interpreted and combined, is used, educational decisions will be much better than decisions made without such information. The chapters in this part of this book are directed toward helping educators use test information in this way.

If you and the students in your school are required to participate in external testing programs, it is important that you do so in a way that makes the results most useful. Then, if you are to use the results, you need to understand how the tests are developed, what they measure, and what the scores mean. You also need to understand the limitations of the tests and how to interpret the results appropriately.

MAJOR TOPICS

Uses of External Group Tests
Types of External Tests
   Achievement Tests
   Tests of Aptitude/Ability
   Interest, Preference, Attitude, and Personality Inventories
   Individual Tests
Selection of Tests
Sources of Information About Published Tests
Administration of Standardized Group Tests
Interpretation and Use of Test Scores

USES OF EXTERNAL GROUP TESTS

Most of the external tests used in schools are *standardized, norm-referenced* tests of achievement that are taken by groups of students, not individually administered. They provide a means of collecting a standardized sample of students' behavior under uniform conditions. The meaning of *standardized* is that we ask all students of a given grade level the same questions, under the same conditions, and that the tests for all students are scored using the same scoring procedures and standards. The goal is to be able to judge the quality of the performance of an individual student or the performance of students in a school or a state, using the same standards for all schools, school districts, and states.

Most external tests have been administered to a norms group so that individual scores can be interpreted in reference to others' scores or a school's average score can be compared with the average scores of a sample of schools. The intent of such comparisons is to help the school staff, the parents, and the public understand how well (or how poorly) their schools and students are doing in comparison with other similar schools and students and to provide an incentive to the schools to improve their educational programs.

There is little debate about whether parents and the public have a right to information about how well schools are doing their job and how well students are learning; and nationally normed, standardized tests are one of the best sources of this information. However, certain requirements must be met if this information is to be valid—that is, if the information is to be an accurate indicator of how well a school is doing. In order to do this well, a test must meet the criteria listed in Table 10.1.

Table 10.1 Criteria for Valid Test Information

1. The tests used must reflect what the school faculty and parents think is important for students of that school to learn.
2. The tests must be good indicators of the important learning.
3. The test results must reflect only student learning, not some other irrelevant information.

Although there is some consensus about the important goals of education, the specific content and skills for all students are still the subject of debate. The most appropriate curriculum for a given group of students depends not only on what is seen as desirable outcomes, but also on where the students are at the moment. Most academic learning is developmental—with advanced courses building on lower level courses. It is ridiculous to expect that a student who cannot read will be able to achieve well in any other course, or to expect that a student whose arithmetic background is poor or lacking will be able to handle calculus or physics.

Students' current achievement is closely related not only to their previous school experience; it is also related to many out-of-school experiences, especially their early childhood experiences. Too often we blame the person (or school) at the end of the line (for example, the teacher), ignoring preconditions that are more important determinants of the achievement outcome and unwilling to direct resources to where the problem really lies.

TYPES OF EXTERNAL TESTS

There are several types of external tests, each type designed to provide a specific kind of information. All of them may be administered either to groups or individuals. The primary difference among them is in whether students are tested simultaneously or whether a single student is tested by an examiner.

Table 10.2 lists the most frequent uses of external tests and indicates the type of test that can serve each purpose. As you can see from this table, all the tests may serve many purposes and all types of tests may contribute to each purpose. The various types of tests are discussed below. Sources of information about various instruments are presented in a later section of this chapter.

Table 10.2 Purposes of External Tests

Purpose	Achievement Tests	Aptitude/Ability Tests	Interest/Attitude/Preference Inventories
Administrative			
Curriculum planning and evaluation	√	√	√
Public relations	√	√	√
Selection and placement	√	√	√
Instructional			
Evaluation of learning outcomes	√	√	√
Evaluation of curriculum	√	√	√
Diagnosis of individual learning needs	√	√	√
Planning students' programs	√	√	
Guidance			
Educational	√	√	√
Vocational	√	√	√
Personal	√	√	√
Research and program evaluation	√	√	√

Achievement Tests

Achievement tests are the most frequently used external tests. Standardized achievement tests were developed and gained widespread usage because many studies indicated that teachers' grades were highly unreliable—different teachers assigned different grades to the same sample of students' work. There was a desire to make grading more objective and to standardize the grading procedures. An early standardized test of educational achievement was a spelling test developed in 1895 by Joseph Mayer Rice and personally administered to more than 13,000 students in grades 4 to 8. Rice developed three forms of the test, in order to check out the results of his findings on more than one sample. He also developed tests in arithmetic and language. Others developed tests in other areas—for example, E. L. Thorndike's *Scale for Handwriting of Children* and C. W. Stone's test of arithmetic reasoning. Thorndike also established a department of educational and psychological testing at

Teachers' College at Columbia University, where most of the early leaders in educational testing were trained, and his students were very active in developing the early standardized achievement tests.

An important contribution of these early leaders was the application of the scientific method to the study of student abilities and achievement and the recognition of the need to control many aspects of the testing situation. They developed tests in which the content was standardized, the instructions were standardized, and the scoring procedures were standardized. They also recognized the importance of having a single standard of comparison against which to judge the students' performance, so they set about collecting "national norms."

Since the first achievement battery, the *Stanford Achievement Test,* was published in 1923, other achievement batteries have been published and have been widely used. The *Stanford Achievement Test* is still being published and has been updated and revised many times. Many of the test publishers offer more than one achievement test battery. Some of the batteries cover all grades, K through 12; others are limited to certain grade levels. In addition, some publishers offer tests in specific subjects, in addition to or in place of a test battery. Some of these tests are designed to be diagnostic. In addition, there are several individually administered achievement tests, used most frequently with students who are having difficulty in school. Various kinds of achievement tests are discussed in Chapter 11. Although most of the national standardized achievement tests are multiple choice, many test publishers now offer performance assessments as well.

Tests of Aptitude/Ability

Achievement tests are designed to indicate an individual's current status. Aptitude tests are intended to indicate an individual's potential. For many years, the most widely used aptitude test was a test of "intelligence," which was thought to be a measure of students' innate ability to learn, which could be compared with their achievement test scores to ascertain whether students were "overachievers," "underachievers," or "normal achievers." However, studies of intelligence have raised serious questions about this concept and led many psychologists to conclude that whatever is measured by "intelligence" tests is also achievement, although it is a more general kind of achievement than that measured by those tests labeled "intelligence."

As early as 1927 Truman Kelley proposed the term *jangle fallacy* for the use of different terms to refer to the same phenomena. Kelley's studies indicated that correlations between measures of "achievement" and "intelligence" were as high as correlations between two achievement measures or two intelligence measures (Kelley, 1927). Later studies corroborated these findings—for example, Coleman and Cureton (1954) and Green (1974).

The finding that scores on intelligence tests are highly correlated with social class, income, and ethnic group has raised questions about the inheritability of intelligence and the extent to which intelligence can be taught. Furthermore, it has been found that the best predictor of subsequent achievement is a measure of current achievement, not an aptitude test. Several writers have attempted to deal with the relationship between achievement and aptitude. For example, the theory of cognitive psychology distinguishes between crystallized and fluid abilities. Snow and Lohman (1989) recommend that school instruction incorporate both types of abilities, and this idea is in keeping with recommendations for teaching high-level thinking skills. Many educators, including the authors of this book, agree that classroom activities should include the teaching of high-level skills and that achievement tests should measure them.

According to Hothersall (1984), "Debates and controversies over testing during the twenties were the forerunners of similar debates and controversies in later decades" (p. 330). In response to these controversies, the terminology used to refer to these tests has been modified to reflect what can be agreed on. Some people would reserve *intelligence* for tests of ability that go beyond the usual classroom activities, such as problem solving and adapting to changing circumstances. Others maintain that what is measured on intelligence tests is only abilities that are related to *school learning,* not abilities that may be equally important in some other situations.

In response to the controversies, many intelligence tests have been renamed and are called tests of "scholastic ability," "scholastic aptitude," or "school ability." In addition, many states and school districts have eliminated such tests altogether, regardless of the term used. Learning-disabled students, however, are still identified primarily through a large discrepancy in aptitude and achievement test scores, although the tests are usually administered individually.

There are also some tests of specific abilities that may be useful for guidance purposes, helping students to make plans for their future. There is also much controversy about the appropriate term to be used for these tests: whether it should be *ability* or *aptitude.* In general, those who prefer *aptitude* define it as "potential." Those who prefer *ability* argue that potential cannot be measured directly, so any test is a measure of "ability," or what an individual *can do,* rather than what he or she *might be able to learn to do.* At any rate, the terminology that is used does not provide much help in understanding what the test is about. Chapter 12 provides a fuller discussion of these issues.

Interest, Preference, Attitude, and Personality Inventories

Achievement and aptitude tests are classified as "cognitive" tests—tests of what a student knows and can do. Interest, attitude, and personality tests are classified as "noncognitive" or "affective" because the items have no right or wrong answers and responses are based on personal preferences. For this reason, many of these instruments are called "inventory" rather than "test." Chapter 13 provides a detailed discussion of these tests.

Some of these inventories were prepared to help identify vocational interests, others address personal interests, and still others ask about attitudes toward various institutions, beliefs, people, and so on. Some were developed to be used as part of the identification of serious personal problems. Some instruments of this type are called "personality tests." The extent to which the various instruments really do what they purport to do varies greatly. For many of the instruments, there is no information that supports the proposed use; others have been studied extensively, so you can find out whether the claims are supported by the studies.

Individual Tests

Most school districts employ specially trained professionals to observe and examine students who are having difficulty in school. These individuals—usually school psychologists—may provide many services in order to help understand the nature of the students' difficulty. An important part of their services involves administering individual tests of intelligence and achievement, as well as other types of instruments, such as development batteries, preference inventories for learning style, tests of specific abilities, behavior scales, neuropsychological scales, and personality scales.

Diagnosis of a student's difficulties cannot be done with a single instrument. Information from a wide range of sources must be used, and all the information must be carefully evaluated. Teachers and sometimes counselors are asked to provide information about their observations of a student; and parents, too, are usually involved in the evaluation. Medical personnel also are frequently consulted.

When an evaluation is completed, an Individualized Education Program (IEP) is prepared to guide the student's educational program. Chapter 16 provides information about the process of referral for special services.

SELECTION OF TESTS

Table 10.3 lists the steps involved in selection of an external test or test battery. The test selection process should start with identification of the purposes for which the test is to be used, followed by specification of the requirements associated with each intended use. Will it be used formatively or summatively? What content and skills should be assessed? What other information will be collected about the students?

Table 10.3 Steps in Selecting an External Test

1. Identify the purposes for the testing.
2. Select the committee.
3. Establish the content and skills to be covered.
4. Identify the technical requirements.
5. Locate possibilities for tests and obtain copies.
6. Locate sources of technical information for the tests and obtain copies.
7. Evaluate the tests for coverage of content and skills and make tentative selection.
8. Evaluate the technical qualities for the selected test.
9. Make the decision.
10. Identify additional tests or information needed, if necessary.

The next decision has to be about who will make the selection. Selection of external tests is usually handled by a committee made up of both curriculum and testing people. Teachers and other curriculum experts identify the purposes and requirements for the coverage of the tests. The test experts then identify the technical requirements for the tests.

After the purpose and requirements are identified, the possibilities are identified through use of some or all of the resources listed in the next section. Then the tests are reviewed. Teachers and other curriculum people look for tests that most closely match the school curriculum. The test experts review the most likely possibilities to see to what extent they meet acceptable technical standards. The final choice will almost always certainly involve some compromise, because it is unlikely that any single test battery or individual test will be completely satisfactory for all purposes. The committee may want to recommend that the chosen tests be supplemented by additional assessments for certain purposes.

SOURCES OF INFORMATION
ABOUT PUBLISHED TESTS

It may surprise and dismay you to learn that published tests vary widely in their technical quality (Hall, 1985, 1986). Many authors and publishers offer little information to help potential users evaluate tests and judge what a given instrument is really measuring and how well it does so. The primary guide for identifying the kind of information you need about tests is the *Standards for Educational and Psychological Testing,* which was developed by the American Educational Research Association (AERA), the American Psychological Association (APA), and the National Council on Measurement in Education (NCME), (1985). The latest edition was published in 1985, and an update is currently in preparation. The *Standards* includes recommendations for both test publishers and test users and describes the kind of evidence that should be provided about validity; reliability; test development and revision; scaling, norming, and equating; and technical manuals and user's guides.

In addition, the *Code of Fair Testing Practices in Education* (Joint Committee on Testing Practices, 1988) provides information especially for schools, school districts, and states. It provides standards for developing and selecting tests, interpreting scores, fairness, and communicating with test takers. (A copy of the *Code* is provided in Appendix C.)

For educators who are charged with selecting published assessment instruments, there are many easily accessible resources. First, there are publications that provide information about which tests are available, and some of these publications also provide reviews by test experts that point out the extent to which the tests meet the standards and discuss the good points of the tests and any problems there may be. There also are some databases that may be accessed for information.

These publications and databases are described below. The addresses and web sites for the various sources are provided in Appendix D.

Buros Institute of Mental Measurement

The Buros Institute of Mental Measurements, located at the University of Nebraska–Lincoln, periodically publishes two books that provide updated information about available tests. The most useful source of critical information about availability of tests of all kinds is the *Mental Measurements Yearbook* (MMY), which was inaugurated by Oscar K. Buros and was first published in 1938 with Dr. Buros as editor. Since then, the yearbooks have been published periodically, although not on any precise schedule. The twelfth edition was published in 1996, the thirteenth MMY in 1998. Test reviews since the eighth *Mental Measurements Yearbook* are available on an on-line computer service. This service is especially useful to secure information about tests published after the latest edition of the yearbook. For the Buros Institute web site address see Appendix D.

The editors of the *Mental Measurements Yearbook* make an attempt to keep up with newly published tests and issue updates on older ones. This is the best single source of technical information about a large number of tests of all kinds. In addition to a description and ordering information, the MMY provides critical reviews written by test specialists, along with comprehensive bibliographies and excerpts from test reviews published in professional journals. The need for critical reviews is illustrated by the following conclusions quoted from some recent reviews in the yearbook:

> "No validity or reliability evidence is provided, there are no norms, and scoring is intuitive. In short, there is little to commend this instrument."

> "The users' manual should be re-written, eliminating useless and misleading information. Users should be cautioned that the test was not designed to diagnose an individual's difficulty."

> "Until these or similar studies are completed, users must be very cautious in making any decisions based on this instrument. The only defensible usage at this time is for exploratory or experimental studies."

Another helpful publication of the Buros Institute is *Tests in Print,* which does not provide critical reviews but does provide a list of currently available tests, with descriptions of each and a reference list of professional literature relevant to the tests. Ordering information is also provided.

Educational Testing Service

The ETS Test Collection (located in Princeton, NJ) has more than 14,000 tests, along with annotated bibliographies. A monthly newsletter serves as a good source for locating new and recently revised tests, and an on-line computer service for this information is provided by Bibliographic Retrieval Services, Inc. See Appendix D for the address.

ERIC Clearinghouse on Tests, Measurement, and Evaluation

The ERIC system was established in 1966 as a nationwide information network of professional literature in education. The ERIC system collects and distributes documents such as research studies, conference papers, curriculum materials, and bibliographies. The ERIC Clearinghouse on Tests, Measurement, and Evaluation (ERIC/TM) includes documents on testing, evaluation, and learning theory. Users may access the ERIC database on-line, on CD-ROM, or through print and microfiche indexes.

The Test Center, Northwest Regional Educational Laboratory

The Test Center is a collection of assessment tools including testing resources, item banks, and curriculum materials. There are also sample computer programs for item banking operations as well as the *Tests in Microfiche* collection from Educational Testing Service, *Released Items* from the *National Assessment of Educational Progress,* and the *Northwest Evaluation Association Item Banks* in science, reading, language arts, and mathematics. Bibliographies and guides are available for most topical areas in education. In addition, the Test Center maintains TESTNET, a database of educators who are available to answer questions about their experience with a specific test or other assessment. To use TESTNET, it is necessary to complete a survey form.

Test Publishers' Catalogs

Test publishers are happy to provide catalogs to prospective purchasers of their tests. These catalogs describe the tests and suggest possible uses for them. In addition, most test companies now have web sites that contain information on test products and services. See Appendix D. However, it is important that the claims of the publishers be checked in one of the independent sources listed above, such as the *Mental Measurements Yearbook,* or some of the journals in educational measurement.

Electronic Databases

In recent years a number of databases have been established that the computer-literate educator can access to get information about available tests. Appendix D contains a list of databases; and new ones are being added almost daily.

ADMINISTRATION OF
STANDARDIZED GROUP TESTS

An important part of making a test standardized is to have the test administered in a standardized way—that is, to see that every student takes the test under the same conditions as every other student. In order for this to happen, all teachers and others who administer the tests must understand the importance of following the instructions exactly.

Teachers who are administering a given test for the first time should participate in a special training session. This training should cover the following material:

Purpose of the test

General test administration procedures

Procedures for the specific test

The purpose of the test and the specific procedures usually cover such information as the following:

How the scores will be used

Overview of the test

Subtests and test level for each grade

Examination of the test booklets and answer sheets

Study of the administrator's manual and directions

Review of the testing schedule by subtests

Review of the time limits

The training should also cover the following information about general procedures in administering standardized tests:

Appropriate assistance for examinees

Appropriate procedures for handling students with special needs

Procedures for preparing materials for return to the testing office

Test security procedures

The reason why examiners need training is to ensure that the administration is standardized, so that students' scores may legitimately be interpreted in reference to the norms. A test may be invalidated at several points. For example, if the administrator gives students more information than they should receive, so that they receive unwarranted help with specific items, their scores will not be valid. Or if students are allowed to take more time than the directions call for, or if they are not allowed the full time, the scores cannot be interpreted by use of the norms tables.

Sometimes special accommodations must be made for handicapped students. The allowable accommodations vary from one program to another. Sometimes the accommodation is simply to excuse the student from the test. Some accommodations involve only provision for use of a wheelchair; others involve the way the test is presented, the way the responses are recorded, or the time limits.

The Americans with Disabilities Act of 1992 requires that all individuals must have access to testing for licensing or credentialing. In school testing programs the way disabled students are handled depends on the purpose of the testing (Fischer, 1994). The decision as to who participates in a large-scale testing program and how they should participate varies from state to state.

The decision about how to handle children on an Individualized Education Program is also made by the IEP team, which under IDEA 1997 decides the conditions under which students are tested. If the team decides the test will not provide valid information it can specify alternative ways to measure the student's progress (Kupper, 1998).

States may only exclude students who are receiving special education services if such a stipulation appears on an Individualized Education Program. One consideration is the percentage of time the student is mainstreamed (Kupper, 1998). A few states make "appropriate accommodations," for other students by considering such factors as the curricular validity for the student, the possibility of adverse effect on the student, and whether the test is likely to yield a valid score.

There is also wide disagreement as to who should make the decision about whether to exclude some students and which students to exclude. Sometimes this decision is made by the testing agency, but often it is left up to the state or local school agency. Some suggest that students with disabilities should be included so the results will be representative of all students, and that accommodations be made for them. Perhaps a better solution would be to exclude those for whom the test is not valid and simply report the number and percentage of students so excluded. At any rate, this dilemma is far from being resolved.

INTERPRETATION AND
USE OF TEST SCORES

In order for tests to be used appropriately to monitor student achievement gains, educators need to understand both the possibilities and the limitations of the test scores. It is essential that scores be interpreted as *indicators,* not as the final answer, and that limitations as to coverage and quality of items be understood. It is also important that we remember that all scores have some degree of error and that we make allowances for it. In subsequent chapters in Part Three we discuss these problems as they relate to the various types of tests, and we suggest ways to handle them.

Also, the public needs a better understanding of how to interpret the scores. Both those who are pushing for high-stakes usage and those who oppose such uses need to become much more sophisticated about the technical issues involved in testing. The public debate in newspapers and in journals and newsletters of various organizations indicates the ignorance on which much of the debate rests.

There are too many variables and factors that are not under teacher control but which affect pupil performance on any test for the tests to be used to evaluate teaching (see, for example, Innes, 1972). However, if the tests are used only as part of the information base about students, rather than for high-stakes decisions about the adequacy of teaching, external tests can be useful to teachers and other school personnel. This part of the book is directed toward providing the information educators need to use the information appropriately.

SUMMARY

- Standardized external tests are widely used in American schools.
- To be useful, tests should meet accepted standards developed by education, psychological, and measurement professionals.
- Test must also be administered and interpreted correctly.
- Teachers may be asked to help select, administer, and interpret scores on external tests.
- Most school districts have a group of specialists who administer and interpret individual tests to students who are having special difficulty.

STUDY QUESTIONS

1. What are the three types of externally created assessments?
2. What are the main reasons why external tests are administered and used by school personnel?
3. Why is it important to involve a variety of persons in the test selection process?

FOR YOUR PROFESSIONAL GROWTH

1. What is the major difference between standardized achievement tests and classroom tests?
2. If you are asked to serve on a test selection committee, what will be your best source of information about the quality of various tests?
3. Have you ever participated in an IEP conference? How did you feel about the outcome? What, if anything, would you have done differently?

11

৯৹

Achievement Tests

PREVIEW

In this chapter we discuss externally developed tests of achievement—that is, achievement tests developed by someone other than the classroom teacher. Most of these tests are developed by commercial testing agencies, but some are developed by state educational agencies, and some accompany textbooks. Sometimes a state selects a commercially developed test battery as a required test for all public schools in the state. Even more often, school districts select such a test and require that it be administered in designated grades in the district. In addition, most school districts have a group of specially trained staff people who administer and interpret individual assessments, including tests of achievement, as a part of diagnosing the learning needs of individual students.

The expectation is that an external test, regardless of who develops it, will provide an impartial evaluation of how well (or how poorly) students in a school, district, or state are doing. The results of these tests are used in making important decisions about large numbers of students and programs. Some of the testing programs are expected to lead to improvement in the educational system.

The issues and concerns that we discussed in the chapters on preparing classroom assessments also arise in the development of external tests. And there are many other issues that do not come up when a test is limited to a single classroom. In this chapter we focus on the issues that are unique to external achievement tests. We start with an overview of external achievement testing and then discuss the selection, administration, and interpretation and use of scores on these tests.

MAJOR TOPICS

Overview of External Achievement Tests
Selection of an External Achievement Test
Administration of Standardized Achievement Tests
Interpretation and Use of Scores on Achievement Tests
Problems with the Use of Achievement Test Scores
Reporting Test Scores
Ethical Considerations in Achievement Testing

OVERVIEW OF
EXTERNAL ACHIEVEMENT TESTS

The most obvious difference between external achievement tests and classroom tests is the extent to which the teacher is involved. Teachers make the decisions about classroom tests—and do all the work! But teachers may have very little to say about what external test is used, what content and skills are covered, how the tests are scored and reported, and how the results are interpreted and used. The teacher's task is primarily to administer tests correctly and to interpret and use the results for the students in his or her own classroom. Counselors and administrators also play a role in interpretation to parents, students, and other educational professionals.

You will do a better job with these tasks if you understand what the external achievement tests are all about. In addition, you may decide to volunteer for committees that make some of the important decisions about the tests—for example, the test selection committee.

We will discuss each of the issues involved in selecting, developing, administering, and using external tests. But first we review some important terms and discuss the sources of the tests.

Terminology

Certain terms are used in specialized ways in discussions of external tests. Unfortunately, sometimes these terms are confused even by people who are supposedly knowledgeable about educational measurement. The most frequently confused terms are listed in Table 11.1. Many of these terms have been introduced in earlier chapters. Check out this table to be sure your understanding of the terms is correct.

Commercially Developed Tests

Many achievement test batteries are available from test publishers. Each of them has many levels, with each level covering only one or two grades. The tests included at each level vary somewhat. Most of the test batteries have a *basic* battery and a *complete* battery. The basic battery usually includes tests in reading, mathematics, and

Table 11.1 Frequently Confused Terms

Test	A procedure that is perceived by both teachers and students as a *formal* assessment device. May be objective, open-ended, or performance.
Assessment	Any procedure used to gather information about students or teachers or both. May be formal or informal. May be *objective, performance,* or *observational.*
External test	A test developed outside the school. May be *objective* or *performance* or both.
Classroom test	An assessment developed by a classroom teacher for use with his or her classes.
Standardized test	An assessment that provides the same items, administered under the same conditions, and is scored with the same procedures for each person who takes the test. May be objective or performance.
Objective test	An assessment that is scored objectively—that is, it does not require any judgment on the part of the scorer. The most usual type of objective test is a multiple-choice test.
Performance test	An assessment that requires the examinee to manipulate materials or equipment in order to accomplish a specified purpose. Requires a trained scorer.
Standards	Preset goals for the performance of a student or group of students.
Norms	A set of scores that indicates how a specified group of pupils actually performed on an assessment and that can be used to evaluate the performance of other, similar, students and groups of students.
Norm-referenced interpretation	Comparison of a test score with the scores made by some appropriate reference group.
Criterion-referenced interpretation	Comparison of a score with the total possible to determine mastery of a list of objectives, the domain of a test, or a preset standard. Also called *domain-referenced* or *objective-referenced.*

language, but the specific subtests vary somewhat. The complete battery includes tests in science, social science (or social studies), and study skills. Table 11.2 provides information about the Stanford Achievement Test Battery that illustrates how this works. Notice that the reading subtests change from kindergarten level to the third grade, then stay the same through Grade 13.0. Also notice that study skills, science, and social science are not tested until later grades. Different publishers use slightly different terms for some of these subtests, but all of the test batteries that extend over a wide range of grades and that include the primary grades use a similar pattern. Many publishers now offer a diagnostic version of some of the tests and some performance tests, especially in writing and mathematics.

The most frequently used achievement batteries are listed in Appendix F, with information about the publisher and the grade levels covered. The Stanford Achievement Test was first published in 1923 and it is still being published, although the coverage has changed over time. This is also true of other early achievement batteries that are still being published, such as the Metropolitan Achievement Tests, California Achievement Tests, Iowa Tests of Basic Skills, Iowa Tests of Educational Development, and Sequential Tests of Educational Progress. The well-known achievement batteries provide norms based on large groups of students who are reasonably representative of the national population.

In addition to the batteries, there are also tests of a single area, such as *Reading, Mathematics, Science,* and *Social Studies.* In addition to the group tests there are

Table 11.2 Content Coverage of Stanford Achievement Test Batteries at Various Levels

Test Level	Early Ach. Test		Primary			Intermediate 1,2,3	Advanced 1,2	Test of Acad. Skills 1,2,3
	1	2	1	2	3			
Grade level	K.0-K.5	K.5-1.5	1.5-2.5	2.5-3.5	3.5-4.5	4.5-7.5	7.5-9.9	9.0-13.0
Reading								
Sounds and letters	X	X						
Word reading	X	X						
Word Study Skills			X	X				
Sentence Reading		X						
Comprehension			X	X	X	X	X	X
Vocabulary				X	X	X	X	X
Total	X	X	X	X	X	X	X	X
Mathematics	X	X						X
Problem Solving			X	X	X	X	X	
Procedures			X	X	X	X	X	
Total			X	X	X	X	X	
Language Form S			X	X	X	X	X	X
Spelling			X	X	X	X	X	X
Listening			X		X	X	X	
Words and stories	X	X		X				
Study Skills						X	X	X
Environment	X	X						
Science					X	X	X	X
Social Science					X	X	X	X

some achievement tests that are administered individually by specially trained examiners. For the individual tests, the norms are not so representative, partly because of the limited use.

Addresses for the publishers are provided in Appendix E. Other information about these tests and about other tests is available from the publishers and from the sources listed in Appendix D.

State Assessments

Many states have had state testing programs or state assessment programs for many years. Initially, many of these programs were "service" programs. The state agency provided one or more test batteries, and the schools or school systems could borrow the reusable booklets and purchase answer sheets from the program. The state agency usually also provided scoring services and, sometimes, some summary reports.

All this changed with the launch of *Sputnik* by the Soviet Union in 1957. That event led both educators and politicians in the United States to scramble in a search for accountability that has continued to the present time. Most of the early leaders in the development of standardized achievement tests had ideas about improvements that might be made in schools as a result of comparing student performance with that of a national sample. However only after the accountability movement became strong did we see the development of state assessment programs with high stakes—where failure to reach a prescribed level resulted in denial of a high school diploma, for example. This problem was discussed in Chapter 2.

Today, some states and districts select a commercially prepared, nationally normed test and simply compare their schools with national norms and with other schools, other districts, or other states. Other states and districts have developed their own tests, using teams of teachers and other educators. Still others use educators to plan for the tests but contract the actual development of the tests to commercial test developers.

National Assessments

National Assessment of Educational Progress. With the assistance of funding from the Carnegie Corporation and the Ford Foundation, the Educational Commission of the States in 1969 set up NAEP, a project to survey the knowledge, skills, and attitudes of young Americans in several subject areas: science, writing, citizenship, reading, literature, music, social studies, mathematics, career and occupational development, and art. Tests in other areas such as basic life skills, health, and energy have been included from time to time. Originally, NAEP reports were designed specifically to provide only information about the nation as a whole, and no information was provided for making comparisons between states. However, that changed in 1988, when Congress passed legislation that allowed state-by-state comparisons on a voluntary basis, beginning in 1990.

America 2000, Goals 2000. In 1989 the *America 2000* program was passed and its successor, *Goals 2000,* was passed in 1994. The purpose of these laws was to develop national goals and standards and to develop national assessments to monitor progress. Although certain precautions were built into the program—for example, no high-stakes purposes for a period of five years—the intent is to improve education and monitor that improvement with a system of assessments.

American Achievement Tests. President Bush proposed the American Achievement Tests in 1991. Because of widespread opposition, Congress created the National Council on Education Standards and Testing (NCEST) in 1991 to consider whether a system of voluntary national tests should be established. The NCEST report was negative toward establishment of national tests but recommended a system of tests to be designed or selected by states. This proposal was not implemented.

Voluntary National Test. The Voluntary National Test (VNT) was proposed by President Clinton in February, 1997 and was supported by the Business Roundtable's Education Task Force, several CEOs and presidents of high-tech companies, and a few governors. It is not so broad as the American Achievement Tests, being limited to one subject in grade 4 (reading) and one in grade 8 (mathematics). For a time the VNT faced little opposition (Linn & Baker, 1997). However, there has been little progress recently.

Both VNT and the American Achievement Tests were tied to NAEP but in different ways. The American Achievement Tests would have been a short version of NAEP. The Voluntary National Test would not use items from NAEP, but NAEP would provide the framework for the specifications of the test and the score scale.

Textbook Tests

Textbook tests are a special case because, like other external tests, they are *used,* not created, by educators and they cannot be easily changed. But, like teacher-generated tests, they provide information on students' achievement of very narrowly defined objectives. Furthermore, if they do not function well, they may be discarded with few consequences. However, textbook tests are subject to some important problems and should be used and interpreted with great care.

If you elect to use a textbook test, look it over carefully, *before* you give it to your students. Look back at our suggestions for preparing tests (Chapter 6). Textbook tests should be as good as your own tests would be if you followed our instructions. Examine each test carefully. Does it adequately cover the content and skills in the chapter or unit? Does it represent what you taught and emphasized? If it does not, discard it. Using such a test, with inadequate content validity, will result in worse than no information. It will create misleading information. Remember, the fact that a test has been published does not mean that the test is of high quality. Be a smart consumer of these tests. They are convenient, but they also must be valid, reliable, and fair.

Individual Achievement Tests

Individual achievement tests are used primarily for evaluating students who are having difficulty in school. Most of the individual tests require that the examiner have a master's degree or special certification or both. The achievement tests are usually administered along with an intelligence (scholastic ability) test and other specialized instruments, and they are usually limited to tests of language, reading, and mathematics. The most commonly used individual achievement tests are listed in Appendix F.

Although the individual tests were developed to serve an important purpose, many of them have serious problems. Often they have not been developed with a solid construct of what content and skills ought to be covered, and there are almost never satisfactory norms for them. These deficiencies mean that the tests must be used with a great deal of caution, and that the norms can seldom be used with great confidence. Often the most useful aspect of an individual test is that a skilled examiner can use it as a standardized observation schedule and from the examiner's experience with many children, he or she can interpret the child's behavior even though the norms are not very useful. In addition to the skills ostensibly covered by the test, a skilled examiner can make inferences about the child's attention span, receptive language, speech, handling of frustration, and thinking strategies.

SELECTION OF AN
EXTERNAL ACHIEVEMENT TEST

If you have an opportunity to participate in the selection of an external achievement test, you should know what the pitfalls are and where you can look for information about commercial tests. Chapter 10 covered much of the general information about selecting tests. Here we discuss specifically the selection of an achievement test:

1. What technical qualities should you look for?
2. What is the purpose of the test?
3. What content and skills should the test cover?

Technical Qualities

Having come this far in this book, you should have a fairly good idea as to the technical qualities tests must have if they are to serve the intended purpose adequately. You should also have a good idea of the time-consuming processes that must be carried out in order to ensure that tests have these qualities. The test should be valid, reliable, and fair. In addition, in order to be interpreted correctly, it must have norms that are truly representative. Although we have already discussed these qualities in general terms, we present a brief review of them as they apply specifically to external achievement tests.

Validity.   The matter of what should be covered on an achievement test is central to validity. You have seen how difficult it can be to decide what is to be covered on a classroom test for a single unit of study. Textbook tests should provide complete coverage of the content and skills presented in each chapter and unit. For state-wide or national tests the decision becomes even more complicated.

In your classroom tests and in textbook tests you are concerned only with what students should have learned in a fairly short period of time. With state or national tests, the concern is with learning over an extended period of time—usually several years. For classroom tests, you can limit your testing to material presented in a single textbook, but state and national tests must be appropriate for all textbooks that might be in use.

As we have discussed in earlier chapters, it is important that any test address higher-level thinking skills, not merely memorization. This is one reason why you may decide to use performance tests as part of your classroom assessment. Many of the commercially published tests, including those accompanying textbooks and mandated state tests, are now including performance tests.

In order to ensure that the items really measure the intended content and skills, they must be well written, and the scoring must be valid and reliable. If you include a few poor items on a classroom test, you will know it immediately, and you can usually re-test using improved items, adjusting the scores in a way that enhance the validity. Teachers also immediately know when a textbook test fails to cover desirable content or emphasizes inappropriate skills. You will not want to use these items or tests if they do not work well. For state-wide and national tests, such choices or corrections are not feasible, so all items must be very carefully written and should be pretested before they are used.

Another important validity issue is the effect on the educational program of having mandated tests that are used to hold teachers and schools accountable. Many studies have demonstrated that, under this condition, teachers limit their teaching to just those things included on the test and spend many hours of instructional time drilling students on specific items and item types.

Reliability. Some other terms for reliability are *dependability* and *consistency*. Poorly written items may lead to problems with reliability. In general, the more assessment information you have, the more confidence you have in the conclusions you draw from it. You can improve the reliability of your classroom assessments by using a great many and a great variety of assessments. This is not possible with state and national tests, so they must be pretested. Training of item writers is also essential.

Fairness. Test items for all external tests, whether textbook, state, or national, should be reviewed and tried out to be sure they are fair to all ethnic and gender groups. Several procedures have been developed to handle this matter. In order to ensure that the procedures are correct and are correctly carried out, the person who directs the project must be familiar with the procedures and know how to carry them out.

Appropriate Norms. Since part of the point of national and state-wide tests is to compare students' scores with norms in order to evaluate their performance and the quality of the schools and the teaching, it is important for the norms to be dependable and representative of the group with whom the students should be compared. With a state test involving only in-state comparison, this is not a serious problem, since all targeted students will be included. For national tests, many norms samples are limited to only those students who are easily accessible, and there is a serious question about whether the norms are truly representative.

At this point you may be wondering whether all national and state testing programs have taken the steps and used people with appropriate training to do the various tasks so that you may feel sure that all external tests have all the desirable qualities. As you may suspect, the answer is *no*. Many articles have been written deploring the quality of the testing that is being done, as well as the undesirable outcomes of this testing. You may want to reread parts of Chapter 2 to refresh your memory about some of these criticisms.

Purpose of the Test

The two often opposing purposes of external achievement testing are (1) to measure and evaluate the *progress of individual students* and (2) to evaluate the educational program for purposes of *program evaluation* and *accountability.*

Measure of Individual Progress.

As we have indicated in previous chapters, the first achievement tests were developed as a method of monitoring the progress of individual students, so they could be retaught material they had failed to learn. This is still the most defensible reason for external testing programs. If you have only the results of your own tests for your classes, you have no way of knowing what is a reasonable expectation and whether your class as a whole and the individual students in the class are making acceptable progress. Of course, after you have taught a few years, you develop a feeling about this, but you may want to know how your students compare with students in other schools. This is the kind of information you can get from well-developed, carefully normed national achievement tests.

Program Evaluation/Accountability.

A legitimate use of test scores is to help educators determine how well an instructional program is working. Most of the early leaders in the development of standardized achievement tests had ideas of improvements that might be made in schools as a result of comparing student performance with a national sample. And when schools or school districts begin an innovative program, there is a need to collect data to see how it is working, and this evaluation nearly always includes test data. It was only after *Sputnik* "launched" the accountability movement that we saw the development of state assessment programs with high stakes.

Many states began their own accountability testing programs, often starting with a "basic skills" or "minimum-competency" test that students had to pass in order to receive a high school diploma. The problem with such limited tests is that the curriculum often became confined to only those skills covered by the tests. This was discussed in Chapter 2.

Content and Skills to Be Covered

If information from a test is to be valid for any purpose, the test must cover the content and skills that are supposed to be taught. The problem is that there are great variations from one district to another and from one state to another as to *what* is to be taught and *when* it is to be taught. For example, some states have adopted a policy that the whole language approach is to be used in teaching primary language arts classes, while other states prescribe the phonetic approach, and still others recommend the eclectic approach. There is also great variation as to when certain concepts are introduced in science and social studies classes. This is one of the reasons for the pressure to adopt a national curriculum.

It would certainly simplify the decision about what should be covered on tests if this decision had been made and all school districts had agreed to use the adopted curriculum. However, many people are opposed to the idea of a national curriculum for many reasons, so test developers face the necessity of developing tests that cut across all curricula. It is up to a school district or a state to select the test that is closest to the philosophy and specific content used in the situation in which the test will be used, or to develop a test if a satisfactory one is not available.

Before test selection or development is done, it is essential that the curriculum has been carefully studied and that there is agreement about what it should be.

Sources of Information About Achievement Tests

The major test publishers are listed in Appendix E, along with their addresses. All of them will provide catalogs that list and describe the tests they publish, and most of them have representatives who are available to meet with test selection committees to assist them in going over the materials. In addition, the test selection committee may consult some of the technical publications, such as those of the Buros Institute, for lists of tests and for critical reviews of the available tests. Chapter 10 listed and described these publications. Information is also provided about web sites in Appendix D.

ADMINISTRATION OF
STANDARDIZED ACHIEVEMENT TESTS

In order to be *standardized,* a test must be administered to all students under the same conditions whenever it is given. Otherwise, a comparison of the scores of students in your school with the national norms might be misleading.

The manual of a good standardized test spells out exactly how the test is to be administered. It provides the exact wording of the instructions and tells what materials students are to have available—for example, whether a calculator may be used for mathematics items, whether a dictionary may be used, and so on. It describes what the teacher may and may not do during the test administration.

Special Accommodations for Students with Disabilities

In school testing programs the way students with disabilities are handled depends on the purpose of the testing. Sometimes they are simply excused from taking the test. Sometimes the instructions are read to a student with a disability, or the time limits are extended. In some cases the student takes a test that was designed for a younger group of students. The school IEP team decides what solution will be used. It should be limited to only those students for whom the test publisher recommends it, and you should follow the publisher's instructions about whether students with disabilities are included in the norms group. Four ways of handling the situation are discussed below.

Exclusion. The decision as to who participates in a large-scale testing program and how individuals should participate varies from state to state. National laws also apply in some situations. Chapter 10 presents a discussion of this situation.

Extending Time Limits. When an individual's difficulty results from a motor problem or from slow cognitive processing or thinking, the solution for accommodation may be to allow more time. Doing this is quite appropriate when the test is a *power* test—that is, a test for which the time limits are expected to be sufficient for all students to finish the test. On the other hand, if speed of performance is a concern in the testing as, for example, in a speeded typing test, this solution is not reasonable.

Reading the Test to the Student. If a student is able to process the material on a test but cannot see well enough to read the materials, arrangements can be made to have someone, perhaps an aide, read the items to the student and record the answers. The person doing the reading and recording must be careful not to give the student any other assistance.

Out-of-Level Testing. In some school districts students who are having academic difficulties are tested with an achievement battery designed for younger students. This strategy seems feasible because most achievement batteries are designed to cover only about three grades. Poor achievers often make scores that are below chance, so their scores cannot be interpreted. A *chance score* is the score a student would make on an objective test by simply marking randomly. On a true-false test or any other test made up of 2-option items, the chance score would be 50 percent, or half of the items. On a 4-option multiple-choice test, the chance score would be 25 percent of the items, and on a 5-option test, the chance score would be 20 percent of the items. Thus, scores at or below chance may have no meaning, because the students could make those scores by simply marking randomly and not reading the items at all. Although some investigators conclude that not many students actually mark their test papers in a completely random fashion, such scores are quite unreliable and do not provide a good indication of a student's achievement level.

The suggestion that poor students should be tested with a lower-level test presupposes that these students will actually read and respond to the items on an easier test. This is a questionable assumption, because many of these students have learned not to try on any test; however, Roland Yoshida (1976) found that out-of-level testing increased the percentage of special education students scoring above the chance level, and some experts recommend that out-of-level testing be tried. Others suggest that testing of these students be limited to individually administered tests.

INTERPRETATION AND USE OF SCORES ON ACHIEVEMENT TESTS

The interpretation of scores on an achievement test may be interpreted in two major ways: criterion referenced or norm referenced, and there are many types of norm-referenced scores. Interpretation of scores involves an understanding of various kinds of norms and of errors of measurement and of how to evaluate gains.

Criterion-Referenced Scores

Criterion-referenced scores are also called *domain-referenced, content-referenced scores* or *curriculum-based assessment scores*. The interpretation of the scores is in terms of the specific information the students have learned and the extent to which a student has mastered the content (or *domain*) or has met a designated *criterion*.

Strictly speaking, a criterion-referenced or curriculum-based test must be *developed,* not simply interpreted. The content must be carefully defined and balanced. We discussed this issue in the chapters in Part Two, so you should understand how difficult this task can be, particularly for a state or national examination.

The intent of a criterion-referenced interpretation is that we will be able to speak of *mastery* of the specified content. This concept works fairly well when we are concerned with only a limited content. However, it makes little sense to speak of mastery of an entire discipline of study, especially if we focus on higher-level thinking skills.

Norm-Referenced Scores

Regardless of whether we can make a criterion-referenced interpretation, it is also useful to know how well a student does in comparison with other students of the same grade or age. We can get this information by referring to a table of norms. It is important to remember that norms simply indicate how the norming sample actually performed; they do *not* indicate how well those students should do. In other words, norms are *not* standards. Standards must be set by human judgment. The term *standard* is usually used to refer to a content-referenced interpretation, but sometimes educational goals are expressed in a way that implies the existence of a standard, as in "Every student will achieve grade level on a nationally normed achievement test in language arts and mathematics."

There are many kinds of norms, and all of them provide useful information to students, their parents, the teacher, and the school administration. The various kinds of normed scores are derived in different ways and have different characteristics. In order to use these scores, you should become thoroughly aware of the kind of information the various scores provide and of the precautions you must take in using the information. We introduced this topic in Chapter 4, and we are revisiting it in this chapter. When you have to interpret scores on external tests, you should read the manual carefully and be sure you understand which scale each type of score uses, so you can interpret it correctly. Figure 4.3 in Chapter 4 helps to clarify the relationship between the most common types of normative scores. You may want to refer back to that figure to refresh your memory about how these various types of scores are related.

The characteristics of each type of normative score are summarized in Table 11.3, and the advantages and disadvantages of each are described below.

Grade Equivalent Scores. *Grade equivalent scores* (GEs) are most useful for elementary school subjects that are studied continuously at increasing levels of skill and complexity over many years. To obtain grade equivalent norms, a test must be given at least twice a year to a large number of students who are representative of each grade. Usually the test is given in October and again in April, and the average raw score (RS) for the grade in October is set equal to $x.3$ and that for April is set equal to $x.8$, where x is the grade at which the test is normed.

For example, if the mean raw score for fourth graders on the October administration of a reading test is 23 and the mean raw score on the April administration of the same test is 35, then a score of 23 would have a GE of 4.2, and a score of 35 would have a GE of 4.8. Suppose that the test has 60 items and we want to get GEs for all scores from 1 to 60. We would need to do some mathematical operations called interpolation and extrapolation.

To estimate the GEs between the scores corresponding to the two means, we use *interpolation,* a process that assumes that average gains in the raw scores will

Table 11.3 Characteristics of Normative Scores

Score	Range	Mean	Meaning of Score	Range of "Average"
Scores based on one grade level				
Standard Scores	–4.0 to +4.0	0	Distance (+ or –) of a score from the mean in terms of SD units	–.1 to +.1
Transformed standard Scores				
T-score	10 to 90	50	M=50, SD=10	40 to 60
DIQ	40 to 160	100	M=100, SD=15	85 to 115
	36 to 164	100	M=100, SD=16	84 to 116
Percentile Rank	1 to 99	50	Percentage of students making that score or below	16 to 84
Stanine	1 to 5	5	Position on a 9 point scale	4 to 6
Scores extending across many grade levels				
Grade Equivalents (GE)	x.0 to x.10 For each grade	x.?	Grade group for which the score is the mean	x.0–x.9 (Depends on date of testing)
Extended Normalized Score Scale	0 to 99 or 0 to 999	Depends on grade level	Position in a distribution that extends across several grade levels	

occur in a smooth pattern. From the example above, there was an average gain in raw score means of 2 points per month over the 6 months, so we can list the values shown in Table 11.4.

Similarly, we can extend our scale by assuming that gains in means before October and after April would occur at the same 2-point per month rate, thus extending our scale. This is called *extrapolation*. Table 11.5 illustrates how scores are interpolated between the actual test dates and extrapolated to one month before and two months after the test was given.

It is easy to see from these examples that grade equivalent scores are not very exact. Furthermore, it has been demonstrated that students do not increase their achievement on a smooth scale of increments but instead proceed by a series of

Table 11.4   Example of Interpolated Scores

Month of Test	RS	GE
October	23	4.1
November	25*	4.2*
December	27*	4.3*
January	29*	4.4*
February	31*	4.5*
March	33*	4.6*
April	35	4.7

*Interpolated score

Table 11.5   Example of Interpolated and Extrapolated Scores for Three Grades

Month of Test	Third Grade		Fourth Grade		Fifth Grade	
	RS	GE	RS	GE	RS	GE
September	1	3.0**	21	4.0**	41	5.0**
October	3	3.1	23	4.1	43	5.1
November	5	3.2*	25	4.2*	45	5.2*
December	7	3.3*	27	4.3*	47	5.3*
January	9	3.4*	29	4.4*	49	5.4*
February	11	3.5*	31	4.5*	51	5.5*
March	13	3.6*	33	4.6*	53	5.6*
April	15	3.7	35	4.7	55	5.7
May	17	3.8**	37	4.8**	57	5.8**
June	19	3.9**	39	4.9**	59	5.9**

*Interpolated score
**Extrapolated score

giant steps. There are some other limitations for grade equivalent scores. These limitations are listed in Table 11.6.

In spite of the limitations, grade equivalent scores do help us to understand approximately how students are achieving.

Table 11.6 Limitations of Grade Equivalent Scores

1. Grade equivalents are *not* standards. They simply tell what a sample of students did. They do *not* tell what these students should do.
2. The units at different parts of the scale are different. A GE gain of 0.1 indicates different gains at different grade levels and at different months of a single year. For example, a GE gain of 1 year at the sixth grade represents a greater gain than 1 year at the second grade level. This is especially true when you are looking at extrapolated scores.
3. A sixth grader who makes a grade equivalent of 8.5 is *not* achieving at the level of eighth grade students. Instead, the sixth grade student is performing as an eighth grade student would have done on this *sixth* grade test, assuming that the gains follow the pattern found in the current grade.
4. The larger the gap between the grade equivalent and the actual grade of the student, the more difficult is the interpretation, because achievement tests are typically normed for only three adjacent grade levels. In the case of a sixth grade test, it would be administered to fifth, sixth, and seventh graders. Eighth grade students would not take the test.

Percentile Ranks. The most common type of derived score is *percentile rank*, which runs from 1 to 99 with a median of 50. The percentile score tells us the position of a score in the entire distribution of scores. For example, if a score has a percentile rank of 60 this indicates that 60 percent of scores for students in the norms group fall at or below that score. To obtain percentile ranks, all students of a given grade who take a given test are placed in rank order, and the number of students at each score level (*frequency* or *f*) is tabulated. The number scoring at or below each score is determined (*cumulative frequency* or *cf*), and the cumulative frequencies are divided by the total number and then multiplied by 100 to eliminate decimals. This process is illustrated in the simple example presented in Figure 11.1.

The concept of percentiles is easy to understand, and the computations are easy and straightforward. However, there is a problem with percentiles: The intervals between percentiles are not equal, so percentile differences at the top and bottom of a scale represent much greater differences in raw score than the same percentile differences in the middle of the scale. In the example shown in Figure 11.1, a gain of one raw score point from 5 to 6 changes the percentile score from 52 to 66, a gain of 14 percentile points. However, a gain of one raw score point from 9 to 10 increases the percentile score only 4 points.

Standard Scores. The most precise method of developing norms is to use standard scores. The process for computing standard scores was explained in Chapter 4 and is reviewed and expanded here. To compute standard scores, the mean and standard deviation must first be computed. Then the difference (plus or minus)

RAW SCORE	f*	cf**	f/cf	PERCENTILE
10	2	50	1.00	100
9	3	48	.96	96
8	5	45	.90	90
7	7	40	.80	80
6	7	33	.66	66
5	8	26	.52	52
4	7	18	.36	36
3	6	11	.22	22
2	4	5	.10	10
1	1	1	.02	2
TOTAL	50			

*Frequency
**Cumulative frequency

FIGURE 11.1 Illustration of the Computation of Percentile Scores

between each score and the mean is computed. Finally, the difference is divided by the standard deviation, so the standard score is expressed as the difference between the score and the mean, in SD units. This yields a set of decimal values, half of which are positive and half negative.

Usually these scores are further transformed in order to eliminate the decimals and negative values. This is done by selecting a convenient number to use as the mean of the transformed distribution, and multiplying the SD units by a convenient constant.

An example of standard scores that is familiar to most college students is the scale on which each part of the *Scholastic Assessment Test* (SAT) score is reported. The mean is set at 500, and the SD difference is multiplied by 100. So a raw score that is 1 standard deviation above the mean is reported as a standard score of 600, while a score 1 standard deviation below the mean is reported as a standard score of 400. A score exactly at the mean is reported as a standard score of 500. Figures 4.2 and 4.3 in Chapter 4 show how this works.

Stanines. The stanine scale is one commonly used system of standard scores that divides the score distribution into nine levels. Levels 2 through 8 are each ½ SD in width, and stanines 1 and 9 split the rest of the distribution. The middle score, stanine 5, covers the range of ¼ SD above and below the mean. Except for stanines 1 and 9, stanine scores have equal units.

Normal Curve Equivalent. The *normal curve equivalent* is a form of standard score that can be interpreted as a position score like the percentile rank. It has a mean of 50 and a standard deviation of approximately 21 points. This value for the standard deviation is used so that the range of NCE scores runs from 1 to 99 and NCE scores of 1, 50, and 99 are equal to the same percentile rank. Percentile and NCE scores vary considerably at other points in the distribution, and the NCE scores are less spread out in the middle and more spread out at the extremes. NCE scores are useful for comparing the achievement of students from year to year. A positive difference in the NCEs is considered evidence of achievement growth.

Normalized Score Scale. The extended normalized score scale was developed to indicate examinee performance on a continuum for a particular area of achievement, such as mathematics problem solving, for all grades for which the test is given. This type of scaling works only when all levels of a test are on a continuum of content; so it is not useful for achievement in many high school courses. Different publishers use different names for the normalized scale score. For the California Achievement Test it is called the "obtained scale score," and for the Terra Nova it is called "scale score." "Standard score" is the term used by the Iowa Test of Basic Skills and the Metropolitan Achievement Test.

The scores are usually three digits, but there is no agreed-on range for the scores. For some tests the range is from 0 to 99 but for others the range is from 0 to 999.

This type of scale score is of greatest interest to evaluators of special programs who need some way to evaluate students' progress across years of the programs' operation. Although these scores are included in the test reports, many teachers and counselors are not sure about how to interpret them, and there is little information about what amount of change should be expected in a year.

Errors of Measurement

Another problem that educators must deal with when we try to interpret a student's scores is that of errors of measurement. We discussed this concept in Chapter 4, and you may want to refer back to that chapter. As we pointed out, there is some error in every measurement. When you are trying to evaluate a student's progress, you want to be sure that any gain the student may have made is real and that it is not simply a chance variation. One way to explore this issue is to look at printouts with percentile bands. They tell you the range within which the "true" score lies. You can look at percentile bands from year to year and check their degree of overlap. See Figure 11.2.

Some achievement tests and test batteries report diagnostic information that may help you find out what is working in your class and where more teaching is needed. Unfortunately, some of this diagnostic information is based on too few items to be really dependable, so you have to look at other indicators as well. Of course, some achievement tests cover a limited area and have been carefully planned to provide quite reliable diagnostic information. Most of the truly diagnostic tests are in reading, although there are a few in mathematics. Also, most of the truly diagnostic tests are individual tests.

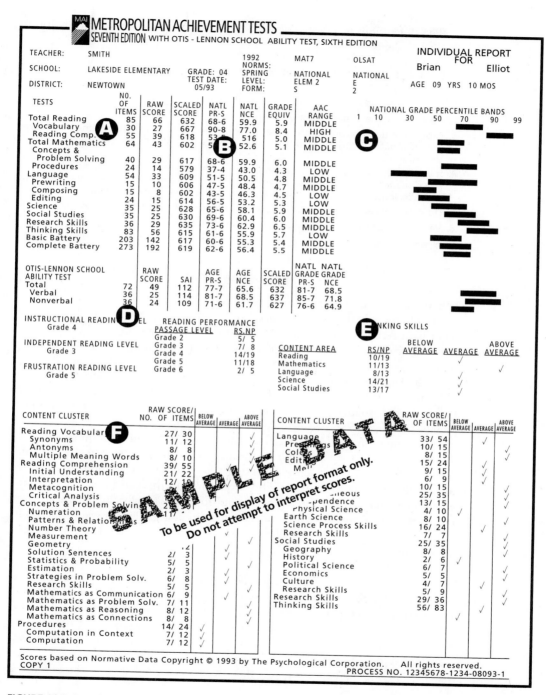

FIGURE 11.2 Sample Report for an Individual Student on an Achievement and School Ability Test

SOURCE: Reprinted with permission of The Psychological Corporation. Copyright © 1992 by The Psychological Corporation. All rights reserved. "Metropolitan Achievement Tests" is a registered trademark of The Psychological Corporation.

The suggestions in Table 11.7 will help in interpreting scores correctly for individual students:

Table 11.7 Suggestions for Interpreting Test Scores for Individuals

1. Be sure you understand what each type of score means.
2. Look for a general pattern in the scores.
3. Expect the tests to confirm the other information you have about students. Compare the information with the results of classroom assessments and your observations of the students.
4. If there are discrepancies—between various tests, between test scores and classroom performance, or between test scores and other information you have in the file—try to make sense of the discrepancies and ask yourself why they occurred.
5. Don't be concerned with small differences. Remember the errors of measurement!
6. Verify the test results by looking at other information.

Evaluating Gains

When we test students more than once over an extended period, we naturally want to know whether there has been any improvement and where the improvement has been. This sounds like a simple matter of subtracting the score made at one time from that made at an earlier date. However, like most procedures in educational testing, the procedure is more complicated than it seems at first. For a carefully developed criterion-referenced test covering a limited domain, it *is* possible to simply subtract the scores and make an interpretation about the gain. However, for broader domains, several conditions must be met before an interpretable gain score can be calculated.

First, the scores must be based on the same test, because the norms for two different tests are based on different norms groups and a difference in scores may simply reflect a difference in norms groups. Second, the scores must be expressed on a scale that has equal units. This requirement eliminates percentiles, grade equivalents, and stanines, leaving only standard scores. Finally, the same scale must run all the way from the earliest grade to the highest grade you want to test. The only kinds of scales that meet all these requirements are standard scores, such as a T-score or the Normal Curve Equivalent (NCE), and something like the Normalized score scale.

If the test you are using does not have such a scale, you can still get information about a student's progress from one year to the next, though not so precisely. For example, you can note whether Landon's percentile score is about the same as it was last year, and whether his grade equivalent score is at or above his actual grade placement. This kind of information helps you know whether Landon is making "normal progress," but it does not answer the question about whether he is doing better this year than in past years, and, if so, how much better he is doing.

Suppose Mariah is in your fourth grade class and this year has a *percentile* score of 55 on Reading Comprehension. You check her record for previous years and find she had a percentile of 47 last year and of 53 in the second grade. Her sta-nines were 3 for each grade. What can you conclude from this information? The answer is that you can conclude that Mariah performed *like an average student* in all three grades. Similarly, if you look at Mariah's *grade equivalent* scores for tests administered in October of each year, you might find that she has a GE of 4.4 this year, with 3.1 last year and 2.3 in second grade. Your conclusion? The same as for the percentiles and stanines: *average performance* in all three grades.

Mariah's scores indicate possible sources of confusion in interpreting scores: On the grade equivalent (GE) and extended normalized scales, progress is in-dicated by scores growing larger. On other scales (percentiles, standard scores, stanines, NCES), scores that stay approximately the same each year indicate progress.

Look again at Table 11.3. This information will help you interpret the scores correctly. Notice especially the column labeled "Range of Average." This indicates the range of scores from approximately -1 SD to +1 SD. Two-thirds of the stu-dents in the norms sample were in that range, and it is important not to over-interpret small differences there. On some of the scales a difference of a few points in the middle of the scale can change the scaled score a lot, as you saw with the percentiles in Figure 11.1. You also have to keep in mind that there is some measurement error in all scores. For the DIQ, on a test with a reliability of .80, the standard error would be approximately 8 points.

Publishers of the major achievement tests try to help you interpret scores by providing "percentile bands" on their report forms, as in Figure 11.2. The only scores that are significantly different are those for which the percentile bands do not overlap. For the student in this example most of the bands are in the middle range, with Vocabulary in the high range, and Mathematics Procedures in the low range. A lot of other information is also provided on this report. Some of it is di-agnostic, indicating the level of performance on specific types of items.

Interpreting a difference in grade equivalents is not so simple. First, you have to think about what the expectation is. For a fifth grader taking the test in the fall, the expected GE is approximately 5.2, plus or minus the error of measure-ment. For a test taken in the spring it would be approximately 5.8, plus or minus the measurement error.

There is no simple way of interpreting a single score precisely. What you have to do is to look at the pattern of scores. When the scores come from an achieve-ment battery, you can look for the general picture. Are most scores in the average range? If not, are they somewhat above, somewhat below, or very high or very low? Are all scores at about the same level? Review Table 11.7 to see what to look for when you are trying to interpret scores. The main point to remember is to get as much information as possible, and look for patterns. Avoid drawing conclusions about limited data.

Figure 11.3 is a report for a school and Figure 11.4 is a district report. These reports differ according to the test publisher and the school district, but there is a lot of valuable information on them which can be very helpful if it is interpreted properly. A more in-depth discussion of interpreting scores will be found in Chapter 15, on creating student profiles.

STANFORD

ACHIEVEMENT TEST SERIES, NINTH EDITION
with OTIS-LENNON SCHOOL ABILITY TEST, SEVENTH EDITION
(SIMULATED DATA)

A

DISTRICT: Newtown - 1234567890
TEST TYPE: Multiple Choice

GRADE: 04
TEST DATE: 04/96

B

ADMINISTRATOR'S DATA SUMMARY FOR LAKESIDE ELEMENTARY
School Code 1234567890

SAMPLE DATA — To be used for display of report format only. Do not attempt to interpret scores.

	READING			MATHEMATICS			LANGUAGE			Spelling	Study Skills	ENVIRONMENT, SCIENCE, SOCIAL SCIENCE		Listening	Using Information	Thnkg Skills	BATTERY TOTALS	
Total Number Tested - 58	Total Reading	Reading Vocab	Reading Comp	Total Math	Problem Solving	Procedures	Language	Mechanics	Expression			Science	Social Science				Basic	Complete
Number Possible	84	43	54	78	48	30	48	24	24	30	30	40	40	40	67	217	310	390
Number Tested	42	43	42	42	42	42	41	41	41	41	40	43	58	42	52	49	40	40
Raw Score Statistics Mean	61.8	26.7	35.2	63.9	18.9	22.4	40.4	21.0	19.4			32.6	26.0	22.6	29.7	62.8	140.2	200.6
Standard Deviation	14.8	7.2	8.8	19.8	5.6	8.4	9.8	4.7	6.1			7.2	8.2	8.3	5.1	15.7	22.1	43.0
Percentiles																		
P90 —90th	81.3	35.4	46.5	91.1	26.8	31.9	52.3		27.0			38.4	38.2	33.9	36.0	84.2	204.5	277.4
Q3 —75th	72.0	32.4	42.8	81.0	23.2	29.7	47.	24.	24.3			36.1	32.7	30.0	30.6	75.7	181.5	259.5
Median—50th	62.5	27.9	35.0	63.0	19.3	25.2		21.	22.6			30.5	26.1	21.8	26.1	62.9	140.5	198.5
Q1 —25th	50.3	20.4	28.0	45.0	14.7			14.				24.9	19.6	14.8	19.6	49.5	99.0	148.5
P10 —10th	40.6	16.2	23.1	36.6	11.0							18.2	15.1	11.5	22.8	42.4	62.5	110.1
Scaled Score Statistics Mean	629.5	633.6	627.	62.			629.3	629.3	629.3	629.0	622.4	633.9	623.6	611.5	637.5	632.3	NA	NA
Standard Deviation	31.6	36.4	32.	2.			39.8	39.8	39.8	39.8	38.2	31.1	28.3	37.2	28.5	24.9		
Percentiles																		
P90 —90th	669.9	675.3	667.3	647.7	6		667.5	663.2	678.3	668.4	673.5	670.0	664.4	660.0	679.1	666.8		
Q3 —75th	645.5	654.6	649.5	631.0	61	608.2	646.5	644.2	652.8	650.9	647.5	657.5	644.0	638.0	653.5	651.2		
Median—50th	626.5	632.0	622.0	605.5	591.3	565.0	628.0	626.0	631.5	630.5	620.5	634.5	622.3	604.2	636.5	631.5		
Q1 —25th	605.0	601.1	601.0	580.3	591.3	565.0	601.0	598.1	597.8	600.5	587.5	610.9	601.9	576.5	611.5	612.0		
P10 —10th	588.7	585.1	586.3	567.6	575.8	538.7	578.8	575.7	574.8	578.8	566.5	588.1	586.3	562.5	601.7	601.3		

D

STANFORD LEVEL/FORM: Intermediate
1995 NORMS: Spring
National

OLSAT LEVEL/FORM: E/3
National

Scores based on normative data copyright© 1996 by Harcourt Brace Educational Measurement. All rights reserved.

Copy 01
Process No. 18904271-8909-10199-5

FIGURE 11.3 Sample Achievement Test Report for a School

SOURCE: Reprinted with permission of the copyright owner, Harcourt Brace Educational Measurement. From Stanford Achievement Test, 9th edition ©1996 by Harcourt Brace & Company.

PROFILE OF SCHOOL DISTRICT PERFORMANCE 1996-97

California   Assessment Program

County—

School District—CALWEST UNIFIED SCHOOL DISTRICT

Grade and Content Area Tested	District Mean Score				State Percentile Rank				
					Of the District Mean Score				Of the Comparison Score Band
	1974-75	1975-76	1976-77		1974-75	1975-76	1976-77		1976-77
Grade 2 Reading	76.3	76.4	76.7		79	77	75		61-78
Grade 3 Reading	87.8	88.4	88.3		73	77	72		60-75
Grade 6 Reading		70.1	70.6			64	68		68-80
Written Expression		67.3	67.9			70	66		66-78
Spelling		66.3	67.2			71	73		63-77
Mathematics		59.9	60.4			63	64		64-81
Grade 12 Reading		65.6	64.5			66	62		63-77
Written Expression		62.6	62.4			57	64		64-79
Spelling		68.2	68.4			59	62		49-81
Mathematics		66.9	67.3			56	65		63-82

Percentile Ranks of the District Mean Score (X) and the Comparison Score Band (0)

Background Factors Used to Develop Comparison Score Bands	District Value			State Percentile Rank of District Value			
	1974-75	1975-76	1976-77	1974-75	1975-76	1976-77	
Grades 2 and 3							
Entry Level Test	28.69	28.64	28.66	65	68	65	
Socioeconomic Index	2.27	2.30	2.30	74	75	75	
Percent AFDC		6.2	5.1		26	23	
Percent Bilingual	9.3	8.3	8.8	51	48	49	
Pupil Mobility	33.8	37.8	34.5	26	40	46	
Grade 6							
Grade 3 Achievement Index		88.0	88.7		74	73	
Percent AFDC		5.3	4.5		24	22	
Percent Bilingual		8.2	6.9		56	51	
Grade 12							
Grade 6 Achievement Index		58.9	66.7		79	68	
Percent AFDC		3.5	3.4		22	25	

Additional Background Factors (Not Used to Develop Comparison Score Bands)	District Value	State Percentile Rank
Percent minority pupils, total	14.3	50
Percent American Indian	0.2	47
Percent Asian American	3.1	88
Percent Black	1.0	68
Percent Spanish-surnamed	9.7	54
Average class size, elementary	28.3	82
Average class size, high school	28.2	83
Average daily attendance	31,312	99
Assessed valuation per unit of a.d.a	$15,112	25	0
General purpose tax rate	$4.20	67	0
Expenditures per unit of a.d.a	$1,129	7	0

FIGURE 11.4 Sample Achievement Test Report for a District

SOURCE: Reprinted with permission of the copyright owner, Harcourt Brace Educational Measurement.

PROBLEMS WITH THE USE
OF ACHIEVEMENT TEST SCORES

By now you should realize that standardized achievement tests can provide useful information that you can get in no other way. That was the intent of the pioneers in the educational testing movement. Unfortunately, a few well-meaning people have encouraged the use of the scores on achievement tests in ways that have led to questionable results and to undesirable practices. Most of the problems have grown out of the attempt to use test scores as the sole information used in making high-stakes decisions about selection and accountability and to try to motivate students. We have discussed these problems before and we will merely summarize them here.

Test results for groups of students are used in three ways: selection, accountability, and motivation. For all these uses, there are both positive and negative effects for the individual involved, and opinion is sharply divided.

Selection

Test scores are sometimes used to classify and sort students. For example, the decision about which students are admitted to colleges or to professional schools is usually based at least in part on test scores. Also, in some schools, tests influence the decision as to whether a child enters first grade or spends another year in kindergarten. Test scores may also be used to assign students to classes that are sorted according to students' achievement levels.

Proponents of sorting and tracking argue that this practice makes it possible for students to be taught on the level that is appropriate, so that their time is not wasted on instruction and activities that they already have mastered or for which they do not have sufficient preparation. Those who are opposed argue that sorting and tracking has many harmful side effects and reduces the opportunity to learn, especially for minorities.

Accountability

Proponents of high-stakes testing programs suggest that these programs focus the curriculum and teaching on desirable goals and thus improve student learning. Studies show that when stakes are high, there is indeed a tendency for schools and teachers to focus on the skills and content covered by the tests. However, this focus can result in narrowing the curriculum and in devoting much instructional time to teaching the specific materials included in the tests, if not the actual test items themselves. Table 11.8 summarizes the undesirable consequences of using test scores as the sole criterion for accountability decisions.

Motivation

Advocates of high-stakes testing programs argue that they motivate students and teachers to work harder in order to avoid low scores. This argument, however, ignores the fact that this kind of motivation works only with people who believe they really have a good chance of attaining the rewards attached to high perform-

Table 11.8   Undesirable Consequences of Using Tests for Accountability

1. **Narrowing of the curriculum.** Sometimes teachers teach only what the test covers. This practice ignores the fact that standardized tests cover a composite of goals from a wide number of school districts and may not exactly fit what is appropriate or desirable for a given school or group of students. Also, when the testing program is limited to "basic skills" or "minimum competency," higher-level skills are not taught.

2. **Ignoring other correlates of student learning.** Many studies demonstrate a strong relationship between test scores and variables such as social class of students and expenditures on education. Accountability projects often ignore these factors. Also, little attention is paid to studies that demonstrate the effect of factors such as providing more time on task for some students.

3. **Overinterpretation of insignificant differences in scores** because the concept of standard error is not understood.

4. **Inappropriate coaching of students,** which invalidates the test results.

ance. For others, there may be serious negative effects. For example, when a district requires passing a competency test for high school graduation, the dropout rate increases.

In spite of these cautions, you will find that the information from an achievement battery can be suggestive of certain problems, and you will certainly want to get all the information you can.

REPORTING TEST SCORES

After a test has been scored, parents and students should be informed about the scores in a manner that will help them interpret the results. Whoever interprets the results must be careful not to overinterpret or misinterpret the information and to explain possible sources of error in the scores.

Written Reports

The most common means of communicating the results of a large-scale test is a written report. Most of these reports present the raw scores on each subtest and one or more derived scores. Usually there is also a profile that makes it possible to compare the various scores visually, as well as a narrative interpretation of the scores. This report is all that many students and their parents want. Figure 11.2 shows a sample of a student's test report from a commercial achievement test battery. Sample reports for a school and a district are presented in Figures 11.3 and 11.4.

Group Meetings

Teachers and counselors sometimes hold a group meeting to help students, their parents, or both interpret the information on the written report. These sessions should be planned to provide adequate time for questions to be asked and answered.

Individual Conferences

An individual conference is usually held when a student's parents request one or when test results suggest there may be a problem that needs further investigation. In the latter case, the individual conference may be a part of, or preparation for, referral to a school psychologist or other specialist for additional evaluation. This process is discussed in Chapters 15 and 16.

If you are asked to discuss test information with students or parents, be sure you understand the information yourself; then try to find a way to interpret it in a manner that the students and parents will understand. Avoid jargon, technical language, stereotypical phrases, and ambiguous terms. If you are asked to make recommendations, be realistic and do not go beyond the information you have. Your best recommendation may be to suggest further study, thus paving the way for referral. Chapter 15 covers additional suggestions and recommended procedures for presenting data to parents, students, and other people.

ETHICAL CONSIDERATIONS IN ACHIEVEMENT TESTING

An external testing program raises many ethical issues. Prior to the test administration, students should be told why the test is being given, what the test is like, and what will be done with the scores. They also should be coached in appropriate test-taking techniques, but they should not be trained on the specific items that will be a part of the test. You may want to refer to Chapter 2 for a discussion of this matter.

There is also an ethical dimension to the actual administration of the test. The matter of whether a given test is valid for a given student must be considered. Should a student whose English is very limited be tested? What about one with a vision problem or a motor problem that makes it difficult to mark an answer sheet? For all students it is important that the testing procedures be followed exactly, except when some type of accommodation is made, in which case some notation should be made about the nature of the accommodation.

All test results must be regarded as private information, and no test results for an individual should be reported to any person or institution without the consent of the test taker or authorized representative, unless such release is required by law. Test data maintained in data files should be adequately protected from improper disclosure.

For a fuller discussion of ethical issues associated with group testing programs, see Chapter 15 as well as Appendix C, *Code of Fair Testing Practices in Education* prepared by the Joint Committee (1988). Also you may want to check out the AERA/APA/NCME *Standards for Educational and Psychological Testing* (1985) from your library.

SUMMARY

- This chapter deals primarily with the selection, administration, and use of standardized group tests of achievement.
- Individual achievement tests were also discussed.
- Score scales and score interpretation were also discussed.
- Scores on standardized achievement tests can be helpful if they are interpreted correctly.
- Achievement test scores are most useful when they are interpreted in the context of other information.

STUDY QUESTIONS

1. What kind of information can you get from a norm-referenced standardized achievement test that you cannot get from your own classroom tests?

2. What are the unique features of textbook tests?

3. What are the advantages and disadvantages of the different score scales?

4. If you want to help your students do well on a statewide achievement test, what should you do?

FOR YOUR PROFESSIONAL GROWTH

1. Select an achievement test battery with which you are familiar.

2. In the library, read the most recent review of the selected battery in the *Mental Measurements Yearbook*. Read some of the articles cited in the reviews. Then answer these questions:

   a. Do the reviews suggest that the battery is appropriate for your students?
   b. What kind of problems might there be in such use?

3. If you have used a test battery with your classes, answer these questions:

   a. What is the general level of achievement in your class(es)?
   b. How many students in your class(es) seem to need special help?
   c. Do the test results support your own observations and conclusions about your students?

12

ॐ

Tests of Aptitude/Ability

PREVIEW

Individual differences is an important concept in psychology and education. An important contribution of psychology and educational measurement to the study of individual differences has been the attempt to identify the nature of the differences between individuals, to identify the relationship between various traits and performance, and to investigate the feasibility of training the traits of interest.

MAJOR TOPICS
Changing Concepts of Intelligence, Aptitude, and Ability
Current Use of General Scholastic Ability Tests in Education
Legal Issues in the Use of Intelligence/Scholastic Ability Tests
Interpreting Scores on General Scholastic Ability Tests
Other General Ability Tests
Readiness and Other Early Screening Tests
Learning Styles Inventories
Tests of Adaptive Behavior
Tests of Creativity
Specific Aptitude and Multiple Aptitude Batteries
Scores and Score Scales
Intelligence Quotient
Deviation IQ
Other Standard Scores
Percentiles and Percentile Ranks
Using the Information

We discussed this history in Chapter 3 and explored some of the controversies related to measures of aptitude and ability as Issue 4 in Chapter 2. The development of the concept of intelligence has been a part of this history. In this chapter we deal with current issues and practices in ability testing. We also discuss special aptitudes and multitrait aptitudes or abilities.

CHANGING CONCEPTS OF INTELLIGENCE, APTITUDE, AND ABILITY

In Chapter 3 we surveyed the early history of attempts to identify and measure traits that differentiate between individuals. The first attempts focused on psychomotor skills, but these studies were abandoned when it was found that differences in these skills were not related to any important "higher" mental process.

Alfred Binet is credited with developing the idea of measuring intelligence by measuring performance on tasks that are samples of intelligent behavior. France's Ministry of Public Instruction commissioned him to develop practical methods of identifying mentally retarded schoolchildren so they might receive special instruction (Wolf, 1973; Hopkins, Stanley, & Hopkins, 1990; Hothersall, 1984)

Psychologists have long been trying to find a workable definition of intelligence. Binet defined it as *inventiveness,* dependent on *comprehension* and marked by *purposefulness* and *corrective judgment* (Binet, 1911). In 1921 the *Journal of Psychology* published a series of articles on the nature of intelligence written by prominent psychologists, who differed widely in their views. More recently, a number of people have recommended the use of operational definitions, and some have proposed that intelligence be defined as "whatever an intelligence test measures."

In spite of the lack of an agreed-on definition, scores on intelligence tests have been very useful in a number of situations, and in recent years there has been a tendency to skip the matter of definition and concentrate on the purpose for which the test is used.

Prediction of ability to function in an educational setting is still an important function served by mental ability tests, but the identification of children with special needs is not as straightforward as it was once thought to be. Because of the problems associated with intelligence testing, some educators recommend that ability tests not be used at all and that identification of children with learning problems be done solely on the basis of achievement scores, along with observation. Others would like to make a distinction between tests of *aptitude* and tests of *ability,* reserving the term *aptitude* to refer to "potential" and using *ability* for developed abilities. However, this is an artificial distinction.

At the present time, it is recognized that both intelligence and achievement tests measure what students have learned. Intelligence tests and other tests of aptitude/ability differ from achievement tests chiefly in the extent to which they reflect knowledge and skills that are directly taught in school. Both types of tests target a spectrum of ability that ranges from skills related to specific areas of the curriculum to generalized skills cutting across many areas and only loosely related to any one area of the curriculum, although they may be important to vocational performance or general living skills. This issue was discussed in Chapter 10. In recent years the term *intelligence test* has been largely supplanted by *ability test* or *aptitude test,* often with a descriptor such as *scholastic* or *mechanical* attached.

Some aptitude tests are very general; others have many specific subtests. In the century since the early work with measures of individual differences, the concept of intelligence has changed dramatically. There are still many viewpoints about what intelligence is and whether or how it may be developed. The Binet tests, for example, have many subtasks, but all are combined into a single score. On the other hand, the Wechsler tests have many subscales and yield both a Verbal and a Nonverbal IQ, as well as a Full Scale IQ. J. P. Guilford (1967) proposed a three-dimensional "structure of the intellect" consisting of content, operations, and products. Howard Gardner (1983) proposed a theory of "multiple intelligences"—linguistic, logical/mathematical, musical, spatial, kinesthetic, interpersonal, and intrapersonal knowledge. Robert Sternberg (1988) criticized Gardner's formulation and proposed a theory based on cognitive theory. Sternberg's "triarchic mind" distinguishes among the internal world (mental processes), experience, and context (relationship to the demands of the external world). Sternberg emphasizes the importance of the concept of necessity to the concept of intelligence. In his schema, those abilities that people require in order to live are part of intelligence, and other abilities are simply specialized talents.

Most general aptitude tests have separate tests of verbal and numerical ability, and some also include a test of spatial perception. Some general aptitude tests sort the tasks into verbal and nonverbal sections (the latter use tasks that require no reading but use diagrams, figures, and performance tasks). There is no general agreement as to how many types of skills there are, but there is much evidence that most of the specific skills are highly correlated. This means that a person who is high on one skill is likely to be fairly high on the others. This finding lends support to the notion of what has been labeled the "g" factor, which is the term used for "general ability." The correlation, however, is not perfect: Some people score significantly higher on one skill than on another.

In any case, the measurement of intelligence (or scholastic ability) is proposed as a method of diagnosis and prescription, leading to training of all the abilities that are part of the construct. This is quite different from early views that saw intelligence as an unchanging attribute. Some instruments are based on the idea of trait-treatment interaction, or aptitude-by-treatment interactions, although there is some disagreement as to what such instruments should be called. We use the term *learning style inventories.* Another type of test, called a test of adaptive behavior, measures an individual's ability to perform the tasks of daily learning.

Some tests were originally developed as aptitude measures to be used as part of the process of selecting students for entry to a university or a professional training program and to predict success in these schools—for example, the *Scholastic Assessment* (formerly *Aptitude*) *Test* (SAT), the *Graduate Record Examination* (GRE), and the *Law School Admissions Test* (LSAT). It is now recognized that these are achievement tests which are useful as predictors of success in college and graduate programs. The American College Testing (ACT) program was always described as an achievement test.

Some aptitude batteries were developed to assist people in planning for a vocation. Most notable of these are the *General Aptitude Test Battery* (GATB) developed by the U.S. Employment Service; the *Differential Aptitude Test Battery* (DAT), developed to be used with high school students; and the *Armed Services Vocational Aptitude Battery* (ASVAB), used in the armed services. For each of several abilities these batteries yield test scores that are designed to be compared to identify an individual's highest and lowest ability areas, thus providing some information to help individuals select an occupational field in which they are likely to be successful.

CURRENT USE OF GENERAL SCHOLASTIC ABILITY TESTS IN EDUCATION

It was once thought that tests of intelligence measured something quite different from achievement tests, that aptitude was an inborn quality, that achievement was developed through education and training, that aptitude tests could be used to predict what a student was capable of achieving, and that achievement tests measured what had been learned. It was recommended that students be tested with both an intelligence and an achievement test, so that the scores could be compared. Discrepancies in the two scores were thought to be diagnostic and resulted in students being classified as "overachievers," "underachievers," or "normal achievers." As we pointed out earlier in this chapter, this interpretation of scores has not been found to be very helpful in working with most students, because the tests are so highly correlated; however, the general concept is still used to identify learning disabled students.

One of the major issues raised by the testing of intelligence is the use of IQ scores in the placement of students in special education classes and in tracking for regular classes. There are two quite contradictory approaches. On the one hand, some school districts eliminated ability tests altogether, because of the possibility that they may be biased against certain ethnic groups. On the other hand, some districts require certain "early identification" or "early screening" instruments to be administered in kindergarten or before, in order to identify children who may possibly have difficulty in the regular program or to identify the learning style of each child. Sometimes children who do not score well on an early screening test are held in kindergarten for another year; sometimes they are referred for individual evaluation by a school psychologist.

Perhaps the most important use of ability tests in education today is to provide additional information about students. As we have tried to stress throughout this book, the more information you have about a student, the more confident you can be that you really understand him or her.

Why might you want to administer or request administration of an ability or aptitude test instead of another achievement test or instead of collecting a lot of observational information? There are several reasons. First, an aptitude test may tap some traits that are not addressed by an achievement test. Second, an aptitude test will sometimes require less time to administer than most achievement batteries. Third, some aptitude tests may be administered to students who have not yet learned to read or to students who have not had any opportunity to learn other material taught in school, because these tests address skills that facilitate learning, not achievement in a specific area. Finally, the most significant reason is that these tests can contribute additional information to help you interpret the information you already have, so you can understand the strengths and weaknesses of your students.

Group tests of scholastic ability are most frequently used with older students, such as those applying for college admission. For young students individual tests are most useful. Appendix F lists the most frequently used individual and group tests of scholastic ability.

Most of the commonly used group tests of scholastic ability provide at least two scores, Verbal and Nonverbal or Performance, as well as a Total score. Some of them also provide subscores which vary widely from test to test. The most widely used group test of scholastic ability in grades 1–12 is the Otis-Lennon School Ability Test (OLSAT), but the other tests listed in Appendix F are also used in some districts. The types of items used in the OLSAT at various grade levels are reported in Table 12.1.

The most widely used individual intelligence tests are the three levels of the Wechsler: The Wechsler Preschool and Primary Scale of Intelligence–Revised (WPPSI-R), the Wechsler Intelligence Scale for Children–Revised (WISC-R/III), and the Wechsler Adult Intelligence Scale–Revised (WAIS-R). An updated version of the Stanford-Binet is also widely used, as is a newer test, the Kaufman Assessment Battery for Children (K-ABC). Other individual intelligence tests are listed in Appendix F. The individual tests differ widely in their constructs, ages covered, and subtests, as Tables 12.2 and 12.3 make clear. These tables report the coverage of the Stanford-Binet and the Wechsler for different levels. The K-ABC differs even more, since it was developed on the construct of *crystallized* and *fluid* intelligence as explicated by Cattell (1943), so there are items for the crystallized scale and the fluid scale. All of them should be checked for technical qualities by consulting one or more of the references discussed in Chapter 10 and listed in Appendix D.

LEGAL ISSUES IN THE USE OF INTELLIGENCE/SCHOLASTIC ABILITY TESTS

Hobson v. Hansen (1967) was the first direct legal challenge to the use of standardized tests as the basis of a tracking system. This case was filed soon after the desegregation of the Washington, DC, public schools. Students were assigned to tracks based on grades, teacher recommendations, and various standardized tests of achievement and ability. The result was that 95% of African American students were in the lower tracks as opposed to actual representation in the population (90%). The plaintiffs alleged that the lower-track programs had poorer facilities,

Table 12.1 Types of Items at Various Levels of the Otis-Lennon School Ability Test (OLSAT)

Levels Grades	A K	B 1	C 2	D 3	E 4–5	F 6–8	G 9–12
Verbal Comprehension							
Following Directions	X	X	X				
Antonyms				X	X	X	X
Sentence Completion				X	X	X	X
Sentence Arrangement				X	X	X	X
Verbal Reasoning							
Aural Reasoning	X	X	X				
Arithmetic Reasoning	X	X	X	X	X	X	X
Logical Selection				X	X	X	X
Word/Letter Matrix				X	X	X	X
Verbal Analogies				X	X	X	X
Verbal Classification				X	X	X	X
Inference					X	X	X
Pictorial Reasoning							
Picture Classification	X	X	X				
Picture Analogies	X	X	X				
Picture Series (K only)	X						
Figural Reasoning							
Figural Classification	X	X	X	X			
Figural Analogies	X	X	X	X			
Pattern Matrix	X	X	X	X			
Figural Series	X	X	X	X			
Quantitative Reasoning				X			
Number Series					X	X	X
Numeric Inference					X	X	X
Number Matrix					X	X	X

poorer instruction, and limited curricula. In ruling for the plaintiffs, the judge apparently understood that tracking was to be based on innate ability. None of the expert witnesses would testify that the mental ability test was a test of innate ability, but they stated that the test reflected to a large extent environmental influences. The judge then enjoined the school from using the tracking system.

Larry P. v. Wilson Riles (1974) dealt with the placement of African American students in classes for the educable mentally retarded (EMR). The argument was made that the intelligence tests used were biased against minorities, and the use of these tests in placement decisions was enjoined.

After these rulings, at least one state stopped the use of mental ability tests altogether, and many school districts have limited their use. But in later court cases the rulings were almost diametrically opposed to early rulings. For example, in *PASE v. Hannon* (1980) the judge upheld the use of ability tests in conjunction with other criteria for the placement of Illinois schoolchildren in EMR classes.

Table 12.2 Types of Items at Various Levels of the Wechsler Intelligence Test

	WPPSI-R Ages 2–11 to 7.3	WISC-III Ages 6.0 to 16.11	WAIS-R Ages 16–69
Verbal			
Information	X	X	X
Comprehension	X	X	X
Arithmetic	X	X	X
Vocabulary	X	X	X
Similarities	X	X	X
Sentences	X (supp)		
Digit Span		X (supp)	X
Letter-Number Sequencing			X (supp)
Total	X	X	X
Performance			
Object Assembly	X	X	X (opt)
Geometric Design	X		
Block Design	X	X	X
Mazes	X	X (supp)	
Picture Completion	X	X	X
Animal Pegs	X (supp)		
Coding		X	
Picture Arrangement		X	X
Picture Completion			X
Symbol Search		X (supp)	X (supp)
Digit Symbol			X
Matrix Reasoning			X
Total	X	X	X

He stated, "Plaintiffs' theory of cultural bias simply ignores the fact that African American children perform differently from each other on the tests. It also fails to explain the fact that some African American children perform better than most whites." In *Marshall et al. v. Georgia* (1984, 1985) and *S-1 v. Turlington* (1986), it was ruled that grouping on the basis of *achievement* has probable benefits to low-scoring students, and that providing instruction on a child's level may have beneficial affects. However, these rulings also stipulate that placement must be flexible and must provide enhanced educational opportunities.

Identification procedures for special education services have been subjected to careful study and discussion since the early decisions. The guidelines for the assessment of students with scholastic difficulties—that serve as the basis for decisions in most court cases and thus are incorporated in the procedures for many states and school districts—are those provided in the classification developed by the American Association of Mental Deficiency (Grossman, 1983).

Table 12.3 Types of Items at Various Levels of the Stanford-Binet Intelligence Test

AGE	2–4	5–9	10–17	18+
Verbal Reasoning				
Vocabulary	X	X	X	X
Comprehension	X	X	X	X
Absurdities	X	X	X	
Verbal Relations			X	X
Quantitative Reasoning				
Quantitative	X	X	X	X
Number Series		X	X	X
Equation Building			X	X
Abstract/Visual Reasoning				
Pattern Analysis	X	X	X	X
Copying	X	X	X	
Matrices		X	X	X
Paper Folding and Cutting			X	X
Short-Term Memory				
Bead Memory	X	X	X	X
Memory for Sentences	X	X	X	X
Memory for Digits		X	X	X
Memory for Objects		X	X	X

There is general agreement that any important decision about a student's placement should be based on multiple sources of information, and that many people should participate in the decision. We address this matter further in Chapters 15 and 16.

INTERPRETING SCORES ON GENERAL SCHOLASTIC ABILITY TESTS

In this section we deal with general ability tests in contrast to tests of specific abilities. We also limit our discussion to tests used in a school setting, so our primary concern is with scholastic ability.

As with all measurement, there are certain precautions you have to observe in interpreting scores on general scholastic ability tests. The first task is to be clear about what the test is measuring. This is a matter of *validity*. As we indicated earlier, tests developed to measure learning ability were once called "intelligence" tests, and this usage is still continued, especially for some individually administered tests. But other terms are now being used, because of conflict about the concept of intelligence and the extent to which intelligence is teachable. Terms such as *learning ability, school ability, cognitive ability,* and *scholastic aptitude* are used to suggest that these tests measure developed abilities that are related to school learning.

The second task is to understand and expect variations in scores from one administration to another, even if the same test is used each time. This concept involves the concept of the "constancy of the IQ." We now know that scores on these tests reflect learning, not aptitude unaffected by life experience, so we expect scores to change as one's experience changes. If intelligence/scholastic ability is believed to be a fixed trait, then an individual should make approximately the same score each time he or she takes the test, and this is generally what happens, especially for older students; however, there are many exceptions. If you take two different tests, you will almost certainly make different scores, and if you take the same test at different times, you will also make different scores. There are several reasons why this is true. First, two different tests almost certainly measure slightly different skills. Second, we know that there is some degree of measurement error in all tests, and this leads to some variation in scores. Measurement error is especially high for early aptitude and screening tests, although the scores become more stable by the time children enter first grade. A third source of variation is the way raw scores are manipulated to compute the ability score or the percentile or whatever other score is reported.

Finally, we need to understand what good performance or poor performance on a given instrument indicates about a student. What makes scores high? What makes them low? To what extent is the ability fixed and to what extent can it be taught? There is much difference of opinion on this issue. What we need to do is to look at the empirical studies and use that information to help us understand how best to work with our students.

OTHER GENERAL ABILITY TESTS

In this section we discuss four additional types of general ability tests.

Readiness and Other Early Screening Tests

One of the first standardized tests a child is likely to take is a readiness test. It is administered either in kindergarten or very early in the first grade. The purpose of the readiness test is to identify the children who are not yet "ready" to begin reading and, perhaps, to group students for reading instruction. Some people view these tests as *aptitude* tests; others consider them to be *achievement* tests. Actually they are both. They are aptitude tests to the extent that they predict how well children will do in learning to read. They are achievement tests of some of the skills that are known to be prereading skills. Readiness tests vary widely in the skills they cover, but usually they cover some of the skills listed in Table 12.4.

Depending on whether the test is group or individual, it may require copying, speaking, pointing, or selection of objects. The available tests vary widely as to which of these skills are used. There is also great variability as to the availability and appropriateness of norms and other interpretive information. If you are planning to select a readiness test, you should study the manual of the test care-

Table 12.4 Skills Covered in Readiness Tests

Motor skills: Draw lines, complete a circle, follow a maze.
Auditory discrimination: Pronounce words, select pictures of "similar-sounding" words.
Visual discrimination: Choose similar or different pairs of words, letters, numbers, or pictures.
Vocabulary: Define a word, name objects, select an appropriate descriptive word.
Memory: Reproduce a simple design from memory, repeat a simple story.
Verbal Comprehension: Restate a verbal statement.
Recognition: Recognize letters, numbers, and words.

---

fully and also consult one of the sources of critical reviews presented in Chapter 10. Most reading specialists agree that a readiness test should be supplemented with other types of information, because they are based on a very restricted view of readiness and they are not impressive as predictors of future achievement test performance (Ellwein, Walsh, Eads, & Miller, 1991).

Some educators support the notion that early school aptitudes should not be tested. Some schools, districts, and states have even gone so far as to postpone both achievement and aptitude testing (except for special education) until the second grade. There is also agreement that these tests are designed to be used only with young children and would not be helpful with, for instance, a seventh grader who cannot read.

There are other early screening instruments that are not so closely related to reading as are the readiness tests. Most of these tests include in their title one or more of the terms "Early," "Preschool," or "Screener."

If you would like to use a readiness or other early screening test, you will have to be very careful in selecting it. Unfortunately, not many of these instruments have a sufficient theoretical or research background to make them really useful. One uses a simple performance task to assess understanding of prepositions. Others are simply standardized observational records. Such instruments may contribute to understanding a child, but they must be interpreted very cautiously and they should be used only in conjunction with other kinds of information. Currently published readiness tests and early screening instruments are listed as part of Appendix F.

Learning Style Inventories

Another type of test that has become popular recently is an inventory of learning styles, although there is no consensus as to which system of learning styles should be used on such inventories. The content of some of the learning style inventories is listed in Table 12.5.

It is obvious from Table 12.5 that the term *learning style* means many things to many people. The use of a learning style inventory is advocated by those who subscribe to the *trait-treatment* or the *Aptitude by Treatment Interaction* (ATI) concept of learning. These concepts are also referred to as *diagnostic-prescriptive* approaches to teaching. Some people have studied the preferred learning styles of

Table 12.5 Content of Some Learning Style Inventories

visual, auditory, or kinesthetic
analytical, categorical, or relational
field dependence vs. field independence
social vs. abstract principles
people vs. ideas
other vs. self
impulsive vs. reflective
leveling vs. sharpening
scanning vs. focusing
conceptual vs. differential
constricted vs. flexible
abstract vs. concrete
random vs. sequential
sequential vs. simultaneous

various ethnic groups, but there is little evidence of consistent differences between groups, and some writers warn against the formation of ethnic stereotypes about learning styles, because large numbers of individuals in all groups do *not* fit any generalization.

If you are interested in finding out about the learning styles of your students, you will first have to be clear about what you mean by the term. Then you will have to find which of the available learning styles instruments use the same definition that you use. Finally, you will want to read some of the critical reviews (see Chapter 10) to see which of the inventories based on "your" definition do the best job of measuring learning style. Be very cautious about using stereotypical information about students in your teaching. The most frequently used tests of learning style are listed in Appendix F.

Tests of Adaptive Behavior

Adaptive behavior is an individual's ability to meet age-appropriate day-to-day living demands, such as self-care, independence, and interpersonal relationships. Although many people argue that academic performance and cognitive ability are crucial components of adaptive behavior, there has been a strong impetus for the use of at least one separate standardized instrument of adaptive behavior as part of the preschool, preplacement assessment and of the assessment of children with learning problems. Some states and school districts now have such a requirement. The fact that some minority children appear to be retarded only in a school setting has led to the questioning of the results of scholastic ability tests. However, students who score poorly on a test of scholastic ability but who score fairly well on a test of adaptive behavior may still need some type of special help in their school work. Tests of adaptive behavior are listed in Appendix F.

Tests of Creativity

Tests of creativity are sometimes used as part of the selection process for gifted/talented programs. One of the leaders in the development of creativity tests was J. P. Guilford, the developer of the three-dimensional "structure of intellect." He suggested that *creativity* is another term for *divergent production,* which is one of the three dimensions of that structure (Guilford, 1967). For a time there was a great deal of interest in developing creativity tests. Items on the tests were open-ended—for example, "What would happen if no one ever had to go to school anymore?" "Make up a story to fit the following title: '_____.'"

Although the tests are interesting, there is little evidence of their practical value, and some people recommend that evaluation of students' creative productions be used instead of a creativity test (Baer, 1994). Others argue that creativity tests can be useful in identifying some aspects of creativity that might be missed otherwise (Cramond, 1994). Tests of creativity are listed in Appendix F.

SPECIFIC APTITUDE AND MULTIPLE APTITUDE BATTERIES

Tests of specific aptitudes are more restricted than general aptitude tests and the aptitudes are usually more precisely defined. Some aptitude tests focus on a single ability; other tests are batteries of many factors. The major use of the multiple aptitude batteries has been in vocational guidance and selection, and some of the single ability tests have the same focus. Other single skill tests are directed toward sensory skills, such as vision and hearing. Teachers may use the sensory tests for screening, but diagnosis and treatment would require a medical or other type of specialist.

The most important use of multiple aptitude batteries is for counseling—to provide additional information to help students think about their strengths and weaknesses and to consider the vocational fields in which they are most likely to do well. Counselors like the idea that students who generally do poorly on most other tests might make average or better scores on one or more of the specific tests. However, it is not likely that there will be as much difference between the various scores as you might think. Studies using the *General Aptitude Test Battery* (GATB), for example, have found that the various tests are highly intercorrelated, lending support to the notion of a "g" factor in ability. However, it has also been found that only modest ability in some of the skill areas is sufficient for an individual to be successful in many endeavors. So the emphasis in vocational guidance is on the *pattern* of abilities. Usually we are interested in the highest-level occupations an individual could be successful in. For example, a student whose verbal ability is at the 90th percentile may consider careers that require a college education, so we may ignore the fact that the student also scores very high on most other skills. But when a student has below-average scores in academic-type skills, the *pattern* of his or her other skills becomes very important.

One of the earliest vocational tests was a test of clerical ability. These tests usually cover such skills as proofreading, perceptual speed, spelling, and grammar. Some of these tests also include typing (or keyboarding) speed. Another type of vocational test involves mechanical skills, such as motor dexterity, eye-hand coordination, and spatial perception. Sometimes a test of mechanical ability will also include a section on mechanical information.

There also are aptitude tests in the arts, including art and music. But many people feel that evaluation of a sample of the student's work is a better measure than the tests.

Tests of specific abilities and multifactor batteries are listed in Appendix F.

SCORES AND SCORE SCALES

In this section we describe various types of scores for aptitude tests.

Intelligence Quotient

The first attempt to score and interpret scores on intelligence tests was the assignment of a "mental level" to a score on the Binet-Simon scales. This became the *mental age*—the age of children for whom a given score was the average score. Examiners informally compared the mental age with a child's chronological age and drew conclusions about how well the child performed. In 1914, the German psychologist William Stern (1914) suggested the use of the IQ (Intelligence Quotient) as an indicator of mental ability. The IQ was the ratio of one's Mental Age (MA) to the Chronological Age (CA). Both ages were expressed in months and the MA was divided by the CA, and the quotient was multiplied by 100 in order to express the result as a whole number rather than as a decimal. See Figure 12.1 for some examples.

Later, when Stern found that IQs were being interpreted as indices of permanent, unchanging, mental ability, he suggested that someone "kill the IQ." The

---

1. MA = 8 years, 1 month (97 months)
   CA = 8 years, 1 month (97 months)
   IQ = 97 ÷ 97 = 1 × 100 = **100**

2. MA = 10 years, 6 months (126 months)
   CA = 8 years, 1 month (97 months)
   IQ = 126 ÷ 97 = 1.33 × 100 = **133**

3. MA = 6 years, 3 months (75 months)
   CA = 8 years, 1 month (97 months)
   IQ = 75 ÷ 97 = .78 × 100 = **78**

FIGURE 12.1   Examples of Ratio IQ Calculations

ratio IQ is no longer used; but, unfortunately, the term is still with us, along with many of the early misconceptions, such as the "constancy of the IQ." Many studies have demonstrated that these scores vary widely from one age to another, so the ratio IQ was replaced in the early 1960s by the deviation IQ, which is a standard score.

Deviation IQ

As you learned in Chapter 10, standard scores are the most precise method of developing norms. In order to compute standard scores, the mean and standard deviation must first be computed. Then the difference (plus or minus) between each score and the mean is computed. Finally, the difference is divided by the standard deviation, so the standard score is expressed as the difference between the score and the mean, in SD units. This yields a set of decimal values, half of which are positive and half negative.

Usually these scores are further transformed in order to eliminate the decimals and negative values. This is done by selecting an arbitrary number to use as the mean of the transformed distribution, and multiplying the SD units by a convenient constant. For the deviation IQ (DIQ), the mean for each age group is set equal to 100 and the standard deviation for each age group is set equal to 15 (Wechsler) or 16 (Stanford Binet). If you look at Figure 4.3 you will see how the DIQ score fits the normal curve and how this score relates to other scaled scores.

Some publishers have tried to eliminate the use of the term *IQ* by coining new terms for this standard score, and a few have advocated the use of percentiles or stanines instead of DIQ.

Other Standard Scores

Another system of standard scores is that of T-scores, which many teachers use for their classroom tests. This scale uses a mean of 50 and a standard deviation of 10. This scale is used in the *Differential Aptitude Test*.

Another scaled score has a mean of 500 and a standard deviation of 100. This scale is used with each part of the *Scholastic Assessment Test* (SAT) and many other tests of this kind.

Percentiles and Percentile Ranks

The most common type of derived score is percentile rank. To obtain the percentile rank of a mental ability score, all students of a given age range who take a given test are placed in rank order; then the number of students at each score level is tabulated. The number scoring at or below each score is determined, and the cumulated frequencies are divided by the total number to find the percentile. This procedure is illustrated in Table 11.5 in Chapter 11.

As we pointed out before, the problem with percentiles is the unequal intervals between rankings.

USING THE INFORMATION

The way you use ability tests will depend on the age of the student and your purpose. The type of information you get will depend on what type of test you have used, although, as we have pointed out, the title of the instrument is not always a good indicator of what it measures.

Furthermore, teachers should never let a low test score be an excuse for not trying to find a way to help a student learn. Most teachers now understand that *all* tests reflect to some extent what children have learned, so they can be useful in helping a teacher decide where to start and, perhaps, in finding an approach that will help. In any case, no test of any kind should be interpreted without reference to whatever other information is available. Furthermore, you should be realistic and not overinterpret the information. Whatever your initial purpose, your best action may be to suggest further study, thus paving the way for referral. Studying a student by creating a profile is discussed in Chapter 15, and the process of referring students for special services is explored in Chapter 16. Two publications may also be helpful. Lorrie Shepard (1989) describes the methods used to identify mildly handicapped students and reviews many of the issues associated with this identification. A handbook published by the National Association of School Psychologists (1994) examines the policies and practices associated with placement in special education classes.

SUMMARY

- Many terms are now used for general mental ability: Intelligence, scholastic ability, scholastic aptitude, learning style, creativity.
- There are also tests of special abilities, both batteries and tests of single skills.
- Ability tests are most useful as a part of a procedure that involves a battery of tests, along with other assessment and observation procedures.

STUDY QUESTIONS

1. What are the major advantages and disadvantages of measuring scholastic aptitude/ability?
2. Why are there so many different terms for aptitude/ability tests?
3. What can educators learn from aptitude/ability tests that is difficult to see in other ways?

FOR YOUR PROFESSIONAL GROWTH

1. Identify a student in your class about whom you would like to have more information.

2. Study the information already available in the student's folder.

3. Identify the type of test that might give you additional useful information.

4. In the library consult the *Mental Measurements Yearbook* to identify some possibilities. Read reviews of tests of the kind you are interested in; then answer these questions:

   a. Do the reviews suggest that any of the tests might be helpful?
   b. Which tests offer the most promise?
   c. What precautions will you have to observe in using these tests?

13

꩜

Inventories of Interests, Attitudes, and Personality

PREVIEW

In Chapter 8 we discussed ways of gathering information about students' interests, attitudes, and personality traits by means of direct observation and retrospective reports.

Most of these instruments are available in a standardized form and national norms are available to help in interpreting them. However, standardization and norming do not eliminate the potential problems you must guard against when using these instruments. It is not likely that the average classroom teacher will administer one of them very often. However, some of them may be used by a counselor or school psychologist, and teachers need to understand and interpret the scores.

MAJOR TOPICS
The Use of Affective Measures in Education
Measurement of Interests
Measurement of Attitudes
Measurement of Personality
Interpreting Affective Measures

THE USE OF AFFECTIVE
MEASURES IN EDUCATION

Most of the time when we talk about measurement in education we are referring to *cognitive* measures—that is, tests of achievement or abilities. On cognitive measures, responses are scored as "right" or "wrong" or as "totally correct," "partially correct," or "incorrect." However, we are also interested in measures of noncognitive traits. The term *affective* is used for these measures. There are no right or wrong answers on affective instruments; the best answer is what a student really thinks or feels about the posed situations. Sometimes this information helps educators understand students' needs and interests so we can find ways to spark their interest or to present information in a more meaningful way. The direct observation and retrospective rating techniques we described in Chapter 8 are directed toward this purpose and are suggested for use by classroom teachers or counselors working with students.

As children get older, they and their parents become concerned about their future, especially their career goals. Some children also need help in handling personal problems. These are the areas in which external affective measures may be especially helpful. However, special training is needed to administer and interpret many of these instruments, so classroom teachers will not usually be directly involved. But they may receive a report of the scores and will want to understand the report. Counselors and school psychologists are expected to be able to use the instruments effectively and to help teachers understand the scores.

The affective traits that these instruments measure are interests (personal and vocational), attitudes, and personality. All are measured in a variety of ways. The simplest and cheapest way is a self-report. Next is retrospective rating by others, which includes the nomination technique, sometimes called *sociometry*. Direct observation is more complicated and requires a trained observer. The technique that requires the greatest sophistication on the part of the examiner is a projective technique. In the rest of this chapter we discuss the measurement of interests, attitudes, and personality and what the measurements mean. Commonly used standardized inventories of interests and attitudes are listed in Appendix F.

MEASUREMENT OF INTERESTS

The concern with measurement of interests began with vocational interests. One of the early vocational interest inventories was the *Strong Vocational Interest Blank* (SVIB), developed by Edward K. Strong, Jr., and first published in 1927. Strong thought that members of an occupational group would have interests that were different from those of other groups and that were similar to those of other members of that group. He prepared a long list of items individuals could use to indicate those activities they preferred, as well as those they thought they were good at. Then he compared the responses of each person with the responses of other members of his occupational group and of men in general (Note: this study did not include women).

From these studies, Strong developed empirically based scoring scales for each of 55 occupational groups, ranging from artist to production manager. The scoring scales were based on the actual choices of identified members of various occupational groups. Other occupational groups have been added, and recently women have been included in the studies. A later version of the SVIB, the *Strong-Campbell Interest Inventory* (SCII) (Strong & Campbell, 1966) has a single form, suitable for both men and women, and 124 occupational scales that can be classified into six "occupational themes" based on Holland's (1966, 1973) theory of occupational choice: realistic, investigative, artistic, social, enterprising, and conventional. For most of the items, which are similar to the examples in Figure 13.1, the examinee indicates Dislike (D), Indifferent (I) or Like (L).

Watching TV	D	I	L
Playing tennis	D	I	L
Painting a picture	D	I	L
Talking with friends	D	I	L

FIGURE 13.1 Examples of Rating Items for a Preference Inventory

Now, there is also an inventory called the *Campbell Interest and Skill Survey* (CISS), published by NCS Assessments. This instrument, developed by David P. Campbell (1989, 1992), provides scores on both self-reported interests and self-reported skills, and it is part of the Campbell Leadership Index. The CISS uses a 6-point rating scale for each item.

The *Kuder Occupational Interest Survey* (KOIS), published by Science Research Associates, was developed by G. Frederick Kuder, using procedures similar to those used by Strong. Other Kuder scales have been developed: The *Kuder Personal Preference Record* (KPPR) (Kuder, 1956, 1963), the *Kuder Preference Record—Vocational* (KPR-V), and the *Kuder General Interest Survey* (KGIS) (1963, 1987). Items on the Kuder inventories are grouped into three choices, and the examinee chooses one of the three as "like most to do." This is the forced-choice technique, which Kuder used in order to overcome *response set*—which is an individual's tendency to mark all items with the same choice, D, I, or L. Examples of two such forced-choice items are presented in Figure 13.2. Other vocational interest inventories have been developed, usually for a limited range of occupations.

In spite of the care with which these instruments were developed, studies have shown that responses can be faked, which could be a serious problem if the instruments are used in an employment situation. In a school setting, where a student's only concern is self-understanding, faking is less likely. Self-reports such as

Which activity from each group would you prefer?

1. ____ Play a piano   2. ____ Read an adventure story
   ____ Tune a piano   ____ Read a travel story
   ____ Move a piano   ____ Read a biography of a famous person

FIGURE 13.2 Examples of Forced-Choice Items for a Preference Inventory

the *Strong-Campbell Interest Inventory* and the Kuder scales are the primary tools for measuring interests. The major concern in administering these instruments is to set the stage in such a way that students have no incentive to lie and have every incentive to be honest.

Interest inventories are of little use if that is all the information you have. However, as part of a package that includes information about aptitudes and achievement, they can be useful in working with students and helping them understand themselves.

MEASUREMENT OF ATTITUDES

Attitude is not an easy concept to define. Attitudes are what makes an individual view some topics (ideas, people, activities) either positively or negatively. We develop our attitudes as a result of our experiences—that is, we generalize our experiences to reach general conclusions, and in doing so we become biased, either favorably or unfavorably, about many matters. There is great overlap between the concepts of interests and attitudes.

Student attitudes that teachers are most interested in are those related to the curriculum and to classroom activities. Counselors and administrators might be concerned with student attitudes toward the school and faculty. In Chapter 8 we presented a variety of forms teachers may prepare for measuring students' attitudes toward subjects and class activities. These "homemade" measures range from direct observation to self-reports of many types. They usually provide the kind of information you want about your students, so you will seldom use a standardized attitude measure.

However, if your school is participating in a special program directed at changing attitudes, you may be asked to administer a standardized attitude survey. For example, if your school has a drug prevention program, your students (and perhaps their parents) may be asked to complete one or more attitude surveys. The survey may be locally developed, or it may be a standardized form used nationally to evaluate the program. Figure 13.3 shows examples of two types of items from an attitude scale.

How far do you expect to go in school? Mark one:

_____ Quit as soon as possible
_____ Graduate from high school
_____ Attend college
_____ Graduate from college
_____ Go to graduate or professional school

Circle "T" if you agree with a statement, "F" if you disagree.

Marijuana is harmless to the body.	T	F
Drinking beer makes me look grown up.	T	F
Alcohol is a dangerous drug.	T	F

FIGURE 13.3 Example of Items from Attitude Scales for Evaluation of a Drug Prevention Program

MEASUREMENT OF PERSONALITY

The term *personality* has been defined in many ways and often the same term is used by different people to mean very different things. Some scholars or researchers take the *trait* approach and list traits that they consider to be part of personality. Figure 13.4 shows two examples of trait lists. Another approach has been an attempt to identify various personality "types," such as those in Figure 13.5.

There is no general agreement as to how many or what the traits or types of personality are, although many studies have been directed toward identifying a simple structure of the determiners of behavior. There is also great disagreement about the role of personality—that is, whether it is the *determiner* or the *result* of behavior. Do you act in certain ways because of your personality? Or is your personality the way it is because of how you act?

Even if the matter of definition were resolved, it is difficult to see how tests of personality could be very useful in schools. While there is some support for desirable personality traits like perseverence and delay of gratification, there is little

Trait List 1	Trait List 2
Achievement	Ambition
Intellect	Friendliness
Perception	Integrity
Sexual orientation	Loyalty
Voice quality	Optimism
Values	Tolerance

FIGURE 13.4 Examples of Trait Lists

warm vs. cold
energetic vs. sluggish
cooperative vs. hostile
happy vs. melancholy
generous vs. stingy
optimistic vs. pessimistic

FIGURE 13.5 Examples of Personality Types

support for the idea that there is a personality type or list of traits that educators would want all people to have, so we would include in our school program the development of such a pattern. What a boring world it would be if everyone had the same personality!

Standardized group inventories of personality are similar in many ways to interest inventories. The content, however, deals with *personal* rather than *vocational* matters. Two examples are the *Edwards Personal Preference Record* (Edwards, 1959) and the *Guilford-Zimmerman Temperament Survey* (Guilford & Zimmerman, 1955).

There is one situation in which a school might be concerned with personality measures—student behavior for which we have no explanation other than a serious personality disorder. But a simple paper-and-pencil test is not likely to identify difficulties of this kind. The first information is likely to come from observation and perhaps from examination of certain products—artwork or writing. The gathering of additional information will require the services of specially trained examiners, such as a school psychologist. These examiners use structured interviews and projective techniques to help them understand how individuals view the world.

Projective techniques require an individual to describe how he or she sees objects, and the person's responses are compared with those of the majority of people. The idea is that how individuals view an object reflects their moods, needs, and perceptions, and that their perceptions are influenced by their values and personal conflicts. In one technique, the individual is shown *structured* pictures or *unstructured* pictures. Structured pictures show a real object or person; unstructured pictures show an image that does not resemble any real object or person. Sometimes both kinds of pictures are used so the responses may be compared. Figure 13.6 provides an example of a structured picture on the left, with an unstructured picture on the right.

A well-known test using unstructured pictures is the Rorschach inkblot test. During World War II, a Swiss psychiatrist, Hermann Rorschach, developed a set of inkblots which he found distinguished between patients with mental disorders and those who were normal. The ten pictures are still in use today, and there is an extensive body of literature relating responses to the inkblots to other aspects of perception and behavior (Beck, 1945, 1949, 1952). A sample of a Rorschach-like inkblot is presented in Figure 13.7.

FIGURE 13.6 Structured Picture (left) and Unstructured Picture (right)

FIGURE 13.7 Example of an Inkblot

Murray (1943) and his associates used a different approach. They developed pictures of people in different settings and asked the examinee to tell a story about the picture. The backgrounds are ambiguous and somewhat indistinct. The person's facial expression is also enigmatic. Sometimes even the age or sex of the person is not apparent. The pictures differ widely. They were planned to elicit responses related to relationships between people in various roles. This test is called the *Thematic Apperception Test* (TAT). In addition to the original set of pictures, there are now many sets, some of them designed specifically for certain age or ethnic groups. Figure 13.8 shows the kind of picture that is used in the TAT.

FIGURE 13.8 Example of the Kind of Picture Used on a Projective Test

In both the Rorschach and the TAT the experience and training of the examiner are of the utmost importance in interpreting the examinee's responses. The examiner not only records what the examinees say but also generalizes and draws conclusions about what is influencing the examinee's response.

Some other projective techniques have also been developed. In one of these the examinee responds to a list of words with whatever word first comes to mind. Imbedded in the list of supposedly neutral words are some words that have been found to provoke emotions of various kinds. The examiner's job is to interpret the responses to the emotion-laden words. Sometimes the examinee is simply handed a list and asked to write a response, and the list is scored. This procedure makes it possible to test several people at the same time. A sample of a section of such a word list is presented in Figure 13.9.

Arm	_____
Chair	_____
Mother	_____
Bed	_____
Automobile	_____
Brother	_____

FIGURE 13.9 Example of a Word List for a Projective Test

Another technique, often used with young children, is to provide dolls and other objects and allow the children to engage in free play while the examiner observes, interprets, and records the behavior. Also, children's artistic productions are sometimes analyzed, as in the Draw-A-Person test.

INTERPRETING AFFECTIVE MEASURES

It is difficult to apply the usual procedures for evaluating validity and reliability to affective measures. There are some good studies of both validity and reliability of the vocational interest inventories, but very few for personality tests. Validity is difficult to assess because often there is no better indicator of the trait than the instrument itself. The traditional ways of evaluating reliability also do not work with most of these instruments. Interpretation requires a very high level of inference. They may generate certain hypotheses that can be tested out as other information is accumulated. At best these instruments suggest possible explanations, which examiners have to interpret cautiously, using all available information. Unfortunately, some people make sweeping claims for some of the instruments, suggesting that scores on one or more of them measure the "whole personality." Many times, however, careful observation by a well-trained observer can provide more meaningful information than the tests do.

The usefulness of self-reports is limited by the individual's willingness and ability to analyze his or her feelings and to label behavior. The usefulness of observation techniques is also limited by the observer's skill and objectivity. And the usefulness of projective techniques is limited by the way traits are defined and by the examiner's skill at interpreting and generalizing examinees' responses.

SUMMARY

- Educators' assessment of affective traits is mostly through informal observation and self-reports.
- In-depth study of affective traits requires specially trained professionals.

STUDY QUESTIONS

1. What information do interest, attitude, and personality inventories provide for educators?
2. Why are some of these instruments of questionable value to teachers?
3. What are the major problems with instruments of this type?

FOR YOUR PROFESSIONAL GROWTH

1. Select a student about whom you would like to have more information.

2. List the kind of information you would like.

3. Consult Appendix F to locate standardized inventories that might provide the information you want.

4. Consult the *Mental Measurements Yearbook* to evaluate possibilities.

5. List some of the problems that reviewers of the various instruments identified.

PART FOUR

ॐ

Putting It All Together

The information in the preceding chapters provides a good foundation for using a wide variety of assessment information. However, assessment information is worth collecting only if you do something with it. Sometimes the use might involve only a single piece of information. For example, a teacher might use a single writing sample to determine instructional activities in writing for students for the next week. A counselor might look at an anecdotal record of a student's inappropriate classroom behavior to create a set of activities to change that behavior. Principals might look only at standardized test scores to plan instructional emphases for the next semester.

However, there are many more times when a single piece of information will not be enough because the behavior is too complex or because you want to summarize the achievements and behaviors in several subject areas or settings or over an extended period of time. An example is assigning grades for report cards. In addition, educators may conduct conferences with students, parents, or other educational professionals for the purpose of helping students improve their achievement and/or behavior. Finally, information may be shared with educational professionals who are external to the school and who are generally consulted for referrals of students for special services such as special education or speech therapy. In all of these situations, the task for an educator is to "paint a picture" of students by putting all the assessment data together.

The chapters in this part of the book deal with three situations, all of which require educators to combine information from a variety of sources, draw a conclusion, and prepare a report of some kind. The purpose of Part Four is to help educators put together the various concepts and assessment techniques in order to describe students for report cards, conferences, and referrals. We covered some of this information in discussing portfolios in Chapter 9, and these chapters will expand on the concepts presented there. Chapter 14 presents a detailed discussion of the processes and controversies grading individual assignments and determining report card grades. In Chapter 15, we discuss the procedures to follow in creating informal case studies of students to be used in conferences of various types. Chapter 16 completes this part of the book with a review of the procedures for referral for special services.

The Rights of Parents and Students. When educators use assessment information about students for *any* purpose, they should do so with the understanding that parents and students have rights that must be considered and protected. There are two often competing concerns about the rights of students and their parents regarding student records: (1) the right of students (over 18) and their parents to have access to the information and (2) their right not to have the information released to unauthorized people. Two documents from the 1970s deal with this dilemma.

Guidelines developed in a conference sponsored by the Russell Sage Foundation in 1970 provide five principles for test use and protection of parents' and students' rights:

1. There should be informed consent for the collection of data. (Informed consent is not required for tests that are a usual part of the school program, such as teacher-made tests and standardized group tests of achievement and aptitude.)
2. Different categories of data should be treated differently in terms of access.
3. All data should be verified for accuracy.
4. Parents and pupils should have access to the data.
5. No agency or persons other than the parents or school personnel who deal with the student should have access to student data without the permission of the parent (or student if the student is over 18).

These principles were incorporated in the Family Educational Rights and Privacy Act of 1974 (Section 513 of Public Law 93-380), also called the Buckley Amendment (Salvia & Ysseldyke, 1995). This law prohibits release of federal funds to any educational institution that fails to make available information about a student to the parents of the student or to the student if he or she is over 18. It also prohibits release of federal funds to educational agencies that release information about individual students to unauthorized persons or agencies.

Most school systems handle the situation by developing a policy that parents may inspect the records of their sons or daughters at a time convenient for the school, that students' records may be shared with professional personnel within the district, but that any other reporting of the information requires a written release from the parent (or student if over 18). Many districts have different policies for different categories of information, which may include grades, attendance, and scores on various categories of assessments, such as achievement, ability, and personality and interests.

In any case, the school has an obligation to provide information to parents and older students and to help them understand whatever information is reported to them. In order to do this, educators themselves need to be sure they understand what the scores mean and the significance of score changes.

14

ॐ

Grades and
Report Cards

PREVIEW

Reporting student progress is one of the most frustrating and controversial tasks a teacher faces. Reports should be based on good assessment data, but the teacher must also exercise a great deal of judgment, because the task not only requires measurement, it also requires evaluation, that is, making a judgment about the quality of the performance. Assigning grades involves a teacher's personal philosophy about the nature of children and the process of learning. It is important to note that there are wide differences of opinion as to how the task should be done—indeed, as to whether it should be done at all. That's right: Some educators believe that teachers should not assign grades at all (e.g., Kohn, 1994)!

MAJOR TOPICS	
The Teacher's Dilemma	Letters to Parents
Purposes of Reports and Grades	Parent-Teacher Conferences
Instructional Uses	Standards of Comparison
Guidance Uses	The Choice Between Normative
Administrative Uses	and Criterion-Based Grading
Motivation	Grading on Ability or Effort
Feedback	Grading on Improvement
Overview of Reporting Methods	Choosing a Grading Standard
Report Cards	Choosing a Procedure
Checklists of Objectives	Methods of Combining Information

THE TEACHER'S DILEMMA

Assigning grades brings into conflict the two primary roles of a teacher: (1) instructional leader and classroom manager and (2) mentor working to understand individual needs and to nurture and support each student. Making judgments about children requires a teacher to maintain some level of objectivity about each child (Seeley, 1994). Doing this is difficult if you genuinely care about your students and if you work hard to motivate and interest them. To some teachers it seems callous or even cruel to consider only *achievement* when assigning grades, especially after working so hard to develop many aspects of students' learning in addition to achievement. The conflict is especially great for elementary teachers. It becomes less pressing for teachers in higher grades and in college; but it is always present to some extent. Here are two scenarios that illustrate this situation:

SCENARIO 1

Marla Jones has been working all year to help three children in her fifth grade class who have been identified as potential dropouts and who have difficult home situations. Now, at the end of the grading period, she must assign grades to each child. One has worked very hard this term in social studies because he found a topic that interested him. But his reading and writing skills are so poor that even under the best conditions his work is of D or even F quality. Marla is afraid that if she gives him a D or F, he will become discouraged and stop working. She wants the grade to reward his effort for the term, and a D won't do that. She thinks about this challenge for several days and finally gives him a B on social studies and a C on everything else.

What would you have done?

SCENARIO 2

Fred Garza teaches both basic and regular classes in tenth grade science. At the end of this nine-week report period, he has to assign student grades.

The students in the basic science classes have worked very hard on a set of activities in ecology that do not require the abstract thinking or the level of reading and writing skills needed for the regular classes. Fred now faces a dilemma. How should he assign grades?

He could base grades for the basic science classes only on the performance of students in those classes and for the regular classes use a scale that covers only that group. Or he could use the same scale for both the basic and the regular classes.

The first choice would mean that A's in the basic and regular classes would not be comparable. This would have implications for students' GPAs, which are used for many administrative purposes and for reporting to parents. The second choice would mean that the effort and motivation of the hardworking basic-class students would not be recognized and might never be recognized with high grades.

What should Fred do?

You can see from these situations that grading may create a conflict for teachers and has many implications for both students and teachers. Grant Wiggins (1994) stated the dilemma concisely:

> Fairness demands that less skilled students not have their work compared to their more talented peers. But honesty demands that we report how all students are doing against high, uniform standards. (p. 33)

The inability to resolve this dilemma has led to the advocacy of many "innovative" methods of reporting student progress, each of which has problems of its own. In this chapter we will take you through the most often proposed grading systems.

Teachers make a lot of assessments that are used only *formatively*—that is, to determine whether students need more work and, if so, what they need. Formative assessment may be used to help teachers plan and to help students check their own progress, usually on individual assignments. As we pointed out in Chapter 9, some portfolios are used to collect information to be used in this way.

In contrast, assigning grades and preparing grade reports are usually *summative* activities, although they also may serve formative purposes. In this chapter, we assume that the teacher is collecting a variety of valid and reliable information about students. The task then is deciding how to put this information together and report it in a form that will be most informative to students, parents, and the school. In this chapter we focus on the summative function. For the formative use of individual assessments, refer to Chapter 6 on scoring paper-and-pencil tasks, Chapter 7 on performance and production tasks, Chapter 8 on direct observation and retrospective ratings, and Chapter 9 on portfolios. Those four chapters focus on the scoring of individual assignments.

To be meaningful, summative reports must be based on good assessments, but good summative reports also display careful and thoughtful integration and interpretation and are presented in a way that makes sense to the individuals to whom they are addressed. Taken together, all elements of a report to students or to parents should paint a verbal picture of student performance that is clear to everyone.

This chapter will help you think about how you view students and your perspective on the best way to assign and report grades. It also will provide you with some information about the most common grading procedures. We explore the issues and provide some guidance for individual teachers and for school faculties in deciding how to handle the task in a specific setting.

This chapter is addressed primarily to teachers, because they do most of the grading and reporting. However, many counselors and administrators find themselves in the position of talking to students and parents about the grades that teachers assign. They also will benefit from studying our suggestions and learning about the grading practices of the teachers with whom they work.

Suppose you are at the end of the grading period or the end of the school year, and you must make a judgment about the academic performance of the students in your classes. You have done your best to create interesting lessons based on sound and appropriate pedagogy and content. You have tried to involve students in interesting activities and to create tests that stimulate and challenge them to learn more. You have collected all of the student work and graded it in what you hope is a valid and reliable manner. Now is the time of reckoning. You must make a summative judgment about the students' work. How will you proceed? What system will you use? If your school or school district has a grading policy, will you use it and in what way?

Suppose you are concerned about and sometimes unsure of your decisions, because you know that grades are taken very seriously in our society. You think that teachers should take the grading process seriously and consider all the ramifications of what they are doing and what the outcomes may be.

There are many philosophies of grading and many systems for assigning grades. Every grading system has certain characteristics that make it better for some students than for others, and for some purposes than for others. To help you make a decision about how to handle grades for your students, we pose some questions for you to ask yourself:

Teachers' Questions About Grades

1. What is my purpose for assigning these grades?
2. Who will see the grades: students, parents, administrators, the general public?
3. What will be the consequences for the students who receive these grades?
4. What is the best procedure for me to use in assigning grades?
5. What problems are likely to arise with this procedure?

The first question addresses the primary purpose for grading. If we do not ask ourselves this question, we may create a convenient, even efficient, system that fails to help students and others. The second question also relates to purpose. We must consider who will see or use the grades and report cards, because we need to communicate accurately and effectively with all these people. The last three questions are extremely important. Because the consequences associated with grades may be very serious, it is important for teachers and other educators to un-

derstand the consequences of the various systems, to know the potential problems associated with each procedure, and to use that information in developing
the system they use.

Part of the difficulty with grading is that often the entire reporting process is
reduced to the assignment of a single symbol that is supposed to convey all the information about a student's performance. At various times, recommendations
about which symbols to use have changed. For example, prior to the 1930s, grades
were reported as numerals intended to represent a percentage, but the problem that
has never been resolved was to identify *what the number was a percentage of.* The most
common set of symbols in use today is a five-letter system: A, B, C, D, and F. From
time to time various school districts have proposed or adopted "Pass/Fail" or the
"H or O/S/U" (Honors or Outstanding/Satisfactory/Unsatisfactory) system.
Sometimes letter grades are referenced to percentages.

Figure 14.1 presents a sample senior high school report card in which a single
letter is used to report grades in each course. Notice that some courses are graded
"Satisfactory" or "Unsatisfactory," although most of the courses are graded on an
A, B, C, D, and F scale. The A, B, C, D, and F grades have a numeric referent,
which supposedly indicates the percentage of the content for a grading period
the student has mastered (we deal with this matter later in the chapter). The report card shown in Figure 14.1 also allows teachers to rate effort, cooperation,
and citizenship behaviors for each course in each grading period. There are also
spaces to indicate numbers of absences and tardies. Comments by teachers may
be added during the year, but the small amount of space makes meaningful comments difficult to write.

In spite of the many criticisms of report cards, no one has found a solution
that would allow schools to do away with them. Instead of simply trying to do
away with report cards, we should look for strategies to accomplish what we need
to do in such a way that we reduce the bad effects of report cards and enhance
the necessary communication with students, parents, and others.

The problem with report cards is not the set of symbols used; it is the fact that
a single symbol is being used to convey too much information. As Grant Wiggins
(1994) says:

> Letter grades per se are not the problem. Using a *single* grade with no clear
> and stable meaning to summarize all aspects of performance *is* a problem. We
> need more, not fewer grades (p. 29).

The solution should be obvious: Either we should report student progress in
more than one way, using the most appropriate method for each aspect of
progress. Or we should define very carefully what the single mark is intended to
convey and make that information known to all teachers, students and parents. In
order for report cards to be meaningful, these decisions must be made:

1. What purposes is the report card to serve?
2. What aspects of a student's behavior will be considered
   in determining the grade?

HIGHLANDS UNIFIED SCHOOL DISTRICT

SCHOOL: _____   GRADE: _____

NAME: _____

SCHOOL YEAR: _____

PROMOTED TO: _____

Subject	Grading Period				Effort **				Cooperation **				Citizenship **			
	1	2	3	4	1	2	3	4	1	2	3	4	1	2	3	4
English*																
Mathematics*																
Science*																
American History*																
Physical Education **																
Music **																

Comments:

	1	2	3	4
Absences				
Tardies				

* A = 91–100   B = 80–90   C = 70–79   D = 60–69   F = Below 60

** S = Satisfactory   U = Unsatisfactory

FIGURE 14.1 Example of a Secondary Report Card

3. What methods of reporting will be used?

4. To what standard will a student's performance be compared?

5. How should various pieces of data be weighted in determining the grade?

PURPOSES OF REPORTS AND GRADES

In spite of the controversies about whether and how grades should be reported, grades serve many important functions. We all know that students, parents, schools, and potential employers take grades seriously. Although teachers make many judgments about students every day, few of these judgments become a matter of public record. Grades, however, do become part of a student's record and are part of the information that may be reported to others authorized to receive it. Not only is the report card used to inform parents and students themselves as to how the student is faring, but the grades are also used in decisions such as whether a student may participate in sports, whether he or she will be admitted to college, whether he or she will obtain a scholarship or other academic honor, and whether he or she will be required to repeat a course or a grade.

Because teachers generally do not like to grade students and find the process very frustrating, you may ask, "Why, then, do we do it?" The simple answer is "Because we are required to." Parents, school administrators, school and other governing boards, and state departments of education require some form of reporting and sometimes prescribe the type of report to be used. All of these groups see grades as being useful for many purposes, often for purposes not intended by the teachers who assign them. Grades provide a basis for important decisions—further education and employment, for example. They are used as a means to stimulate, direct, and reward the educational efforts of students. They are reported to the public and to foundations and state and federal educational agencies as evidence of the success of educational programs.

A grading system should take into account all likely uses and should serve the most important functions for particular groups of students and for specific circumstances. Grades for first grade students are used primarily to inform parents of students' progress toward mastery of some basic skills. Grades for secondary and college students are often used to certify that students have reached a level of mastery much beyond the basic level. Some of the ways in which grades are used are reviewed briefly below.

Instructional Uses

The most useful type of reporting for instructional purposes is a *formative* report. The teacher gives a test on a specific unit and reports the scores to students, also providing an explanation of the correct answers. Or the teacher rates students' speeches or research reports, and the rating scale indicates the strong or weak points. Or the teacher uses a checklist to identify skills attained. The teacher may use any or all of this information in a conference with students. Similar reports may be made to parents, or teachers may use a conference or telephone call to inform parents about students' progress. These grades may be part of a report card grade but are not listed separately.

Reporting methods of this type are used most frequently in elementary schools, where teachers have a relatively small number of students for long periods of time. In secondary schools, there is a tendency for teachers to assign a single grade based on some type of average of test scores and scores on other assignments, unless the school has specifically developed some additional or alternative reporting system. This procedure is changing in some schools with the advent of educational reforms that involve combining subject areas such as mathematics and science or English and history. In these situations students may be with the same teacher or teachers for extended parts of the day, and teachers may use reporting methods similar to those in elementary schools.

Guidance Uses

Reports of progress in specific courses can help students and their parents make decisions about the students' educational future. Should they consider higher education? Do they seem to be better in one area of study than in others? Do they have vocational goals that will require some additional strengthening in certain areas? Counselors use this information as well as the grade-point average to help a student decide whether to apply to specific colleges or universities. Counselors may also look at the types of courses taken and the grades in those specific courses. For example, in helping a student who wants to become an engineer, a counselor might look at the mathematics and science courses the student has taken and the grades the student received.

Administrative Uses

Many administrative functions involve the use of student grades. Perhaps the first and most important use is to report to parents. Schools must find ways to let parents know how their children are doing in school, because children often do not talk about school and teachers are not usually in frequent communication with parents. Communication about the grading system is also important because parents sometimes do not understand the system being used at their children's school (Waltman & Frisbie, 1994).

Report cards and conferences are among the most commonly used methods of communication. Grades on report cards are expected to indicate student success and areas that need more work. These grades often stimulate conversations between parents and their children about the reasons for the students' performance. In addition, a report card might cause a parent to ask for a teacher conference to discuss a child's achievement.

Grades are also widely used for making administrative decisions, not all of which are considered appropriate by some measurement experts. Grades often determine whether students "pass" or "fail" the grade in elementary schools, whether they get credit for a course in secondary schools and college, and even whether they graduate from high school. Grades may be used to determine whether students are admitted to advanced courses. And in some schools grades are used to determine which "track" of studies students are allowed to pursue.

Along with test scores, secondary school grades are often among the criteria that determine whether a student is admitted to a college or university. Grades also may determine whether a student is awarded a scholarship. For decisions of this type, the concern often is not so much whether students have mastered the basic content of a course, but how their performance compares with that of other students.

Two other administrative uses of grades have become common in recent years. One is in district reports cards—reports created to inform the public about the quality of schools. Figure 14.2 shows an outline of such a report. In addition to providing descriptive information about the school plant and the staff, these reports may include information about student enrollments, attendance, and the distribution of grades in various courses. The reports may also include information about test scores, graduation and dropout rates, and students' college entrance rates, as well as demographic information about students and information about teachers' degrees, credentials, and years of experience. If there are mandated state or district standards, the district report card may also include a section on progress in meeting those standards.

**SCHOOL ACCOUNTABILITY REPORT CARD
CENTRAL HIGH SCHOOL
1997**

Message from the Principal
Contents
  School Facilities and Safety
  Teacher Education, Experience, and Assignments
  Counseling and Other Support Services
  Student Profile
    Enrollment and Grades in All Courses
    Enrollment and Grades in Upper Level Courses
    Attendance
    Graduation Rates
    Honors to Graduates
    College Admission of Graduates

FIGURE 14.2 Outline of a District Report Card

Another, lesser known, use of grades is in the evaluation of programs funded with state and federal money. Evaluators of programs in mathematics and science, or of programs to prevent students from dropping out of school, may use information about students' course grades to determine whether they are improving in their course work and whether an innovative program seems to be related to such improvement. Since the 1960s, such grant-funded programs have become more common, and the use of grades as an indicator of success has also increased.

Motivation

Educators often hope that students will be motivated to work harder in order to receive good grades. State legislatures and local school boards frequently "raise standards" by raising the GPA required for students to play on sports teams or even to graduate. The intent is to motivate students to work harder. What these people do not realize is that the results are likely to be very different from what they are hoping for.

In the first place, the dropout rate is likely to go up because some students believe they will not be able to meet the new standards. This effect may be ignored, however, because grades do go up somewhat as teachers adjust to the new standards and either limit the coverage of their assessments so students will score higher on criteria-based assessments or change their expectations in keeping with reality. Grades also may go up as those students who struggle and earn lower grades leave school, reducing the proportion of students with low grades.

Sometimes grades are used in an attempt to improve behavior or attendance—they are lowered for absences or incidents of misbehavior. This strategy does not often work. If grades motivate at all, they motivate students who routinely make good grades. Students with poor grades are not motivated by the possibility of improved grades or by the threat of having their grades lowered further. And even the good students for whom grades are important, when faced with a new task or assignment, frequently ask, "Does it count on our grade?" If the answer is "No," they may refuse to participate in the activity or expend little effort.

Grades are at best an *extrinsic* motivator and are not as effective as an *intrinsic* motivator that impels an individual to value learning for its own sake. Interestingly, numerous studies in various settings demonstrate that extrinsic motivators may actually decrease performance (Kohn, 1994). Thomas R. Guskey (1994) suggested an alternative to using grades as a negative reinforcer:

> Rather than attempting to punish students with a low mark, teachers can better motivate students by regarding their work as incomplete and requiring additional effort. (p. 16)

Feedback

Notwithstanding the difficulties addressed above, it is difficult for students to improve unless they know how they are doing. And it is possible that feedback might motivate students if they receive *positive* reinforcement for some extra effort. Sometimes, however, the motivation is only to try to improve *grades,* not the learning that grades are supposed to represent. Furthermore, grades for a grading period may be given weeks after a student completes an assignment. For many students, the feedback is too little and too late. Most students need detailed information on the ways their work needs to improve, and they appreciate commendations for areas in which they are doing well or have improved. And they need this information at the time they do the work, not weeks later.

Susan Brookhart (1993) recommends the use of an immediate feedback sheet in scoring writing assessments and cites the improved validity and reliability of the scoring as well as the provision of information to students about their strengths and weaknesses. Similar procedures could be used in other courses. We presented many such procedures in Part Two of this book.

In some schools the report card includes grades or a checklist to cover nonachievement variables such as attitude, effort, work habits, and social skills. In addition, many schools now use a checklist for subskills or subcontent, such as quality of writing, clarity of thinking, and organization. Other report cards provide a space for teachers to make comments.

OVERVIEW OF REPORTING METHODS

After you decide that you know what standards you want to follow and the purpose you hope your grades will serve, how do you decide what method of reporting to use? Report cards are the most commonly used vehicle for reporting student progress, and many types of report cards have been developed. However, some schools use other methods instead of, or in addition to, report cards. The various procedures are discussed below.

Report Cards

The most common type of report card uses a single symbol for each course or subject to summarize all aspects of a student's progress. The most commonly used symbols are A, B, C, D, and F, although the numerals 5, 4, 3, 2, and 1 may be used instead. Sometimes pluses and minuses are added.

Other systems use different sets of symbols, such as "H or O/S/U," or "S/U," or "E, S, U," or "Pass/Fail." Sometimes grades of this kind are used only for elective courses, which the school wants to encourage students to take, but which students avoid out of concern about lowering their GPAs. At other times, these marks are used for behavior and participation. When a school uses both the standard grading system and a pass/fail or satisfactory/unsatisfactory system, the pass/fail or S/U grades are usually not considered when the GPA is computed.

As noted above, the report card is sometimes modified to allow separate reporting of achievement, effort, and behavior. Some report cards provide a checklist of skills or content or a place for teachers to write comments. Figure14.3 shows a report card with spaces to check many aspects of achievement. Figure 14.4 shows a report card with spaces for teacher comments. Figure 14.5 is an example of a report card with a place for separate grades for attitude, effort, citizenship, and cooperation. Attendance is also reported.

Checklist of Objectives

Instead of assigning a single grade in each course, some schools, particularly in the primary grades, use a checklist, similar to the one shown in Figure 14.6, which lists desired skills for each course and provides a space to check whether the student has attained each skill. Checklists similar to those presented in Chapters 7 and 8 could also be used.

A checklist may be very useful for formative purposes, to guide students' practice, but it usually is not sufficient to serve the purpose of summarizing a student's progress and providing a permanent record of his or her status at a given time. Nevertheless, checklists are useful for daily work and projects, and they may be used to supplement report cards. Progress toward meeting state or district standards may also be noted on a checklist.

Letters to Parents

Many schools use letters to parents to replace or supplement the report card, especially in the early grades. The hope is that a letter will provide information about the unique strengths, weaknesses, and needs of each pupil, along with some suggestions for improvement. A letter may provide important information for parents, and it may be a useful supplement to a report card, but there are some serious drawbacks to the use of letters as the sole source of information for parents.

First, writing comprehensive and thoughtful letters requires a lot of time, and some important information may be overlooked. Second, many teachers do not have the skill to write letters that convey exactly what needs to be said without angering parents. Third, parents often misinterpret even skillfully written letters. Finally, records of this type are difficult to maintain in a permanent file, to summarize, and to maintain continuity from term-to-term or year-to-year.

Letters should be written when the teacher needs to provide some additional information to help the parent understand the report card. We believe they are not appropriate as the sole method of reporting.

Parent-Teacher Conferences

Conferences offer an opportunity for two-way communication between teachers and parents and may be a useful supplement to report cards. However, this method of reporting has the same drawbacks as letters—large time and skill requirements, possibility of misunderstandings, and failure to provide a permanent, consistent record.

NAME: _____ TEACHER: _____ GRADE: _____ SCHOOL YEAR: _____

EXPLANATION OF MARKS:

A = Excellent B = Good C = Satisfactory D = Needs Improvement F = Failure S = Satisfactory U = Unsatisfactory

	Quarters			
	1	2	3	4
Language Arts				
Reading Grade				
Reads with understanding				
Uses word recognition skills				
Reads well orally				
Shows growth in vocabulary				
Writing Grade				
Expresses thoughts well in writing				
Uses proper language mechanics				
Uses dictionary				
Spells words correctly in writing				
Spells assigned words correctly				
Listening: Listens actively				
Speaking: Expresses thoughts orally				
Uses correct speech				
Mathematics Grade				
Understands basic concepts				
Knows mathematics processes				
Reasons well in problems				
Social Studies Grade				
Participates in projects and activities				
Uses globes and maps				
Uses reference materials				

	Quarters			
	1	2	3	4
Science				
Participates in activities				
Understands scientific concepts				
Experiments to find answers				
Art				
Physical Education				
Develops physical skills				
Participates in activities				
Music				
Citizenship Problems				
Needs To:				
Respect school property				
Respect property of others				
Complete homework				
Listen in class				
Follow directions				
Cooperate with others				
Show good sportsmanship				
Come to class promptly after recess				
Attendance				
Total days absent				
Total days tardy				

FIGURE 14.3 Example of a Report Card Including a Checklist

NAME: _____   TEACHER: _____   GRADE: _____   SCHOOL YEAR: _____

EXPLANATION OF MARKS:

A = Excellent   B = Good   C = Needs Improvement   F = Failure   S = Satisfactory   U = Unsatisfactory

	Quarters				Comments
	1	2	3	4	
Language					First Quarter
Reading					
Writing					
Listening					
Speaking					Second Quarter
Mathematics					
Social Studies					
Science/Health					
Physical Education					Third Quarter
Art					
Music					
Citizenship					
Attendance					Fourth Quarter
Total days absent					
Total days tardy					

FIGURE 14.4 Example of a Report Card Including Space for Comments

NAME: _____   TEACHER: _____

GRADE: _____   SCHOOL YEAR: _____

EXPLANATION OF MARKS:

A = Excellent   B = Good   C = Satisfactory   D = Needs Improvement   F = Failure
S = Satisfactory   U = Unsatisfactory

Achievement

	Quarters						Quarters			
	1	2	3	4			1	2	3	4
Language Arts						Attitude				
Reading						Effort				
Writing						Citizenship				
Listening						Attendance				
Speaking										
Mathematics										
Social Studies										
Science/Health										
Physical Education										
Art										
Music										

FIGURE 14.5 Example of a Report Card Including Grades on Attitude, Effort, and Citizenship

STANDARDS OF COMPARISON

When evaluating the quality of student performance, teachers must use some kind of standard to help them decide how good the performance is and to convey that information to students and their parents. Consider these statements about Tom J.; then answer the questions that follow.

"Tom J. is in the top 1 percent of his grade on a nationally normed achievement test."

"Tom has mastered 75 percent of the state-adopted curriculum framework."

"Tom's IQ score indicates that he should be able to work at a grade level two years above his current placement.

Questions

1. Which statement provides correct information about Tom?
2. Which information should be reported on Tom's report card?
3. What should be entered in Tom's permanent record?

NAME: _____

TEACHER: _____   GRADE: _____   SCHOOL YEAR: _____

EXPLANATION OF MARKS: A check mark (√) indicates the student has acquired the skill.

	Quarters			
	1	2	3	4
READING				
Reads silently with understanding				
Uses word recognition skills				
Reads orally with expression				
Uses dictionary to build vocabulary				
WRITING				
Expresses thoughts in writing				
Uses dictionary to correct spelling				
Uses proper language mechanics				
Uses dictionary to find better words				
Spells words correctly in writing				
Spells assigned words correctly				
SPEAKING				
Prepares a speech				
Expresses thoughts orally				
Answers questions about speech				
MATHEMATICS				
Understands basic concepts				
Knows which process to use				
Reasons well in problems				
Solves problems accurately				
SOCIAL STUDIES				
Participates in projects and activities				
Uses globes and maps				
Uses reference materials				
DAYS ABSENT				

FIGURE 14.6 Example of a Checklist Report

The answer to question 1 is that each of the statements could be correct. For question 2, the answer depends at least partly on the purposes of the grades to be given to Tom. If he is in an honors algebra course, his grades may be used in making a decision about his admission to college or obtaining a scholarship. In that case, his achievement may be compared with a larger national sample of students, and the teacher should base Tom's grade on a comparison of his accomplishments with those of other honors algebra students. But if Tom is a young child, his parents and future teachers are more likely to be concerned with the specific skills he has mastered and with whether he is being challenged by the curriculum in his class. In this case, Tom's teacher might assign his grade on an absolute or criterion basis in which his grade would be based on the percentage of the curriculum he has mastered.

Whatever the basis on which Tom's grades are determined, both Tom and his parents need to understand exactly what kind of information is being reported. Some schools try to convey all of the information by providing several grades for each course or content area. Other schools use teacher comments or parent-teacher conferences to explain the meaning of the reported grade and to add other kinds of information. According to Wiggins (1994), confusion arises because teachers do not make clear what the basis for the grades is—that is, with what standard the student is being compared. As you can see, making a decision about the standard and using the appropriate procedures is much more complicated than it might at first seem. The answer to the third question is that all information should be entered in the appropriate place on Tom's student record.

The standard that you decide to use will reflect your philosophical ideas about students and the learning experience and will be based on your belief about the purposes grades should serve. For example, if you view learners as being on a long continuum of achievement, then a grading system using a scale comparing a student's achievement with that of other students in your class or in the school is in order. If you view grades as being an indicator of how much of a specified content students have learned, then a grade indicating a proportion of how much they learned is appropriate. If you view grades as tools to be used as rewards or punishments, you might wish to think about the consequences of making grades indicate how hard students have worked—that is, the amount of effort they have put forth. Or you might want to use grades to indicate improvement rather than current achievement. Regardless of your position, you must choose a standard—whether you are grading a student's daily assignment or deciding which grade goes on the report card—and you need to make your position clear to your students and their parents. Table 14.1 summarizes several standards used in assigning grades, indicating the type of information provided, giving examples, and reviewing the results. Notice how the results or consequences differ from standard to standard.

The Choice Between
Normative and Criterion-Based Grading

With *normative grading,* the standard against which each student's performance is compared is the performance of a group of students of which the student is a legitimate part. The group may be a national grade-level sample, as it is in nationally normed achievement testing, or it may be the tenth grade mathematics students of Central High School. It also may be ESL students enrolled in an English class. The point is that each student is compared with the designated group, and an individual student's performance is evaluated in terms of how his or her performance compares with the performance of that group. This kind of grading is fairly easy to handle, but it may not provide the kind of information that students and their parents need and want.

Table 14.1 Standards of Comparison as the Basis for Assigning Grades

Standard	Type of Information	Examples	Results or Consequences
Normative or Relative Grading	Performance of other pupils Grades are set so a fixed percentage of students earn A's, B's, etc.	Percentile rank of students on a test Grading on the curve	A certain percentage of students get A's, B's, C's, D's, and F's regardless of the overall performance of the class or group.
Criterion or Absolute Grading	Predefined standards Percentage of objectives mastered Specific objectives mastered All students who meet the criteria for A's, B's, etc., receive them	Percentage of state-adopted "minimum standards" mastered Percentage of national curricula mastered Tests scored as a percentage of total Grade expressed as percentage	Students earn grades by meeting criteria for the A's, B's, etc. Therefore, it is possible that all students in the group might get A's or all might get F's.
Aptitude or Ability Grading	Performance in comparison with ability Performance in comparison with others in a "tracked" course (honors, basic, etc.)	Comparison with prediction from mental age Comparison only with students in a "tracked" course	The grade has no meaning unless the ability score is known or inferred. This procedure assumes that we have an accurate measure of aptitude. All students could get A's if they are working at their correct ability level.
Relative Improvement Grading	Performance showing improvement over time	Change from previous achievement	Only those with the greatest improvement may earn A's. Those who already know the subject well may show only a small improvement, so they would not get A's.
Amount of Effort Grading	Amount of effort expended	Comparison of effort required versus actual effort used in assignment	Only those with the greatest effort may earn A's, although their performance may be poor. Those who already know the subject well may be highly skilled but would get lower grades. This procedure also assumes that we have an accurate measure of effort.
Pass/Fail Grading	Like criterion grading with one set of criteria	Grades in physical education or music class Vocational courses Work study or internship	Gradations of quality of performances are not rewarded. As a result, participation and attendance become factors.

With *criterion-based grading,* each student's performance is compared with a standard of mastery, so criterion-based grading is most useful when a mastery learning approach to teaching and learning is used. Grades are defined in terms of what percentage of the objectives students have achieved. This approach requires many conditions that are difficult to meet.

Both approaches are discussed further in the next sections of this chapter.

Normative Grading.   Advocates of normative grading argue that the best basis we have for deciding what students *should learn* is information about what they actually *do learn.* That is the thinking that has led to the use of *norms.* Norms are developed by testing a representative group of students and using the distribution of their scores as the criteria for judging how well others do on the test. A problem is that we get very different information depending on which norms group we use for our comparison: A student may be at the top of a group of "basic" students but be only average in a regular class. Or a student may be in the top 10 percent of regular students but be only average when compared with a group enrolled in an honors class. However, as long as we use the same group for comparison, we can get derived scores that have similar means and ranges.

So our first decision in using normative grading must be, "With what group will we compare students in this class?" Usually normative grading works best for classes that are taken by very large numbers of students who may be considered "average" students—for instance, students in a required class in English, mathematics, history, or science. However, we may use normative methods of converting scores and then adjust our grading system to fit nontypical situations, as we will show you in the latter part of this chapter.

Criterion-Based Grading.   An alternative to normative grading is to score and grade students' work in terms of the extent to which they have mastered the objectives of the course, or at least that part of it that has been covered during a grading period. In a criterion-based system, a given score on one assignment should indicate the same level of proficiency as the same score on another assignment.

Implementing this system is difficult; and sometimes when a grading system is criterion referenced, the objectives are so limited that many important high-level objectives are omitted (this problem has been discussed in earlier chapters). But in spite of the difficulties and possible pitfalls, there is good reason for trying to help students understand how they are doing in terms of what they should be learning, rather than how they compare with other students. The first task is to get all the scores on a common scale. One method that has traditionally been used to do this is to convert all scores to percentages. Another method is to use a point system, and a third is to use rubrics.

Grading on Ability or Effort

Assigning grades that reflect ability, effort, or both requires a judgment about students' ability and effort. But there seldom is any real information on which to base the judgment. What usually happens is that the teacher scores the assessments and then adjusts the scores in some way based on his or her informal observation of how hard a student tries or how hard the material is for a student.

A student who seems to be having a hard time but who always turns in homework may have a plus added to the grade, or the grade may even be raised to the next letter. A student who does well on tests but frequently fails to turn in assignments or often creates a disturbance in class may have his or her grade lowered. Grades assigned in this way are impossible to interpret without a careful description of the considerations that were used. It is much more informative to assign grades either normatively or with reference to a criterion then to rate "effort" separately, as required by the report card in Figure 14.5.

Grading on Improvement

Improvement grading is closely related to grading on effort and raises the same issues. To really assess improvement, you would need a preassessment and a postassessment, and you would have to check the difference between them for statistical significance. These assessments are not likely to be available, so teachers who want to base grades on improvement have to depend on their informal observations.

In this case, too, it is better to let the grades simply reflect achievement. If a student really is improving, grades for this period should be better than grades for the preceding period.

CHOOSING A GRADING STANDARD

On the one hand, teachers cite the "unfairness" of giving an A to both the best student in an advanced placement physics course and to a student in a remedial reading course, when these grades may be part of an average to determine who gets a scholarship or whether a student is admitted to college. On the other hand, there is concern about the self-image of a student who never receives an A or B simply because he or she takes only basic courses for which C is the highest grade. And what about the fact that some students can make A's with very little effort, while others work very hard and are only able to make a C? This issue must be resolved by consideration of the purpose the grades will serve.

Interestingly, when faculty members in a school are questioned, they do not always agree about their grading standards—a situation that greatly confuses students and parents (Stiggins, Frisbie, & Duke, 1989). Furthermore, even though many schools and districts have developed and published their grading policies, our experience at all levels of education indicates that teachers often do not know about the school policy or simply choose to ignore it. So it is not surprising if students and their parents, too, do not understand school policy.

Questions such as those raised above have led some schools to decide that some courses, such as physical education, art, or music, will not be graded or will carry only S/U or pass/fail grades and will not be considered when grade-point averages are computed. This practice has consequences if the school or students need those grades for other purposes.

One university of which we are aware does not award any grades unless students request them. Instead, students receive written summaries of their achievements. This arrangement is acceptable if the students seek no further education. But if they apply for admission to graduate school, they need GPAs. This university's graduates have no GPAs unless students have requested course grades. Instead, graduate schools receive written summaries of the students' work toward bachelor's degrees. Unfortunately for the students, graduate admissions offices are not equipped to handle such records. Therefore, applicants with no GPA must take the *Graduate Record Examination* (GRE) or some other appropriate entrance examination even though it may be waived for other applicants who have GPAs that meet the entrance requirements.

Because grades are used in making such important decisions, the basis of the grades should be carefully considered, and the type of standards on which they are based must be made clear. We discuss some of the considerations below. Then we present seven methods of computing grades from the same data so you can see the results of each method.

CHOOSING A PROCEDURE

Let's go back to the original issue: What kind of grades shall we report? How shall we report them? Your answers to these questions will reflect your philosophy and may put you in a difficult professional position. To help you resolve your position on this issue, here are some guidelines for developing your grading system: A grading system should be

- *Fair* to all students
- *Accurate* in representing what students have learned
- *Consistent* in its application to all students
- *Defensible* to others, including students, other faculty, administrators, and the general public

To help ensure that your grading system meets those guidelines, we suggest the following rules for assigning grades.

Rule 1: Determine the Purpose for Your Grading System in Advance of Assigning Grades.   As we have emphasized numerous times, you always must be certain of your purpose. In this instance, the uses for the grades and for your grading system must be clear before you start assigning grades. For example, if your purpose is to motivate students with your grades, then you probably will not want a normative system. With a normative system, most students would not get high grades no matter how hard they worked. Unless your students are unusual, getting a low grade even though they tried hard would be very unmotivating. The criterion or absolute system will probably work best in this situation.

Perhaps you are assigning grades that will be used for selection to a program or for determining whether a student will move to a higher-level course. In this case, a normative or relative system might work best. Whatever you choose, your choice should be based on the purpose for which the grades will be used.

Rule 2: Include Only Achievement in the Academic Grade. The issue of what teachers should consider when computing grades is very controversial. It is closely related to the purpose for assigning grades. If the purpose of the grade is to report what a student is learning and how well he or she is achieving, then including other criteria in the calculation of the grade may convey misinformation. Many teachers think that including attendance, participation, effort, preparedness for class (having pencils, pens, etc.), and submission of homework in a course grade motivates students. It may do that, but it may also cause confusion. Figure 14.7 illustrates this point. When you look at the distribution of points for Betty and Fred you see that Betty consistently performed at a lower level than Fred. If the purpose of the grades that Ms. Wood gives is to show the amount of English that students have learned, the grades as she has designed them do not reveal the real difference in the performance of Betty and Fred. When the ratings for attendance and preparation are omitted, there is an *8-point difference* in their totals.

Ms. Wood uses a 10-point spread of scores for each grade level, so an 8-point difference could make a difference in the letter grades that Betty and Fred receive. Even more important, grades for Ms. Wood's classes are impossible to interpret to students, parents, other teachers, administrators, or the public unless an explanation is provided. Furthermore, grades assigned by other teachers in Ms. Wood's school who consider only achievement are not comparable to the grades that Ms. Wood assigns.

English teacher Sandra Wood includes points for attendance and preparedness when calculating total points for her students' course grades. She uses a system in which 90 to 100 points are worth an A, 80 to 89 a B, 70 to 79 a C, 60 to 69 a D, and 59 or less an F. Two of Ms. Wood's students, Betty and Fred, each earned 82 points for their five assignments, attendance, and preparedness. Betty, however, consistently performed at a lower level than Fred.

Point Distribution for Two Students, Including Points for Attendance and Preparedness

Student	Research Paper 1	Research Paper 2	Weekly Assignments	Midterm Exam	Final Exam	Attendance	Preparedness	Total Points
Betty	12	12	8	15	25	5	5	82
Fred	13	14	9	17	27	1	1	82
Maximum points	15	15	10	20	30	5	5	100

FIGURE 14.7 Effect of Including Attendance and Preparation in Computing Grades

Also, there are other, more subtle issues. Why did a student of Fred's achievement level not come to class or bring the necessary materials for class? Was Fred unable to attend class because of personal illness or difficulties at home? Did he not need to come to class because he found the course material easily learnable without the teacher? Did he lack money to purchase the necessary school supplies? Raising these questions and finding the answers require more information than is provided by a simple letter grade. When information is buried in a composite grade for the course, such questions might not even be raised.

If there is only a single grade for a course, and if that grade reflects only achievement, how do you provide feedback for nonachievement factors such as attendance and preparedness? As we suggested earlier, you can supplement the report with checklists, letters to parents, or conferences. Some schools require separate reporting of several aspects of a student's performance in addition to the achievement grade. Figure 14.5 is a sample of such a report card: There is a grade on "Attitude," "Effort," and "Citizenship," with "Attendance" reported separately. Critics of this system argue that teachers have no way of knowing how hard a student has worked and that attitudes are much more difficult to assess validly than is achievement. Also, some teachers say that students are concerned only with the achievement grade and have no incentive to improve their attitude, effort, or attendance unless the achievement grade is subject to being cut. It is an interesting dilemma.

In spite of this argument, we believe that a report card should convey, as a minimum, information about students' achievement in the usual academic courses and that this information should not be contaminated by other considerations. Wiggins (1994) reports that parents' greatest concern is with how well their daughter or son is learning. Whether students should be permitted to take courses in which achievement is not a consideration is a different matter, as is the question of how to handle additional information. Sometimes the academic grade is broken down into several categories, and the student receives a rating or check mark for those categories, in addition to the grade for the course, or there is space for the teacher to make comments about other variables. See Figure 14.3 and Figure 14.4.

Rule 3: Communicate Your Grading System at the Beginning of the Term or Year and When an Assignment is Made.

Students should be able to judge the importance of various assignments by looking at the criteria for grades. We recommend that teachers develop rubrics for each grade that describe the expectations students must meet to receive each grade. Students can participate in developing the rubrics, and they should have a copy of them so they understand what is expected.

Rule 4: Avoid Changing the Grading Criteria During the Term.

This rule follows from Rule 3. Once you have set up a grading procedure, stick to it unless a major event happens to cause you to reevaluate your procedure. One such event would be the realization that the course you planned is far too difficult for your students. You would have to rethink your criteria and weights for some assignments. Other events necessitating reevaluation would be the occurrence of a natural disaster in which tests and term papers are lost, or a fire in the library that makes library research for a paper impossible. In such cases you would have to make some adjustment. But be careful! Nothing angers students and parents more or causes more confusion than changing the rules in midstream.

In addition, you should assign grades consistently. If you have decided to use criterion-based grading, be sure to use it for all your assessments. If you decided to use relative grades, your grades on the various assessments should reflect that decision, even though you decide to supplement those grades with checklists, comments, conferences, and the like.

Rule 5: Include Variables That are Relevant to the Assignments in the Computation of the Grade. As Rule 3 indicates, you may want to report performance on more than one type of assessment. If you must combine all assessments into a single grade, you can indicate the weights you will assign to various assessments, as in the Sandra Wood example in Figure 14.7

Rule 6: Try to Match Your Grading System to That of the School or District in Which You Work. This rule is probably an expectation, either written or unwritten, of your district or school. Usually a district has a grading policy and a report card that all teachers are expected to use. The advantage of a single policy and report card is that when students move from one school to another within the district, the meaning of their grades remains the same. Sometimes, however, there are special reporting systems for the primary grades and for students with disabilities.

METHODS OF COMBINING INFORMATION

Our assumption in this section is that you have decided what kind of information you want to include in students' grades and that you have a valid method of assessment so that you have a score for each piece of information. But what, you may be asking, are the most common and best ways to combine information? Table 14.2 summarizes the seven approaches that we cover in this chapter. As you can see from the table, each procedure has advantages and disadvantages. Some are easy to calculate but provide inaccurate or invalid combinations of scores for end-of-semester or end-of-year grades.

The first two methods of simply adding raw scores or multiplying raw scores by the course point value (a form of weighting)—are the ones that teachers most often use. They are also the *least* desirable in terms of validity or fairness. Next, we list two methods of deriving normative scores. Converting raw scores to standard scores (listed third in Table 14.2) is the best and most valid procedure for combining grades that have a relative interpretation. This method ensures the most valid and fair outcomes for students. However, it is also the most mathematically complex. Although we recommend it, we know that teachers often think they do not have the time or expertise to use it, but we offer it as a kind of gold

Table 14.2 Methods of Combining Assignment Scores to Calculate Course Grades

Method	Procedure	Advantages	Disadvantages
Addition of unweighted scores	Add all assignment raw scores regardless of importance to course and total possible score	Easy to calculate	Emphasizes large point assignments and masks impact of small point assignments
Addition of scores weighted by their course point value	Multiply each score by its point value for the course Add all of the weighted scores	Moderately easy to calculate Increases the importance of assignments by their course value	Magnifies impact of large point assignments and reduces value of small point assignments Unequal means and SDs
Relative grading: converting raw scores to standard scores	Calculate means and standard deviations Calculate standard scores Multiply standard scores by weights for course	Puts all assignments on a common scale for combining scores Weights all assignments by importance	Difficult to calculate Requires calculation of means and standard deviations for each assignment.
Relative grading: converting raw scores to letter grades	Convert raw scores to letter grades Assign points to letter grades Multiply points by weights for course	Easy to calculate Creates a common scale for combining scores Weights all assignments by importance	Requires several steps for each assignment score Only works if converted means and standard deviations are about the same for every assignment
Criterion grading: converting raw scores to percentages	Convert raw scores or letter grades to percentages Multiply percentages by weights for course	Moderately easy to calculate Puts all assignments on a common scale for combining scores	Only works if converted means and standard deviations are about the same for every assignment
Criterion grading: converting raw scores to a point system	Multiply (or divide) raw score points by multiplying them by assignment course weights	Easy to calculate	Only works if converted means and standard deviations are about the same for every assignment
Criterion grading: converting raw scores to rubric scores	Create a common rubric scale for all assignments Multiply rubric scores by weights for the course	Requires preparation of rubrics Easy to calculate Puts all assignments on a common scale for combining scores	All rubrics must use same number of points Only works if converted means and standard deviations are about the same for every assignment

standard against which the other procedures may be judged. The use of letter grades as equating scores is the fourth method listed in Table 14.2. The final three methods are less rigorous but quite usable.

Each teacher must decide which procedure works best and is most defensible and which limitations he or she is willing to accept. To help you make that decision, we discuss each method in detail.

Method 1: Adding Unweighted Raw Scores

We discussed this method in the previous section. However, the example used in that discussion included items other than achievement. In Figure 14.8 we present fictional data for two other students, Susan and Henry, and combine the scores by simply adding them.

In this example, the two students receive the same number of points but differ greatly as to their actual performance. Susan's work on her papers and weekly assignments is barely acceptable, but she scores well on the midterm and final exams. Henry produces better papers and weekly work throughout the term but scores lower than Susan on the midterm and final exams. Over the course of the term, Henry appears to be the better student, showing more consistent learning. However, his achievements on the research papers and weekly assignments do not count as much as the midterm and final exams, on which he does not do well.

The differences between Susan and Henry are masked by the addition of the unweighted scores. Furthermore, the teacher's treatment of these two students should be quite different. The teacher might want answers to these questions: Why did Susan accomplish mediocre achievement in class yet "ace" the exams, and why did Henry display the opposite behavior? Did Susan cheat or just finally apply herself? Did Henry freeze up during the examinations? What about Henry's and Susan's motivation to work hard? What messages do students get when different patterns in their work result in the same grades?

In Figure 14.9 we present fictional raw score data for a class of 20 students, and we will use the same raw scores for Methods 2 through 7. To simplify the computations, we used a class of 20 students, and we limited the number of as-

Student	Assignments			Midterm Exam	Final Exam	Total Points
	Research Paper 1	Research Paper 2	Weekly Assignments			
Susan	12	13	6	20	29	80
Henry	20	19	9	12	20	80
Maximum points	20	20	10	20	30	100

FIGURE 14.8 Raw Scores for Two Students

Class Size: 20

Data to be Combined and Weights:

Data	Items	Point Weights
3 unit tests (UT 1, 2, 3)	20 each	10 each
Final examination	100	50
Research paper (graded A–F = 5–1)		20

	UT1	UT2	UT3	FINAL EXAM	RES. PAPER Grade	RES. PAPER Score	TOTAL RAW SC	TOTAL WGTD SCORE
Alice	13	8	11	53	F	1	86	2990
Bob	15	11	13	71	C	3	113	4000
Charles	17	12	14	78	C	3	124	4390
Doris	17	13	15	79	B	4	128	4480
Elizabeth	15	12	14	63	D	2	106	3600
Frances	16	12	14	76	C	3	121	4280
Geraldine	14	9	13	61	D	2	99	3450
Harry	19	14	17	94	A	5	179	5300
Inga	14	8	12	68	D	2	104	3780
John	18	10	15	85	F	1	129	4700
Kathy	13	8	12	47	C	3	83	2740
Louise	16	11	14	76	D	2	119	4250
Mary	16	11	14	74	C	3	118	4170
Nat	17	13	15	78	B	4	127	4430
Orpha	20	15	16	91	A	5	147	5160
Pat	17	11	15	81	B	4	128	4560
Ricky	15	10	13	72	C	3	113	4040
Sara	18	14	16	88	A	5	141	4980
Tom	17	14	18	76	B	4	129	4190
Virginia	14	7	13	71	C	3	108	3950
Sum	321	223	284	1482		62	2402	83,440
Mean	16	11	14	74		3.1	120.1	4172
SD	1.87	2.16	1.45	11.48		1.18	20.82	636
Range	13–20	7–15	11–17	47–94		1–5	83–179	2470–5300

FIGURE 14.9 Grading Problem: Raw Scores

sessments to five. We have converted the letter grades on the research paper to numbers, assigning a value of 1 to an F, 5 to an A. We listed the sum of the un-weighted raw scores in the next-to-last column, labeled "Total Raw SC."

In our discussion of Methods 2 through 6 we assume that you wish to weight the scores in some manner and that you also know how much weight you want each of these measures to have in the final grade. At the top of Figure 14.9 we provide the weights we will use for all these methods. Now the problem is how to put the information together to come up with the grade itself.

We will use the data in Figure 14.9 to show how to combine the scores in a variety of ways and how the grades come out with each procedure. In addition, we will discuss the advantages and disadvantages of each method and point out some serious problems with some of them. We will also provide instructions for handling the problems, offering two methods for *relative* grading and three methods for *criterion-based* grades. And we will discuss variations that will make either method work for the most common forms of grading.

Method 2: Adding Raw Scores
Weighted by Their Course Point Value

For this method we will use the weight for each piece of information, assigning the weights in such a way that the highest possible total of the weights is 100. In Figure 14.9 we use the same raw scores as in Method 1, but we multiply them by their point weights. The information about the weights is reported at the top of Figure 14.9. The totals of the weighted scores are reported in the last column of the figure, labeled "Total Wgtd Score."

We started working with the data in Figure 14.9 by multiplying the *raw scores* for each assignment by the number of points each assignment is worth for the entire course. In Figure 14.10 we use Alice's scores to show how the weighting works. Alice received a raw score of 13 on the first unit test (UT1). If we multiply her score by its weight in the course (10 points), the weighted score for UT1 is 130. We multiply the rest of her raw scores by their weights and arrive at a total weighted score of 2,990.

We do this for all the raw scores of all 20 students and get total weighted scores for all of them. These scores are reported in the last column of Figure 14.9.

Now we are ready to assign grades. But are we? Study the total weighted scores. The numbers are all much larger than 100. And there are some other problems, too. Who gets A's? Who gets B's? Why does John, who made an F on his research paper ("Res Paper"), have a higher total score than Doris, who made a B on her research paper? You might surmise that the reason is that John's final examination score is higher than Doris's and the final exam is more heavily weighted than the research paper. That is true, but it is only part of the answer.

Assignment	Raw Score	Weight	Weighted Score
UT1	13	10	130
UT2	8	10	80
UT3	11	10	110
Final exam	53	50	2,650
Research paper	1	20	20
TOTAL	86		2,990

FIGURE 14.10 Computation of Weighted Raw Scores: Alice

The main problem is that the scores on the final exam are much larger and have a wider range than the scores for the research paper. When we simply added the scores without weighting, there was only one point difference: Doris at 128 and John at 129. But now what we are doing is like adding inches and feet. Simply weighting the feet is not going to make them equal to inches unless our weight includes an equating factor. But how can we equate a letter grade on a 1-to-5-point scale with a examination grade that can run from 1 to 100?

If you wish to see how this could work out, look at the means and standard deviations for each of the assignments in raw score form. They are quite different. Scores on the final exam and the research paper look very different when their statistics are compared. How do we make them more comparable?

After calculating Alice's score and her total weighted score and looking at the total weighted scores of the other students, it should be obvious to you that the final examination really carries all of the weight in the course and the other assignments are quite minor. Is this what the teacher intended? No, it is not! So, we must find a better way to handle this problem.

There are several possibilities. Some are easier than others, and some give better results than others. The procedure that we use for converting scores on all the assessments to a common scale must yield scores with a similar mean and range for each assignment. We present the various possibilities in Methods 3 through 7 and show you how they work out. Unfortunately, the easiest method is not usually the best.

Method 3: Converting Raw Scores to Standard Scores

Most measurement experts advocate the use of standard scores for putting a variety of assessments on a common scale so they can be weighted and combined accurately. The procedure is as follows:

1. Compute the mean and standard deviation for each assignment. We did this for you in Figure 14.9. Some test scoring programs will do this at the time a test is scored. Of course, you would have to do it yourself for term papers and for hand-scored tests. In case you are interested, we provide instructions and a simple worksheet in Appendix A.

2. Find the difference between each student's score and the mean. Differences for scores below the mean have a minus sign. Scores at the mean would have a difference score of 0, and those above the mean have a plus difference score.

3. Divide the difference score by the standard deviation. Some scores will be negative and some positive. This calculation gives you a "standard score" and puts scores on all the assignments on the same scale, as long as all of them are based on the same group.

To eliminate the negative scores, many people like to convert the standard score to a scaled score using a convenient mean and standard deviation, such as

50 and 10. These scores are T-scores. That is how we got the scores reported in Figure 14.11.

Once the scores are converted to standard scores, each piece of information has the same mean and the same standard deviation, and the ranges are very similar. The scores now can be weighted with no problem, and the weights will reflect the weights you want. For this reason Method 3 is the method recommended by many experts. When we discuss the other methods, we will evaluate them by comparing the results with the results produced by Method 3.

Now that the scores are in the same units, they can be weighted, and the weights can be properly added to get the total score. If you can get the T-scores from a scoring program or from a computer program, or if you are comfortable with handling the fairly simple mathematics involved, this is the best way to handle the weighting and adding of the scores for a *relative* grading system.

You still have the problem of deciding such questions as whether the top grade will be an A or a C, whether there will be any F's, and what the most com-

	UT1	UT2	UT3	FINAL EXAM	RES PAPER	TOTAL WGTD SCORE	GRADE
Alice	34	36	30	32	36	340	F
Bob	45	50	43	47	47	467	C
Charles	55	55	50	53	53	531	C
Doris	55	59	54	57	61	577	B
Elizabeth	45	55	50	41	44	449	C
Frances	50	55	50	52	50	511	C
Geraldine	39	41	43	39	39	396	D
Harry	34	64	70	67	67	637	B
Inga	39	36	36	45	41	410	D
John	61	45	57	59	33	472	C
Kathy	34	36	36	26	47	372	D
Louise	50	50	50	52	39	462	C
Mary	50	50	50	50	50	500	C
Nat	55	59	57	53	56	554	B
Orpha	71	69	64	65	64	655	A
Pat	55	50	57	56	56	554	B
Ricky	45	45	43	48	44	453	C
Sara	61	64	64	68	67	643	B
Tom	50	50	50	50	59	536	C
Virginia	39	31	43	47	47	442	D
Mean	50	50	50	50	50	498	
SD	10	10	10	10	10	87	
Range	34–71	31–69	30–70	26–68	33–67	340–655	

FIGURE 14.11 Grading Problem: T-Scores

mon grade will be. In a strictly norm-referenced grading situation, the percentages of each grade are preset, and the teacher simply follows the guidelines. The
distribution may look something like this:

A = 5%   B = 20%   C = 50%   D = 20%   F = 5%

However, there are problems if, for instance, the class is an honors class in which
most of the students seldom make any grade lower than B. Should some of these
students make F's? Or suppose the class is a basic mathematics class that is made
up of students who have failed previous classes or who are being mainstreamed
and has a curriculum very different from that of the regular classes. What kind of
grade distribution should you have for this class? When you consider questions
like these, it is obvious that assigning grades is not simply a matter of handling the
mathematics correctly.

We like to use a combination of a visual display and professional judgment
that takes into account the group with which the individuals are being compared.
For the data in Figure 14.11 we started by tallying the distribution of weighted
T-scores as reported in Figure 14.12.

If this is a regular class with a full range of students, we would expect about
half of the students to make C's, which would be anchored around the mean of
498 (approximately 500). So we would assign C's to total scores ranging from 450
through 549. We assign an A to the person with a total score of 655 and B's for
scores between 550 and 650. Similarly, we assign an F to the person with a total
score between 300 and 349 and D's for scores between 350 and 450. So we have
the following grade distribution:

A 1 (5%)   B 5 (25%)   C 8 (40%)   D 5 (25%)   F 1 (5%)

This distribution is fairly close to what is usually recommended for relative grading. These are the grades reported in Figure 14.11. But we are not required to follow preset percentages. If our class is not a regular class, we can change our
procedure.

T-Score Ranges	Number of Students
300–349	1
350–399	2
400–449	3
450–499	4
500–549	4
550–599	3
600–649	2
650–699	1

FIGURE 14.12 Distribution of Weighted T-Scores

In an honors class, we could have approximately 75% A's, 15% B's and the rest C's. For some classes, our top grade might be C, D might be the grade made by most students, and there might be many F's. Or we might decide that no student in this class is doing poorly enough to deserve an F. In other words, our grading system is not completely norm based, because we use some criterion information to help us decide what the final grades will be. Studies show that most teachers also make value judgments about how hard each student tries when assigning grades (Brookhart, 1993).

Method 4: Converting Letter Grades to Points

Some teachers handle the matter of deriving equivalent scores for the different assignments by converting the scores on each test and on the term paper to letter grades; then they translate the letters to numbers and multiply the numbers by the desired weights. This method works fairly well if the grade distributions for all assignments are similar and close to a normal distribution; otherwise, we have the same problem as for raw scores. In Figure 14.13 we have converted all the

	UT1	UT2	UT3	FINAL EXAM	RES PAPER	TOTAL WGTD SCORE	GRADE
Alice	2	2	2	1	1	130	F
Bob	3	3	3	3	3	300	C
Charles	3	3	3	3	3	300	C
Doris	3	4	4	3	4	340	C
Elizabeth	3	3	3	2	2	230	D
Frances	3	3	3	3	3	300	C
Geraldine	2	2	2	2	2	200	D
Harry	5	4	4	5	5	480	A
Inga	2	2	2	3	2	250	D
John	4	3	3	4	1	320	C
Kathy	2	2	2	1	3	170	D
Louise	3	3	3	3	2	280	C
Mary	3	3	3	3	3	300	C
Nat	3	4	4	3	4	340	C
Orpha	5	5	5	5	5	500	A
Pat	3	3	3	2	4	270	C
Ricky	3	3	3	3	3	300	C
Sara	4	4	4	4	5	420	B
Tom	3	3	3	3	4	320	C
Virginia	2	2	3	3	3	280	C
Mean	3.05	3.05	3.05	3.0	3.1	305	
Range	2–5	1–5	2–5	1–5	1–5	130–500	

FIGURE 14.13 Grading Problem: Letter Grades

scores to a numerical scale from 5 to 1, corresponding to letter grades from A to F, using a quasi-normative procedure similar to the one described above. Our distribution of total scores is reported in Figure 14.14.

Point Ranges	Number of Students
100–149	1
150–199	1
200–249	2
250–299	4
300–349	9
350–399	—
400–449	1
450–499	2

FIGURE 14.14 Distribution of Total Weighted Points from Letter Grades

Using the same procedures we used for the T-scores, we assigned A's to scores above 450, B's to scores from 350 to 449, C's to scores between 250 and 349, D's to scores from 150 to 249, and F's to scores 149 and below, giving us this distribution of grades:

   A 2 (10%)   B 1 (5%)   C 13 (65%)   D 3 (15%)   F 1(5%)

This distribution is very similar to what we got using T-scores, but our distribution is not as symmetrical. Harry would like this system better, but Doris, Elizabeth, Nat, and Pat would not like it as well. It would not make any difference to the rest of the class.

Method 5: Converting Scores to Percentages

Percentage grading is one of the oldest methods of trying to assign grades on a common scale across several variables. The percentages are usually interpreted as being the percentage of content or objectives the student has mastered. However, this is a very doubtful interpretation unless the objectives have been carefully defined and each assessment has been carefully constructed to represent the objectives. Furthermore, two assessments may both represent the domain very well, but if one is much more difficult than the other, the distributions of the percentages may differ grossly, which results in the same kind of problem with raw scores that we saw in Method 1.

The percentage scores for our data are reported in Figure 14.15. In using our data for this criterion-based procedure, we have assumed that the tests are well constructed and measure the curriculum very well. Since we had only letter grades and no numerical scores for the research paper, we used the bottom of the percentage equivalent for each letter grade.

	UT1	UT2	UT3	FINAL EXAM	RES PAPER	TOTAL WGTD SCORE	GRADE
Alice	65	40	55	53	50	525	F
Bob	75	55	65	71	70	690	D
Charles	85	60	70	78	70	745	C
Doris	85	65	75	79	80	780	C
Elizabeth	75	60	70	63	60	640	D
Frances	80	60	70	76	70	730	C
Geraldine	70	45	65	61	60	605	D
Harry	95	70	85	94	90	900	A
Inga	70	40	60	68	60	630	D
John	90	50	75	85	50	740	C
Kathy	65	40	60	47	70	540	F
Louise	80	55	70	76	60	715	C
Mary	80	55	70	74	70	715	C
Nat	85	65	75	78	80	775	C
Orpha	100	75	80	91	90	890	B
Pat	85	55	75	81	80	780	C
Ricky	75	50	65	72	70	690	D
Sara	90	70	80	88	90	860	B
Tom	80	55	70	74	80	735	C
Virginia	70	35	65	71	70	665	D
Median	80	55	70	74	71	717.5	
Range	65–100	40–75	55–85	47–94	50–90	525–900	

FIGURE 14.15   Grading Problem: Percentage Scores

Look at the medians and ranges for percentage scores for the three unit tests as reported in Figure 14.15. It may be that Unit 2 should be retaught. Or it may be that the items for that test are poorly written or that they call for isolated pieces of information that were not really parts of the classroom work. The use of norm-referenced grading takes care of the problem of differences in test scores that are caused by this kind of problem. However, as we pointed out earlier, it may mask a genuine problem of the students' missing some important information.

We still have the problem of what letter grade to assign for the final grade. One way to simplify the task is to divide the total weighted score by 10, which gives us a distribution like the one in Figure 14.16. How will we assign the letter grades now? If we use the traditional standard that 75% is passing, then only six of these students will make a passing score. If we lower the passing score to 70%, we still have only 12 passing. And how will we split the other grades?

Percentage Ranges	Number of Students
50–54	2
55–59	—
60–64	3
65–69	3
70–74	6
75–79	3
80–84	—
85–89	2
90–95	1

FIGURE 14.16 Distribution of Total Weighted Percentage Scores

Unless this is a singularly poor class, it does not make sense for our grade distribution to follow this pattern. What we need for each test is a set of criteria that will indicate the extent to which students have mastered the objectives covered by that test, so we can get a grade on each test that is based on the extent to which the content covered by the test has been mastered, rather than using percentages that are very dependent on the difficulty level of the individual items. We describe this procedure in a later section. If we want to stick with our percentage system, we will probably want to change to a normative system now and set up a system similar to the others:

A 1 (5%)   B 2 (10%)   C 9 (45%)   D 6 (30%)   F 2 (10%)

Method 6: The Point System for Raw Scores

Suppose, instead of using percentage scores, we go back to our original point system. After all, we have already made a decision about what weight each variable should have, so all we have to do is to determine what portion of each weight the various scores get. Since each unit test is worth 10 points, and each test has 20 items, we will divide the scores by 2. Similarly, with the final exam, there are 100 items, and the test is worth 50 points, so we will also divide those scores by 2. But what about the research paper? The maximum score is 5 (for an A), and the research paper is to be worth 20 points, so we will have to multiply those scores by 4. Now all we have to do is to add up the points for each person. Figure 14.17 shows the results.

Notice that we still have the problem of unequal means and ranges. Our distribution of total scores is shown in Figure 14.18. We used the same criteria for assigning grades as we used for the percentages. Now our distribution looks like this:

A 2 (10%)   B 1 (5%)   C 13 (65%)   D 2 (10%)   F 1 (10%)

	UT1 10	UT2 10	UT3 50	FINAL EXAM 50	RES PAPER 20		TOTAL PTS	GRADE
Alice	6.5	4	5.5	26.5	F	4	46.5	F
Bob	7.5	5.5	6.5	35.5	C	12	67	D
Charles	8.5	6	7	39	C	12	72.5	C
Doris	8.5	6.5	7.5	39.5	B	16	78	C
Elizabeth	7.5	6	7	31.5	D	8	60	D
Frances	8	6	7	38	C	12	71	C
Geraldine	7	4.5	6.5	30.5	D	8	48.5	F
Harry	9.5	7	8.5	47	A	20	92	A
Inga	7	4	6	34	D	8	59	F
John	9	5	7.5	42.5	F	4	68	D
Kathy	6.5	4	6	23.5	C	12	52	F
Louise	8	5.5	7	38	D	8	66.5	D
Mary	8	5.5	7	37	C	12	69.5	D
Nat	8.5	6.5	7.5	39	B	16	77.5	C
Orpha	10	7.5	8	45.5	A	20	91	A
Pat	8.5	5.5	7.5	40.5	B	16	78	C
Ricky	7.5	5	6.5	38	C	12	69	D
Sara	9	7	8	44	A	20	88	B
Tom	8	5.5	7	37	B	16	73.5	C
Virginia	7	3.5	6.5	35.5	C	12	64.5	D
Sum	160	110	140	740		248	1392	
Mean	8	5.5	7	37		12.4	69.6	
SD	.93	1.08	.72	5.87		4.71	12.38	
Range	6.5–10	3.5–7.5	5.5–8.5	23.5–47		4–20	46.5–92	

FIGURE 14.17 Grading Problem: Weighted Point System

Point Ranges	Number of Students
45–49	2
50–54	1
55–59	1
60–64	2
65–69	5
70–74	3
75–79	3
80–84	—
85–89	1
90–94	2

FIGURE 14.18 Distribution of Total Weighted Point System Scores

Method 7: Use of Rubrics

If you are discouraged about the possibility of finding a defensible system of assigning grades, perhaps you would like to consider a system that builds in judgment but does so in a carefully defined manner. This is the use of rubrics to define each grade.

There are many approaches to preparing rubrics for criterion-based grades. One approach is to use a set of general rubrics and rewrite it to include the specifics of the requirements for each grade and subject. The rubric describes the examinees who should receive the various grades. For classroom grading you need a common set of rubrics that will work for all assignments and that have the same total point values. A set of general rubrics might look like the one in Table 14.3.

Table 14.3 General Rubrics for Grades

Grade	Point Value	Meaning
A	5	**Outstanding:** Has mastered all major and minor objectives. May have a few incorrect items, but the options chosen are at least partially correct.
B	4	**Very Good:** Has mastered all major objectives and most minor ones.
C	3	**Satisfactory:** Has almost mastered all major objectives but still needs work on minor objectives.
D	2	**Very Weak:** Needs remedial instruction. Mastered less than half of the major objectives and very few of the minor objectives.
F	1	**Unsatisfactory:** Has not mastered any of the objectives. Any items correctly marked seem due to chance, not real understanding.

Many systems of rubrics for scoring writing samples and essays have been developed. You will find several in Chapters 7 and 8, and you might be able to adapt some of them to your own scoring and grading situation. Some rubrics are criterion based, like the one in Table 14.3. Others may provide normative scores, and some could be written in a way that would indicate improvement.

No distribution is presented for grades based on rubrics, because we do not have information about how the scores would look.

CONCLUSION

In the figures above we have used fictional data on 5 assignments for a class of 20 students to illustrate how various methods of computing grades work. In all but one method, we weighted our assignments the way we said we wanted them weighted. But we got somewhat different results depending on the process we used.

Figure 14.19 makes clear how grades based on the same student products can vary widely, depending on the philosophy of grading and on the method used to combine the various pieces. This figure reports the grade each student would make with Methods 3 through 6. Some students would make the same grade no matter how the grades are assigned, and the grades for each person are fairly close regardless of the method used. However, the consequences of making an F instead of a D may be severe in some cases.

It should be clear that no matter how we process the numbers, we still have to exercise some professional judgment in deciding which total scores get the A's and which the F's. Or, maybe there won't be any A's—or, perhaps, not any F's. Or there might be only A's, C's, and F's. Making a distribution table of the total scores helps us see how the students compare with each other. Analyzing the content and skill level of the items helps us see which objectives the class and each student has mastered.

| | Grades | | | |
| | Relative | | Criterion | |
Method	T Score 3	Letter Score 4	Percentage 5	Weighted Points 6
Alice	F	F	F	F
Bob	C	C	C	D
Charles	C	C	C	C
Doris	B	C	C	C
Elizabeth	C	D	D	D
Frances	C	C	C	C
Geraldine	D	D	D	F
Harry	B	A	A	A
Inga	D	D	D	F
John	C	C	C	D
Kathy	D	D	F	F
Louise	C	C	C	D
Mary	C	C	C	D
Nat	B	C	C	C
Orpha	A	A	B	A
Pat	B	C	C	C
Ricky	C	C	D	D
Sara	B	B	B	B
Tom	C	C	C	C
Virginia	D	C	D	D

FIGURE 14.19 Comparison of Grades Derived by Methods 3, 4, 5, and 6

It is useful to try several methods of scaling, weighting, and evaluating performance as a check on your final product. It is also a good idea to play around with scores on the tests you give and check the relative performance of the students. Is the mean about what you think it should be? Are the most knowledgeable students getting the A's? The more information you have about your class and your tests and other assessments, the more confidence you will have in your grading procedures and the better you will be able to explain and defend them.

SUMMARY

- Grades are used for many important purposes in education.
- The most important information conveyed by grades is how well the student is learning.
- Other information reported should be clearly labeled.
- Report cards should indicate what the grades mean.

STUDY QUESTIONS

1. What do you think should be included in a course grade?

2. You want your grades to indicate how students compare with other students in the class. Which method will you use to assign grades?

3. You want your grades to indicate how much progress students are making in mastering objectives. Which method will you use to assign grades?

4. What is the most difficult problem to handle when you are trying to use a criterion-based system of grading?

FOR YOUR PROFESSIONAL GROWTH

1. Take a unit in a course that you are teaching or have taught and write rubrics for each grade, A through F.

2. Prepare at least one assessment for the unit, administer it to your students, and assign grades to the assessments using your rubrics.

3. How did this work out?

15

స౹

Student Profiles

PREVIEW

Teachers regularly collect and use a wide variety of data on their students. In fact, teachers generally possess extensive knowledge of their students' abilities, achievements, and behaviors. These data come from both formal assessments, such as test scores and grades, and informal assessments, such as observations of students' work habits and classroom behavior. When a student is not progressing academically or is exhibiting behavioral problems that interfere with learning, we need to look even more closely at that student.

Teachers, who are usually the first to notice a problem, should start by trying to determine the nature of the problem for themselves. Doing this requires them to gather information and make sense of it. We call this process preparing a student profile.

Counselors and principals, too, may need to develop a clear picture of students' behavior and achievement because they must regularly share information about students with each other, other school personnel, parents, and even the students themselves.

Creating a picture, or profile, of a student to explain his or her difficulties and set a course of action can be a complex task. What information should be used, and how can it best be presented? In this chapter we describe a systematic, efficient method for collecting, analyzing, and assembling information into a student profile, which resembles a case study but is less formal. A student profile may be a one-page summary or a set of notes that describes a student in detail. Other documents may accompany it.

In this chapter, we provide background information on student achievement factors, present a general model for developing student profiles, identify sources of information, and explain methods for presenting the information to others. Where appropriate, we refer to other chapters for details of assessment techniques.

<table>
<tr><td align="center">**MAJOR TOPICS**</td></tr>
</table>

Reasons for Creating Student Profiles
  Poor Overall Achievement
  Deficits in Prerequisite Knowledge and Skills
  Failure to Master End-of-Instruction Objectives
  Frequent Errors in Classroom Work
  Unproductive Behaviors That Interfere with Student Achievement
  Errors in Students' Cognitive Organization of Concepts
Model of a Student Profile
Procedures for Creating a Student Profile
  Steps in Creating a Student Profile

REASONS FOR CREATING A STUDENT PROFILE

You may use a student profile for many purposes. It can be used as a source of information for a discussion with a parent or student about student progress or possible curricular or program changes. Teachers or counselors create profiles to prepare for conferences with students to review achievement progress or behavior problems. They may also use a profile with another teacher, counselor, or the school principal for the purpose of requesting help with a student from other professionals. A profile could be the basis for a discussion of the need for new grade-level or course placements or for a parent conference where educators and parents together make important decisions about matters such as a student's referral for special services or suspension or expulsion.

A teacher may create profiles at the beginning of instruction to diagnose student needs, as a means to monitor progress (formative evaluation), or as a summative evaluation over a long instructional period such as a semester. Usually you will create a profile only when there is some kind of problem that you want to understand. In Table 15.1 we present types of student behavior, or *presenting problems,* that might lead you to decide to prepare a profile of a student. For each problem, we provide possible data sources. A discussion of each presenting problem follows.

Poor Overall Achievement

You might decide to prepare a profile if a student's test scores and the quality of his or her class work are much lower than those of other students. In this case, the data sources would be all available test data as well as scores on class work.

Table 15.1 Reasons for Preparing Student Profiles

Presenting Problem	Possible Sources of Data
Poor overall achievement	Aptitude tests
	Individual and group achievement tests
	Diagnostic subject area tests
	Student work samples
Deficits in prerequisite knowledge and skills	Individual and group achievement tests
	Diagnostic subject area tests
	Entry-level skills checklists
Failure to master end-of-instruction objectives	Individual and group achievement tests
	Textbook tests
	Student work samples
Error patterns in classroom work	Individual and group achievement tests
	Diagnostic subject area tests
	Textbook tests
	Student work samples
	Nomination techniques
Unproductive behaviors that interfere with student achievement	Observation
	Anecdotal records
	Student work samples
	Student interviews
	Rating scales
	Nomination techniques
Errors in students' cognitive organization of concepts	Student interviews
	Student work samples
	Observations of student
	Rating scales
	Nomination techniques

Deficits in Prerequisite Knowledge and Skills

This is one of the most common reasons why you might want to prepare a profile, because past achievement is directly tied to current achievement. Achievement test data, especially data from good diagnostic tests, can help you identify how bad the deficit is. Another useful technique is a checklist of skills. You may construct the checklist yourself or you may look for checklists that are commercially available. See Chapters 7 and 8.

Failure to Master End-of-Instruction Objectives

Another common reason why you might want to prepare a profile of a student is failure to master the objectives of what you have tried to teach. Nonmastery is explored through tests and student work samples. You might collect student work showing end-of-instruction activities and look for the places where mastery was and was not achieved.

Error Patterns in Classroom Work

Examination of consistent errors in achievement such as frequent place value mistakes, inability to find main idea or inability to write a topic sentence for a paragraph can help a teacher to plan the next instructional phase.

Unproductive Behaviors That Interfere with Student Achievement

Some student behaviors interfere with learning because they keep students from focusing on a task. They may also distract other students. Some unproductive behaviors are more subtle. Some individuals may be unwilling to take risks on problem tasks, or they may adopt a rigid approach to solutions. Some may not feel secure when working with other students in cooperative group activities, or they may try to dominate a group with their own ideas. Exploration of such behavior problems might require systematic observation or a collection of anecdotal records by one or more teachers and other professionals.

Errors in Students' Cognitive Organization of Concepts

Some students seem to have problems in *cognitive organization*—a concept based on the cognitive psychology precept that every individual structures or organizes knowledge in unique ways. Students with faulty cognitive organization might be unable to access appropriate information when they need it. Investigating the problem requires a sophisticated analysis of interviews with the student, work samples by the student, and observations of the student. To investigate this situation you need a deep understanding of the knowledge and structural organization of a subject area and of the principles of cognitive psychology. This type of information is essential for working with students who struggle academically and for whom other types of analyses offer few clues. For some students we might get some valuable information by collecting works-in-progress and looking for individual error patterns.

MODEL OF LEARNING FACTORS

Because creating a student profile can be a complicated process requiring a major investment of time, the effort should be systematic. To assist you, we are providing information about factors that affect learning processes and outcomes. Some or all of these factors may be explored in a profile. Keller (1983) identified three elements in instruction: person inputs, instructional factors, and learning outcomes. In Figure 15.1 we start with those three elements and try to show how all the elements are interrelated.

Learning outcomes is usually where educators begin their profile analysis because failures in these areas trigger concerns. In this scheme, *effort* is a *learning outcome*. It is influenced by emotional or affective factors such as *motives and expectations* (Swaby, 1989; Reutzel & Cooter, 1992), and it has a great deal to with the other *learning outcomes*.

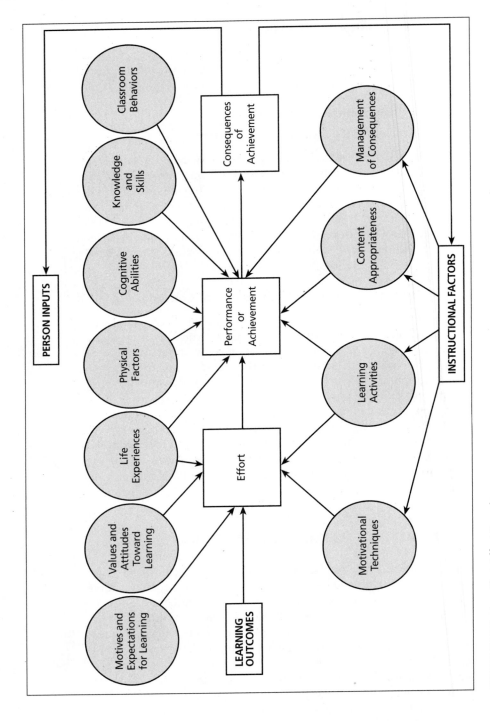

FIGURE 15.1 Factors That Affect Learning

Instructional factors are aspects of the classroom environment that are primarily under the control of the teacher. The *motivational techniques, learning activities, content appropriateness,* and *management of consequences* should match the person inputs. In other words, they should be explored for the degree to which they suit the student. While the first three are often considered by teachers, management of consequences is often not considered. By consequences, we mean the consequences for students and teachers if students succeed *or* fail to learn.

Consequences of achievement are outcomes of performances or achievements and involve both teacher actions and students' perception of the effects of success or failure to learn. If a student succeeds in learning the information, what is the reward? Is the reward really reinforcing to this student? What are the consequences of failure? Is there punishment, encouragement to try again, reassurance from concerned adults?

The way a teacher reinforces students' successes and handles their failures is an important aspect of instruction. Some students may be afraid to take risks in learning activities because they fear ridicule by the teacher or other students. Others may not try to succeed because they do not wish to attract the attention of the teacher's praise. Furthermore, reactions to teachers' praise or rebuffs are often based in the culture of the student.

It should be clear from Figure 15.1 that the reasons for a student's failure to learn may be complex and are not likely to have a single explanation.

Person inputs refers to the components students bring to school which impact one or more learning outcomes. These include both cognitive and noncognitive factors and they involve both in-school and out-of-school experiences. *Motives and expectations for learning* influence whether students want to learn and whether they think they can learn the materials and skills that are being taught. *Values and attitudes toward learning* focus on students' like or dislike of the materials and activities and whether they think the information is worth learning. These emotions are strong influences on their desire and effort to learn.

Life experiences involve all of the out-of-school life of the student, including family circumstances, access to various experiences such as travel and library visits, and the educational levels of parents. Problems in a student's family circumstances include inattention to physical care, poor development of literacy, and little provision for concept and language development experiences (Swaby, 1989).

Physical condition may also affect learning. This includes basic health such as general physical development, chronic health issues such as ear infections or asthma, and any disabilities. Disabilities may be physical problems such as poor vision, hearing problems, or physical handicaps; they may also be less apparent as with learning disabilities or mental retardation.

Two of the *person inputs* are especially school related: *Cognitive abilities* are typically what we think of as scholastic ability. *Knowledge and skills* encompass what the student already knows and has learned how to do.

Finally, *classroom behaviors* include the habits that a student brings to a learning task. Desired behaviors include perseverance, planning, risk taking, metacognition, and self-reinforcement. They may also involve general studying behaviors such as note taking, dictionary and library skills, and study skills. Undesirable behaviors include self-distraction, trial-and-error approaches to problems, poor listening skills, and inappropriate attention-getting behavior.

STEPS IN CREATING A STUDENT PROFILE

The procedures we are presenting for creating a student profile were developed in the context of the learning factors model we have already presented. A completed student profile is presented in Figure 15.2. It was prepared by a teacher who was a student in a class taught by one of the authors. This profile shows you what the final product might look like.

The steps in preparing a profile are listed below and then discussed one by one. Each of the steps is illustrated with examples drawn from Figure 15.2 and from three other profiles also prepared by teachers. These profiles are presented in sections to illustrate the development of each section of the profile.

Steps in Creating a Profile

1. Describe the student and circumstances that led you to create the profile.
2. Generate questions that you will attempt to answer as a rationale for the profile.
3. Collect data that will best address the questions.
4. Answer the questions generated in Step 2.
5. Draw conclusions about the data you have collected.

Step 1: Describe the Student and Circumstances That Led You to Create the Profile. Your first step is to choose one or more of the six reasons for profile development listed in Table 15.1 and briefly describe the student, his or her behavior, and other relevant information that supports your reason for the profile. The key point to remember is that you are going to collect and analyze the information in the profile based on this description. Focus on one or more of the components identified in Figure 15.1. In which areas is the student not successful?

The teacher who wrote the profile shown in Figure 15.2 was primarily concerned about Don's achievement in relation to other students' achievement and his non-mastery of behavioral objectives. Figure 15.3 provides descriptions from the profiles of three other students: Bobby, Tasmin, and Amelia.★

★ These three student profiles were created by three teachers and master's degree graduates in the School of Education at California Lutheran University: Profile 1 (Bobby): Kathleen Bordner, Curriculum and Instruction Program; Profile 2 (Tasmin): Gayle Pinkston, Curriculum and Instruction Program; Profile 3 (Amelia): Linda S. Johnson, Educational Administration. Reprinted with permission.

SAMPLE STUDENT PROFILE

Description: Don, a 13-year-old 8th grade male student, shows consistently low academic performance in all his classes; appears unconcerned about his achievement; is slow to complete his work, if at all; is disorganized and distracted when he is working; makes inappropriate comments in class.

Questions: 1. Is this student academically misplaced in courses that are too difficult for him?

2. What is the cause of his academic difficulties? (Prior school experience, learning disability, etc.)

Data:

Test Scores: *Metropolitan Readiness Test:* (First Grade)

Extremely low language and quantitative skills levels

Stanford Achievement Test:

Scores throughout elementary school below 5th stanine in listening and comprehension, reading comprehension consistently at 2nd or 3rd stanine.

Report Cards: Past grades consistently C's and D's. Comments on report cards reflect previous teachers' concerns with listening, attention, and inability to stay focused on tasks.

Observations and Anecdotal Information: Other current teachers concerned about his academic performance and inability to stay focused and "on task." Student disorganized and unfocused in the classroom and in oral presentations and discussions. Is easily distracted from his work.

Student Work: His work shows difficulty in applying, interpreting, and analyzing information. He loses his train of thought even in the middle of a written essay. Handwriting is also poor.

Answer to Questions:

1. Don's previous grades and classroom behavior do indicate that he is misplaced in his classes.

2. Teachers consistently report his lack of focus, distractibility, and inattention as a possible cause of the problem.

Conclusions: Don's consistently poor academic performance seems to be related to his lack of focus and distractibility. Report information and teachers' comments all support these findings.

Don's current poor performance in junior high has its roots in his early school experiences. His inattention in class may be caused by attention deficit disorder. His inability to handle higher-order thinking tasks also should be explored.

In view of these findings, I feel that screening him for special education would seem to be in order.

FIGURE 15.2   Sample of a Completed Student Profile: Don

SOURCE: Created by Elizabeth Brown, teacher and graduate of the Pupil Personnel Master's Degree Program at California Lutheran University, School of Education. Reprinted with permission.

In Profile 1 in Figure 15.3, Bobby's overall mastery of content is poor in all areas. However, his test scores indicate average ability, so his problem does not seem to be general in relation to achievement among his peers. His distractibility disappears only when he works on a task he enjoys.

Tasmin (Profile 2) displays good classroom achievement in mathematics and reading, although she works slowly in reading. Her low achievement test scores make sense when you consider the time constraints placed on students on a test of this kind. Tasmin's problem may also be one of self-confidence, as the teacher points out in mentioning parental comparisons with siblings and Tasmin's lack of confidence in the classroom.

Profile 1: Bobby

Bobby is a second grade boy who has low achievement in all academic areas. Test scores indicate average reading and mathematics achievement. Has a short attention span. Does significantly better on class tasks when one-on-one with the teacher. Has trouble concentrating except when doing drawing and design tasks. Already identified as ADHD (Attention Deficit with Hyperactivity Disorder).

Profile 2: Tasmin

Tasmin is a sixth grade girl with CTBS scores in math, science, and social studies at about 25th percentile. Is a slow reader with good comprehension skills, excellent mathematics achievement. Is being compared with other siblings who are strong students. Lacks confidence in work except in mathematics.

Profile 3: Amelia

Amelia, a seventh grade female is earning D's and F's on current classroom tests in college prep mathematics. Classroom responses reflect little understanding of mathematics. Is motivated to learn, a hard worker, and does homework. Previous report cards show her earning A's. Conversations with the parent and school counselor reveal a shy student.

FIGURE 15.3   Three Sample Profile Descriptions

Amelia (Profile 3) is not mastering content and seems to be lacking the prerequisite skills. The puzzling part of this description is the past report cards filled with A's.

Step 2: Generate Questions That You Will Attempt to Answer as a Rationale for the Profile. In this step, you should look at your description to guide you in formulating your questions. Look again at the completed profile in Figure 15.2. The teacher who developed Don's profile used the description to create two questions. Because of her observations about Don's current work and reports from other current teachers, the teacher first focused on Don's possible misplacement. The second question was a more general one about the cause of the problem. It allowed the teacher to explore several data sources.

The questions may be about *person inputs, instructional factors,* or both. Questions about *person inputs* may include those concerning the student's *motives and expectations for learning, values and attitudes toward learning, life experiences, cognitive abilities, knowledge and skills, physical factors,* and *classroom behaviors.* See Figure 15.1. Many person inputs are developed through family and life circumstances.

Instructional factors are controlled by the teacher. It is important for us to question ourselves as professionals about how well we are meeting students' needs. We should especially examine how we manage the consequences of success or failure in our classrooms. *Instructional factors* create an environment in which students may or may not feel safe or welcome.

In Figure 15.4, we present questions generated from the descriptions of Bobby, Tasmin, and Amelia provided in Figure 15.3. There are some interesting patterns in these questions. All three teachers responded to discrepancies in either past general achievement tests and current classroom performances or in the tests

---

Profile 1: Bobby

1. What are the differences between tasks on general achievement tests and classroom activities?
2. Why is Bobby's performance so different in the one-on-one situation than in classroom activity situations?
3. How do the drawing and design tasks differ from more traditional classroom tasks?

Profile 2: Tasmin

1. What differences in the general achievement test situation and in regular classroom activities could affect Tasmin's performance on the tests?
2. Is there a relationship between Tasmin's level of confidence in her mathematics and reading skill levels and her achievement in these areas?
3. Are the parents' reactions to Tasmin's accomplishments affecting her achievement?

Profile 3: Amelia

1. Why is Amelia's current level of mastery so low?
2. Why are Amelia's responses not indicative of an A student who has mastered previous content?
3. Why did Amelia go from being an A student to a D and F student almost overnight?
4. Is there any possible connection between her shyness and her performance?

FIGURE 15.4 Questions Generated by the Profile Descriptions in Figure 15.3

and past performances noted on report cards. These discrepancies led the teachers to look for differences in the ways the tasks were structured and presented to the students. More subtle are differences in environmental conditions in testing and regular classroom tasks. For example, in testing situations students are generally allowed no assistance and may be under tight time constraints. These conditions usually are not present in classroom working environments.

The teachers also identified possible *person factors* in student performance. In Profile 1, the teacher wanted to know why Bobby acted so differently in one-on-one work with the teacher than he did when he worked alone or with other students. The teachers who wrote Profiles 2 and 3 were curious about possible affective student characteristics and conditions and their relationships to student behavior in learning activities.

Step 3: Collect Data That Will Best Address the Questions. After you have decided on the questions you wish to address in the profile, you should determine which data sources to use. Some assessment information has already been collected; other information must be collected by you. Sources of data in schools are numerous and varied. Some data, such as test scores and report cards, are readily available in files. Other data must be collected from other educators in your building or school system or from students' work files and portfolios. To answer your questions, you should choose the *best* and *most direct* sources of data. For example, if you want to know about general achievement in an area, you should collect test scores that summarize learning, such as standardized and textbook tests. More specific learning is best explored through student work such as writing samples, worksheets, and projects.

The first step is to understand the meaning of each separate piece of information. Then you should look for patterns across the various pieces of data. The questions with each type of data may help you think of things to look for as you study a student's record.

Table 15.2 lists various types of information that you may wish to use and where that information is most likely to be found. Of course, you also may find data in other places. Table 15.2 shows that much information about students is concentrated in the cumulative record. In addition, information may be found in student portfolios and work folders. Information from interviews and observation must be purposefully collected. The cumulative record, student work, and all other data sources are discussed in detail below.

Table 15.2 Sources and Location of Information About Students

Type of Information	Location/Source
Student family information	Cumulative record file
	Parent interviews
	Student interviews
First language	Cumulative record file
	Parent interviews
	Student interviews
Health information	Cumulative record file
	Health office records
	Parent interviews
Past attendance information	Cumulative record file
	Report cards from previous years
Current school-year attendance records	Attendance register
Promotions/retentions	Cumulative record file
	Past-year report cards
Past report card grades	Cumulative record file
	Past-year report cards
Past achievement test scores	Cumulative record file
Textbook and semester examination scores	Teacher grade book
	Classroom student files
	Student portfolios
Student work records	Classroom student files
	Student portfolios
Enrollment in special service programs (such as special education, remedial academic programs, bilingual programs)	Cumulative record file
IEPs and other special prescriptions	Cumulative record file
Psychological and other professional reports	Counselor's files

The Cumulative Record. Most of the information that a school regularly collects about students is filed in the cumulative record, also known as the "cum folder." This file contains personal information, attendance information, grades for all the years the student has been in school, and scores on all standardized tests the student has taken. It may also include anecdotal and observational records, as well as reports of administrative and guidance actions. In some schools samples of student work are also included, although many schools put this material in a separate portfolio file.

To help teachers plan the year's activities, we recommend that they study the cum folders of their students carefully before the students arrive. Some teachers reject this suggestion, because they think looking at the cum folder might bias them against some students. We believe that the more information teachers have about their students, the better they will understand their needs and be able to meet them. Careful study done correctly can help overcome biases.

In earlier chapters we discussed the interpretation of the various kinds of information that might be in a student's folder. Grades are discussed in Chapter 14, standardized achievement tests in Chapter 11, aptitude and ability tests in Chapter 12, and the other standardized instruments in Chapter 13.

Figure 15.5 suggests questions that may guide you when you examine the cumulative record.

---

1. What is the student's general achievement level as indicated by
   - grades
   - achievement test scores
2. Is achievement higher (lower) in some areas than in others?
3. If there are differences, are they *significant?* (See Chapter 11 for suggestions.)
4. Do the test results and the grades present the same picture, or are there discrepancies? If so, what are they?
5. Is the student's achievement generally
   - at about grade level   ____
   - above grade level   ____
   - well above grade level   ____
   - below grade level   ____
   - well below grade level   ____
   - varying from one test or one grade to another ____
6. How does the student's scholastic ability score compare with the achievement test results? Is one much higher (lower) than the other? If so, which is higher? Remember to allow for errors of measurement. (See Chapters 4 and 11 to refresh your memory about errors of measurement.)
7. If there are discrepancies in the scores and grades, does any information in the folder suggest a possible cause? Possibilities include medical problems, family problems, behavioral problems.
8. Do you need more information? To answer what question(s)? Where might you get it?

FIGURE 15.5   Questions to Be Answered by Examining the Student's Cumulative Record

Student Work. Student work provides a huge, rich source of information about the achievements and problems of students. Unlike annually administered achievement tests, which assess general knowledge in subject areas, student work provides detailed information on the presence or absence of basic skills such as knowledge of multiplication tables, growth trends in the attainment and use of knowledge and skills, and patterns of errors. An extensive list of types of student work is provided in Chapter 9 on portfolios.

The key to strategic use of student work in preparing the student profile is to focus on the questions. The following suggestions should focus your search for the best information:

Collect items that will best reveal answers to your questions.

Look for patterns in the information.

What are the trends in achievement?

What are the most consistent individual behaviors?

Are there major inconsistencies in the student's work (e.g., the student knows something one day but not the next)?

Determine whether you need other student work to answer your questions.

Other Data Sources. Other data sources include observations collected through checklists and rating scales, anecdotal records, and informal observations. Chapter 8 provides many practical suggestions for using and creating these data sources. Other information may be collected from interviews with other interested professionals—other teachers, counselors, the principal, or community members. In addition, parents may provide insights not found in the cumulative record—about matters such as recent changes in the student's health or in family composition. A serious illness, the death of a family member, the birth of a sibling, divorce, or marriage can and do affect a student's work. In looking at information of this kind, keep the following points in mind:

Determine who has the best information for interviews and observations.

Determine what behaviors and situations you would like to observe or discuss with others.

Try to discuss these specific points consistently with all the people you consult.

Look for patterns in the information you receive from others.

What trends are evident in the student's behavior or achievement?

Are there major inconsistencies in the observations or feedback that you receive from others (e.g., problem behaviors that are seen by only one person or by all but one person)?

Determine whether you need to conduct other observations or to consult other persons to answer your questions.

Look again at Table 15.1 and Figure 15.5 to identify the data sources that Don's teacher may use to answer her questions about Don's cognitive abilities, knowledge and skills, and effort and attitude toward learning. These data include standardized test scores, report cards, current student class work, and observations and anecdotal information from other school professionals.

Data sources for the profiles of Bobby, Tasmin, and Amelia are listed in Figure 15.6. Recall that Bobby (Profile 1 in Figure 15.3), the second grade student, has problems functioning in classroom activities and works best in a one-on-one situation with the teacher. The teacher used the test tasks and conditions as points of comparison for everyday learning conditions in the classroom. In addition, she observed the student while he worked on drawing and on other tasks, and she talked to previous teachers and to Bobby's parents.

Tasmin's teacher (Profile 2) wanted to explore the reasons for her low achievement test scores in all areas. In class Tasmin was a slow but accurate reader and an excellent mathematics student. The teacher compared the tasks on the standardized test with tasks and conditions on daily classroom assignments. She also collected samples of the student's work and observed the student. To verify the shyness and problems with siblings, this teacher talked to other teachers and Tasmin's parents.

For Amelia's profile (Profile 3), the teacher examined all her previous standardized achievement test scores and samples of her work. She also interviewed Amelia's parents and personnel in the student's previous school.

Profile 1: Bobby

Previous standardized achievement test scores

Tasks and conditions of test situations

Samples of student work

Observation of student while engaged in classroom activities and in drawing and designing tasks

Interviews with parents and previous teachers

Review of reports identifying student as having ADHD

Profile 2: Tasmin

Previous standardized achievement test scores

Tasks and conditions of test situations

Samples of student work

Observation of student while engaged in classroom activities

Interview with student and parents

Interviews with previous classroom teachers

Profile 3: Amelia

Previous standardized achievement test scores

Samples of student work

Interviews with previous teachers concerning report card grades

Interview with student and parents

FIGURE 15.6   Data Sources for Sample Student Profiles

Step 4: Answer the Questions Generated in Step 2. After you collect all the relevant data, the next step is to complete the analysis suggested in the section on collecting information and find a tentative answer to the questions generated by the profile description.

Let's return to Don's profile (see Figure 15.2). The teacher used her information to answer the two questions she had posed. She had asked if Don were misplaced in his courses and what the cause of his academic difficulties was. Don's test scores, grades, and current classroom behavior all supported the misplacement conclusion. Interviews with previous teachers confirmed the student's difficulty with focusing on a task and his distractibility. The cumulative record showed no evidence of referral to special services, and the parent interview confirmed this fact.

The teachers who created the three other student profiles followed the same procedures. The results are presented in Figures 15.7, 15.8, and 15.9. The data in Bobby's, Tasmin's, and Amelia's profiles raise some interesting issues.

In Bobby's profile, the teacher reported that she observed the distractibility of the child and his interactions with students. Exploration of test scores revealed that Bobby excels at tasks involving drawing and spatial ability. Reading and other tasks may be harder for him because he does not have as strong an aptitude for them. His disruption of class activities and his preference for working alone with the teacher may be at least partially explained by his distress about his parents' divorce and new family arrangements. Bobby may need more personal attention at this time. His profile clearly shows the relationship between test scores and actual classroom work. It also illustrates the potential power of family circumstances to affect student learning.

Tasmin is a good example of a child who excels at one task or content area but not another. This disparity may be related to aptitude, experience, or even

---

1. What are the differences between the tasks on a general achievement test and classroom activities?

Bobby's achievement and aptitude scores are in the average range. Although there are differences in the tasks, his performance is consistent in testing situations. In the classroom, he is distracted by other students' activities, fails to complete work and distracts others.

2. Why is Bobby's performance so different in the one-on-one situation than in classroom activity situations?

Bobby's parents indicated that he lives with his mother in a newly blended family after the divorce of his parents and his mother's remarriage. The divorce was difficult for Bobby, and he misses his father's attention. He may be seeking attention from the one-on-one situations with the teacher and other students.

3. How do the drawing and design tasks differ from other more traditional classroom tasks?

The drawing tasks are easy for Bobby because he excels in test tasks involving reproducing designs, completing mazes, and spatial relationships.

FIGURE 15.7 Tentative Answers to Questions About Student Profile 1: Bobby

1. What differences in the general achievement test situation and in regular classroom activities could affect Tasmin's performance on the tests?

Tasmin performed at low levels on all achievement tests in all areas. An informal reading inventory revealed that she is a slow oral reader but maintains good comprehension. It is possible that the timed nature of the tests affected her scores. In the classroom, Tasmin dislikes reading, but she excels in mathematics. Although reluctant to participate in reading, she readily responds in mathematics lessons. Again, the timed nature of the test situation could explain the differences in test scores and classroom performance in mathematics.

2. Is there a relationship between Tasmin's level of confidence in her mathematics and reading skill levels and her achievement in these areas?

It is difficult to answer this question directly. Tasmin does struggle with reading. She does not like to read, as do her mother and sisters. Her work in mathematics seems to be a unique achievement among her siblings. She seems to be succeeding in an area in which she is not compared with her sisters.

3. Are the parents' reactions to Tasmin's accomplishments affecting her achievement?

Interviews with the mother indicate that she is frustrated with her daughter's achievement and "shy" personality. The mother also compares Tasmin's reading ability with her sisters'. The comparisons and the mother's verbalized frustration with Tasmin could be affecting Tasmin's progress in reading. They also may create some stress in the testing situation when performance is measured in a summative manner and may be used for other comparisons.

FIGURE 15.8   Tentative Answers to Questions About Student Profile 2: Tasmin

1. Why is Amelia's current level of mastery so low?

The cumulative record revealed some unusual findings. First, her test scores were exceptionally high in mathematics. The last entries were not placed on an official sticker but were written in by hand. Investigation by the counselor indicated that the scores had been hand-recorded at her previous school from a master printout of test scores. The person who had recorded them made a clerical error.

2. Why are Amelia's responses not indicative of an A student who has mastered previous content?

Amelia's classroom responses to questions and work in mathematics were definitely not those of an A student. When the report card was examined by the teacher and counselor, they discovered Amelia's grades had been received in a special remedial mathematics program that was not preparation for an honors math course. The teacher gave Amelia the A's because she felt she had worked hard and deserved them.

3. Why did Amelia go from being an A student to a D and F student almost overnight?

This question was answered with the discoveries made in questions 1 and 2.

4. Is there any possible connection between Amelia's shyness and her performance?

There was a connection between her shyness and her performance, but it was related to her actual achievement in mathematics. An interview with Amelia revealed that she felt uncomfortable in the honors class and did not want to call attention to herself.

FIGURE 15.9   Tentative Answers to Questions About Student Profile 3: Amelia

lack of family competition in mathematics achievement. Unfortunately, the teacher has no tests that would help her eliminate that possible cause. However, the parents' comments in the interview help the teacher to understand their frustration and possible pressure on Tasmin. Pressure to perform may be one of the reasons why she has not demonstrated high achievement on a standardized test in mathematics. The timed nature of the task and the possibility of being compared unfavorably with her sisters might also be impeding Tasmin's performance.

Amelia's profile presents an interesting look at validity issues in data. The sole reason for this profile was that Amelia's reputation as an A student did not make sense in light of her current classroom performance. Exploration of her report card grades through an interview with the previous math teacher revealed that she awarded the grades primarily on effort and not achievement. This made their interpretation and comparability to other math grades unclear. The standardized test scores also did not make sense to Amelia's current teacher. Discussions with the counselor at the previous school revealed that the score stickers never arrived at the school, so a clerk transferred the scores by hand to the cumulative records. Amelia's scores were not valid because of clerical error.

In each of these profiles, the data that were collected helped to answer important questions related to student achievement. Each type of data worked with other data to create a clearer picture of the student and allowed the teachers to make better, more informed decisions. These decisions are presented in Step 5, drawing conclusions from the data.

Step 5: Draw Conclusions About the Data You Have Collected. After you have collected all the data you need and have found tentative answers to your questions, revisit your original description of the student and the situation. What do you now know, and what will you need to do next to help the student? To illustrate, we return one last time to each of the profiles to examine the teachers' conclusions.

In the complete profile of Don in Figure 15.2, the teacher fit all of the pieces of information together to conclude that her initial observations about the student's distractibility were confirmed by test scores and previous teachers' comments and grades. Don's distractibility was even apparent in current work—in writing samples that revealed his tendency to lose his train of thought. In view of these findings, the teacher felt that Don should be screened for special education. Preparation of the profile permitted her to make specific statements about his classroom behavior and achievement. All of this information, carefully analyzed and presented, strengthened the teacher's case.

The other student profiles also led to important conclusions and decisions for the students. In Profile 1 (Bobby's) the teacher concluded that the ADHD classification seemed correct but that the situation was more complicated. The student's distractibility and disruption of other students occurred when he was supposed to be working on tasks he disliked. The differences in his behavior and concentration in one-on-one situations and general class activity gave the teacher some additional clues for action.

She started by setting up a situation in which drawing tasks were used as rewards for other work. She also tried to incorporate more hands-on activities in Bobby's class experiences and used his spatial relations aptitude as a means to help him understand complex mathematics concepts. His need for attention was also used to help him. Whenever possible, the teacher worked with Bobby alone and used two other strategies to meet his need for attention. She enlisted the help of an older tutor in the upper grade levels, and she placed Bobby in a cooperative group of students whom he liked.

After preparing Tasmin's profile, the teacher initiated a program of praising Tasmin for her work in mathematics and deemphasizing the reading problems. She also increased the amount of time Tasmin spent in reading. To work on the confidence issue, the teacher made Tasmin a math tutor for younger children. She also began a long-term discussion with the parents about focusing on Tasmin's strength in mathematics and making reading a more family-oriented activity with less competition.

Amelia, the student in Profile 3, was moved to a lower-level mathematics course. The parents were not happy about this placement at first, but when the pressure on Amelia decreased, her achievement and shyness began to improve. The problem with the report card caused the teacher who created Amelia's profile to rethink her own grading practices. The whole faculty at Amelia's school entered into a discussion of this issue and plans to explore the problem in future faculty meetings. The clerical error on the test scores caused the principal of Amelia's current school to examine the school's data-recording procedures, and the staff and faculty are discussing ways to avoid such recording errors in their school records.

The profiles clarified achievement issues and behavior problems. Each profile helped the teachers, working with the counselor, to make key changes in students' programs and, as a result, help the students learn more. In the case of Amelia, the profile prompted the current school staff to reexamine their procedures.

SUMMARY

- Student profiles help teachers make decisions about what students need.
- The steps in creating student profiles were described in this chapter.
- Profiles of four students were presented to illustrate the process.

STUDY QUESTIONS

1. What are the most common reasons why educators create profiles?
2. Compare cumulative records, student work, and other data sources in terms of their usefulness to teachers.

FOR YOUR PROFESSIONAL GROWTH

1. Look at cumulative record forms for several students. Ask questions about items with which you are not familiar.

2. Talk to other teachers about using profiles. In what situations would you find them useful at your school?

3. Create a profile for a student about whom you are concerned. Show it to another teacher, the counselor, or the principal for help in clarifying your ideas and procedures. Use a profile at an upcoming important meeting concerning a student.

16

❧

Referral for
Special Services

PREVIEW

In Chapter 15, we discussed the use of student profiles to examine and attempt to explain a student's difficulties. In this chapter, we extend the profile concept to the referral of students for services that are not provided by regular classroom teachers. These special services may include remedial reading instruction, bilingual training, speech therapy, physical therapy, gifted education programs, and special education programs for students with cognitive, learning, emotional, or physical disabilities.

MAJOR TOPICS

Background Information
   Important Laws
   The Roles of Educators
   Questions to Be Addressed
The Referral Process
Preparing a Referral
Designing an Individualized Education Program

BACKGROUND INFORMATION

Regardless of the type of instruction, special services should only be provided when traditional classroom techniques and strategies have failed. Special services generally cost more than traditional instruction and may result in a dramatically different educational experience for the student, so educators should ensure that any services that are requested are actually the ones the student needs. Referrals must be based on a precisely identified problem, clearly described and supported by a body of valid information. Creation of a portfolio and a student profile helps the teacher to develop this information, but that is only the beginning of the referral process. The teacher and other educational professionals must collect data to monitor the effectiveness of services and to determine whether instructional goals are being achieved.

The roles of educators in the referral process and the procedures to be followed are spelled out in state and federal laws and regulations. Federal and state funded remedial reading and mathematics, bilingual education, gifted education, and special education programs are regulated programs.

We devote this chapter to the process of referring students to special programs, stressing the importance of valid data and the essential role that all educators play. It is important to note that the rules, laws, and judicial decisions guiding these processes change from time to time. Educators should always check the policies and rules in their schools before undertaking a referral.

Important Laws

The referral or identification of any student for special services is generally guided by federal and state regulations and laws. Among the programs affected by such rules are remedial programs in reading, language arts, and mathematics, bilingual programs, and gifted education programs. We can not list all of the federal laws and regulations here, but educators should consult with administrators about the availability of programs and the legal procedures that the school or district needs to follow.

Special education faces very rigorous and restrictive rules. Table 16.1 lists and describes the most important laws pertaining to special education. As the table indicates, special education has been modified over the years to broaden the definition of *disability* and to provide a wider range of services. In addition, Congress has prescribed at least two conditions for delivery of services. Services are to be provided to students in the Least Restrictive Environment (LRE) that is appropriate, by means of Individualized Education Programs (IEPs). Settings in which special education takes place range from placement in a full care facility to "mainstreamed" placement in a regular classroom environment. In 1994, Congress stressed the need for more service delivery in the regular classroom environment, and the concept of *mainstreaming*—placing students with special needs in the mainstream with other students, in the regular classroom—was introduced.

Table 16.1 Important Legislation Affecting Special Education

Date	Act	Purpose
1975	Education of Handicapped Children Act (P.L. 94-142)	Required that all handicapped children receive a free and appropriate education in the least restrictive environment (LRE) with an Individualized Education Program (IEP) for every student
1983	P.L. 98-199	Required plans for transition services for secondary children, parent training, and information services
1986	P.L. 99-457	Amended P.L. 94-142 to include early interventions for children ages 5 or younger
1990–1991	Individuals with Disabilities Education Act (IDEA) (P.L. 102-119 and P.L. 101-476)	Expanded the definition of disabilities (not handicaps) to include autism and traumatic brain injury and added therapeutic recreation, assistive technology, social work, and rehabilitative counseling services
1994	Congressional reauthorization of IDEA	Added provision for inclusion of disabled in regular classrooms

Source: Based on information from "Full Inclusion Is Neither Free Nor Appropriate," by A. Shanker, 1994/1995, *Educational Leadership, 52* (4) pp. 18–21.

Other laws also affect the referral process and options for services. The Americans with Disabilities Act (1990) requires schools and employers to provide many types of accommodations for all disabled persons regardless of the nature of the disability. Among the accommodations are modification of tests and test procedures (Fischer, 1994). We discussed the nature and implications of these accommodations for achievement testing in Chapter 10.

The Roles of Educators

All educators at some point in their careers are involved in the referral of students for special services of various types. Teachers play a primary role in identifying students in need of such services and in planning and monitoring the intervention, using information gathered from observation, classroom work, and test scores. Counselors play a supportive role in the collection of data about students for identification and monitoring progress. In some cases, a counselor may chair the Child Study Team for special education referrals (described later in this chapter). Principals are responsible for ensuring that the entire procedure follows the applicable laws, safeguarding the rights of students and their families, and acting as liaison to parents.

Teachers and the way in which they use student data play a central role in any referral. Figure 16.1 lists activities a teacher carries out when creating a student profile. As Chapter 15 pointed out, the profile is an essential tool in preparing for a referral and in monitoring student progress after the placement has been made. Another profile or an extension of the first one could be used to evaluate the effectiveness of the placement.

---

1. Formulate a preliminary description of the student and his or her problems and questions regarding student achievement and behavior.
2. Collect preliminary student data, including
   - Class work
   - Student observations
   - Textbook test scores
   - Interviews with parents and with other educators
   - Standardized test scores and background information usually found in the cumulative record
   - Contents of portfolios
3. Document previous unsuccessful interventions.
4. Use the data to make a preliminary diagnosis of the student's difficulties.
5. Consult with other professionals such as the school psychologist to
   - Share information
   - Verify data collected from other sources
6. Explain data and observations to parents.
7. Document student progress after the referral, using the data sources listed above.
8. Use data to determine the effectiveness of placement in the service, and suggest continuation, discontinuation, or change of service.

FIGURE 16.1 Teacher's Role in Referrals

Questions to Be Addressed

The posing of appropriate questions is an extremely important step in constructing a profile that will document the nature of the difficulty a student is experiencing. When teachers ask for help outside the classroom, they must be able to articulate what is going on in class. The questions the teacher formulates in the profile determine what types of data are collected and should target the problem clearly.

J. H. McMillan (1997) developed an excellent and comprehensive list of questions organized by type of problem addressed in special education. In Table 16.2 we expand that list to include questions that need to be answered before referral to various types of programs. The questions are of three types. Some deal with the exact nature of the problem; some ask about contributing causes; and some explore the effect of the problem on academic performance and classroom behaviors.

Table 16.2 Questions for Specific Types of Problems

Problem	Questions
Primary language/ Cultural differences	Does the student command the language of instruction well enough to increase knowledge and skills?
	Does the student understand and use appropriate cultural norms in the classroom?
	Does the cultural or linguistic background of the student contribute to deficits in academic performance?
Basic reading or mathematics skills deficiency	What is the nature of the basic skills deficiency?
	Is the deficiency severe enough to impede the student's general academic progress?
	Are the deficiencies related to language and/or cultural differences?
	Have disabilities of various types been ruled out as possible causes of the problem?
Mental disability	How well does the student function in everyday life?
	Do deficits in daily living skills affect academic performance?
	Have other disabilities or health problems been ruled out as possible causes of the problem?
Sensory disability	Is there adequate eye/hand coordination?
	Is the student able to see text and classroom materials well enough to use them?
	Does the student hear classroom directions and discussions well enough to participate in class activities?
	Is the student able to speak clearly enough to participate in discussions and interact with others?
Physical disability	Does the disability affect classroom performance?
	In what ways is classroom performance affected?
Learning disability	Does the student have average or above-average intelligence?
	Is there a discrepancy between aptitude and achievement?
	How is the disability affecting student achievement?
	Are sensory, physical, mental, and other disabilities ruled out?
Emotional disturbance	What inappropriate behaviors and feelings are exhibited?
	How well does the student interact with others?
	Is the student upset, depressed, or withdrawn much of the time?
	Is the behavior or feeling fleeting or consistent?
	Are any other disabilities responsible for the behavior or feelings?
	How does the behavior or feeling interfere with classroom performance?

Another area of interest is the interaction of a student's primary language and culture with achievement and aptitude. Duran (1989) states that language and cultural differences have profound impacts on the achievement of students and their performance on aptitude tests, causing students to appear less knowledgeable or intelligent than they are or to exhibit inappropriate or undesirable classroom behaviors that interfere with instruction.

THE ROLE OF THE TEACHER
AND OTHERS IN THE REFERRAL PROCESS

The classroom teacher is the person most likely to recognize that a student has special needs and is the person responsible for starting the process that will lead to appropriate placement for the student. The referral process might start at the beginning of the year, after the teacher has reviewed the cumulative records and portfolio records. The teacher may decide at that time that he does not know how to handle one or more of his students and needs to ask for help from other teachers and professionals. Another situation might arise later in the year. Even though information in a student's cum folder does not suggest any problems, the teacher's own observations lead her at some point during the year to request help.

When should teachers ask for help in working with a student? The answer is: When they feel that they are not handling the student and the classroom situation adequately even after trying other interventions. Those interventions could include isolating the student, providing more work time, moving the student to another place in the classroom or to a different room.

It has been estimated that about half of all students, at some point in their school career, will have some difficulty and approximately 10% of students will have difficulties severe enough to require referral to a program in addition to, or in place of, the regular education program (Shepard, 1989). Some of these students have physical problems—low vision, poor hearing, a debilitating illness, for example—that require services that must be provided under the Americans with Disabilities Act. Other students have problems that are not so easily identified but which may interfere with their learning unless they are properly diagnosed and handled by special education or integrated services. Information about three students is presented in Figure 16.2.

If one of these students were in your class, which of them should you consider referring to a study team? What questions would you want to have addressed by the study team?

PREPARING A REFERRAL

In most school districts and individual schools a formal referral procedure is used to request additional help for a student. In this section we provide a general model of referral procedures and then discuss the specific procedures for referral for special education.

General Referral Procedures

In most schools, the process of referral for special services requires the teacher to complete these steps:

1. Collect preliminary data on the student, including information prior to intervention.

Joey, Age 7, Grade 2

Joey is in the second grade. He has trouble staying on task and attending to the teacher, but he likes to read and to write stories and read them to the class. His handwriting is almost illegible, and the spelling is mostly "invented." In arithmetic he quickly does the worksheets and problems the teacher assigns, but his work is sloppy and inaccurate. He likes to use manipulatives to show other students how to do something.

When the teacher is talking to the class, Joey often interrupts, asking irrelevant questions. He usually finishes his work before the other students, and then he wanders around the room and disturbs the other students, in spite of numerous reprimands.

At the end of first grade, Joey took the *Stanford Achievement Test* and received the following scores:

Grade	Test Date	Subtest	Percentile	GE	Stanine
1	5/96	Reading Total	95	3.0	9
		Mathematics	65	2.1	6

Carlos, Age 10, Grade 5

All of Carlos's scores on the *California Test Battery* have been at the 98th or 99th percentile level each year. The school system has an optional program that would permit Carlos to remain in the elementary school for the sixth grade, rather than transferring to the middle school as most of the students will do. His mother asks for your advice. She feels Carlos is immature and thinks he will achieve better under the supervision of a single teacher than he would if he changes teachers each period.

You have also found that Carlos is immature. He often fails to complete his homework, and he requires a lot of your attention to keep him on task. He frequently disrupts the class and complains that other students are bothering him.

George, Age 14, Grade 9

George is quiet and is not any problem in his classes except that he seldom does his homework and he does not participate in class activities unless he is forced to.

George's attendance is poor, and he and some of his friends have been seen "hanging out" in a part of town that is home to known drug dealers.

George likes to draw cartoons, which he sometimes shares with the other students if the teacher asks him to. George's achievement test record is presented below:

Grade	Test Date	Subtest	Percentile	GE	Stanine
1	5/89	Reading Total	46	1.7	5
		Mathematics Total	50	1.8	5
2	5/90	Different school—No data			
3	5/91	Absent—No data			
4	5/92	Reading Total	47	4.6	5
		Mathematics Total	49	4.7	5
5	5/93	Reading Total	47	5.2	5
		Mathematics Total	57	5.7	5
6	5/94	Reading Total	37	5.1	3
		Mathematics Total	33	5.2	3
7	5/95	Absent—No data			
8	5/96	Reading Total	27	4.2	2
		Mathematics	25	4.3	2

FIGURE 16.2 Sample Student Profile

2. Create a profile to clarify your observations and assessment of the problem.

3. Review the student's profile with the appropriate administrator to discuss the situation, review program or service options and the requirements of these options, and establish a plan of action.

4. Complete the necessary forms, notify the appropriate persons, and secure parental permission for any required testing.

5. After establishing a program plan for the student, use the student's class work, observation, and other information to monitor progress and determine the effectiveness of the services.

These steps require use of data for a variety of purposes. In collecting and analyzing these data, you may enlist the help of counselors and other school professionals. The main point is that assessment is involved at every step of the referral process.

Referral for Special Education

There are usually several additional steps in the referral process for special education. They are quite specific and may involve the participation of professionals such as a school psychologist, medical doctor, and other evaluation specialists such as audiologists. The steps are

Prereferral

Child (or student) study team conference

In-school interventions

External referral

Evaluation by specialists

Development of the Individualized Education Program (IEP)

Prereferral. Many schools have a standard form for making referrals for special education. Recall that this process is largely dictated by federal laws, but state and local requirements may also apply. In most cases, the teacher and perhaps the counselor are asked to excerpt information from the student's record for the referral form. Both persons may also need to report their observations of the child. The student profile is an excellent tool for completing this task. If the school routinely uses portfolios, there should already be valuable information there, but the information may need to be supplemented with a profile.

Figure 16.3 is a sample of a form that might be used to request the start of the referral process. The form is easily completed from data in a student profile or portfolio.

Student _____ Date of Birth _____ Grade _____

Reason for referral:

Interventions used to date: (Description, duration, and result)

Special services the student is now receiving:

Referring teacher:

_____

FIGURE 16.3 Sample of a Request for Referral Form

Child (or Student) Study Team Conference. Referrals usually start with a study by a team at the school. The Child Study Team (CST) or Student Study Team (SST) is usually composed of the people who know the student best. These persons may include any or all of the following: classroom teachers, counselors, school psychologists, school workers, intervention specialists, administrators, and parents. At the middle school and secondary level it is also valuable for the student to participate in the SST—at least part of it. It depends on the issue.

At the conference, assessment results are reported and used for planning the initial IEP or other changes in instruction. It is important that all participants understand the information reported. Some procedural guidelines help to keep the conference on track. The beginning and ending time of the conference should be specified and it should be of reasonable duration. The length of the conference will vary from one to four hours, depending on whether it is the initial meeting or a transitional one. Everyone should have a written copy of all assessment reports. The Chair should arrange for introductions and direct the discussion. Each person should report the results of his or her own assessments to the group, but they should not read their portion of the report verbatim. The main points to be covered are: the reason for the referral, the student's behavior during assessment, a brief summary of the results, and implications for instructional services. Samples of the student's work and responses to specific items from the assessments may be used to illustrate certain points. The parents should have an opportunity to ask questions, but usually it is better to have all the information reported before questions and comments. However, some parents need to have each piece of information explained and illustrated through examples. Sometimes it is possible to arrive at a plan for the student at the first conference, but it is often necessary to have at least one more meeting to decide whether the next step will be an in-school intervention of some sort, or whether further study is needed and, if so who should do it.

In-School Interventions.   Some authorities prefer not to use the term *intervention* because they believe it has negative connotations. However, the policy manual of the National Association of School Psychologists (1994) uses the term and defines it thus:

> Interventions are a type of specific *supports* designed to meet specific needs of children. Interventions can include activities to increase children's competence and skills. They can also include environmental or instructional modifications designed to facilitate the acquisition of such skills. A classroom placement alone (e.g., special education) is *not* an intervention. (p. 3)

The child study team in the school will help you explore the situation with the student and, perhaps, help work out some in-school interventions. These interventions may involve anything from finding a place for the student to spend part of the day to providing a helping teacher to work in the classroom along with the regular classroom teacher to try to develop different ways of working with the student. The interventions are usually a compromise between the child's needs and what the school is able to offer. In most cases the interventions are instituted on a trial basis, and whether they are retained depends on how they work out. It may take several meetings of the CST/SST to find a solution.

External Referral.   At some point you and the CST/SST may decide you need additional help and institute a referral to a school psychologist or evaluation team. A form similar to the one shown in Figure 16.3 may be used for this referral, but information from the cum folder and other student profile information should accompany the form, so the specialists will have as much information as possible. The teacher and the CST/SST should also formulate carefully the questions they want answered. Review Chapter 15 for examples of questions that might be asked. Depending on the nature of the problem, parents, too, may be asked to provide certain information, such as medical reports, and they must be asked for their permission for individual testing if it is needed.

Evaluation by Specialists.   The school psychologist or evaluation specialist is able to do a much more intensive study of the student than is possible in a classroom setting, although some of the evaluation may involve on-site observation. Several tests of different kinds may be administered. There is usually at least one individual ability test, and often there are inventories of learning styles, prefer-

ences, interests, and personality. Individual achievement tests are usually administered if additional information is needed (as in the case of a learning disability diagnosis), or if there is some reason to question the accuracy of the scores of
standardized tests on file. The psychologist prepares a written report of the findings. This report is made available to the teacher and the parents, as well as to
other members of the CST/SST.

As a result of these evaluations, a recommendation may be made to provide
some kind of special education for the student. An IEP to outline the proposed
program is developed by the child study team.

DESIGNING AN
INDIVIDUALIZED EDUCATION PROGRAM

An Individualized Education Program (IEP) may be prepared by the CST/SST
for interventions within the current school, or it may be prepared by another
team after all the testing is completed. MacMillan (1988) recommends that the
classroom teacher coordinate and moderate the meeting. Regardless of who runs
the meeting, the teacher's input is very valuable, because the teacher is the one
who will carry out the plan. Furthermore, the teacher's impressions of the child
are extremely important in understanding the student's difficulties. It has been
found, for example, that classroom teachers' ratings correlate in the .8 to .9 range
with scores obtained from good standardized reading achievement tests (Hopkins,
Stanley, & Hopkins, 1990). However, a well-trained psychologist, special evaluator, or counselor can use instruments and make observations that a teacher is unable to do in the classroom situation.

If you are in charge of the meeting, you need to make some preparation in
advance. You must be certain that you receive the reports from all of the specialists well in advance, so that you have time to digest the information before you
contact the parents. Then you should contact the parents to set up the meeting. If
you do not already know them, introduce yourself, explain the purpose of the
meeting, and explain what will happen. In addition, share with the parents as
much information as possible. MacMillan (1988) thinks parents should have *all*
the reports in advance, so that they will have time to read and react to them. She
acknowledges that many of the reports include terms and acronyms that parents
may not understand, so she suggests that the teacher call the parents before the
meeting to respond to any questions that occurred to them while they read the
reports.

During the meeting, you may choose to sit near the parents, rather than with
the specialists, so that you will be in a good position to sense what the parents are
feeling and to ask clarifying questions to help clear up any questions or confusion
about the tests and conclusions. Remember that under federal law (P.L. 94–192
and P.L. 102–119) or (IDEA), the parents are equal members of the IEP team
(Vaughn, Bos, Harrell, & Lasky, 1988).

After the presentation of the information, possibilities for the child's program are discussed. Someone should be prepared to discuss the activities that are proposed and explain how each activity addresses the child's needs. At this point, the parents have probably heard mostly negative comments and need something positive. This is a good time to address the child's strengths—such as enthusiasm for a certain activity, generosity, neatness in written work. It is also sometimes helpful to ask parents about the child's preferences and fears. Vaughn et al. (1988) suggest that the conference should also address how to communicate with the child about the situation.

The person in charge of the meeting should be sure to see that everyone—specialists and parents—is clear about what will happen and what is expected. If there is disagreement about some of the details, you may have to take a brief break and then try to resolve the matter or, perhaps, schedule another meeting.

After the IEP is signed, invite the parents to call you if they need additional information or if they are confused about anything. Also, be sure the parents receive a clearly written copy of the IEP. Figure 16.4 is a sample of a simple in-school IEP. Some IEPs are much more complicated and detailed.

NAME: Joseph Cowan   GRADE: 8   DoB: 10-3-84

REFERRAL INITIATED BY: Thomas Ramirez

REASON FOR REFERRAL: To develop behavior strategies

IN ATTENDANCE: Thomas Ramirez (teacher), Gloria Johnson (principal), John Woo (counselor), George Svec (school psychologist), Fred and Marsha Cowan (parents)

DATE: 11/14/97

Area of Concern	Action Plan	Person Responsible	When
Inability to work in group	Switch math and science classes to move away from friends	Counselor	Immediately
Inability to focus and concentrate on assignments	Psychiatric evaluation	Parent	By 2/1/98
	Reward system at home	Parent	By 1/30/98
Student expresses frustration	Reward system at school	Teacher and student	12/15/97

FIGURE 16.4 Sample of an Individualized Education Program

SUMMARY

- A referral for special services may be needed if a student is having severe difficulties.
- The child study team includes the parents, the teacher, other educators, and specialists.
- Much useful information will be found in the cumulative record and in portfolios and profiles.
- Additional information may need to be gathered through other assessments, interviews, and observations.

STUDY QUESTIONS

1. What is an IEP? How is it used?
2. Who serves on the child study team or the student study team?
3. What is the purpose of a child study or student study conference?

FOR YOUR PROFESSIONAL GROWTH

1. Figures 16.5 through 16.7 present material that came from the cum folders of three students: Samuel D., Alice J., and Fred G. Read each figure, and select one of the students. Study and interpret the information about the student you have chosen, following the procedures described in Chapters 15 and 16. Think about these questions, and decide how you would handle the situation:
   a. What is the student's general level of achievement?
   b. Are there any differences from the general pattern?
   c. What additional information do you want?
   d. Should the student be referred to the child study team?

2. Check with the administration in your school or school system about the special services that are available. Choose one service with which you are *not* familiar, and study the referral process, including qualification requirements, roles of the school professional staff, and the procedures for the referral.

NAME: SAMUEL D.   **AGE:** 16   **GRADE:** 10   **SCHOOL:** X HIGH SCHOOL

REPORT CARD INFORMATION*

Grade 10

	Grading Period							
	1		**2**		**3**		**4**	
COURSE	**GR**	**ABS**	**GR**	**ABS**	**GR**	**ABS**	**GR**	**ABS**
SCI/HEALTH	C		F	2	D	1		
MATH BASIC	D		D–	3	D	1		
PE	C–		C	2	D			
LANG ARTS	D		D	2	D			
US HISTORY	D–		D–	2	F			
MUSIC	C		C	2	C			

Grade 9

	Grading Period							
	1		**2**		**3**		**4**	
COURSE	**GR**	**ABS**	**GR**	**ABS**	**GR**	**ABS**	**GR**	**ABS**
SCI/HEALTH	C		C	1	D	1	D	2
MATH BASIC	D		D	1	D	1	D–	2
PE	B		B	1	B	1	B	2
LANG ARTS	C		C	1	C	1	C	2
HISTORY	D		D	1	D	1	D	2
ART	B		B	1	B	1	B	1
MUSIC	B		B	1	B	1	B	1

*(A = Excellent   B = Above Average   C = Average   D = Poor   F = Failing)

CTBS Achievement Tests*

Grade

	1		2		3		4		5		6		7		8		9	
	GE	**NP**	**GE**	**NP**	**GE**	**NP**	**GE**	**NP**	**GE**	**NP**	**GE**	**NP**	**GE**	**NP**	**GE**	**NP**	**GE**	**NP**
LA	.9	49	1.9	49	2.9	48	3.2	30	3.2	20	4.8	30	5.2	20	5.8	19	6.5	8
MATH	.7	35	1.6	39	2.5	40	2.9	28	3.7	25	5.1	35	5.5	25	6.1	20	6.8	10

*(GE = Grade Equivalent   NP = National Percentile)

FIGURE 16.5   Case Study 1: Samuel D.

NAME: <u>ALICE J.</u>   AGE: <u>11</u>   GRADE: <u>4</u>   SCHOOL: <u>W ELEMENTARY</u>

Report Card Information*

Kindergarten:		1990–1991				1991–1992		
Grading Period:	1	2	3	4	1	2	3	4
LA ARTS	/	N	S–	S–	/	S	S–	S
MATH READ	/	N	S–	S	/	S	S	S
FINE MOTOR	N	S–	S–	S	S	S	S	S
GROSS MOT	S–	N	S–	S	S–	S–	S	S
FINE ARTS	S	S	S	S	S	S	S	S
EMOT/SOC	S	S	S	S+	S	S	S	S

			Grade 1				Grade 2	
Grading Period:	1	2	3	4	1	2	3	4
L ARTS	C	C+	B–	B–	C–	C–	C–	C–
WRIT	S	S	S	S	S–	S–	S–	S–
MATH	C+	C+	C+	C	C–	C–	D+	D+
SOC ST	S	S	S	S	S–	S–	S–	S–
SCI/HEAL	S	S	S	S	S	S	S	S
HAND WR	N	N	N	N+	S–	N	N	N+
ART	S	S	S	S	S	S+	S+	S+
MUSIC	S	S	S	S	S	S+	S+	S+
PE	S	S	S	S	O	O	O	O
SOC SK	O	O	O	O	O	O	O	O
WK HAB	S	S	S	S	S	S	S	S

*(O=Outstanding, N=Needs Improvement, S=Satisfactory, / = Not Assessed)
 (A=Excellent   B=Above Average   C=Average   D=Poor   F=Failing)

FIGURE 16.6 Case Study 2: Alice J.

Source: Case study prepared by Maureen Everakes and Maxine Fowles, teachers and graduates of the Pupil Personnel Master's Degree Program at California Lutheran University, School of Education. Reprinted with permission.

	Grade 3				Grade 4			
	Grading Period				**Grading Period**			
	1	**2**	**3**	**4**	**1**	**2**	**3**	**4**
L ARTS*	2	2	2	2	2	2		
WRIT*	2	2	2	2	2	2		
MATH**	C	C	C−	D	C	C		
SOC ST**	C	B−	B	C	C	B		
SCI/HEAL**	B−	C	C	C	C	C−		
HAND WR**	S	S	S	S	S−	N		
ART**	S	S	S	S	S	S+		
MUSIC**	S	S	S	S	S	S		
PE**	S	S	S	S	S	S		
SOC SK**	S	S	S	S	O	O		
WK HAB**	S	S	S	S	S+	S+		

*Resource Teacher (4=Outstanding, 3=Satisfactory, 2=Needs Improvement, 1= Unsatisfactory)
**Classroom Teacher (O=Outstanding, S=Satisfactory, N=Needs Improvement, U=Unsatisfactory)

(A=Excellent   B=Above Average   C=Average   D=Poor   F=Failing)

Standardized Test Report—CTBS*

Grade:	**1**		**2**		**3**	
	S	NP	S	NP	S	NP
COMPRE	4	53				
LANG EXP	4	35				
CONC & APP	3	12				
TOT RD			3	16	3	16
TOT LANG			3	21	3	21
TOT MATH			3	22	3	22
TOT BATT			3	17	3	14

* (S = Stanine   NP = National Percentile)

FIGURE 16.6 Case Study 2 (Page 2)

NAME: <u>FRED G.</u>   AGE: <u>5</u>   GRADE: <u>1</u>   SCHOOL: <u>Z ELEMENTARY</u>

Report Card Information*

Grades:	Kindergarten: 1995–1996				Grade 1 1996–1997			
Grading Period:	1	2	3	4	1	2	3	4
LA ARTS	/	N	S–	S–	S–	N+		
MATH	/	N	S–	S	S	S–		
FINE MOT	N	S–	S–	S	N+	N		
GR MOT	S–	N	S–	S–	S–	S–		
F ARTS	N	N	N	N	N	N		
EMT/SOC	S–	S–	S–	S–	N	N		

*(N = Needs Improvement, S= Satisfactory, / = Not Assessed)

STANDARDIZED ACHIEVEMENT TEST REPORT—CTBS

GRADE K

	Stanine	National Percentile
COMPRE	4	53
LANG EXP	4	35
CONC & APP	3	12

FIGURE 16.7 Case Study 3: Fred G.

APPENDIX A

༄

Worksheet for Computing Mean and Standard Deviation

Mean

The mean is simply the *arithmetic average* of a group of scores. One way to compute the mean is to add all the scores and divide by the number. This operation is expressed by the following formula:

$$M = \frac{\text{Sum of Scores}}{\text{Number of Scores}}$$

or

$$M = \frac{\Sigma X}{N}$$

in which
$\Sigma X = $ the sum of scores
$X = $ any score
$N = $ number of scores

If you have such a large number of scores that adding them is inconvenient and apt to be incorrect, you can save a lot of time by tabulating the scores.

Example: Scores 34, 31, 34, 33

When we add these scores and divide by 4, the number, we get

$$132 \div 4 = 33.$$

Here are the steps we would use if we had a large number of scores.

1. Make a vertical list of all the possible scores in numerical order. A form similar to Form A1 will assist you in this task.
2. For each score, place a tally mark beside the score.

Score (X)	Tally
34	||
33	|
32	
31	|

3. Count the tallies for each score and record the number (*N*) who made each score. For the data above, the numbers would be:

Score (X)	N
34	2
33	1
32	
31	1

4. When all scores are tallied and all tallies are counted and recorded, multiply each score by *N* and record the results. Then add the *NX* column. This gives you the total sum of the scores, just as if you had added all the scores.

Score (X)	N	NX
34	2	68
33	1	33
32		
31	1	31
TOTAL	4	132

Form A1 is a worksheet for handling this distribution or one even larger. To use Form A1, you first enter all the possible scores in the first column. Notice that the scores must be in numeric order—either *ascending* or *descending*. Then you tally the scores and count the tallies. For each score, you multiply the number by the score. Then you add up the *N*'s to get the total number and add the *NX*'s to get the sum of scores. Finally, you divide the sum of scores by the number of scores and that will give you the mean.

Practice Problem

For the problem, we have provided a set of numbers which might be the way a set of test scores would look. You may add all these scores and divide by 50, which is the total number of the scores. This gives you the MEAN, which in this case is equal to 34.32.

However, you may prefer to use Form A1 and get the mean by using the tallies and counts as we did in the example. Also, since you sometimes may have a large number of scores covering a fairly wide range, you may want to group them into intervals of five, as we do on our sample worksheet. The Form has some columns we will not use now, but we will use them when we calculate the standard deviation.

Scores:									
23	45	35	46	39	34	49	33	32	27
31	25	36	40	33	37	41	29	33	37
41	32	39	43	25	32	35	39	29	31
37	40	35	33	29	38	35	47	36	29
25	38	39	29	18	39	20	41	33	24

Sample Worksheet							
SCORE	TALLY	N	NX	d	d^2	Nd^2	
15–19	I	1	17	−17	289	289	
20–24	III	3	66	−12	144	432	
25–29	⊬⊬⊤ IIII	9	243	−7	49	441	
30–34	⊬⊬⊤⊬⊬⊤ I	11	352	−2	4	44	
35–39	⊬⊬⊤⊬⊬⊤⊬⊬⊤ I	16	592	3	9	144	
40–44	⊬⊬⊤ I	6	252	8	64	384	
45–49	IIII	4	188	13	169	676	
50–							
TOTALS		50	1710			2410	

Notice that our sum is slightly different from the sum we got when we simply added up the scores. That is because we multiply the number by the midpoint of the interval, rather than by the actual score. Using the grouped data, we get a mean of 34.20, which is not too different from what we got when we used the actual scores.

Standard Deviation

With the same worksheet we used for the mean, we can also calculate the standard deviation, using the last three columns. This is what we do:

1. Find the difference between the midpoint of each interval and the mean. To simplify calculations, we rounded the mean to 34. Notice that if the score is higher than the mean, the difference is positive, but if the score is lower than the mean, the difference is negative. Record these differences in column d.
2. Square the differences. Record the squares in the d^2 column.
3. Multiply the squares by the N and record the product in the Nd^2 column.
4. Add the Nd^2 column, divide by the total number of cases (ΣN), and take the square root.

For these data, our standard deviation is 6.94.

Form A1. Worksheet For Mean and Standard Deviation

Score Interval	Tally	N	NX	d	d^2	Nd^2	
Totals							

APPENDIX B

༵

Standards for Teacher Competence in Educational Assessment of Students

DEVELOPED BY THE AMERICAN FEDERATION OF TEACHERS, NATIONAL COUNCIL ON MEASUREMENT IN EDUCATION, AND NATIONAL EDUCATION ASSOCIATION

The professional education associations began working in 1987 to develop standards for teacher competence in student assessment out of concern that the potential educational benefits of student assessments be fully realized. The Committee[1] appointed to this project completed its work in 1990 following reviews of earlier drafts by members of the measurement, teaching, and teacher preparation and certification communities. Parallel committees of affected associations are encouraged to develop similar statements of qualifications for school administrators, counselors, testing directors, supervisors, and other educators in the near future. These statements are intended to guide the preservice and inservice preparation of educators, the accreditation of preparation programs, and the future certification of all educators.

A standard is defined here as a principle generally accepted by the professional associations responsible for this document. Assessment is defined as the process of ob-

---

[1]The Committee that developed this statement was appointed by the collaborating professional associations: James R. Sanders, (Western Michigan University) chaired the Committee and represented NCME along with John R. Hills (Florida State University) and Anthony J. Nitko (University of Pittsburgh). Jack C. Merwin (University of Minnesota) represented the American Association of Colleges for Teacher Education, Carolyn Trice represented the American Federation of Teachers, and Marcella Dianda and Jeffrey Schneider represented the National Education Association.

taining information that is used to make educational decisions about students, to give feedback to the student about his or her progress, strengths, and weaknesses, to judge instructional effectiveness and curricular adequacy, and to inform policy. The various assessment techniques include, but are not limited to, formal and informal observation, qualitative analysis of pupil performance and products, paper-and-pencil tests, oral questioning, and analysis of student records. The assessment competencies included here are the knowledge and skills critical to a teacher's role as educator. It is understood that there are many competencies beyond assessment competencies which teachers must possess.

By establishing standards for teacher competence in student assessment, the associations subscribe to the view that student assessment is an essential part of teaching and that good teaching cannot exist without good student assessment. Training to develop the competencies covered in the standards should be an integral part of preservice preparation. Further, such assessment training should be widely available to practicing teachers through staff development programs at the district and building levels.

The standards are intended for use as:

- a guide for teacher educators as they design and approve programs for teacher preparation
- a self-assessment guide for teachers in identifying their needs for professional development in student assessment
- a guide for workshop instructors as they design professional development experiences for in-service teachers
- an impetus for educational measurement specialists and teacher trainers to conceptualize student assessment and teacher training in student assessment more broadly than has been the case in the past.

The standards should be incorporated into future teacher training and certification programs. Teachers who have not had the preparation these standards imply should have the opportunity and support to develop these competencies before the standards enter into the evaluation of these teachers.

The Approach Used to Develop the Standards

The members of the associations that supported this work are professional educators involved in teaching, teacher education, and student assessment. Members of these associations are concerned about the inadequacy with which teachers are prepared for assessing the educational progress of their students, and thus sought to address this concern effectively. A committee named by the associations first met in September 1987 and affirmed its commitment to defining standards for teacher preparation in student assessment. The committee then undertook a review of the research literature to identify needs in student assessment, current levels of teacher training in student assessment, areas of teacher activities requiring competence in using assessments, and current levels of teacher competence in student assessment.

The members of the committee used their collective experience and expertise to formulate and then revise statements of important assessment competencies. Drafts of these competencies went through several revisions by the Committee before the standards were released for public review. Comments by reviewers from each of the associations were then used to prepare a final statement.

The Scope of a Teacher's Professional Role and Responsibilities for Student Assessment

There are seven standards in this document. In recognizing the critical need to revitalize classroom assessment, some standards focus on classroom-based competencies. Because of teachers' growing roles in education and policy decisions beyond the classroom, other standards address assessment competencies underlying teacher participation in decisions related to assessment at the school, district, state, and national levels.

The scope of a teacher's professional role and responsibilities for student assessment may be described in terms of the following activities. These activities imply that teachers need competence in student assessment and sufficient time and resources to complete them in a professional manner.

Activities Occurring Prior to Instruction

(a) Understanding students' cultural backgrounds, interests, skills, and abilities as they apply across a range of learning domains and/or subject areas; (b) understanding students' motivations and their interests in specific class content; (c) clarifying and articulating the performance outcomes expected of pupils; and (d) planning instruction for individuals or groups of students.

Activities Occurring During Instruction

(a) Monitoring pupil progress toward instructional goals; (b) identifying gains and difficulties pupils are experiencing in learning and performing; (c) adjusting instruction; (d) giving contingent, specific, and credible praise and feedback; (e) motivating students to learn; and (f) judging the extent of pupil attainment of instructional outcomes.

Activities Occurring After the Appropriate Instructional Segment (e.g., Lesson, Class, Semester, Grade)

(a) Describing the extent to which each pupil has attained both short- and long-term instructional goals; (b) communicating strengths and weaknesses based on assessment results to students, and parents or guardians; (c) recording and reporting assessment results for school-level analysis, evaluation, and decision-making; (d) analyzing assessment information gathered before and during instruction to understand each students' progress to date and to inform future instructional planning; (e) evaluating the effectiveness of instruction; and (f) evaluating the effectiveness of the curriculum and materials in use.

Activities Associated with a Teacher's Involvement in School Building and School District Decision Making

(a) Serving on a school or district committee examining the school's and district's strengths and weaknesses in the development of its students; (b) working on the development or selection of assessment methods for school building or school district use; (c) evaluating school district curriculum; and (d) other related activities.

Activities Associated with a Teacher's Involvement in a Wider Community of Educators

(a) Serving on a state committee asked to develop learning goals and associated assessment methods; (b) participating in reviews of the appropriateness of district, state, or national student goals and associated assessment methods; and (c) interpreting the results of state and national student assessment programs.

Each standard that follows is an expectation for assessment knowledge or skill that a teacher should possess in order to perform well in the five areas just described. As a set, the standards call on teachers to demonstrate skill at selecting, developing, applying, using, communicating, and evaluating student assessment information and student assessment practices. A brief rationale and illustrative behaviors follow each standard.

The standards represent a conceptual framework or scaffolding from which specific skills can be derived. Work to make these standards operational will be needed even after they have been published. It is also expected that experience in the application of these standards should lead to their improvement and further development.

1. Teachers should be skilled in *choosing* assessment methods appropriate for instructional decisions.

Skills in choosing appropriate, useful, administratively convenient, technically adequate, and fair assessment methods are prerequisite to good use of information to support instructional decisions. Teachers need to be well-acquainted with the kinds of information provided by a broad range of assessment alternatives and their strengths and weaknesses. In particular, they should be familiar with criteria for evaluating and selecting assessment methods in light of instructional plans.

Teachers who meet this standard will have the conceptual and application skills that follow. They will be able to use the concepts of assessment error and validity when developing or selecting their approaches to classroom assessment of students. They will understand how valid assessment data can support instructional activities such as providing appropriate feedback to students, diagnosing group and individual learning needs, planning for individualized educational programs, motivating students, and evaluating instructional procedures. They will understand how invalid information can affect instructional decisions about students. They will also be able to use and evaluate assessment options available to them, considering among other things, the cultural, social, economic, and language backgrounds of students. They will be aware that different assessment approaches can be incompatible with certain instructional goals and may impact quite differently on their teaching.

Teachers will know, for each assessment approach they use, its appropriateness for making decisions about their pupils. Moreover, teachers will know of where to find information about and/or reviews of various assessment methods. Assessment options are diverse and include text- and curriculum-embedded questions and tests, standardized criterion-referenced and norm-referenced tests, oral questioning, spontaneous and structured performance assessments, portfolios, exhibitions, demonstrations, rating scales, writing samples, paper-and-pencil tests, seatwork and homework, peer- and self-assessments, student records, observations, questionnaires, interviews, projects, products, and others' opinions.

2. Teachers should be skilled in *developing* assessment methods appropriate for instructional decisions.

While teachers often use published or other external assessment tools, the bulk of the assessment information they use for decision-making comes from approaches they create and implement. Indeed, the assessment demands of the classroom go well beyond readily available instruments.

Teachers who meet this standard will have the conceptual and application skills that follow. Teachers will be skilled in planning the collection of information that facilitates the decisions they will make. They will know and follow appropriate principles for developing and using assessment methods in their teaching, avoiding common pitfalls in student assessment. Such techniques may include several of the options listed at the end of the first standard. The teacher will select the techniques which are appropriate to the intent of the teacher's instruction.

Teachers meeting this standard will also be skilled in using student data to analyze the quality of each assessment technique they use. Since most teachers do not have access to assessment specialists, they must be prepared to do these analyses themselves.

3. The teacher should be skilled in administering, scoring, and interpreting the results of both externally produced and teacher-produced assessment methods.

It is not enough that teachers are able to select and develop good assessment methods; they must also be able to apply them properly. Teachers should be skilled in administering, scoring, and interpreting results from diverse assessment methods.

Teachers who meet this standard will have the conceptual and application skills that follow. They will be skilled in interpreting informal and formal teacher-produced assessment results, including pupils' performances in class and on homework assignments. Teachers will be able to use guides for scoring essay questions and projects, stencils for scoring response-choice questions, and scales for rating performance assessments. They will be able to use these in ways that produce consistent results.

Teachers will be able to administer standardized achievement tests and be able to interpret the commonly reported scores: percentile ranks, percentile band scores, standard scores, and grade equivalents. They will have a conceptual understanding of the summary indexes commonly reported with assessment results: measures of central tendency, dispersion, relationships, reliability, and errors of measurement.

Teachers will be able to apply these concepts of score and summary indices in ways that enhance their use of the assessments that they develop. They will be able to analyze assessment results to identify pupils' strengths and errors. If they get inconsistent results, they will seek other explanations for the discrepancy or other data to attempt to resolve the uncertainty before arriving at a decision. They will be able to use assessment methods in ways that encourage students' educational development and that do not inappropriately increase students' anxiety levels.

4. Teachers should be skilled in using assessment results when making decisions about individual students, planning teaching, developing curriculum, and school improvement.

Assessment results are used to make educational decisions at several levels: in the classroom about students, in the community about a school and a school district, and in society, generally, about the purposes and outcomes of the educational enterprise. Teachers play a vital role when participating in decision-making at each of these levels and must be able to use assessment results effectively.

Teachers who meet this standard will have the conceptual and application skills that follow. They will be able to use accumulated assessment information to organize a sound instructional plan for facilitating students' educational development. When using assessment results to plan and/or evaluate instruction and curriculum, teachers will interpret the results correctly and avoid common misinterpretations, such as basing decisions on scores that lack curriculum validity. They will be informed about the results of local, regional, state, and national assessments and about their appropriate use for pupil, classroom, school, district, state, and national educational improvement.

5. Teachers should be skilled in developing valid pupil grading procedures which use pupil assessments.

Grading students is an important part of professional practice for teachers. Grading is defined as indicating both a student's level of performance and a teacher's valuing of that performance. The principles for using assessments to obtain valid grades are known and teachers should employ them.

Teachers who meet this standard will have the conceptual and application skills that follow. They will be able to devise, implement, and explain a procedure for developing grades composed of marks from various assignments, projects, in-class activities, quizzes, tests, and/or other assessments that they may use. Teachers will understand and be able to articulate why the grades they assign are rational, justified, and fair, acknowledging that such grades reflect their preferences and judgments. Teachers will be able to recognize and to avoid faulty grading procedures such as using grades as punishment. They will be able to evaluate and to modify their grading procedures in order to improve the validity of the interpretations made from them about students' attainments.

6. Teachers should be skilled in communicating assessment results to students, parents, other lay audiences, and other educators.

Teachers must routinely report assessment results to students and to parents or guardians. In addition, they are frequently asked to report or to discuss assessment results with other educators and with diverse lay audiences. If the results are not communicated effectively, they may be misused or not used. To communicate effectively with others on matters of student assessment, teachers must be able to use assessment terminology appropriately and must be able to articulate the meaning, limitations, and implications of assessment results. Furthermore, teachers will sometimes be in a position that will require them to defend their own assessment procedures and their interpretations of them. At other times, teachers may need to help the public to interpret assessment results appropriately.

Teachers who meet this standard will have the conceptual and application skills that follow. Teachers will understand and be able to give appropriate explanations of how the interpretation of student assessments must be moderated by the student's socio-economic, cultural, language, and other background factors. Teachers will be able to explain that assessment results do not imply that such background factors limit a student's ultimate educational development. They will be able to communicate to students and to their parents or guardians how they may assess the student's educational progress. Teachers will understand and be able to explain the importance of taking measurement errors into account when using assessments to make decisions about individual students. Teachers will be able to explain the limitations of different informal and formal assessment methods. They will be able to explain printed reports of the results of pupil assessments at the classroom, school district, state, and national levels.

7. Teachers should be skilled in recognizing unethical, illegal, and otherwise inappropriate assessment methods and uses of assessment information.

Fairness, the rights of all concerned, and professional ethical behavior must undergird all student assessment activities, from the initial planning for and gathering of information to the interpretation, use, and communication of the results. Teachers must be well-versed in their own ethical and legal responsibilities in assessment. In addition, they should also attempt to have the inappropriate assessment practices of others discontinued whenever they are encountered. Teachers should also participate with the wider educational community in defining the limits of appropriate professional behavior in assessment.

Teachers who meet this standard will have the conceptual and application skills that follow. They will know those laws and case decisions which affect their classroom, school district, and state assessment practices. Teachers will be aware that various assessment procedures can be misused or overused resulting in harmful consequences such as embarrassing students, violating a student's right to confidentiality, and inappropriately using students' standardized achievement test scores to measure teaching effectiveness.

APPENDIX C

୬୭

Code of Fair Testing Practices in Education

PREPARED BY THE JOINT COMMITTEE ON TESTING PRACTICES

The Code of Fair Testing Practices in Education states the major obligations to test takers of professionals who develop or use educational tests. The Code is meant to apply broadly to the use of tests in education (admissions, educational assessment, educational diagnosis, and student placement). The Code is not designed to cover employment testing, licensure or certification testing, or other types of testing. Although the Code has relevance to many types of educational tests, it is directed primarily at professionally developed tests such as those sold by commercial test publishers or used in formally administered testing programs. The Code is not intended to cover tests made by individual teachers for use in their own classrooms.

The Code addresses the roles of test developers and test users separately. Test users are people who select tests, commission test development services, or make decisions on the basis of test scores. Test developers are people who actually construct tests as well as those who set policies for particular testing programs. The roles may, of course, overlap as when a state education agency commissions test development services, sets policies that control the test development process, and makes decisions on the basis of the test scores.

The Code presents standards for educational test developers and users in four areas:

A. Developing/Selecting Tests
B. Interpreting Scores
C. Striving for Fairness
D. Informing Test Takers

Organizations, institutions, and individual professionals who endorse the Code commit themselves to safeguarding the rights of test takers by following the principles listed. The Code is intended to be consistent with the relevant parts of

The Code has been developed by the Joint Committee on Testing Practices, a cooperative effort of several professional organizations, that has as its aim the advancement, in the public interest, of the quality of testing practices. The Joint Committee was initiated by the American Educational Research Association, the American Psychological Association, and the National Council on Measurement in Education. In addition to these three groups, the American Association for Counseling and Development/ Association for Measurement and Evaluation in Counseling and Development, and the American Speech-Language-Hearing Association are now also sponsors of the Joint Committee.

This is not copyrighted material. Reproduction and dissemination are encouraged. Please cite this document as follows:

Code of Fair Testing Practices in Education. (1988) Washington, DC: Joint Committee on Testing Practices. (Mailing Address: Joint Committee on Testing Practices, American Psychological Association, 750 First Avenue, NE, Washington, DC 20002-4242.

the *Standards for Educational and Psychological Testing* (AERA, APA, NCME, 1985). However, the Code differs from the Standards in both audience and purpose. The Code is meant to be understood by the general public; it is limited to educational tests; and the primary focus is on those issues that affect the proper use of tests. The Code is not meant to add new principles over and above those in the Standards or to change the meaning of the Standards. The goal is rather to represent the spirit of a selected portion of the Standards in a way that is meaningful to test takers and/or their parents or guardians. It is the hope of the Joint Committee that the Code will also be judged to be consistent with existing codes of conduct and standards of other professional groups who use educational tests.

A. Developing/Selecting Appropriate Tests*

Test developers should provide the information that test users need to select appropriate tests.

Test Developers Should:

1. Define what each test measures and what the test should be used for. Describe the population(s) for which the test is appropriate.
2. Accurately represent the characteristics, usefulness, and limitations of tests for their intended purposes.
3. Explain relevant measurement concepts as necessary for clarity at the level of detail that is appropriate for the intended audience(s).
4. Describe the process of test development. Explain how the content and skills to be tested were selected.
5. Provide evidence that the test meets its intended purpose(s).
6. Provide either representative samples or complete copies of test questions, directions, answer sheets, manuals, and score reports to qualified users.

7. Indicate the nature of the evidence obtained concerning the appropriateness of each test for groups of different racial, ethnic, or linguistic backgrounds who are likely to be tested.
8. Identify and publish any specialized skills needed to administer each test and to interpret scores correctly.

Test users should select tests that meet the purpose for which they are to be used and that are appropriate for the intended test-taking populations.

Test Users Should:

1. First define the purpose for testing and the population to be tested. Then, select a test for that purpose and that population based on a thorough review of the available information.
2. Investigate potentially useful sources of information, in addition to test scores, to corroborate the information provided by tests.
3. Read the materials provided by test developers and avoid using tests for which unclear or incomplete information is provided.
4. Become familiar with how and when the test was developed and tried out.
5. Read independent evaluations of a test and of possible alternative measures. Look for evidence required to support the claims of test developers.
6. Examine specimen sets, disclosed tests or samples of questions, directions, answer sheets, manuals, and score reports before selecting a test.
7. Ascertain whether the test content and norms group(s) or comparison group(s) are appropriate for the intended test takers.
8. Select and use only those tests for which the skills needed to administer the test and interpret scores correctly are available.

---

*Many of the statements in the Code refer to the selection of existing tests. However, in customized testing programs test developers are engaged to construct new tests. In those situations, the test development process should be designed to help ensure that the completed tests will be in compliance with the Code.

B. Interpreting Scores

Test developers should help users interpret scores correctly.

Test Developers Should:

9. Provide timely and easily understood score reports that describe test performance clearly and accurately. Also explain the meaning and limitations of reported scores.
10. Describe the population(s) represented by any norms or comparison group(s), the dates the data were gathered, and the process used to select the samples of test takers.
11. Warn users to avoid specific, reasonably anticipated misuses of test scores.
12. Provide information that will help users follow reasonable procedures for setting passing scores when it is appropriate to use such scores with the test.
13. Provide information that will help users gather evidence to show that the test is meeting its intended purpose(s).

Test users should interpret scores correctly.

Test Users Should:

9. Obtain information about the scale used for reporting scores, the characteristics of any norms or comparison group(s), and the limitations of the scores.
10. Interpret scores taking into account any major differences between the norms or comparison groups and the actual test takers. Also take into account any differences in test administration practices or familiarity with the specific questions in the test.
11. Avoid using tests for purposes not specifically recommended by the test developer unless evidence is obtained to support the intended use.
12. Explain how any passing scores were set and gather evidence to support the appropriateness of the scores.
13. Obtain evidence to help show that the test is meeting its intended purpose(s).

C. Striving for Fairness

Test developers should strive to make tests that are as fair as possible for test takers of different races, gender, ethnic backgrounds, or handicapping conditions.

Test Developers Should:

14. Review and revise test questions and related materials to avoid potentially insensitive content or language.
15. Investigate the performance of test takers of different races, gender, and ethnic backgrounds when samples of sufficient size are available. Enact procedures that help to ensure that differences in performance are related primarily to the skills under assessment rather than to irrelevant factors.
16. When feasible, make appropriately modified forms of tests or administration procedures available for test takers with handicapping conditions. Warn test users of potential problems in using standard norms with modified tests or administration procedures that result in non-comparable scores.

Test users should select tests that have been developed in ways that attempt to make them as fair as possible for test takers of different races, gender, ethnic backgrounds, or handicapping conditions.

Test Users Should:

14. Evaluate the procedures used by test developers to avoid potentially insensitive content or language.
15. Review the performance of test takers of different races, gender, and ethnic backgrounds when samples of sufficient size are available. Evaluate the extent to which performance differences may have been caused by inappropriate characteristics of the test.
16. When necessary and feasible, use appropriately modified forms of tests or administration procedures for test takers with handicapping conditions. Interpret standard norms with care in the light of the modifications that were made.

D. Informing Test Takers

Under some circumstances, test developers have direct communication with test takers. Under other circumstances, test users communicate directly with test takers. Whichever group communicates directly with test takers should provide the information described below.

Test Developers or Test Users Should:

17. When a test is optional, provide test takers or their parents/guardians with information to help them judge whether the test should be taken, or if an available alternative to the test should be used.
18. Provide test takers the information they need to be familiar with the coverage of the test, the types of question formats, the directions, and appropriate test-taking strategies. Strive to make such information equally available to all test takers.

Under some circumstances, test developers have direct control of tests and test scores. Under other circumstances, test users have such control. Whichever group has direct control of tests and test scores should take the steps described below.

Test Developers or Test Users Should:

19. Provide test takers or their parents/guardians with information about rights test takers may have to obtain copies of tests and completed answer sheets, retake tests, have tests rescored, or cancel scores.
20. Tell test takers or their parents/guardians how long scores will be kept on file and indicate to whom and under what circumstances test scores will or will not be released.
21. Describe the procedures that test takers or their parents/guardians may use to register complaints and have problems resolved.

NOTE: The membership of the Working Group that developed the Code of Fair Testing Practices in Education and of the Joint Committee on Testing Practices that guided the Working Group was as follows:

Theodore P. Bartell
John R. Bergan
Esther E. Diamond
Richard P. Duran
Lorraine D. Eyde
Raymond D. Fowler
John J. Fremer (Co-chair, JCTP; and Chair, Code Working Group)
Edmund W. Gordon
Jo-Ida C. Hansen
James B. Lingwall
George F. Madaus (Co-chair, JCTP)
Kevin L. Moreland
Jo-Ellen V. Perez
Robert J. Solomon
John T. Stewart
Carol Kehr Tittle (Co-chair, JCTP)
Nicholas A. Vacc
Michael J. Zieky

Debra Boltas and Wayne Camara of the American Psychological Association served as staff liaisons

Additional copies of the Code may be obtained from the National Council on Measurement in Education, 1230 Seventeenth Street, NW, Washington, DC 20036. Single copies are free.

APPENDIX D

༄

Selected Assessment Web Sites

This appendix presents selected web sites that feature information on assessment and related topics. The list has been arranged by type or organization, and each entry includes the web site address (URL) and a brief summary of the site's content. Where possible, mailing addresses have also been provided. Please note that web site owners do occasionally change their addresses and contents. The information in this appendix was the most current available at the time of this printing.

Research and Professional Organizations

Organization and Mailing Address	Web Site/URL	Available Information
American Council on Education (ACE) One Dupont Circle Washington, DC 20036	http://www.ACENET.edu	Assessment and other research topics, services, and publications
American Educational Research Association (AERA) 1230 Seventeenth Street, NW Washington, DC 20036-3078	http://aera.net	AERA's assessment and other research activities and publications
American Psychological Association 750 First Street, NE Washington, DC 20002-4242	http://www.apa.org	Current test and professional standards and draft of new standards
Argus Clearinghouse No address given	http://www.clearinghouse.net.	Research information on assessment, evaluation, educational standards

Organization and Mailing Address	Web Site/URL	Available Information
Buros Institute on Mental Measurements University of Nebraska at Lincoln 135 Bancroft Hall Lincoln, NE 68588-0348	http://www.unl.edu/buros/	Information database on tests and research instruments, links to test company web sites
Council of Chief State School Officers (CCSSO) One Massachusetts Ave., NW, Suite 700 Washington, DC 20001-1431	http://www.ccsso.org/	Information on interstate teacher assessment and licensure, standards for school leaders, and assessment standards for various educators
Education Commission of the States 707 17th Street, #2700 Denver, CO 80202-3427	http://www.ecs.org/ecs/ecsweb.nsf	Reports and direct searching for assessment and other information by state, region, and grade level
Education Week 6935 Arlington Road, Suite 100 Bethesda, MD 20814-5233	http://www.edweek.org	Assessment and other information from *Education Week;* searchable by topic, links to products
Eisenhower National Clearinghouse for Mathematics and Science Ohio State University 1929 Kenny Road Columbus, OH 43210-1079	http://www.enc.org	Teachers' professional standards for creating assessments and obtaining and using assessment results in math and science
ERIC Clearinghouse on Assessment and Evaluation a.k.a. Educational Testing Service (ETS) Test File Catholic University of America 210 O'Boyle Hall, Dept. of Education Washington, DC 20064	http:ericae.net http://ericae.net/testcol.html (Access through http://ericae.net then click on "test Locator")	Facts on assessment, links to ERIC searching, full text library, and information database on more than 10,000 tests and research instruments
International Reading Association (IRA) 800 Barksdale Road Newark, DE 19714-8139	http://www.reading.org	Order information for new reading standards including standards for assessment procedures and use of results
National Board of Professional Teaching Standards 26555 Evergreen Road, Suite 400 Southfield, MI 48076	http://www.nbpts.org	Teaching standards including those on the use of assessment information for instruction and meeting students' needs

Organization and Mailing Address	Web Site/URL	Available Information
National Council of Teachers of English (NCTE) 1111 West Kenton Road Urbana, IL 61801	http://www.ncte.org	Assessment and other standards for English education
National Council of Teachers of Mathematics (NCTM) 1906 Association Drive Reston, VA 20191-1593	http://www.nctm.org	Assessment and other standards for mathematics education
National Council on Measurement in Education (NCME) 1230 Seventeenth Street, NW Washington, DC 20036-3078	http://www.assessment.iupui.edu/ncme/ncme/html	*Code of Fair Testing Practices* and association assessment activities
U.S. National Center for Educational Statistics (NCES) 555 New Jersey Avenue, NW Room 400 Washington, DC 20208	http://nces.ed.gov/	Information on testing programs, research projects and results, and laws and policy
National Center for Research on Evaluation, Standards, and Student Testing (CRESST) University of California at Los Angeles (UCLA) GSE&IS Box 951522 Los Angeles, CA 90095-1522	http://cresst96.cse.ucla.edu/	Research programs and results, links to other projects and test web sites
National Institute on Student Achievement, Curriculum and Assessment (Sponsored by OERI)	http://www.ed.gov./offices/OREI/SAI/	Links to nationally funded educational research institutes dealing with various assessment and other research topics
National Network of Regional Educational Laboratories (through) Brown University Providence, RI 02903	http://www.lab.brown.edu/public/national/national.shtml	Provides direct access to all 10 national educational labs, several of which have major assessment projects and collections of instruments and materials
Northeast and Islands Regional Educational Laboratory Brown University 222 Richmond Street, Suite 300 Providence, RI 02903-4226	http://www.lab.brown.edu/public/index.shtml	Information on portfolio and assessments standards

Organization and Mailing Address	Web Site/URL	Available Information
Northwest Regional Educational Laboratory 101 SW Main Street, Suite 500 Portland, OR 97204	http://www.nwrel.org/	Information on tests, test bibliographies, portfolios, and curricula and materials
U.S. Office of Education (Office of Education and Research Information) (OERI) 600 Independence Ave., SW Washington, DC 20202-0498	http://www.ed.gov/	Wide variety of information on assessment and other educational topics, research projects, standards, and policies
U.S. Office of Education Consumer's Guides 600 Independence Ave., SW Washington, DC 20202-0498	http://www.ed.gov/pubs/OR/ConsumerGuides/ (Type in after getting to U.S. Office of Edu. Homepage)	Information for the general public on performance assessment methods, research findings, and examples
U.S. Office of Education State Resources Directory No address given	http://www.ed.gov/BASISDB/EROD/direct/SF	Provides links to all state departments of education, research institutes and regional educational laboratories, many of which contain projects and information on assessment research, standards and materials

Testing Organizations and Companies

Organization and Mailing Address	Web Site/URL	Available Information
American College Testing Program (ACT) 2201 North Dodge Street PO Box 168 Iowa City, Iowa 52243-0168	http://www.act.org/	Information on tests and assessment research created by the ACT
College Board 11911 Freedom Drive, Suite 400 Reston, VA 20190	http://www.collegeboard.org/	Information on tests and assessment research created by the College Board
CTB-Macmillan/McGraw-Hill 20 Ryan Ranch Road Monterey, CA 93940	http://www.ctb.com	Testing company information on products and services
Educational Testing Service (ETS) Rosedale Road Princeton, NJ 08541	http://www.ets.org	Assessment and other research topics, services, research, and publications created by ETS
Harcourt Brace (Psychological Corporation) 555 Academic Court San Antonio, TX 78204	http://www.hbtpc.com	Testing company information on products and services, and test standards

Organization and Mailing Address	Web Site/URL	Available Information
Riverside Testing Corporation (Houghton Mifflin) 425 Spring Lake Drive Itasca, IL 60143-2079	http://www.riverpub.com/	Testing company information on products and services

Selected State Departments of Education

California Department of Education 721 Capitol Mall Sacramento, CA 94244-2720	http://www.cde.ca.gov/	Information on educational standards, testing programs, and research results
Florida Department of Education Capitol Building Tallahassee, FL 32399-0400	http://www.firn.edu/doe/index.html	Information on educational standards, testing programs, and research results
Kentucky Department of Education 1930 Capitol Plaza Tower 500 Mero Street Frankfort, KY 40601	http://www.kde.state.ky.us	Information on educational standards, testing programs, and research results
Texas Education Agency William B. Travis Building 1701 North Congress Ave. Austin, TX 78701-1494	http://www.tea.state.tx.us/	Information on educational standards, testing programs, and research results
Vermont Department of Education 120 State Street Montpelier, VT 05620-2501	http://www.state.vt.us/educ	Information on educational standards, testing programs, and research results
Washington Office of Public Instruction Old Capitol Building 600 South Washington P.O. Box 47200 Olympia, WA 98504-7200	http://www.ospi.wednet.edu	Information on educational standards, testing programs, and research results

APPENDIX E

ॐ

Names and Addresses
of Test Publishers

Academic Therapy Publications
20 Commercial Blvd.
Novato, CA 94944-6191

American College Testing Program
2201 N. Dodge St.
P.O. Box 4060
Iowa City, IA 52243-4060

American Council on Education
One Dupont Circle
Washington, DC 20036

American Guidance Services, Inc.
4201 Woodland Rd.
P.O. Box 99
Circle Pines, MN 55014-1796

Clinical Psychology Publishing Co., Inc.
4 Conant Square
Brandon, NJ 05733

The College Board
45 Columbus Ave.
New York, NY 10023-6992

Consulting Psychologists Press, Inc.
3903 Bayshore Rd.
P.O. Box 10096
Palo Alto, CA 94303

Creative Learning Press, Inc.
P.O. Box 320
Mansfield Center, CT 06250

CTB-Macmillan/McGraw-Hill
20 Ryan Ranch Rd.
Monterey, CA 93940-5703

Curriculum Associates
5 Esquire Rd.
North Billerica, MA 01862-2589

Educational Testing Service (ETS)
P.O. Box 6736
Princeton, NJ 08541-6736

GED Testing Service of the
    American Council on Education
One Dupont Circle
Suite 20
Washington, DC 20036-1193

Gesell Developmental Test Materials, Inc.
P.O. Box 272391
Houston, TX 77227-2391

Gregorc Associates
15 Doubleday Rd.
P.O. 351
Columbia, CT 06237

Grune & Stratton
465 S. Lincoln Dr.
Troy, MO 63379

Hanson, Silver, Strong, and Associates
34 Washington Rd.
Princeton Junction, NJ 08550

Harcourt Brace Educational Measurement
555 Academic Court
San Antonio, TX 78204-2498

Institute for Personality and Ability Testing, Inc.
P.O. Box 1188
Champaign, IL 61824-1188

IOX Assessment Asso.
5301 Beethoven St., Suite 109
Los Angeles, CA 90066-1061

Jastak/Wide Range, Inc.
P.O. Box 3410
Wilmington, DE 19807-0250

Kendall-Hunt Publishing Co.
4050 Westmark Drive
Dubuque, IA 52004-1840

McBer & Company
116 Huntington Ave.
Boston, MA 02116

McCarron-Dial Systems
P.O. Box 45628
Dallas, TX 75245

National Association of
   Secondary School Principals
1904 Association Dr.
P.O. Box 3250
Reston, VA 22091-1598

NCS Assessments
5605 Green Circle Dr.
Minnetonka, MN 55343

Price Systems, Inc.
P.O. Box 1818
Lawrence, KS 66044

PRO-ED Inc.
8700 Shoal Creek
Austin, TX 78757-6897

Psychological Assessment Resources (PAR)
P.O. Box 998
Odessa, FL 33556-9908

The Psychological Corporation
555 Academic Court
San Antonio, TX 78204-2498

Riverside Publishing Co.
425 Spring Lake Dr.
Itasca, IL 60143-2079

Scholastic Testing Service
480 Meyer Rd.
Bensenville, IL 60106-1617

Science Research Associates, Inc.
9701 W. Higgins Rd.
Rosemont, IL 60018

Slosson Educational Publications
P.O. Box 280
East Aurora, NY 14052-0280

Stoelting Co.
Oakwood Center
620 Wheat Lane
Wood Dale, IL 60191

Teachers College Press
Teachers College
Columbia University
New York, NY 10027

Touchstone Applied Science Associates, Inc.
   (TASA)
Fields Lane
P.O. Box 382
Brewster, NY 10509

U.S. Department of Labor
Employment and Training Administration
200 Constitution Ave.
Washington, DC 20210

U.S. Military Entrance Processing
Department of Defense
2500 Green Bay Rd.
Washington, DC 20305

Variety Pre-Schoolers' Workshop
47 Humphrey Dr.
Syosset, NY 11791-4098

Western Psychological Services
12031 Wilshire Blvd.
Los Angeles, CA 90025-1251

Wonderlic Personnel Test, Inc.
1509 Milwaukee Ave.
Libertyville, IL 60048-1387

APPENDIX F

༉

Published Tests

In this appendix we have listed some of the commercially available tests, along with information about the age or grade level for which the test is intended and the publishers. We have listed the instruments most often found in the professional literature and on lists from some state departments of education. However, we caution the reader not to rely entirely on our list but to consult the sources listed in Appendix D and the latest edition of *Tests in Print*.

In order to assist you in using the list, we have sorted the instruments into the categories we use in the book, and we have indicated the chapter in which most of the discussion of the category is covered.

Achievement Tests (Chapter 11)

Group Tests: Batteries

Test	Grade/Age	Publisher
Adult Basic Learning Examination 2nd ed. (ABLE)	Adult	Harcourt Brace Educational Measurement
Aprenda 2	K–7	Harcourt Brace Educational Measurement
California Achievement Tests	K–12	CTB-Macmillan/McGraw-Hill
Iowa Tests of Basic Skills	K–9	Riverside Publishing
Iowa Tests of Educational Development	Gr. 9–12	Riverside Publishing
Life Skills	Gr. 9–12, Adult	Riverside Publishing
Metropolitan Achievement Tests	K–12	Harcourt Brace Educational Measurement
National Educational Development Tests	Gr. 9–10	Science Research Associates

Achievement Tests (Chapter 11)

Group Tests: Batteries (continued)

Test	Grade/Age	Publisher
Sequential Tests of Educational Progress (STEP)	K–12	Dist.: CTB-Macmillan/McGraw-Hill
Spanish Assessment of Basic Education II/(SABE/II)	1–8	CTB-Macmillan/McGraw-Hill
Stanford Achievement Tests	K–12	Harcourt Brace Educational Measurement
Stanford Early School Achievement Test	K–1	Harcourt Brace Educational Measurement
Supera	1–9/10	CTB-Macmillan/McGraw-Hill
Terra Nova	K–12	CTB-Macmillan/McGraw-Hill
Tests of General Educational Development (GED)	Adult	GED Testing Service of American Council on Education
The 3-Rs Test	K–12	Riverside Publishing
USES Basic Occupational Literacy Test (BOLT)	Adult Disadvantaged	U.S. Department of Labor, Employment and Training Administration
Wonderlic Basic Skills Test	Teen–Adult	Wonderlic Personnel Test, Inc.

Achievement Tests in Specific Subjects

Test	Grade/Age	Publisher
ACT Proficiency Examination Program	Adult	American College Testing Program
Advanced Placement Program	High school	ETS (for the College Board)
College Board Achievement Tests	High school	ETS (for the College Board)
College Level Examination Program	High school	ETS (for the College Board)
STEP-III End of Course Tests	High school	Dist.: CTB-Macmillan/McGraw-Hill

Reading

Test	Grade/Age	Publisher
Basic Reading Inventory	P–10	Kendall-Hunt Publishing Co.
Degrees of Reading Power	Gr. 1–12	Touchstone
Diagnostic Reading Scales	Gr. 1–12	CTB-Macmillan/McGraw-Hill
Durrell Analysis of Reading Difficulty III	Gr. 1–6	Harcourt Brace Educational Measurement
Gates-McGinitie Reading Tests (Diagnostic)	K–12	Riverside Publishing

Achievement Tests (Chapter 11)

Achievement Tests in Specific Subjects (continued)

Test	Grade/Age	Publisher
Gray Oral Reading Test (III)	Age 7–18	Harcourt Brace Educational Measurement
MAT6 Reading Diagnostic Tests	K.5–9.9	Harcourt Brace Educational Measurement
Nelson-Denny Reading Test	Gr. 9–16, Adult	Riverside Publishing
Nelson Reading Skills Test	Gr. 3–9	Riverside Publishing
Slosson Oral Reading Test (I)	K–1	Slosson Educational Publications
Stanford Diagnostic Reading Test	1.5–13	Harcourt Brace Educational Measurement
Test of Early Reading Ability (I) (Deaf and Hard of Hearing)	Age 3-12	PRO-ED
Woodcock Reading Mastery Test	K–12	American Guidance Services
Mathematics		
California Diagnostic Mathematics Test	Gr. 1–12	CTB-Macmillan/McGraw Hill
Key Math Diagnostic Arithmetic Test	K–9	American Guidance Services
MAT6 Mathematics Diagnostic Tests	Gr. 1.5–13	Harcourt Brace Educational Measurement
Orleans-Hanna Algebra Prognosis Test, Third Edition	Gr. 7–12	Harcourt Brace Educational Measurement
Stanford Diagnostic Mathematics Test	1.5–13	Harcourt Brace Educational Measurement
Test of Early Mathematics Ability	Age 3–11	PRO-ED
Language Development		
Bilingual Syntax Measure	PreK–12	Harcourt Brace Educational Measurement
Communications Abilities Diagnostic Test	Age 3–11	Riverside Publishing
Language Assessment Scales—Oral	Gr. 1–12	CTB-Macmillan/McGraw-Hill
Lista de Destrez as en Des arrollo	PreK–K	CTB-Macmillan/McGraw-Hill
Secondary-Level English Proficiency Test	High School	Educational Testing Service
Test of Early Language Development	Age 2–11	PRO-ED
Woodcock Language Proficiency Battery	Age 2–90+	Riverside Publishing
Woodcock-Munoz Language Survey	Age 4–Adult	Riverside Publishing

Achievement Tests (Chapter 11)

Achievement Tests in Specific Subjects *(continued)*

Test	Grade/Age	Publisher
Social Studies		
Cultural Literacy Test	Gr. 11–12	Riverside Publishing

Open-Ended and Performance Achievement Tests

Test	Grade/Age	Publisher
Basic Achievement Skills	Gr. 1–12	Harcourt Brace Educational Measurement
GOALS	Gr. 1–12	Harcourt Brace Educational Measurement
Integrated Assessment System (IAS)	Gr. 1–8	Harcourt Brace Educational Measurement
Language Arts	Gr. 1–8	
Language Arts—Spanish	Gr. 1–8	
Mathematics	Gr. 1–9	
Science	Gr. 1–8	
Wide Range Achievement Tests	Age 5–Adult	Jastak/Wide Range (Harcourt Brace, dist.)

Readiness and Development Scales (Chapter 12)

Test	Grade/Age	Publisher
Analysis of Readiness Skills: Reading and Mathematics	K–1	Riverside Publishing
Bayley Scales of Infant Development	1–42 mos.	Harcourt Brace Educational Measurement
Boehm Test of Basic Concepts	K–2	Harcourt Brace Educational Measurement
BRIGANCE Screener	K–1/2–2.5	Curriculum Associates
Children at Risk Screener (CARS)	P–K	Dist.: CTB-Macmillan/McGraw-Hill
CIRCUS (and El Circo)	Age 3–8	Dist.: CTB-Macmillan/McGraw-Hill
Cooperative Preschool Inventory	Age 3–6	Dist.: CTB-Macmillan/McGraw-Hill
Early School Assessment (ESA)	K–1	CTB-Macmillan/McGraw-Hill
Early Screening Inventory	Age 3–6	Teachers College Press
First STEP	Age 3–6	Harcourt Brace Educational Measurement
The Five P's Screener	P–K	Variety Pre-Schooler's Workshop
The Gesell Child Development Scale	Age 2–10	Psychological and Educational Publications

Readiness and Development Scales (Chapter 12)

Test	Grade/Age	Publisher
Harrison–Stroud Reading Readiness Profiles	K–1	Riverside Publishing
Metropolitan Readiness Tests	K–1	Harcourt Brace Educational Measurement
New Standards Reference Examination English Language Arts Mathematics	Elem., MS, HS	Harcourt Brace Educational Measurement
Stanford 9 Open-Ended Reading Assessment Mathematics Assessment Science Assessment Social Science Assessment	Gr. 1.5–13	Harcourt Brace Educational Measurement

Individual Achievement Tests

Test	Grade/Age	Publisher
Adult Basic Learning Examination (ABLE)	Adult	Harcourt Brace Educational Measurement
Basic Achievement Skills Individual Screener (BASIS)	Gr. 1–12	Harcourt Brace Educational Measurement
Durrell Analysis of Reading	Gr. 1–12	Harcourt Brace Educational Measurement
Early School Assessment	K–1	CTB-Macmillan/McGraw-Hill
Kaufman Survey of Early Academic and Language Skills	Age 3–7	American Guidance Services
Key Math Diagnostic Arithmetic Test	P–6	American Guidance Services
Key Math Revised	K–9	American Guidance Services
M-KIDS	Age 4–7	Harcourt Brace Educational Measurement
Multilevel Academic Survey Tests (MAST)	K–12	Harcourt Brace Educational Measurement
Peabody Individual Achievement Test	K–Adult	American Guidance Services
Stanford Early School Achievement Test (III)	K–1.5	Harcourt Brace Educational Measurement
Tests of Basic Experience (TOBE)	P–1	CTB-Macmillan/McGraw-Hill
Wechsler Individual Achievement Test	Age 5–19	Harcourt Brace Educational Measurement

General Scholastic Abilities (Chapter 12)

Individual Tests

Test	Grade/Age	Publisher
Arthur Point Scale of Performance	4.5–Adult	Stoelting Co.
Beta II (Nonverbal)	Age 16–Adult	Harcourt Brace Educational Measurement
Cognitive Behavior Rating Scales	Neurological Patients	Psychological Assessment Resources
Columbia Mental Maturity Scales	Age 3–6	Psychological Corporation
Culture-Fair Intelligence Test	Age 4–8	Institute for Personality and Ability Testing
Kaufman Assessment Battery for Children (K–ABC)	Age 2.5–12.5	American Guidance Services
Leiter International Performance Scale	Age 2–18	Stoelting Co.
McCarthy Scale of Children's Abilities	Age 2–4	Psychological Corporation
Peabody Picture Vocabulary Test	Age 2.5–10	American Guidance Services
Porteus Maze	Age 3–17, Adult	Psychological Corporation
Raven's Progressive Matrices	Age 5–11, Impaired adults	Harcourt Brace Educational Measurement
Stanford-Binet Intelligence Scale	P–Adult	Riverside Publishing
System of Multicultural Pluralistic Assessment (SOMPA)	Age 5–11	Psychological Corporation
Wechsler Adult Intelligence Scale (WAIS)	Adult	Psychological Corporation
Wechsler Intelligence Scale for Children (WISC) III	Age 6–18	Psychological Corporation
Wechsler Pre-School and Primary Scale of Intelligence (WPPSI)	2 yr 11 mo–7 yr 3 mo	Psychological Corporation
Woodcock–Johnson Psychlinguistic Battery	Age 2–90	Riverside Publishing

Group Tests

Test	Grade/Age	Publisher
Cognitive Abilities Test	K–12	Riverside Publishing
Culture-Fair Intelligence Test	Gr. 4–16, Adult	Institute for Personality and Ability Testing
Detroit Tests of Learning Aptitude	Age 3–Adult	PRO-ED
Goodenough-Harris Drawing Test	Age 3–15	Psychological Corporation

General Scholastic Abilities (Chapter 12)

Group Tests (continued)

Test	Grade/Age	Publisher
Henmon-Nelson Tests of Mental Ability	K–12	Riverside Publishing
Kuhlmann-Anderson Tests of Mental Ability	K–12	Scholastic Testing Service
Naglieri Nonverbal Ability Test	K–12	Harcourt Brace Educational Measurement
Otis-Lennon School Ability Test	Gr. 1–12	Harcourt Brace Educational Measurement
Raven's Progressive Matrices	Age 5–11, Adult	Harcourt Brace Educational Measurement
Slosson Intelligence Test	Age 4+	Slosson Educational Publication
Tests of Cognitive Skills	Gr. 2–12	CTB-Macmillan/McGraw-Hill

Multiple Aptitude Batteries (Chapter 12)

Test	Grade/Age	Publisher
Armed Services Vocational Aptitude Battery	Adult	U.S. Military Entrance Processing Dept. of Defense
Differential Aptitude Battery (DAT)	Gr. 7–12, Adults	Harcourt Brace Educational Measurement
Flanagan Aptitude Classification Battery	Gr. 9–12, Adults	Science Research Associates
Planning Career Goals: Ability Measures	HS, Adult	CTB-Macmillan/McGraw-Hill
USES General Aptitude Test Battery	HS, Adult	U.S Department of Labor, Employment and Training Administration
USES Nonreading Aptitude Test Battery	HS, Adult	U.S. Department of Labor, Employment and Training Administration

Learning Styles Inventories (Chapter 12)

Test	Grade/Age	Publisher
Assessment of Individual Learning Style	Age 4+	McCarron-Dial Systems
Canfield Learning Style Inventory	M, S, Adult	Western Psychological Services
Gregorc Style Delineator	Adult	Gregorc Associates
Kaufman Assessment Battery for Children	Age 2.5–12.5	American Guidance Services
Learning Efficiency Test II	Age 5–75	Academic Therapy Publications
Learning Preference Inventory	Elem to Adult	Hanson, Silver, Strong, and Associates

Learning Styles Inventories (Chapter 12)

Test	Grade/Age	Publisher
Learning Style Inventory	Gr. 3–12	Price Systems
Learning Style Inventory	Gr. 6–Adult	McBer & Company
Learning Style Profile	Gr. 6–12	National Association of Secondary School Principals
Learning Styles Inventory	Gr. 4–12	Creative Learning Press

Tests of Creativity (Chapter 12)

Test	Grade/Age	Publisher
Alternate Uses	Age 6–16, Adult	Dist.: Consulting Psychologists Press
Christensen-Guilford Fluency Test	MS, HS, Adult	Dist.: Consulting Psychologists Press
Consequences	Age 9–16	Dist.: Consulting Psychologists Press
Thinking Creatively in Action and Movement	Age 3–8	Scholastic Testing Service
Torrance Tests of Creative Thinking	K–Adult	Scholastic Testing Service
Watson-Glaser Critical Thinking Appraisal	Gr. 9–12, Adult	Harcourt Brace Educational Measurement

Adaptive Behavior Inventories (Chapter 12)

Test	Grade/Age	Publisher
AAMR Adaptive Behavior Scale—Public School Version	Age 3–21	PRO-ED
Adaptive Behavior Inventory for Children (ABIC)	Age 5–11	Psychological Corporation
Checklist of Adaptive Living Skills	Infant–Adult	Riverside Publishing
Coping Resources Inventory	HS, Adult	Consulting Psychologists Press
Survey of Functional Adaptive Behavior	Age 16+	McCarron-Dial Systems
Vineland Adaptive Behavior Scales	Birth–Adult	American Guidance Services
Ways of Coping Questionnaire	Adult	Consulting Psychologists Press

Inventories of Interests and Attitudes (Chapter 13)

Test	Grade/Age	Publisher
Campbell Interest and Skill Survey	Age 15–Adult	NCS Assessments
Career Assessment Inventory	Gr. 9–Adult	NCS Assessments
Career Development Inventory	Gr. 8–12, Adult	Consulting Psychologists Press

Inventories of Interests and Attitudes (Chapter 13)

Test	Grade/Age	Publisher
Dimensions of Self-Concept	Gr. 4–12, Adult	Educational and Industrial Testing
Guilford–Zimmerman Interest Inventory	College/Adult	Consulting Psychologists Press
Kuder General Interest Survey	Gr. 6–12	CTB-Macmillan/McGraw-Hill
Kuder Preference Record—Vocational	Gr. 9–16, Adult	Science Research Associates
Ohio Vocational Interest Survey	Gr. 7+	Harcourt Brace Educational Measurement
Rokeach Value Survey	Age 11+	Consulting Psychologists Press
Study of Values	Gr. 10–12, Adult	Riverside Publishing
USES Interest Inventory	Adult	U.S. Department of Labor, Employment and Training Administration

APPENDIX G

༉

Item Banks and Item Banking Programs

Item Banking Programs

Vendor	Program
Addison–Wesley Publishing Co. 2725 Sand Hill Road Menlo Park, CA 94025	Test Authoring Program (TAP)
Assessment Systems Corporation 2233 University Ave., #440 St. Paul, MN 55114	MICROCAT ASTEC ITEMAN ASCAL RASCAL
A. U. Software 1735 S Street, NW Washington, DC 20036	EXAM BUILDER
Chariot Software Group 3659 India Street San Diego, CA 92103	MICRO TEST and MICRO GRADE
Compu-tations, Inc. P.O. Box 487 Southfield, MI 48037	TESTS MADE EASY

Note: This list is for information only. It does not constitute a recommendation. All item banks and item banking programs should be carefully evaluated by the potential purchaser. For more information, see Naccarato, R. W. (1988), *A Guide to Item Banking in Education* (3rd ed.), Northwest Regional Education Laboratory, Portland, OR 97204 or Ward & Murray-Ward (1994a, 1994b).

Item Banking Programs

Vendor	Program
Concourse 7668 West 78th St. Bloomington, MN 55439	GENIE
Cross Educational Software 504 E. Kentucky Ave., P.O. Box 1536 Ruston, LA 71270	THE GRAND INQUISITOR CREATE-A-TEST
Data Assist, Inc. P.O. Box 26114 Columbus, OH 43216	PC-QUIZZER

Economics Research, Inc.
2925 College Ave.
Costa Mesa, CA 92929
	PAR System
	  PARTEST
	  PARSCORE

Educational Clearinghouse, Inc. Box 3951 Tallahassee, FL 32315	TEST CONSTRUCTION AND P.O. REVIEW
Edusoft P.O. Box 2560-OK Berkeley, CA 94702	PC GRADE BOOK DELUXE and PC TEST IT! DELUXE
Goal Systems/Legent Corp. 7965 North High St. Columbus, OH 43235	PHOENIX
Harcourt Brace Educational Measurement 555 Academic Court San Antonio, TX 78204-2498	AIMS
IPS Publishing Company 12606 N.E. 95th St., C-110 Vancouver, WA 98682	EXAM IN A CAN
Midwest Agribusiness Services 6739 Glacier Drive West Bend, WI 53095	Quizwriter Plus
Midwest Software 22500 Orchard Lake Road, Suite 1 Farmington, MI 48024	TESTMASTER
National Computer Systems P.O. Box 9365 Minneapolis, MN 55440	EXAM System
Teaching Technologies 3889 N. Van Ness Blvd. Fresno, CA 93704	QBANK and VIDEO TEST

Item Banks

Vendor	Title	Areas	Grade Level
CTB–Macmillan/McGraw-Hill 20 Ryan Ranch Rd. Monterey, CA 93940–5703	CTB–Macmillan/ McGraw-Hill Item Bank		
Harcourt Brace Educational Measurement 555 Academic Court San Antonio, TX 78204–2498	AIMS	Mathematics Reading Language Arts	
IPS Publishing Company 12606 N.E. 95th St., C–110 Vancouver, WA 98682	EXAM IN A CAN (Algorithm item generator not item bank)	Basic Mathematics Applications in Basic Mathematics Algebra I, Algebra II Pre-Algebra Geometry Calculus Pre-Calculus Chemistry Statistics	HS
Midwest Agribusiness Services 6739 Glacier Drive West Bend, WI 53095	Agri Quiz Series Business Quiz Series Home Ec Quiz Series Biology Series Career Quiz		Gr. 7–12 Gr. 9–College Gr. 7–12 Gr. 7–12 Gr. 7–12
Riverside Publishing Co. 425 Spring Lake Dr. Itasca, IL 60106	MULTISCORE		
Science Research Associates, Inc. 9701 W. Higgins Rd. Rosemont, IL 60018	SRA Objective Item Bank		

Glossary

ability, ability test. An ability test measures the present level of functioning and may provide an estimate of future functioning.

academic aptitude. The abilities needed for school learning. Also called *scholastic aptitude, scholastic ability.*

accountability. An effort to require students to meet defined standards of performance and to evaluate teachers and schools according to how their students perform.

achievement, achievement test. An achievement test measures what one has learned, usually as the result of direct instruction.

adaptive behavior. Ability to handle day-to-day requirements of living.

affective domain. Behavior related to feelings, values, attitudes, interests, and personality.

age norms. Score scale based on average performance for persons of various age groups.

alternative assessment. An assessment other than multiple-choice tests. May include performance testing and portfolios.

analytic scoring. Scoring of a product by giving separate scores or ratings for specific aspects of the product.

anecdotal record. A written description of an observation of an incident in an individual's behavior. The description should be significant for understanding of the individual. It should be reported objectively and should be non-judgmental.

aptitude, aptitude test. An aptitude test measures ability to learn to perform particular tasks or skills. Often used as a synonym for *ability.*

assessment. Any measurement device. Includes tests, observations, ratings, performances, portfolios.

attribute. A characteristic of a person. Also called *trait* or *variable.*

authentic assessment. Assessment that grows out of instruction and is a part of it. Often includes assessment of real-world tasks.

battery of tests. A group of tests standardized on the same norm sample so that there is a common set of norms for all tests in the battery.

behavioral objective. Behavioral objectives are specified in terms of observable behavior, and the conditions of the observations are given.

bias. A measurement is said to be biased when some groups or individuals have an advantage because of some feature of the measurement that is not related to ability on the variable being measured.

blueprint. Specifies the outline of skills and content to be covered by an assessment.

central tendency. A score indicating where the center of distribution of scores is located. Measures of central tendency include *mean, median,* and *mode.*

cognitive domain. Behavior related to such processes as memorizing, thinking, reasoning, analyzing, and solving problems.

completion item. An item for which the examinee must write the response, rather than choosing from a group of responses presented as part of the item. See also *constructed-response item, open-ended item, open-response item,* and *unstructured-response item.*

construct. In testing, a construct is the trait being measured. Construct definition requires use of a theory or definition that makes clear what the trait is and how it operates.

constructed-response item. An item for which the examinee must write the response, rather than choosing from a group of responses presented as part of the item. See also *completion item, open-ended item, open-response item,* and *unstructured-response item.*

correlation, coefficient of correlation. Correlation is the relationship between two or more sets of scores for the same group of individuals. The correlation coefficient is a *measure* of the relationship. Correlation co-efficients may be either *positive* or *negative* and range in size from −1.00 to +1.00.

creativity. Usually includes such traits as flexibility, fluency, and originality.

criterion-referenced measurement. Scores are interpreted in reference to a pre-established standard of mastery. Contrast with *norm-referenced measurement.*

critical thinking. Use of higher-level thinking skills, such as evaluation and problem solving.

deviation IQ (DIQ). A standard score used for mental ability or intelligence tests. It places the average score for a given age equal to 100 and expresses other scores in units of the standard deviation. See also *intelligence quotient.*

diagnostic test. A test designed to identify an individual's specific areas of strength or weakness.

direct observation. Observing and recording behavior at the time it is occurring.

dispersion. The degree to which a score distribution spreads out from the center of the distribution. Synonymous with *variability.*

distractor. An incorrect option for a multiple-choice item.

distribution. A tabulation showing the number of individuals making each score or making scores within the range of each score interval.

domain, domain sampling. The term *domain* is used in two different ways. It may refer to the general area of a measurement, such as *cognitive, affective,* or *psychomotor.* Or it may refer to the universe of possible items that might be asked about a defined area, such as a curriculum course, from which a given assessment is supposed to be a representative sample.

domain scoring. Method of scoring a product or performance in which several scores are used to assess three or four major aspects of the product or performance.

ecological assessment. An assessment of students' skills that is taken during or directly from the students' classroom work and activities.

educational objective. The goal of the educational process. Also defined as the difference between the obtained score and the true score. Includes both content and skills.

error of measurement. The random error present in all test scores. See also *standard error of measurement.*

evaluation. Evaluation is the process of making judgments about the quality of behavior or a performance.

external test. A test prepared by someone or some agency other than the classroom teacher.

extrapolation. The process of estimating values of scores outside the actual range of the available distribution—for example, grade placement scores for grades not tested in the norms sample.

fairness. Related to absence of bias. The most usual concern is with ethnic or gender bias.

formative assessment. Assessment for the purpose of evaluating the status and planning the next steps.

frequency distribution. See *distribution*.

grade equivalents (GEs), grade placements (GPs). The grade level for which a given score is the real or estimated average score.

group test. A test administered to a group of examinees at the same time.

high-level skills. Skills that require more than simple recognition. May include analysis, evaluation, and problem solving.

holistic scoring. Method of scoring a product or performance in which a single score is given for all aspects of the product or performance.

Individualized Education Program (IEP). A formal plan for handling the education of a specific student. Also called *individual educational plan* or *individualized education plan*.

individual test. A test administered to only one individual at a time.

instructional objective. See *educational objective*.

intelligence quotient (IQ). Originally the ratio of mental age to chronological age and considered an index of brightness. Now replaced by the deviation IQ (DIQ), which is a standard score with a mean of 100 and standard deviation of 15 or 16. (See *deviation IQ*.)

intelligence test. An assessment to measure abilities that are thought to be related to learning, especially in academic and vocational areas. Now also sometimes called *school ability, scholastic ability, scholastic aptitude*.

item. A question or exercise in an assessment.

item specification. A set of rules for creating items.

interest inventory. An inventory directed at vocational or personal interests.

interpolation. Estimation of values of scores between the known points in the distribution, as with scores lying between the means of the fall and spring administration of an achievement test.

interquartile range. The measure of dispersion used for scores on a percentile scale.

inventory. An assessment instrument usually used for affective traits such as interests or attitudes, rather than achievement.

learning style. An individual's preferred style of learning. There is no commonly accepted system for organizing and discussing learning styles.

mastery. A construct of achievement that is based on the concept of specifying what each student should know at certain points and expressing a student's score as a percentage of that goal or as mastery/nonmastery.

matching test. Items presented in two lists. Items in one list are matched to options in the other list.

mean. The arithmetic average: the sum of the scores divided by the number of scores.

measurement. Measurement is the act of assigning a number or other symbol to the amount or extent of a characteristic of a person or object.

median. The middle score when the scores are arranged in numerical order.

mode. The most frequent score. Usually used for categorical data.

multiple-choice test. The most common type of objective test or structured-response test. The items consist of the stem and several options for the answers, from which the examinee makes a selection. May be scored by machine.

narrative report. A descriptive report of observations. May be either individual or group (as a classroom).

nominations. Use of direct votes or of such techniques as "Guess Who?" to identify people with defined characteristics.

normal curve. The shape of a normal distribution when placed in line graph form. Also called a bell-shaped curve.

normal curve equivalent (NCE). A normalized percentile score used for all levels of an achievement battery, ranging from 1 to 99, with a mean of 50.

normal distribution. An ideal frequency distribution of scores or other measures that forms a bell-shaped curve when displayed in a graph. It is symmetrically distributed about the mean, and approximately two-thirds of the scores lie within the area between +1 standard deviation and -1 standard deviation.

norm-referenced measurement. Measurement that is interpreted by reference to a table of norms.

norm-referenced test. A test that has been administered to a representative sample of people so that the performance of those individuals in the norms sample may be used to develop norms. The scores of examinees are compared with the norms in order to evaluate their performance. (See *norms*.)

norms. Scores based on the actual performance of students in specified age or grade groups.

objective item. An item that may be scored completely objectively, as by a machine. The item presents options from which the examinee selects. The most common objective item is *multiple choice*. Other objective items are *true-false* and *matching*. Also called *structured-response item*.

objective test. A test made up of objective items.

open-ended item. See *open-response item*.

open-response item. An item for which the examinee constructs the response, rather than having choices among possibilities offered. Also called *open-ended* or *completion* item.

operational definition. The definition of a variable using the description of the procedures used to measure it.

percentile/percentile rank. A transformed score that indicates the percentage of students who score at or lower than a given score.

performance assessment. Requires the examinee to actually carry out a procedure or a series of procedures in as near a real-life situation as possible.

personality test. A test designed to obtain information about an individual's *affective* characteristics, as distinguished from *cognitive* abilities. Also sometimes called *personality inventory*.

portfolio. A purposeful collection of a student's products that represent what he or she is able to do.

practicality. The extent to which an assessment procedure is doable in terms of time and money. Also referred to as *usability*.

preference record. A questionnaire to assist individuals in identifying their personal or occupational preferences.

primary trait scoring. A scoring system based on the premise that all writing is addressed to a specific audience for a specific purpose. Those qualities are then built into the scoring criteria.

product assessment. The assessment of a product that results from a performance—for example, an evaluation of a lab report from a science experiment.

profile. A meaningful collection of information about a student, including specific questions addressed and answered.

projective techniques. A method of studying personality using a series of stimuli for which there are no predetermined correct answers.

quartile deviation. One-half of the interquartile range.

range. The difference between the highest and lowest score in a distribution of scores.

rating scale. A rating scale may be a self-report, or others may rate one. The traits rated vary widely, and rating scales are directed at the kind of information that is needed.

raw score. Number of items correct or number of points earned. Also called the *obtained score*.

readiness, readiness test. A readiness test measures an individual's ability to profit from instruction. The most frequently used readiness tests are administered to young children to ascertain their readiness for reading, but there are also readiness tests for various mathematics and science courses.

relevance. Part of the concept of validity. Measurement must be *relevant* to the variable of interest.

reliability. The consistency or dependability of scores on an assessment. May involve consistency between different parts or forms of a test. It may also involve consistency of scores obtained at different time periods, or agreement between different raters of a performance or product.

retrospective rating measures. Assessments that are taken by remembering events, rather than at the time the events occur.

rubric. A scoring guide that describes the qualities and the indicators for scoring student products or performances.

scaled scores. Transformation of raw scores into scores on a scale that helps to interpret the individual's ability in comparison with some norm group.

sociometry. Measurement of interpersonal relationships among the members of a group. May be handled by direct observation or by use of a questionnaire.

specifications. A set of rules for creating an assessment or items. See *item specification*.

standard deviation. A measure of dispersion of scores away from the mean of a distribution.

standard error of measurement (SEM). An estimate of the amount of error in a score. It is the standard deviation of the error of measurement.

standardized test. A test designed to be administered under the same conditions every time it is given—same directions, same time limits, and so on.

standard score. A transformed score based on the mean and standard deviation of a designated group.

standards. Criteria of performance. Should be distinguished from *norms*, which are actual performance of a specified group.

stanine. A type of scaled score that divides the distribution into 9 parts with a mean of 5. Each stanine is one-half of a standard deviation, except for 1 and 9 at the ends of the distribution.

structured-response item. An item presenting the examinees with a choice of options from which they select the correct or best answer. See also *objective test*.

summative assessment. Assessment for the purpose of decision making, such as assigning grades, promotion, and placement.

taxonomy. A classification system that arranges the items in a systematic, ordered way. The term originated in the sciences but is now also used in education as a way of organizing educational objectives.

test. A set of items or tasks that is scored to measure achievement, ability, or other variables. Also called an *assessment*.

traditional assessment. Usually refers to multiple-choice tests. May include other types of written tests.

trait. A characteristic of an individual. May also be called an *ability*, an *achievement,* a *characteristic,* or a *preference.*

true-false item. A two-choice test item that is a statement which examinees evaluate and mark either "true" or "false."

true score. A hypothetical value of what an individual's score would be on a given test if the score were entirely free of error. True scores can only be estimated, because all actual scores involve some error.

T-score. A normalized score with the mean set at 50 and the standard deviation set at 10.

unstructured-response item, unstructured-response test. Item or test on which a judge decides whether the responses are right and to what extent they are right. Also called *open-response test*.

usability. As used in reference to educational measures, the practicality of being able to obtain the measures and/or to get them scored properly. Also called *practicality.*

validity. The extent to which an assessment measures the intended trait and for which the inferences are meaningful, appropriate, and useful for the assessment's purpose. Evaluation of validity requires a variety of evidence.

variability. The degree to which a distribution spreads out around a measure of central tendency. Synonymous with *dispersion*.

variable. A trait or characteristic. What is intended to be measured by a given assessment.

z-score. A scale of transformed scores derived by subtracting each score from the mean and dividing the difference by the standard deviation. The scores range from approximately -3.00 to 3.00. z-scores are usually converted to scores with all positive values such as T-scores.

References

Airasian, P.W. (1991). Perspectives on measurement instruction. Educational Measurement: *Issues and Practice, 10*(1), 13–16.

American Educational Research Association, American Psychological Association, & National Council on Measurement in Education. (1985). *Standards for educational and psychological testing.* Washington, DC: American Psychological Association.

American Federation of Teachers, National Council on Measurement in Education & National Education Association. (1990). *Standards for teacher competence in educational assessment of students.* Washington, DC: Author.

Anastasi, A. (1988). *Psychological testing.* (6th ed.). New York: Macmillan.

Arter, J.A. (1992). Alternative assessment: Promise and perils. In J. Bamber (Ed.), *Assessment: How do we know what they know?* Union, WA: Washington State Association for Supervision and Curriculum Development.

Arter, J.A. (1993). *Science and mathematics alternative assessment: State-of-the-Art.* Paper presented at the annual meeting of the California Educational Research Association, Long Beach.

Arter, J.A., & Spandel, V. (1992) Using portfolios of student work in instruction and assessment. *Educational Measurement: Issues and Practice, 11*(1), 36–44.

Ausubel, D.P. (1963). *The psychology of meaningful verbal learning.* New York: Grune & Stratton.

Baer, J. (1994, October). Why you *still* shouldn't trust creativity tests. *Educational Leadership, 52*(2), 72–73.

Barrett, H.C. (1994). Technology-supported assessment portfolios. *The Computing Teacher, 21*(6), 6–12.

Beck, S.J. (1945, 1949, 1952). *Rorschach's test.* New York: Grune & Stratton.

Berliner, D.C., & Biddle, B.J. (1995). *The manufactured crisis: Myths, fraud, and the attack on America's public schools.* Reading, MA: Addison-Wesley.

Binet, A. (1911). *Les idées modernes sur les enfants.* Paris: Flammarion.

Bloom, B.S. (1968, May). Learning for mastery. *Evaluation Comment, 1*(2). Center for the Study of Evaluation of Instructional Programs. Los Angeles: University of California at Los Angeles.

Bloom, B.S., Engelhart, M.D., Furst, E.J., Hill, W.H., & Krathwohl, D.R. (1956). *Taxonomy of educational objectives. Handbook 1. The cognitive domain.* New York: McKay.

Bracey, G.W. (1992). The second Bracey report on the condition of public education. *Phi Delta Kappan, 74,* 104–105, 117.

Bracey, G.W. (1993). The third Bracey report on the condition of public education. *Phi Delta Kappan, 75,* 104–112, 114–118.

Brandt, R. (1992). On performance assessment: A conversation with Grant Wiggins. *Educational Leadership, 49*(8), 35–37.

Brookhart, S.M. (1993). Teachers' grading practices: Meaning and values. *Journal of Educational Measurement, 30*(2) 123–142.

Bruner, J.S. (1966). *Toward a theory of instruction.* Cambridge, MA: Harvard University Press.

Cadenhead, K. & Robinson, R. (1987). Fisher's "Scale-book": An early attempt at educational measurement, *Educational Measurement: Issues and Practice, 6*(4), 15–18.

Calkins, C. (1986). *The art of teaching writing.* Portsmouth: NH: Heineman.

Campbell, D.P. (1989, 1992). *Campbell interest and skill survey.* Ann Arbor, MI: NCS Assessments.

Cannell, J.J. (1988). Nationally normed elementary achievement testing in America's public schools: How 50 states are above the national average. *Educational Measurement: Issues and Practice. 7*(2) 5–9.

Carlson, S.B., Bridgeman, B., Camp, R. & Waanders, J. (1983). *Relationship of admission test scores to writing performance of native and non-native speakers of English.* Princeton, NJ: Educational Testing Service.

Carr R. (1991, May 2). Markets can't fix schools' problems. *Wall Street Journal,* p. A-17.

Carroll, J.B. (1963). A model of school learning. *Teachers College Record, 64,* 723–733.

Carroll, J.B. (1989). The Carroll Model: A 25-year retrospective and prospective view. *Educational Researcher, 18*(1), 26–31.

Carter, K. (1984). Do teachers understand principles for writing tests? *Journal of Teacher Education, 35,* 57–60.

Cattell, R.B. (1943). The measurement of adult intelligence. *Psychological Bulletin, 40,* 153–193.

Cheney, L. (1991). *National tests: What other countries expect their students to know.* Washington: National Endowment for the Humanities.

Cheong, J.L. & Shively, A.H. (1991). *Issues and reflections on implementing portfolio assessment systems, K-12.* A paper presented at the annual meeting of the California Education Research Association at Santa Barbara, CA.

Chipman, S.F., Brush, L.R., & Wilson, D.M. (1985). *Women and mathematics: Balancing the equation.* Hillsdale, NJ: Lawrence Erlbaum.

Clay, M.M. (1991) The early detection of reading difficulties (3rd ed.). Portsmouth, NH: Heineman.

Clemmons, J., Laase, L., Cooper, D., Areglado, N., & Dill, M. (1993). *Portfolios in the classroom: A teacher's sourcebook.* New York: Scholastic.

Cogan, J., Tourney-Purta, J., & Anderson, D. (1988). Knowledge and attitudes toward global issues: Students in Japan and the United States, *Comparative Education Review, 32,* 282–297.

Cole, N.S. and Moss, P.A. (1989). Bias in test use. In Robert L. Linn (Ed.), *Educational measurement,* 3rd edition, (pp. 201–219). New York: American Council on Education.

Coleman, W. & Cureton, E. E. (1954). Intelligence and achievement: The "jangle fallacy" again. *Educational and Psychological Measurement, 14,* 347–51.

Coleman, W. & Ward, A.W. (1955). A comparison of Davis Eells and Kuhlmann-Finch scores of children from high and low socio-economic status. *Journal of Educational Psychology, 46,* 463–469.

Cramond, B. (1994, October). We *can* trust creativity tests. *Educational Leadership, 52* (2), 70–71.

Cronbach, L.J. (1971). Test validation. In R.L. Thorndike (Ed.). *Educational Measurement* (2nd ed., pp. 443–507). Washington, DC: American Council on Education.

Cronbach, L.J. (1990). *Educational psychology* (5th ed.). New York: Harper and Row.

Curry, J. (1989). Role of reading instruction in mathematics. In D. Lapp, J. Flood & N. Farnan (Eds.) *Content area reading and learning: Instructional strategies,* (pp. 187–197). Englewood Cliffs, NJ: Prentice-Hall.

Diana v. State Board of Education, No. C:70–37 RFP N.D. Cal. (June 7, 1970).

Drummond, R.J. (1992). *Appraisal procedures for counselors and helping professionals.* New York: Macmillan.

Dubois, P.H. (1964). A test-dominated society: China, 1115 B.C.–1905 A.D. *Proceedings of the 1964 Invitational Conference on Testing Problems.* Princeton: Educational Testing Service.

Dubois, P.H. (1970). *A History of psychological testing.* Boston: Allyn and Bacon.

Duran, R.P. (1989). Testing of linguistic minorities. In R. L. Linn (Ed.), *Educational Measurement* (3rd ed., pp. 573–587). New York: American Council on Education and Macmillan.

Ebel, R.L. (1965). *Measuring educational achievement.* Englewood Cliffs, NJ: Prentice-Hall.

Ebel, R.L. (1980). *Practical problems in educational measurement.* Lexington, MA: D.C. Heath.

Ebel, R.L. & Frisbie, D.A. (1991). *Essentials of educational measurement* (5th ed.). Englewood Cliffs, NJ: Prentice Hall.

Edwards, A.L. (1957). *Techniques of attitude scale construction.* New York: Appleton-Century-Crofts.

Edwards, A.L. (1959). *Edwards Personal Preference Record.* San Antonio, TX: Psychological Corporation.

Edwards, P.R. (1992). Using dialectic journals to teach thinking skills. *Journal of Reading, 35,* 312–316.

Eisner, E.W. (1993). Invitational conference on the hidden consequences of a national curriculum. *Educational Researcher, 22*(7), 38–39.

Ellwein, M.C., Walsh, D.J., Eads, G.M., II, & Miller, A. (1991). Using readiness tests to route kindergarten students: The snarled intersection of psychometrics, policy, and practice. *Educational Evaluation and Policy Analysis, 13*(2), 159–175.

Farr, R. (1990). Trends: Reading; Setting directions for language arts portfolios. *Educational Leadership, 48,* 103.

Farr, R. & Tone, B. (1994). *Portfolio performance assessment: Helping students evaluate their progress as readers and writers.* Fort Worth: Harcourt.

Feuerstein, R. (1980). *Instrumental Enrichment: An intervention program for cognitive modifiability.* Glenview, IL: Scott Foresman.

Findley, W.G. (1963). Purposes of school testing programs and their efficient development. In W.G. Findley, (Ed.) *The impact and improvement of school testing programs: The sixty-second yearbook of the National Society for the Study of Education, Part II* (pp. 1–27). Chicago: University of Chicago Press.

Fischer, R.J. (1994). The American with Disabilities Act: Implication for measurement. *Educational Measurement: Issues and Practice, 13*(3), 17–26, 37.

Flanagan, J.C. (1982). Analyzing changes in school levels of achievement for men and women using Project TALENT ten- and fifteen-year retests. In G.R. Austin, & H. Garber (Eds.), *The rise and fall of national test scores.* (pp. 35–49). New York: Academic Press.

Fosnot, C.T. (1993). Foreword. In J. Grennon Brooks & M.G. Brooks (Eds.) *The case for constructivist classrooms* (pp. vii–viii). Alexandria, VA: Association for Supervision and Curriculum Development.

Frieze, I.H. (1975). Women's expectations for causal attributions of success and failure. In M.T.S. Mednick, S.S. Tangrit, & L.W. Hoffman (Eds.), *Women and achievement: Social and motivational analyses* (pp. 158–171). Washington, DC: Hemisphere Publishing Corporation.

Gardner, H. (1983). *Frames of mind: The theory of multiple intelligences.* New York: Basic Books.

Gearhart, M., & Herman, J.L. (1995, Winter). Portfolio assessment: Whose work is it? Issues in the use of classroom assignments for accountability. *Evaluation Comment,* 2–16.

Gillespie, C.S., Ford, K.L., Gillespie, R.D. & Leavell, A.G. (1996). Portfolio assessment: Some questions, some answers, some recommendations. *Journal of Adolescent & Adult Literacy, 39,* 480–491.

Glaser, R. (1963). Instructional technology and the measurement of learning outcomes—some questions. *American Psychologist, 18,* 519–21.

Glaser, R., Lesgold, A., & Lajoie, S. (1987). Toward a cognitive theory for the measurement of achievement. In R.R. Ronning, J.A. Glover, J.C. Conoley & J.C. Witt, (Eds.), *The influence of cognitive psychology on testing and measurement.* (pp. 41–82). Hillsdale, N.J.: Erlbaum.

Godshalk, F.I., Swineford, F., & Coffman, W.E. (1996). *The measurement of writing ability.* New York: College Entrance Examination Board.

Graves, D. H. (1983). *Writing: Teachers and children at work.* Portsmouth, NH: Heineman.

Green, D. R. (1974). *The aptitude-achievement distinction.* Monterey, CA: CTB/McGraw-Hill.

Gronlund, N.E., & Linn R.L. (1990). *Measurement and evaluation in teaching* (6th ed.). New York: Macmillan.

Grossman, H.J. (1983). *Classification in mental retardation.* Washington, DC: American Association on Mental Deficiency.

Guilford, J.P. (1957). *A revised structure of the intellect.* (Psychological Laboratory of the University of Southern California Rep. No. 19). Los Angeles, CA: University of Southern California.

Guilford, J.P. (1967). *The nature of human intelligence.* New York: McGraw-Hill.

Guilford, J.P. & Zimmerman, W.S. (1955). *The Guilford-Zimmerman Temperament Survey.* Manual. Beverly Hills: Sheridan Psychological Services.

Gullickson, A.R. (1986). Teacher education and teacher-perceived needs in educational measurement and evaluation. *Journal of Educational Measurement, 23,* 347–354.

Guskey, T.R. (1994). Making the grade: What benefits students? *Educational Leadership, 52*(2), 14–20.

Hall, B.W. (1985). Survey of the technical characteristics of published educational achievement tests. *Educational Measurement: Issues and Practice, 4*(1), 6–14.

Hall, B.W. (1986). Validity, reliability, and norms of popular versus less popular published educational achievement tests. *Journal of Educational Research, 79*(3), 145–150.

Hart, D. (1994). *Authentic assessment: A handbook for educators.* Menlo Park, CA: Addison-Wesley.

Haney, W.M. (1988). Editorial. *Educational Measurement: Issues and Practices, 7*(2), 4, 32.

Harris, A.M. & Carlton, S.T. (1993). Patterns of gender differences on mathematics items on the Scholastic Aptitude Test. *Applied Measurement in Education, 6*(2), 137–151.

Haywood, H.C., Brook, P.H. & Burns, S. (1992). *Bright start: Cognitive curriculum for young children.* Watertown, PA: Charles Bridge Press.

Herman, J.L. & Golan, S. (1993). The effects of standardized testing on teaching and schools. *Educational Measurement and Practice, 12*(4), 20–25, 41–42.

Herman, J.L. & Winters, L. (1994). Portfolio research: A slim collection. *Educational Leadership, 52*(2), 48–55.

Herrnstein, R.J. & Murray, C. (1994). *The bell curve: Intelligence and class structure in American life.* New York: The Free Press.

Hiscox, M.D. & Brezinski, E.J. (1980). *A guide to item banking in education.* Portland, OR: Northwest Regional Laboratory.

Hobson v. Hansen. 269 S. Supp. 401, (D.D.C. 1967).

Holland, J.L. (1966). *The psychology of vocational choice: A theory of personality types and work environments.* Waltham, MA: Blaisdell.

Holland, J.L. (1973). *Making vocational choices: A theory of careers.* Englewood Cliffs, NJ: Prentice-Hall.

Hopkins, K.D., Stanley, J.C., & Hopkins, B.R. (1990). *Educational and psychological measurement and evaluation* (7th ed.). Needham Heights, MA: Allyn and Bacon.

Horner, M.S. (1970). Femininity and successful achievement: A basic inconsistency. In J.M. Bardwick, et al. (Eds.). *Feminine personality and conflict* (pp. 45–76). Monterey, CA: Brooks/Cole.

Hothersall, D. (1984). *History of psychology.* Philadelphia: Temple University Press.

Impara, J.C., Divine, K.P., Bruce, F.A., Liverman, M.R., & Gay, A. (1991). Does interpretive test score information help teachers? *Educational Measurement: Issues and Practice, 10*(4), 16–18.

Innes, T.C. (1972). *The prediction of achievement means of schools from non-school factors through criterion scaling.* Invited address at Southeastern Invitational Conference on Testing. Athens, GA.

Jaeger, R.M. (1992). Weak measurement serving presumptive policy. *Phi Delta Kappan, 74*(2), 118–128.

Jaeger, R.M. & Tittle, C.K. (Eds.) (1980). *Minimum competency achievement testing: Motives, models, measures, and consequences.* Berkeley, CA: McCutchan.

Jensen, M.R, & Feuerstein, R. (1986). Cultural difference and cultural deprivation: A theoretical framework for differential intervention. In R.M. Gupta and P. Coxhead (Eds.) *Cultural diversity and learning efficiency.* London: The Macmillan Press.

Joint Committee on Testing Practices. (1988). *Code of fair testing practices in education.* Washington, DC: American Psychological Association.

Judges 12:5–6. *The Holy Bible,* Revised Standard Version.

Keller, J.M. (1983). Motivation design of instruction. In C.M. Reigeluth (Ed.) *Instructional-design theories and models: An overview of their current status* (pp. 386–434). Hillsdale: NJ: Lawrence Erlbaum.

Kelley, T.L. (1927). *Interpretation of educational measurements.* New York: World.

King-Sears, M.E. (1994). *Curriculum-based assessment in special education.* San Diego, CA: Singular Publishing Group.

Kohn, A. (1994). Grading: The issue is not how but why. *Educational Leadership, 52*(2), 38–41.

Koretz, D. (1992). What happened to test scores, and why? *Educational Measurement: Issues and Practice, 11*(4), 7–11.

Koretz, D., Stecher, B., Klein, S., & McCaffrey, D. (1994). The Vermont portfolio assessment program: Findings and implications. *Educational Measurement: Issues and Practice. 13*(3), 5–16.

Kuder, G.F. (1956). *Kuder Preference Record—Vocational.* Chicago: Science Research Associates.

Kuder, G.F. (1963). A rationale for evaluating interests. *Educational and Psychological Measurement, 23,* 3–12.

Kuder General Interest Survey. (1963, 1987). Ann Arbor: NCS Assessments

Kupper, L. (1998, June). The IDEA Amendments of 1997 (revised edition). *National Information Center for Children and Youth with Disabilities News Digest, 26.*

Lam, T.C., & Gordon, W.I. (1992). State policies for standardized achievement testing of limited English proficient students. *Educational Measurement: Issues and Practice, 11*(4), 18–20.

Lane, S. (1989). Implications of cognitive psychology on measurement and testing. *Educational Measurement: Issues and Practice, 8*(1), 17–19.

Larry P. v. Wilson Riles. 343 F. Supp. 1306 (Cal., 1972), aff'd 502 F. 2d 963 (9th Cir. 1974); 495 Supp. 926 (N.D. Cal. 1979) (decision on merits) aff'd (9th Cir. No. 80–427, January 23, 1984). Order modifying judgment, C-71-2270 RFP, September 25, 1986.

Lehmann, I.J. (1990). The state of NCME: Remembering the past, looking to the future. *Measurement: Issues and Practice, 9*(1), 3–10.

Linn, R.L., & Baker, E.L. (1992, Fall). Portfolios and accountability. *The CRESST Line.*

Linn, R.L., & Baker, E.L. (1997, Summer). National tests in reading and mathematics. *The CRESST Line.*

Linn, R.L., & Dunbar, S.B. (1990). The nation's report card goes home: Good news and bad news about trends in achievement. *Phi Delta Kappan, 72,* 127–133.

Linn, R.L., Graue, M.E., & Sanders, N.M. (1990). Comparing state and district test results to national norms: The validity of claims that "everyone is above average." *Educational Measurement: Issues and Practices, 10*(3), 5–14.

Linn R.L., & Gronlund, N.E. (1995). *Measurement and evaluation in teaching* (7th ed.). New York: Merrill.

Linn, R.L., & Werts, C.E. (1971). Considerations for studies of test bias. *Journal of Educational Measurement, 8*, 1–4.

Lohman, D.F. (1993). Teaching and testing to develop fluid abilities. *Educational Researcher, 22*(7), 12–23.

Madaus, G.F. (Ed.). (1983). *The courts, validity, and minimum competency testing.* Boston: Kluwer-Nijhoff.

Madaus, G.F., & Kellaghan, T. (1992). In P.W. Jackson (Ed.), *Handbook of research on curriculum* (pp. 134–147). Washington, DC: American Educational Research Association.

MacMillan, C. (1988). Suggestions to classroom teachers about designing the IEP. *The Exceptional Parent, 18,* 90–92.

Mager, R.E. (1962). *Preparing instructional objectives.* Palo Alto, CA: Fearon.

Marshall et al. v. Georgia. U.S. District Court for the Southern District of Georgia, CV482-233, June 28, 1984; Aff'd (11th Cir. No. 84-8771, October 29, 1985).

Mathematical Sciences Education Board (1991). *A summary of the regional presummit forums.* Paper, National Summit on Mathematics Assessment, Washington, DC: National Research Council.

Mattie T. v. Holladay. No. D.C.: 75:31 (N.D. Miss., January 26, 1979).

McLaughlin, M.W. (1991). Test-based accountability as a reform strategy. *Phi Delta Kappan 73*(3), 248–251.

McMillan, J.H. (1997). *Classroom assessment: Principles and practice for effective instruction.* Boston: Allyn and Bacon.

Miller, E., Murray-Ward, M., & Harder, H. (1996). *Reading and language arts for all students: A practical guide for content area teachers.* Dubuque, Iowa: Kendall-Hunt.

Millman, J., Bishop, C.H., & Ebel, R.L. (1965). An analysis of test wiseness. *Educational and Psychological Measurement, 25,* 707–726.

Morrison, H.C. (1926). *The practice of teaching in the secondary school.* Chicago: University of Chicago Press.

Moss, P.A., Beck, J.S., Ebbs, C., Matson, B., Muchmore, J., Steele, D., & Taylor, C.

(1992). Portfolios, accountability, and an interpretive approach to validity. *Educational Measurement: Issues and Practice, 11*(3), 12–21.

Mumme, J. (1990). *Portfolio assessment in mathematics.* Santa Barbara: University of California at Santa Barbara.

Murray, H.A. (1943). *Thematic apperception test.* Cambridge, MA: Harvard University Press.

National Association of School Psychologists. (1994). *Assessment and eligibility in special education: An examination of policy and practice with proposals for change.* Alexandria, VA: National Association of State Directors of Special Education.

National Center for Educational Statistics. (1996, 1997, 1998). The third international math and science study (TIMSS). Washington, DC: Author.

National Commission on Excellence in Education. (1983). *A nation at risk: The imperative for educational reform.* Washington, DC: Author.

National Commission on Testing and Public Policy. (1990). *From gatekeeper to gateway: Transforming testing in America.* Chestnut Hill, MA.: Author.

National Council of Teachers of Mathematics. (1989). *Curriculum and evaluation standards for school mathematics.* Reston, VA: Author.

National Council on Measurement in Education. (1995). *Code of professional responsibilities in educational measurement.* Washington, DC: Author.

National Education Association. (1983). *Teachers' views about student assessment.* Washington, DC: Author.

National Education Goals Panel. (1991). *Measuring progress toward the national educational goals: Potential indicators and measurement strategies.* Washington, DC: Author.

National Education Goals Panel. (1997). *National education goals report: Building a nation of learners.* Washington, DC: U.S. Government Printing Office.

Nitko, A.J. (1996). *Educational assessment of students.* Englewood Cliffs, NJ: Merrill.

Nunnally, J.C. (1972). *Educational measurement and evaluation.* New York: McGraw-Hill.

Oosterhof, A.C. (1990). *Classroom applications of educational measurement.* Columbus, OH: Merrill.

O'Sullivan, R., & Chalnick, M.K. (1991). Measurement related course work requirements for teacher certification and recertification. *Educational Measurement: Issues and Practice, 10*(1), 17–19.

Pallas, A.M., Natriello, G., & McDill, E.L. (1989). The changing nature of the disadvantaged population: Current dimensions and future trends. *Educational Researcher, 18*(5), 16–22.

PASE v. Joseph P. Hannon. U.S. District Court, Northern District of Illinois, Eastern Division, No. 74 (3586), July 1980.

Phillips, G.W., & Finn, C.E., Jr. (1988). The Lake Wobegon effect: A skeleton in the testing closet? *Educational Measurement: Issues and Practice, 7*(2), 10–12.

Popham, W.J. (1981). *Modern educational measurement.* Englewood Cliffs, NJ: Prentice-Hall, Inc.

Popham, W.J. (1995). *Classroom assessment: What teachers need to know.* Boston: Allyn and Bacon.

Resnick, D.P., & Resnick, L.B. (1985). Standards, curriculum, and performance: A historical and comparative perspective. *Educational Research, 14*(4), 5–20.

Resnick, L.B., & Resnick D.P. (1992). Assessing the thinking curriculum: New tools for educational reform. In B.R. Gifford & M.C. O'Connor (Eds.), *Changing assessments: Alternative views of aptitudes, achievement and instruction* (pp. 37–75). Boston: Kluwer Academic.

Reutzel, D.R., & Cooter, R.B. (1992). *Teaching children to read—From basals to books.* New York: Macmillan.

Revak, M.A. (1995). A call for improved teacher assessment training. *Florida Journal of Educational Research, 35*(1), 63–71.

Roid, G.H. (1989). Item writing and item banking by microcomputer: An update. *Educational Measurement: Issues and Practice, 8*(3), 17–20, 38.

Roid, G.H., & Haladyna, T. M. (1982). *A technology for test-item writing.* Orlando, FL: Academic Press.

Rosenfeld, M., Thornton, R.F., & Skurnik, L.S. (1987). *Relationships between job functions and the NTE Core Battery* (Research Rep. 86–8). Princeton, NJ: Educational Testing Service.

Royer, J.M., & Carlo, M.S. (1991). Assessing the language acquisition progress of limited English proficient students: Problems and a new alternative. *Applied Measurement in Education, 4*(2), 85–113.

Russell Sage Foundation. (1970). *Guidelines for the collection, maintenance, and dissemination of pupil records.* New York: Author.

S-1 v. Turlington., 636 S.2d 342 (5th Cir. 1981), 646 F. Supp. 1179, 1986 U.S. Dist.

Sadker, M., & Sadker, D. (1986). Sexism in the classroom: From grade school to graduate school. *Phi Delta Kappan, 67*(5) 512–515.

Salvia J., & Ysseldyke, J.E. (1995). *Assessment* (6th ed.). Boston: Houghton Mifflin.

Santayana, G. (1905). *Life of Reason. I, 12.*

Schafer, W. (1991). Essential assessment skills in professional education of teachers. *Educational Measurement: Issues and Practice, 10*(1), 3–6.

Schafer, W.D., & Lissitz, R. W. (1987). Measurement training for school personnel: Recommendations and reality. *Journal of Teacher Education, 38*(3), 57–63.

Schnitzer, S. (1993). Designing an authentic assessment. *Educational Leadership 50*(7), 32–35.

Schwarz, P.A. (1971). Prediction instruments for educational outcomes. In R.L. Thorndike (Ed.), *Educational measurement* (2nd ed., pp. 303–331). Washington, DC: American Council on Education.

Scruggs, T.E., & Lifson, S.A. (1985). Current conceptions of test wiseness: Myths and realities. *School Psychology Review, 14*, 339–350.

Scruggs, T.E., White, K.R., & Bennion, K. (1986). Teaching test-taking skills to elementary grade students: A meta-analysis. *Elementary School Journal, 87*(1), 68–82.

Seeley, M.M. (1994). The mismatch between assessment and grading. *Educational Leadership, 52*(2), 4–6.

Shanker, A. (1994/1995). Full inclusion is neither free nor appropriate. *Educational Leadership, 52*(4), 18–21.

Shavelson, R.J., Baxter, G.P., & Pine, J. (1992). Performance assessments: Political rhetoric and measurement reality. *Educational Researcher, 21*(5), 23–27.

Shepard, L.A. (1989). Identification of mild handicaps. In Robert L. Linn (Ed.), *Educational measurement*(3rd ed., pp. 545–572). New York: American Council on Education and Macmillan.

Shepard, L.A. (1990). Inflated test score gains: Is the problem old norms or teaching to the test? *Educational Measurement: Issues and Practices, 9*(3), 15–22.

Shepard, L. (1991). Will national tests improve student learning? *Phi Delta Kappan, 73,* 232–238.

Smith, M.L., & Rottenberg, C. (1991). Unintended consequences of external testing in elementary schools. *Educational Measurement: Issues and Practice, 11*(1), 7–11.

Snow, R. E. (1980). Aptitude and achievement. *New Directions for Testing and Measurement, 5,* 39–59.

Snow, R.E., & Lohman, D.F. (1989). Implications of cognitive psychology for educational measurement. In R.L. Linn (Ed.), *Educational measurement* (3rd ed., pp. 263–331). New York: American Council on Education and Macmillan.

Spearman, C. (1904). The proof and measurement of association between two things. *American Journal of Psychology, 15,* 72–101.

Starch, D., & Elliott, E.C. (1912). Reliability of grading high school work in English. *School Review, 20,* 442–457.

Starch, D., & Elliott, E.C. (1913a). Reliability of grading high school work in mathematics. *School Review, 21,* 254–259.

Starch, D., & Elliott, E.C. (1913b). Reliability of grading high school work in history. *School Review, 21,* 676–681.

Stern, W. (1914). *The psychological methods of testing intelligence* (G. M. Whipple, Trans.) (Educational Psychology Monographs, No. 13). Baltimore: Warwick & York.

Sternberg, R.J. (1984). Toward a triarchic theory of human intelligence. *The Behavioral and Brain Sciences, 7,* 269–315.

Sternberg, R.J. (1985). *Beyond IQ: A triarchic theory of human intelligence.* Cambridge, MA: Harvard University Press.

Sternberg, R.J. (1988). *The triarchic mind: A new theory of human intelligence.* New York: Viking.

Stevens, S.S. (1946). On the theory of scales of measurement. *Science, 103*(2684), 677–680.

Stiggins, R. (1987). *Profiling classroom assessment environments.* Paper presented at the annual meeting of the National Council on Measurement in Education, San Francisco.

Stiggins, R. (1988). Revitalizing classroom assessment: The highest instructional priority. *Phi Delta Kappan, 69,* 363–368.

Stiggins, R.J. (1991a). Facing the challenges of a new era of educational assessments. *Applied Measurement in Education, 4*(4), 263–273.

Stiggins, R.J. (1991b). Relevant classroom assessment training for teachers. *Educational Measurement: Issues and Practice, 10*(1), 7–12.

Stiggins, R.J., & Bridgeford, N.J. (1985). The ecology of classroom assessment. *Journal of Educational Measurement, 22*(4), 271–286.

Stiggins, R., Conklin, N.F., & Bridgeford, N.J. (1986). Classroom assessment: A key to effective education. *Educational Measurement: Issues and Practice, 5*(2), 5–17.

Stiggins, R.J., Frisbie, D.A., & Duke, D.L. (1989). Inside high school grading practices: Building research agenda. *Educational Measurement: Issues and Practice, 8*(2), 5–14.

Strong, E.K., & Campbell, D.P. (1966). *Manual for Strong Vocational Interest Blanks.* Stanford, CA: Stanford University Press.

Swaby, B. (1989). *Diagnosis and correction of reading difficulties.* Boston: Allyn and Bacon.

Thorndike, E.L. (1920). Intelligence and its uses. *Harper's Magazine, 140,* 227–235.

Thorndike R.M., Cunningham, G.K., Thorndike, R.L., & Hagen, E. (1991). *Measurement and evaluation in psychology and education.* New York: Macmillan.

Thurstone, L.L. (1938). *Primary mental abilities* (Psychometric Monograph, No. 1). Chicago: University of Chicago Press.

Tierney, R.J., Carter, M.A., & Desai, L.E. (1991). Portfolio assessment in the reading-writing classroom. Norwood, MA: Christopher-Gordon.

Torres, J. (1991). Equity in education and the language minority student. *Forum, 14*(4), 1–3.

U.S. Office of Education. (1991). *America 2000: An education strategy.* Washington, DC: Author.

Valencia, S.W. (1990). A portfolio approach to classroom reading assessment: The whys, whats and hows. *The Reading Teacher, 44,* 338–340.

Valencia, S.W., & Calfee, R. (1991). The development and use of literacy portfolios for students, classes, and teachers. *Applied Measurement in Education, 4*(4), 333–345.

Vaughn, S., Bos, C.S., Harrell, J.E., & Lasky, B.A. (1988). Parent participation in the initial placement/IEP conference ten years after mandated involvement. *Journal of Learning Disabilities, 21*(2), 82–89.

Waltman, K.K., & Frisbie, D.S. (1994). Parents' understanding of their children's report card grades. *Applied Measurement in Education, 7*(3), 223–240.

Ward, A.W., & Murray-Ward, M. (1992). *Generic specifications and sample items.* Daytona Beach, FL: Techne Group.

Ward, A.W., & Murray-Ward, M. (1994a). Guidelines for the development of item banks: An instructional module. *Educational Measurement: Issues and Practice, 13*(1), 3–39.

Ward, A.W., & Murray-Ward, M. (1994b). *Item banks and item banking.* Daytona Beach, FL: Techne Group.

Washburne, C.W. (1922). Educational measurements as a key to individualizing instruction and promotions. *Journal of Educational Research, 5,* 195–206.

Weiner, B., Frieze, I.H., Kukla, A., Reed, S., & Rosenbaum, R.M. (1971). *Perceiving the causes of success and failure.* Morristown, NJ: General Learning Press.

Wiggins, G. (1989). A true test: Toward more authentic and equitable assessment. *Phi Delta Kappan, 70,* 703–713.

Wiggins, G. (1994). Toward better report cards. *Educational Leadership, 52*(2), 28–37.

Wilder, G.Z., & Powell, K. (1989). *Sex differences in test performance: A survey of the literature* (College Board Rep. No. 89–3). New York: College Entrance Examination Board.

Winograd, P., Paris, S., & Bridge, C. (1991). Improving the assessment of literacy. *The Reading Teacher, 45,* 108–116.

Wirth, A. (1992). *Education and work for the year 2000: Choices we face.* San Francisco: Jossey-Bass.

Wolf, D.P. (1989). Portfolio assessment: Sampling student work. *Educational Leadership, 46,* 35–39.

Wolf, R.M. (1992). What can we learn from state NAEP? *Educational Measurement: Issues and Practice, 11*(4), 12.

Wolf, T.H. (1973). *Alfred Binet.* Chicago: University of Chicago Press.

Yoshida, R.K. (1976). Out-of-level testing of special education students with a standardized achievement battery. *Journal of Educational Measurement, 3*(3), 215–220.

Zill, N. (1985). *Happy, healthy, and insecure: A portrait of middle childhood in the United States.* New York: Cambridge University Press.

Author Index

Subject Index